The Eccentric Core

The Eccentric Core

The Thought of Seth Benardete

Edited by

Ronna Burger and Patrick Goodin

ST. AUGUSTINE'S PRESS
South Bend, Indiana

Manufactured in the United States of America

1 2 3 4 5 6   24 23 22 21 20 19 18

Library of Congress Cataloging in Publication Data
Names: Benardete, Seth, honoree. Burger, Ronna, 1947– editor.
Title: The eccentric core: the thought of Seth Benardete
edited by Ronna Burger and Patrick Goodin.
Description: 1st [edition].
South Bend, Indiana: St. Augustine's Press, 2016.
Includes bibliographical references and bibliography.
Identifiers: LCCN 2016012558
ISBN 9781587315800 (paperbound: alk. paper)
Subjects: LCSH: Philosophy, Ancient—Congresses.
Classification: LCC B171 .E33 2016 | DDC 180–dc23
LC record available at https://lccn.loc.gov/2016012558

∞ The paper used in this publication meets the minimum requirements of the
American National Standard for Information Sciences
Permanence of Paper for Printed Materials, ANSI Z39.48-1984.

ST. AUGUSTINE'S PRESS
www.staugustine.net

Contents

Foreword

This volume is a tribute to the thought of Seth Benardete as it left its mark on those of us who had the rare good fortune of studying with him or those who discovered the treasure of his writings. Benardete's classical scholarship and remarkable knowledge of Greek served his philosophic quest to understand the nature of things, which he pursued through a brilliant practice of interpretation of texts. He found in the Platonic dialogue—in the action through which the argument unfolds—the key to philosophic thinking, and this enabled him, in turn, to read the poets philosophically. He was fully immersed in the world of the ancients, starting with Homer, but their works opened up for him a way to the fundamental questions—about justice and love, nature and law, the city and the gods. Recognizing, as he once put it, that "the problem of the human good is grounded in the city, and the problem of being in god," he came to the conclusion that "Political philosophy is the eccentric core of philosophy." Benardete wrote this statement reflecting on "the political-theological issue" in the work of his teacher, Leo Strauss (see his 1974 memorial speech for Strauss and his 1978 review of *The City and Man*). But the paradoxical notion of an "eccentric core" expresses as well the characteristic way his own thinking so often moves from an off-center observation to disclose, unexpectedly, the illuminating focal point of a whole.

This collection had its origin in a small conference on "The Thought of Seth Benardete," organized by Patrick Goodin in the spring of 2005 at Howard University. It expanded to include papers based on talks at earlier memorial conferences for Benardete, at New York University in February 2002 and the New School University in December 2002. The essays about or inspired by Benardete's thought—on the Bible and Homer, Parmenides and Plato, Aristotle and the Roman writers—indicate the range of his teaching and studies. The centrality of Plato is evident, at the same time, not only in those essays but also in the reviews reprinted here, by readers who appreciate the importance of Benardete's work, its subtlety and its depth. The volume closes with three of Benardete's previously unpublished essays and a bibliography of his writings.

Acknowledgments

We wish to thank all the journals and presses that granted rights to reprint previously published pieces, and we appreciate Seth Appelbaum's help with those arrangements. Specific bibliographic information, where relevant, appears on the first page of the chapter. Jane Benardete kindly gave us permission to publish the three essays by Benardete included in this volume and we were sorry to learn of her passing before she could see it appear in print. Those manuscripts can be found in the Seth Benardete Papers, New School for Social Research Archives and Special Collections. We would like to take this occasion to express gratitude to Susan P. Johnson for her careful work on the Collection Guide to the Papers as well as for her skillful editorial assistance in the production of this book. We are indebted to Robert Berman for suggestions on the revision of several essays and to Michael Davis for his advice at many stages, especially his proposal for the title of the collection. Finally, we feel fortunate to have had Bruce Fingerhut's encouragement and the continuing support of St. Augustine's Press.

Recognizing the deep and lasting influence he had on all of us, we offer this collection in memory of Seth Benardete.

Chapter One

Seth Benardete, 1930–2001

Harvey Mansfield

Last week Seth Benardete died, a most extraordinary man, a scholar and a philosopher. His post in life was to be a classics professor at New York University, but he was not an especially prominent professor. Nor was he much known in the world of intellectuals, a realm he never tried to enter. He wrote books on Greek poetry and philosophy, and before he died he was the most learned man alive, and I venture to assert, the deepest thinker as well.

To me, he was both friend and hero. The hero got in the way of our friendship because he was in every way my superior and the best I could offer him was unspoken admiration. I first met him in 1957 when he arrived at the Society of Fellows at Harvard, a group of very bright or highly praised young persons who are given the run of the university for three years. He had received his B.A. in classics from the University of Chicago in 1949 and his Ph.D. from the Committee on Social Thought in 1955, with a dissertation on "Achilles and Hector: The Homeric Hero." I was introduced to Benardete by his fellow student at Chicago and our common friend Allan Bloom. All three of us were in the company of those who saw something quite remarkable in the teaching of Leo Strauss.

Bloom in his brilliance went on to become a best-selling author and a figure of renown. Benardete did not. Because of his obvious gifts he received high honors when he was young, but then he settled in as a professor at N.Y.U. in 1964. When in 1984 his books began to appear in a steady stream, he was largely ignored. He was held in awe by some Straussians, and he had a select following from the courses on Plato that he taught over the years at the New School for Social Research as well as devotees elsewhere who sensed his greatness.

Reprinted from *The Weekly Standard*, December 3, 2001, and expanded in a talk presented at the memorial service for Seth Benardete, New York University, February 1, 2002.

Not surprisingly, the classics profession never gave him recognition or honor for the books in which he showed how little they knew, and from which they could have begun to think. Classicists are only somewhat more insular and thick-headed than most professors, and their neglect did not bother Benardete a whit. He left the task of punishing lesser scholars to others. His books have no anger in them. They are there for people who want to fly to strange places without buying a ticket and without being frisked by security guards.

Actually, in Benardete's view it's very important that flights to strange places are protected by security guards. Benardete was extremely learned in the details of philology, more so indeed than those who know nothing else and are proud of it. But if you want to know his specialty, it was the whole. The whole is depicted to us by poetry and explained to us by philosophy. The depiction by poets tells us the extra-large sized beliefs we need to hold in order to live as we do. Philosophers call these beliefs into question and to the extent possible replace them with rational explanations.

This might sound like "the old quarrel between philosophy and poetry" featured in Plato's *Republic*. But without denying the existence of such a quarrel, Benardete found philosophy in poetry and poetry in philosophy. That was the theme of his many books on Homer, Plato, and Sophocles. Poetry with its image-making aims at, and depends on, the nature of things that is the object of philosophy. And philosophy with its logic cannot simply reject the conceits and the plotting of the poet. It must "learn from our mistakes"— not so much to avoid them as to see why we make them. This re-learning is what Benardete called, following Plato, the "second sailing": it is at the heart of all serious thinking.

My summary does not convey the adventurous sparkle of Benardete's prose as he alternately plunges into the deep and returns to the surface. His books have been published by the University of Chicago Press, a faithful friend to him and his readers. Those who have never read Seth Benardete might begin with a volume of his essays, *The Argument of the Action*. Soon to come is a book of reminiscence and self-summary, *Encounters and Reflections: Conversations with Seth Benardete*.[1] When he died, this family man, a scholar who worked seven days a week, left the world, as do the best human beings, richer for his having lived and poorer for his being gone.

---

1. Editor's note: *The Argument of the Action* appeared in 2000, *Encounters and Reflections* in 2002. See "Works by Seth Benardete" at the end of this volume.

Chapter Two

Definitional Law in the Bible

Ronna Burger

"Shame is the law's expression of man's ignorance by way of prohibition. The law completes man by saying no to man. The law
clothes man and thus turns philosophy—man's awareness of his
own ignorance—into shame."

I. The Noetic Human

The remarks above are from the "Second Thoughts" that Seth Benardete
added to his book on Herodotus when it was reprinted in 1999.[1] He is suggesting, if I understand him, something like this: the awareness of our deficiency that amounts, philosophically, to knowledge of ignorance, takes the
form, morally and politically, of shame, which makes the "clothing" of the
law necessary. This suggestion provides an illuminating key, I believe, to a
central theme of the Book of Genesis, which through its portrayal of the
defective character of the human condition implies in advance an argument
for the necessity of divine law.[2]

Originally presented at the conference on "The Thought of Seth Benardete," Howard
University, April 2005.

1. *Herodotean Inquiries*, "Second Thoughts" (South Bend: St. Augustine's Press,
    1999), 216. Cf. note 19 below.

2. Although not topics of Benardete's published work, the Hebrew Bible and the
    New Testament in Greek were regular subjects of his teaching and conversation.
    He gave a great deal of thought in particular to the biblical understanding of law
    and its status. Some of Benardete's ideas that inspire my reflections in this essay
    were ones he shared at a conference on biblical law and the work of David Daube,
    sponsored by the Liberty Fund, June 1999, in Princeton, N.J.

The law is a response to the defective human condition, but not itself the standard of which the defective falls short. That standard is furnished by the original human being of Genesis 1, the primordial Adam created in the image of God—in Benardete's words, the "noetic human."[3] After first setting out that standard, the Book of Genesis goes on to develop an account of the human being who fails to live up to it. That account begins with the division of the androgynous Adam into two partial beings, man and woman, whose limits are set by the most basic divine prohibition, forbidding the acquisition of knowledge of good and evil. What is presented as divine punishment of man and woman for the violation of that prohibition is in fact a characterization of the essential features of the human condition. The development of those features once human beings have brought about their own expulsion from paradise makes it increasingly clear why life under divine law is necessary.

In beginning, however, with the standard of the noetic human being, created in the image of God, the Bible invites the attempt to return to that starting point. That is an attempt, as Benardete sometimes put it, to do an end-run around the law. In this way, the law—perhaps above all divine law—fosters its own antithesis, in the form of mysticism.[4] The threat is not just to the commands and prohibitions that make political life possible; what is at stake on a deeper level is the law insofar as it replaces the noetically defined human being with its own attempt to define what it is to be human. What Benardete calls

---

3. Cf. *Encounters and Reflections:Conversations with Seth Benardete*, ed. Ronna Burger (Chicago: University of Chicago Press, 2002), 165. Maimonides begins the *Guide of the Perplexed* with this identification of the original human: "It was because of this something, I mean because of the divine intellect conjoined with man, that it is said of the latter that he is *in the image of God and in His likeness*, not that God, may He be exalted, is a body and possesses a shape." *Guide* I.1, trans. Shlomo Pines (Chicago: The University of Chicago Press, 1963), 23.

4. In his analysis of the Athenian Stranger's first prelude to the laws, Benardete refers to Leo Strauss regarding "the two possible forms religion can take, either a religion of law, in which man does what god tells him to do... or a religion of imitation in which man does what god does." See "On the *Euthyphron*," in *The Rebirth of Classical Political Rationalism* (Chicago: University of Chicago Press, 1989), 197–98. If, Benardete goes on, the moderation to which the Stranger appeals in the second form is some notion of sanity, its contrary would be madness, and "the Stranger would thus imply that mysticism in some form is the ultimate consequence of emulation." *Plato's "Laws": The Discovery of Being* (Chicago: University of Chicago Press, 2000), 139.

"definitional law" expresses a universal human awareness that "man is not man unless he does not do everything of which he is capable."[5]

A hint of these thoughts appears in the two places, as far as I know, where Benardete puts into print some brief remarks about the Bible, one in his essay "On Plato's *Symposium*," the other in his commentary on Plato's *Laws*. I would like to try to draw out what I see as some of the implications of those discussions, which are, in all their brevity, remarkably rich and provocative.

II. Genesis and Aristophanes

Benardete was intrigued by David Daube's discussion of a tradition of Rabbinic interpretation that suggests a parallel between the biblical account of the primordial Adam of Genesis 1 and the original whole humans of Aristophanes' speech on eros in Plato's *Symposium*.[6] In very different contexts, with different purposes, each account attempts to explain the human as a partial and defective being, the product of the splitting in two of an original being that was whole and complete. Beyond this structural parallel, the resonance between the accounts extends to the dynamic of the plots that animate each story. As Benardete proposes:

> Aristophanes seems to assign the soul two layers, an original pride and a subsequent shame, that cannot but remind us of the biblical Fall. Pride made man scale heaven, shame made him realize his defectiveness. Eros, then, is an ever-to-be-thwarted longing for a second try on heaven. We turn to each other in lieu of our rebellion against the gods.[7]

The speech of Aristophanes, like the account in Genesis, sets out to elucidate a present reality by means of what is supposedly a lost original, to which, per-

---

5. *Plato's "Laws,"* 95.

6. On the notion of the androgynous Adam invoked in rabbinic commentary on the Book of Genesis, see note 12 below. Daube analyzes the role this notion plays for Mark (10:2–12) and Matthew (19:3–9) in supporting the rejection of divorce. *The New Testament and Rabbinic Judaism* (Salem, N.H.: Ayer Co. Publishers, 1984), 71–79. For a more detailed analysis, see my essay, "Male and Female Created He Them: Some Platonic Reflections on Genesis 1–3," in *The Nature of Woman and the Art of Politics*, ed. Eduardo Velasquez (Lanham, Md.: Rowman and Littlefield Press, 2000), 1–18.

7. "On Plato's *Symposium*," in *The Argument of the Action*, eds. Ronna Burger and Michael Davis (Chicago: University of Chicago Press, 2000), 174.

haps, we cannot help but desire to return. Both are "myths," in the sense that they offer, as Benardete would put it, a genetic account, which can be reconstructed into an eidetic account.[8] Of course, recognizing the common ground of the biblical and the Greek text is only the condition for bringing to light the contrasts between the two that may shed light on each.

The original human of the biblical account is a complete whole, in the image and likeness of its creator. Its completeness is expressed as the union of male and female in one being: "In the image of God created He him, male and female created He them" (Gen.1:27). The recreation of this original in a corporeal form requires the union of two individuals, man and woman. Aristophanes' speech, in contrast, articulates three species of original humans—male-male, female-female, and male-female, who are identified as offspring of the sun, the moon, and the earth, respectively. The distinction of these three human types serves to explain differences in sexual orientation among human beings as we know them. In fact, it is this typology that proves to be the realistic subject of Aristophanes' account of eros: when the experience of love for an absolutely unique individual, which the speech captures so vividly, shows itself to be only a powerful illusion, the reality offered in the end is the second best hope of finding some male half or female half who could be one's favorite.[9]

Aristophanes assigns the highest rank to the male-male type, as the source of the political men whose lives most exemplify the ambitious spirit that marks our primitive nature. But despite the differences in rank of the three genders, all of the original humans are aware of their completeness—their being in the image of the cosmic gods—which fills them with "big thoughts" (199b). "Big thoughts," with an eye to the heavenly bodies, could have suggested cosmology, or more generally, some conception of contemplation, or the desire for knowledge of the whole. But that is not what Aristophanes recognizes as the primordial human impulse. For the poet, being filled with "big thoughts" is the ambition that moves the original humans to scale the heavens, like

---

8. In his study of Plato's *Laws*, Benardete aims to uncover the dialogue's problematic translation of the "eidetic structure of the good" into the "genetic structure of the law." As he formulates the distinction most generally, "'Eidetic' is short for what results from an analysis of something into its kinds, 'genetic' stands for the result of examining the coming into being of a genus or one genus from another." *Plato's "Laws,"* 18 n.18.

9. See *Symposium* 191b.

Homer's giants, in rebellion against the authority of the Olympian gods.[10] The effort, of course, fails, and Zeus comes up with a response that confirms the power of the gods of the city and the law: by splitting the original humans in half, he can weaken each one while multiplying his worshippers. The traces of this act of divine punishment are forever encoded in our comic shape. In particular, our wrinkled belly button displays Apollo's fulfillment of Zeus's command to draw together the skin of the fragmented human half, like a purse string, and the turning of our faces to the front side compels us to look down always on that mark of our humiliation. The shame provoked by our very shape is accompanied by fear, in the face of Zeus's threat to cut us in half once more, if in any way we should express our rebellious spirit.

Eros, according to Aristophanes, is just the desire to overcome our defective state and return to our ancient nature by finding the other half who would make us whole again. This longing is so demanding, and insatiable, that the human race began dying out until Zeus took pity, or rather, as Aristophanes explains, began to worry about losing all his worshippers. His solution was one last make-over: by turning the genitals of his half-beings around to the front, he made possible the momentary satiation of sexual union. But the longing that defines the human condition is a wound, Aristophanes indicates, that cannot be healed—at least not after the first generation of fallen humans; and if it could, it would be only in a state that would destroy the individuality eros was supposed to restore. The comic poet's depiction of the human condition has the tragedy of eros at its core.

The Aristophanic individual as the fragmented half of an original whole has its counterpart in the human being represented in the opening chapters of Genesis; but the sequence of the plot of Aristophanes' speech fits more precisely the story of the tower of Babel, which brings to a close, in Genesis 11, the Bible's universal history of humanity. Like Aristophanes' spherical humans, this community of mankind, in all its completeness, is filled with proud thoughts: "Come, let us build us a city, and a tower, with its top in

---

10. The pride of the original human beings, and their assault on the heavens, signifies, as Benardete sees it, "man's will to be himself." But the basis for that will is a sense of being superior to the Olympian gods, "who somehow or other managed to gain control of the cosmic elements." Here Benardete finds "the deepest difficulty in Aristophanes' account": "the strict individuality that he detects to be the secret spring of eros is not of the same order as man's cosmic origin. Because eros is for Aristophanes not original with man it is divorced from man's rationality." "On Plato's *Symposium*," *The Argument of the Action*, 175.

heaven, and let us make us a name; lest we be scattered abroad upon the face of the whole earth" (11:4). The biblical God, like Zeus, recognizes the great danger: "This is what they begin to do; and now nothing will be withholden from them, which they purpose to do" (11:6). God's punitive response, like that of Aristophanes' Zeus, is to fragment the unitary subject whose wholeness has made it so ambitious: "So the Lord scattered them abroad from thence upon the face of all the earth; and they left off to build the city" (11:8).[11]

The division of humanity in the tower of Babel looks like a political reflection of the natural division into male and female of the whole human of Genesis 1. That whole human being is the counterpart of Aristophanes' spherical humans, but the primordial Adam is not engaged in an act of rebelliousness, motivated by a sense of completeness. Hence, when the biblical God splits this original being in two to produce human beings as we know them, it is not an act of divine punishment for a deed of human ambition. The biblical God seems concerned, rather, for the well-being of his creature. Or, one might wonder, is it possible that the biblical God is just more prescient than Aristophanes' Zeus, and He foresees the need for a preemptive strike, necessary to prevent the human being from becoming, as God eventually puts it, "one of us" (3:22)?

The story of the division of the human being is told in the second chapter of Genesis. Of course the Adam of Genesis 2 is already something other than the Adam of Genesis 1. YHVH, who has taken the place of Elohim, is a potter who molds his Adam from the dust of the earth (*adamah*), then breathes life into his nostrils. The human being of Genesis 1, who could be identified with mind, has been replaced by a compound of earth and breath, body and soul. YHVH sets Adam down in a garden that supplies all his needs, with only one restriction imposed: man is forbidden to eat the fruit of the tree of knowledge of good and evil, with the warning that, on the day he does, he shall surely die. If this genetic account were translated into an eidetic one, the prohibition and consequences of its disobedience would be understood, rather, as the essential characterization of the loss of a life of simple innocence.

Looking upon the earthly paradise He has created, and in particular the solitary human being who belongs in it, God for the first time declares something not good: it is not good for Adam to be alone, presumably because of his incompleteness. Or could it be that what God finds not good is precisely

---

11. This recalls the political image with which Aristophanes concludes his speech on eros: the splitting of the original humans, as punishment for their "injustice," is like the dispersion of the Arcadians by the Lacedaemonians (193a).

the wholeness of this first human, which could indicate potential ambition? What he needs turns out to be an other, brought into being, however, not by an addition to him, but by a separation from him. Adam is put into a deep sleep—a kind of death—from which he will awaken a new being: out of his "rib"—meaning, according to the Rabbis, one side[12]—God forms woman, and with that, two partial beings in place of one whole.

If the fragmented being of man and woman is a form of defectiveness, they have no realization of it: they are naked but not ashamed. Rather, Adam recognizes the other as his own—"flesh of my flesh and bone of my bones."[13] At the moment he bestows on her the name "woman" (*esha*), he becomes for the first time "man" (*esh*). From this unique event, a universal principle is drawn: "Therefore a man leaves his father and mother and clings to his wife and they become one flesh" (2:24)—a momentary corporeal reenactment of the whole being God created in His image.

While it was Aristophanes' self-sufficient humans who rebelled against the ruling gods, in Genesis, it is the partial being, more precisely, the woman, who commits the act of disobedience. We are given some insight into the motivation of the woman through her exchange with the serpent, who appears mysteriously on the scene to initiate the Bible's first dialogue. Discounting God's warning about the certainty of death, the serpent promises that whoever eats the forbidden fruit of knowledge will have his eyes opened and become like God. It is a jealous God who prevents humans from sharing in such knowledge. The woman listens to the serpent, but she also looks for her-

---

12. In the collection of rabbinic commentary, *Genesis Rabbah*, Rabbi Jeremiah ben Eleazar observes: "When the Holy One, blessed be He, created Adam, He created him a hermaphrodite, for it is said, 'Male and female created He them and called their name Adam' (Gen. 5:2)." Rabbi Samuel ben Nahman adds: "When the Lord created Adam, he created him double-faced, then He split him and made him of two backs, one back on this side and one back on the other side." And when the objection is raised that God only took one of Adam's ribs, he responds that this term means one of his sides, referring to Exodus 26, where "the rib of the Taber-nacle" means the side (*Gen. R.* 8:1, cf. the Talmudic tractate, *Erubin* 18a). Alluding to this idea, Maimonides comments, "Understand in what way it has been explained that they were two in a certain respect and that they were also one; as it says: bone of my bones, and flesh of my flesh." *Guide* II.30, 355–56.

13. It is at this moment, Philo notes, that love supervenes and brings together into one the divided halves, as it were, of one being. See "On the Creation of the World" 53, *The Works of Philo Judaeus* Vol. I, trans. C. D. Yonge (London: Irving Bohn, 1854), 45.

self; and what she sees is fruit, not only good for food and a delight to the eyes, like that of all the trees in the garden (2:9), but also desirable to make one wise (3:6). The serpent's promise of becoming like God may sound like the voice of spiritedness; but what the woman discovers on her own, which leads her to disobey the prohibition, is the desire for wisdom.

After eating the forbidden fruit, as the serpent predicted, the eyes of man and woman are opened. What they see is their nakedness, which was already before their eyes, but now in a new light—the light of shame, from which they try to hide by covering themselves with fig leaves. The sign of their knowledge of good and evil is shame at their defectiveness: to be man or woman, they now realize, is to fall short of the human as such, the human in the image and likeness of God.[14] Their acquisition of knowledge looks like a negative development, if shame is its primary consequence. But awareness of defectiveness, which elicits this shame, is the principle that shows up, in another form, as knowledge of ignorance: the woman, in acting on the desire for wisdom, has brought about a new human possibility that was unavailable, and unnecessary, for the complete "noetic human" of Genesis 1.

Whatever may have motivated the desire for knowledge of good and evil, seeking that knowledge, in the biblical account, is the transgression of a prohibition, and the shame it provokes in man and woman before each other is followed by fear before God: when God calls to him, "Where are you?," Adam responds, "I heard Your voice in the garden and I was afraid because I was naked, and I hid myself" (3:8-10).[15] While Adam has been hiding himself, God is present to him only as a voice. There is a concealment of God at the same time as man. And this is the necessary condition for the new human situation about to be established—life under the law.[16]

---

14. The biblical man and woman experience shame in discovering their unlikeness to God, which is their failure to embody the human as such. Aristophanes' human beings experience shame, Benardete remarks, in being subject to gods in whose image they have been reconstructed. "On Plato's *Symposium*," *The Argument of the Action*, 174.

15. Philo asks why Adam makes this claim, when he and the woman have already covered themselves with "girdles." It must indicate, he suggests, that what is at stake is not nakedness of the body, but nakedness of the mind deficient in virtue. "The Allegories of the Sacred Laws" III.18, in *The Works of Philo Judaeus* Vol. I, 121.

16. Moses, the lawgiver, on re-ascent to acquire the tables of stone after the episode of the golden calf, will beg God to reveal to him His glory. "Thou canst not see My face," God responds, "for man shall not see Me and live" (Ex. 33:20). God

God's response to man and woman, after their deed of disobedience, fundamentally alters the relation between them and the life they will lead together. Originally they were to become one flesh as the corporeal recreation of the whole human of Genesis 1. Now that union is reinterpreted and becomes a punishment of the woman: your desire, God announces, will be unto your husband, and he shall rule over you (3:16). The desire for wisdom that motivated woman is redirected toward man and serves to subordinate her. What initially looked like the joining of two equal partners has become the primordial relation of ruler and ruled. The new role of woman is giver of life, as Adam recognizes when he now names her "Eve" (Hava); but as a product of divine punishment, this is to be an experience of terrible pain and suffering. The counterpart for man will be toil by the sweat of his brow, on ground now cursed, until Adam returns to *adamah*, "for dust thou art, and unto dust shalt thou return" (3:19). The Bible's genetic account presents as punishment what would be, if translated into an eidetic account, a description of the necessities of human life as we know it[17]—painful childbirth, toilsome labor, and most fundamentally, mortality.

God concludes his encounter with Adam and Eve and prepares to send them into the world with one last puzzling gesture: he produces skins from animals and clothes the humans in them (3:21). The Hebrew Bible, it is said, has no word for nature, *phusis*, in opposition to *nomos* or convention;[18] but the clothing of man and woman, in its function of covering over their natural nakedness, seems to represent just that distinction.[19] The need for such cloth-

---

allows Moses only to see His back as he passes out of sight (33:23). See Maimonides' analysis, *Guide* I.54.

17. Benardete finds this distinction at the end of Aristotle's account of wisdom and philosophy. After acknowledging that the acquisition of wisdom "would justly be thought to be not human, for the nature of men is in many ways enslaved," Aristotle adds the poet's line, "God alone would have this honor." While poet and philosopher agree, Benardete observes, on how unlikely the attainment of wisdom is, "divine jealousy is the poets', natural enslavement is the philosopher's explanation." "On Wisdom and Philosophy: The First Two Chapters of Aristotle's *Metaphysics A*," in *The Argument of the Action*, 406.

18. See Leo Strauss, "Jerusalem and Athens: Some Preliminary Reflections," *Studies in Platonic Political Philosophy*, with an Introduction by Thomas Pangle (Chicago: University of Chicago Press, 1983), 151.

19. Compare Benardete's account of Herodotus's story of Gyges, who was commanded by the king, Candaules, to look at his own wife naked, in violation of

ing is something human beings come to realize on their own, when their nakedness elicits shame and they cover themselves with fig leaves. Why, then, does God find it necessary to re-clothe them?

The most obvious answer is that the law, symbolized by this clothing, is not to be the product of human autonomy, but must have a divine source. Still, we might wonder, why must God replace the fig leaves by the skins of an animal?[20] Adam and Eve, Benardete once observed, now look like the beasts with whose skins they have been covered. Does this mean that the law bestializes the human being?[21] There is, perhaps, another way to think about this. In the chapters of Genesis that follow, we hear of the increasing depravity of the human race living in the absence of divine law. Could the clothing of animal skins be understood as an image of what the human being is or would be were it not for the law? The clothing itself might represent the divine law; but it could disclose at the same time the potential bestiality in human nature that makes the law necessary. This double meaning opens up what one might call the ultimate paradox of the law. On the one hand, it covers up and forbids us from uncovering what it has concealed; on the other hand, the law aims to express some understanding of the nature of things. This is the potential of the law Benardete wanted to indicate by the subtitle he gave to his study of Plato's *Laws*: "the discovery of being."

III. Noah and the First Law in Genesis

In choosing this formula for his reading of the *Laws* Benardete was guided by Plato's *Minos*, where Socrates proposes that "law wants to be the discovery

---

Lydian laws. "Laws," Benardete observes, "are like clothes: they too conceal from us the way things are. All laws say that certain things cannot be seen; before certain things one must have shame." But as Benardete goes on to argue, "if Gyges unwillingly violates a Lydian law, Herodotus willingly violates the universal prohibition which Gyges himself has formulated. The *Inquiries* of Herodotus continually show him looking at alien things." *Herodotean Inquiries*, 12.

20. Discussing the doctrines and opinions of the Sabians, Maimonides refers to the "story they tell about Adam and the serpent and the tree of knowledge of good and evil, a story that also alludes to unusual clothing." *Guide*, III.29, 520.

21. When God clothes man, Benardete remarks, "He makes him in appearance into a beast. He makes them forget that they are naked and turns them into beasts." Reading Notes on Genesis 3:21, 2001, SB 01–92, p. 58, Seth Benardete Papers, NA.0005.01, New School Archives and Special Collections, The New School, New York, New York.

of being."[22] The anonymous companion with whom Socrates is speaking in the *Minos* ignores the important qualification "wants to be" and wonders why, if law *is* the discovery of being, different peoples have such different laws or customs. The examples are sacrifice and burial (315b–d). Socrates does not dispute the evidence that the Carthaginians unlike the Greeks sacrifice human beings, nor that the Athenians long ago buried their dead in a different place than they later came to do. Distinctive customs of this sort define "our way" and differentiate one tribe from another, or one people over time. But what Socrates' companion does not realize, Benardete argues, is the universal status of the verbs, "to sacrifice" or "to bury." These practices, in whatever special form they might take, are a way of addressing the most fundamental questions: rituals of sacrifice exhibit some "answer" to the question, What is god?, rituals of burial to the question, What is the soul? Ultimately, they are a response to the primary question, What is the human? Benardete speaks of sacrifice and burial as the "pillars of definitional law":

> Definitional law says what man is or what he is not through his regular performance of some rite. Sacrifice denies that man is a god, burial denies that man is either a beast or carrion. Man is both soul and body, and there are gods. These two actions are the plainest evidence that law wants to be the discovery of what is.[23]

In the context of discussing this notion of "definitional law" as it appears in the *Laws* (cf. 716d–718a), Benardete makes a brief digression to Genesis and ponders the account of God's interaction with Noah after the flood, which brings with it the first biblical law (8.20).[24] In promulgating this law, God is responding to what appears to be His new realization about the human being. It is inspired, apparently, by the burnt animal sacrifice Noah offers upon emerging from the ark: "And the Lord smelled the sweet savor; and the

---

22. While the *Minos* begins with Socrates' proposal that law wants to be the discovery of being, it ends with the question, What are the things that make the soul better when the good legislator and shepherd distributes them to us? Plato's *Laws* takes up this question when it proposes a psychology for interpretation of law; but the primary purpose of his commentary on the dialogue, as Benardete puts it at the outset, is "to try to uncover the concealed ontological dimension, and explain why it is concealed and how it comes to light." *Plato's "Laws,"* xii.

23. *Plato's "Laws,"* 139.

24. *Plato's "Laws,"* 140–41.

Lord said in His heart: 'I will not again curse the ground any more for man's sake; for the imagination of man's heart is evil from his youth'" (8:21). An almost identical insight had earlier led God to His plan of total destruction: "The Lord saw that the wickedness of man was great in his heart, and that every imagination of the thoughts of his heart was only evil continually" (6:5). Now, however, God has come to a slight, but important difference in his understanding of the evil in the human heart: it is not only continual, but "from youth," which seems to mean, from birth, that is, a condition that cannot be eradicated. Noah's sacrifice has appeased God—He will never again destroy His creation—but it has also led Him to realize the futility of starting over again. The new beginning with Noah will not change anything in the human heart. The only possible, if imperfect, solution is the law, which is concerned with behavior, not intention. Law is the "second sailing" that comes with the realization of the impossibility of solving the human problem by a new nature.

The first law is a prohibition against murder. The first crime—or the first non-symbolic crime—was murder, Cain's murder of his brother. For that deed, Cain was only condemned to exile—a sentence he carried out by settling in Nod, "the land of wandering," and becoming the founder of a city. The first law now brings with it a specific threat of punishment: in requital for killing a human being, a human agent must be permitted to kill the perpetrator. The prohibition against murder, Benardete proposes, should be understood in connection with man as a political being: the model of Cain, the fratricide who founds the first city, suggests that the prohibition against murder is a requirement of the city, despite, or because, its own foundation lies in murder.[25] Behind the political law against murder, however, Benardete sees a concealed prohibition that is not just political, but a determination of what it is to be human as such.[26]

What seems to have led him to this conclusion is the puzzling way in which the first law is introduced. As the smell of Noah's burnt offering wafts toward him, God responds, not by immediately announcing the prohibition

---

25. Reading Notes on Genesis 4, 2001, SB 01–92, pp. 58-59, Seth Benardete Papers.

26. In the Preface to his translation of and commentary on Plato's *Philebus*, Benardete uses this distinction between political law and "definitional law" in order to characterize the opposition between philosophy and poetry: "There is for philosophy a divide between man as man and man as political animal that poetry denies." *The Tragedy and Comedy of Life: Plato's "Philebus"* (Chicago: University of Chicago Press, 1993), ix.

against murder, but rather, by granting a new permission to human beings. Originally, man and woman, along with the rest of the animals, were granted "the green herb" for food; only now, after the flood, are they permitted to kill and eat animals. In the beginning, the human being was to have dominion over the animals and the rest of nature; now, God announces, every beast and fowl and fish will be filled with fear and dread of man (9:2-3). The permission to kill and eat animals looks like a concession to the ineradicable evil God has discerned in the human heart. But how is the carnivorous way of life connected with the prohibition against murder that follows?

Benardete found a clue in the qualification God sets on the permission He grants:

> Every moving thing that liveth shall be for food for you.... Only flesh with the life thereof, which is the blood thereof, shall ye not eat. (9:4)

This qualification then slides into the warning:

> And surely your blood of your lives will I require.... Whoso sheddeth man's blood, by man shall his blood be shed; for in the image of God made He man. (9:5-6)

To murder is to shed a man's blood and the human punishment of the perpetrator is to shed his blood. What links the prohibition against murder with the permission to kill and eat animals is blood. While animal flesh is now permitted, it is forbidden to eat the blood. For blood *is* life. And it runs, of course, through the veins of humans as much as any other animal. To eat the blood of an animal, then, is tantamount to eating a human being. Hence, Benardete seems to have reasoned, the restriction on eating the blood of animals, which slides into the prohibition against shedding the blood of a human, could be seen as a concealed prohibition against cannibalism. And while taking the prohibition against murder, with the threat of capital punishment, to be a political law, Benardete understands the prohibition against cannibalism to be a definitional law.[27] It signifies that the human is not flesh, to be eaten

---

27. Reading Notes on Genesis IX: 4–6, 2001, SB 01–92, p. 51, Seth Benardete Papers. While Benardete characterizes the prohibition of murder as a political law, it seems that it too could be understood, in Genesis 9, as a definitional law. More precisely, the permission to human beings to punish the murderer by killing him is justified by an appeal to the status of the human being created in the image of

like any other animal; and only the human being who would do such a deed, not any other animal, is truly bestial.

The characterization of the human that the Bible's definitional law has begun to reveal through God's interaction with Noah is developed by two stories that follow. The first, which comes almost immediately, is the obscure but disturbing story of Noah's son coming upon his father in a drunken stupor and failing to cover over his nakedness (9:20-27). It is a violation of shame to look behind what has been, or should be, clothed—above all, for a son to look upon the nakedness of his progenitor. The theme of incest, which seems to be darkly implied here, becomes explicit several chapters later in the story of Lot and his daughters, after their escape from the destruction of Sodom and Gomorrah. Dwelling in a mountain cave, isolated from all others, they get their father drunk and initiate sexual relations with him, considering it the only way to preserve the race (19:30-38). This story has an echo in Book III of Plato's *Laws*, where the Stranger describes the isolated life of Cyclopean mountain dwellers, characterized, he implies, by incest and cannibalism (680b-d). Such practices, Benardete comments, are originally done out of dire need; only when necessity lets up a little are they reinterpreted, so that they come to be understood as the mark of bestiality, and hence the prohibition against them as a case of definitional law.[28]

A passage from the end of Deuteronomy seems to express this notion, in fact, this example, of definitional law. Reflecting, in this final speech, on the law as a whole, Moses recites all the blessings that will come to his people from observing God's commandments and all the curses if they do not. Among those curses is one that warns: "And thou shalt eat the fruit of thine own body, the flesh of thy sons and of thy daughters whom the Lord thy God hath given thee" (28:53).[29] What is presented here in genetic form, as the punishment for violation of a prohibition, would be understood, eidetically, as a description of what the human being would be in the absence of law.

Law clothes the naked human being and forbids uncovering what it has concealed, while it "wants to be" the discovery of being. It thus inevitably provokes its subjects to circumvent its commands and try to get back to its source. These reflections on the Bible, inspired by Benardete, lead to this

---

God: to be in the image of God must mean either a being not to be killed or a being who can kill another human in punishment for killing a human, or both.

28. See *Plato's "Laws,"* 188.

29. A Greek counterpart appears in the story of Atreus's revenge against his brother Thyestes, by serving him the cooked bodies of his own children.

striking conclusion: in trying to get back to the noetic human being of Genesis 1, behind the clothing of the law, we discover, instead, the bestiality of the human without the law.

Chapter Three

Extending the History of Philosophy Back to Homer: Seth Benardete's *Odyssey*

Laurence Lampert

> Some day my belief that Homer started it all and that there was a continuous tradition from Homer until the end of the 18th century will be vindicated.
>
> — Leo Strauss to Seth Benardete, November 15, 1957

Seth Benardete stands out as the most rewarding of Leo Strauss's followers, if the most difficult. He concentrated on Plato but his perhaps most accessible book, by no means easy, is *The Bow and the Lyre: A Platonic Reading of the* Odyssey, a book that vindicates Strauss's belief that Homer started it all.[1] Reading Homer as a master of the exoteric art recovered by Strauss, Benardete discovered in Homer, the first known author of our tradition, its first philosopher and political philosopher.

Strauss began his introduction to the *History of Political Philosophy* with the origins of political philosophy in philosophy and states that

> [t]he primary theme of philosophy . . . is "nature." What is nature? The first Greek whose work has come down to us, Homer himself, mentions "nature" only a single time; this first mention of

---

Reprinted (with some revision by the author) from Laurence Lampert, *The Enduring Importance of Leo Strauss* (Chicago: University of Chicago Press, 2013).

1. *The Bow and the Lyre: A Platonic Reading of the* Odyssey (Lanham, Md.: Rowman and Littlefield, 1997). References to this book will be by page numbers in parentheses in the text.

"nature" gives us a most important hint as to what the Greek philosophers understood by "nature."[2]

He then cites the event in the tenth book of the *Odyssey* whose treatment by Benardete will be a chief theme of my essay, Hermes revealing the nature of the herb *moly* to Odysseus. Strauss's quotation of Homer ends with this: "Hard is it to dig for mortal men, but the gods can do everything." The gods are omnipotent, Strauss concludes, not because they know everything, for they don't, but because they are "knowers of the natures of the things... 'Nature' means here the character of a thing, or of a kind of thing, the way in which a thing or a kind of thing looks and acts, and the thing, or kind of thing, is taken not to have been made by gods or men." Strauss's final comment takes Homer literally: "the first man we know who spoke of nature was the Wily Odysseus who had seen the towns of many men and had thus come to know how much the thoughts of men differ from town to town or from tribe to tribe." Homer's Odysseus was the first to come to know the nature of man and to act on that knowledge. The first philosopher and political philosopher, Strauss intimates to open his history of political philosophy, was wily Odysseus, because, learning what only the gods had known, he came into the knowledge that gave them their power.

Benardete devoted considerable attention to Homer, writing his dissertation on the *Iliad* and publishing articles on it. *The Bow and the Lyre*, written in 1994, is the ripened fruit of his lifelong attention to Homer. In its preface he describes learning from Plato in a way that he could not learn from Homer and the tragic poets. His failure was "no fault" of the older authors: we lost knowledge of how to read them. Plato's famous remark on "the ancient quarrel between poetry and philosophy," Benardete says, cast a spell over him that kept him from wondering whether Plato himself had learned from the poets. But it was Plato himself, he then reports, who led him over time to questions that allowed him to recover the lost art of reading Homer and other wise poets—*wise poets* being redundant in Benardete's usage, for he distinguishes poets from versifiers (153n.2).

Nearing the end of his preface, Benardete reports a view he finds expressed in Plato's *Phaedrus*: "the ascent to the beings always passes divergently through the fiction of the Olympian gods" (xiv). And he asks whether the poets, poetizers of the Olympian gods, understood their own doing or

---

2.   Leo Strauss and Joseph Cropsey, eds., *History of Political Philosophy*, Third Edition (Chicago: University of Chicago Press, 1987 [1963]), 3.

making. If they did, they would not be simply the preface to philosophy but would have entered philosophy itself, knowledge of the beings. It is on this issue that Benardete, for the only time in his book, mentions "[m]y teacher, the late Leo Strauss": Strauss "had often spoken to me about this possibility, but I did not know then what he really meant, and I do not know now whether what I think I now understand was what he really meant." Benardete's book on the *Odyssey* presents his mature view on the ancient quarrel between poetry and philosophy, an issue on which he was set to thinking by Leo Strauss; according to that view, Plato recovered from the poets "a way of thinking that is not on the way to philosophy but is philosophy." Therefore, when Benardete adds that on this view "the apparent tension between Plato the poet and Plato the philosopher would disappear," he implies the same of Homer: Homer the poet of the *Odyssey* is one with Homer the philosopher.

I single out two sections of Benardete's book, "Nature" and "Hades," for the obvious reason: they treat in turn philosophy and political philosophy in a way that displays the harmonious relation between them when poetry is understood in the most expansive sense. Singling out two sections, tearing them out of Benardete's developing narrative, comes at a high cost: they treat episodes within two tightly woven Homeric narratives, Odysseus's own story of his odyssey as told to wise Alcinous, and Homer's story, which he presents as having being told to him by the Muse. These broader narratives enclose the two episodes I discuss and are essential to Odysseus's total odyssey as Homer relates it. I tear out these two because they show that in Homer too philosophy and political philosophy are related by sequential implication: fundamental insight entails comprehensive action.

The last sentences of Benardete's beautiful book have always meant the most to me: "Odysseus is free to submit to his fate and begin his second journey. He should now know that his destiny is to establish belief and not knowledge." Benardete's book-long argument is condensed into these sentences, for his argument reenacts a becoming. The "wisest of men"[3] becomes truly wise only after he has understood the meaning of the war won at Troy, the moral war and its warriors. Following the complex thread of the Muse's chosen way of presenting the complex odyssey of Odysseus, Benardete reveals the stages whereby this reflective man of understanding enters philosophy and political philosophy.

---

3. *Republic* 390a.

"Nature"

"A mighty necessity is upon me." So says Odysseus as he sets out for the house of Circe, a setting out that leads to what Benardete calls a "revelation" that "[f]rom every point of view, both intrinsically and extrinsically... is the peak of the *Odyssey*" (84). Presented as the gift of Hermes, the revelation "that things have natures" stands as the peak, the indispensable insight with which philosophy gains its true ground. But what is the *mighty necessity* that led to the revelation? Many preparatory steps were involved, including all four episodes already related in the nine-stage odyssey Odysseus is describing for Alcinous, wise king of the Phaeacians. The immediate trigger of the mighty necessity, however, is Odysseus's recognition of his "negligence or dereliction of duty," his unprecedented withdrawal from command that caused the Laestrygonian disaster: having surrendered command, Odysseus allowed eleven of his twelve ships to sail into the harbor of the Laestrygonians while he, with "characteristic caution," moored his own ship outside the harbor, leaving himself and his crew the chance to escape. Why did Odysseus withdraw command and in this passive way cause the destruction of over ninety percent of his men? The preceding episode, Aeolus and his gift of winds, explains why. These three episodes, Aeolus, the Laestrygonians, and Circe, Benardete placed together under the title "Nature": the discovery of nature in the Circe episode came about because of what the Aeolus and Laestrygonian events did to Odysseus.[4]

---

4. No one will ever visit an actual island of Circe or Aeolus or any other place in the imaginary geography invented by Odysseus to convey to wise Alcinous his odyssey to philosophy and political philosophy. But thanks to the inspired and obsessive labors of Robert Bittlestone, assisted by the academic expertise of Cambridge University philologist James Diggle and Edinburgh University geologist John Underhill, we can now knowingly visit Odysseus's actual Ithaca for the first time since antiquity. It is not the western Ionian island now called Ithaca but the northwest peninsula of nearby Cephalonia, a peninsula formerly separated from Cephalonia proper by a strait. We can now walk up again from the sandy beach of Phorkys Bay to the site of Eumaeus's pig farm and from there on up to the commanding height where Odysseus's palace once stood, marveling that the origins of Western philosophy, Western civilization, got part of their impetus in these very hills and harbors. See Robert Bittlestone, *Odysseus Unbound: The Search for Homer's Ithaca* (Cambridge: Cambridge University Press, 2005), and www.odysseus-unbound.org.

Aeolus, steward of the winds, gave Odysseus a bag in which he had sewn up all the winds but Zephyr, allowing him the apparently unimpeded opportunity to sail home to Ithaca. Having decided that he could trust only himself on that sail home, Odysseus stayed awake nine days and nights guiding the ships. On the tenth day, sighting Ithaca and close enough to see men tending fires, he was overcome by sleep. With Odysseus asleep, his crew opened the bag suspecting, reasonably enough, that it contained treasure that Aeolus had given Odysseus and that he had not shared with them; the released winds blew them away from Ithaca. Benardete reports Odysseus's reconstruction of the speech of his crew as "Odysseus's understanding of their resentment, which he expresses as their coming home emptyhanded even though they accomplished the same journey as he did" (80–81)—a deeply mistaken view of Odysseus's journey, if an understandable one. Benardete focuses on Odysseus's report of his thoughts on awakening far from Ithaca: in despair, he ponders suicide. Rather than slip over the side and under the waves, however, Odysseus "endured in silence: he gives up control of his ships and men. He asks no questions.... He lets things take their course. He becomes indifferent" (81). He chooses "resignation."

Blown back to Aeolus's island, Odysseus hears Aeolus's curse on him as "an object of enmity to the immortals" (82), and Benardete observes that Odysseus too seems to have concluded that "[h]e does not deserve to exist unless either he himself is perfect or he commands total trust on the part of his crew." Aeolus's curse causes a "decisive change" in Odysseus, for he now knows that he is "on his own, and no divine support is to be expected." Benardete's word choice highlights the singular importance of this change: "This turn to complete self-reliance emerges as the necessity for his men to row for six days straight." The turn to rowing reminds Benardete of "the proverb 'second sailing,' which applies to those who cannot employ the best means possible but must be content with whatever means are available." This *turn*, this *second sailing*, means that "[t]he feasible replaces the ideal." Benardete makes no mention of Socrates when using his famous words from Plato's *Phaedo* (99d) but his preface spoke of "Socrates' 'second sailing'" as Socrates' "own term for the turnaround in his own thinking when he abandoned a direct approach to cosmology and turned instead to speeches rather than to the beings" (xii). Benardete invites his reader to think of the events he is now describing in the *Odyssey* as Homer's version of the Socratic turn, a turn leading in Homer too to the discovery of nature.

After saying that "the feasible replaces the ideal," Benardete goes on to describe a sequence of two alterations caused by this replacement. First, it "alters the very character of Odysseus's narration" (82): Odysseus narrates the Laestrygonian episode differently. Second, "[t]he Laestrygonian disaster alters Odysseus" (84): it is an altered Odysseus who sets out for Circe's house in order to rescue his men and to whom Hermes reveals the nature of the *moly*. These alterations in the narrative and in Odysseus show that the feasible new way is the way to philosophy after the abandonment of the ideal way.

Benardete reports Odysseus's narration in the altered terms Odysseus gave it: "Odysseus does not say a word about [the] injustice or wickedness [of the Laestrygonians]. He does not even pray for their destruction. His account is as neutral as Homer's description of the carnage of war" (82–83).[5] Odysseus's neutral narration is "stripped . . . of any mention of the gods" (83). Neutrality allows the acts of the Laestrygonians to be viewed from *their* perspective: seeing eleven alien warships enter their harbor, they act to defend themselves against what looks like an invasion force. And neutrality allows a different perspective on Odysseus: abandoning rule of his men, tying up his own ship outside the harbor, not even advising them to be as cautious as he knew it was necessary to be—could this mean that Odysseus's "neutral tone" arises "from a resentment against his own men and a corresponding satisfaction in their 'punishment'"?[6] Regarding his relationship to these men, Benardete says, it is inconceivable that Odysseus's "negligence or dereliction of duty could be defended at home if any managed to survive." Finally, neutrality may reflect the fact that "Odysseus has had a potentially grave problem solved for him, to which he himself called attention when he reconstructed the speech of his own crew"; he had them express their resentment against him "as their coming home emptyhanded even though they accomplished the same journey as he did" (81). The "grave problem" they represent, then, is that even though they cannot have understood everything Odysseus under-

---

5. Benardete emphasizes the altered narration by repeatedly invoking Odysseus's previous narration of the Polyphemus episode. He shows Homer's corresponding neutrality by citing *Iliad* 16.404–10: Homer applied to the actions of heroic Patroclus the image Odysseus applied to the actions of the Laestrygonians, spearing fish.

6. Benardete thus suggests that Odysseus's action could be based in anger, the meaning of his name given to him by Autolycus, his grandfather on his mother's side, a most telling name when added to the name he gave himself in the Polyphemus episode, *outis*—nobody. Benardete's accounts of Odysseus's names are continuously instructive (3, 43–44, 76–79, 129–30).

stood, "their experiences have made them wiser"; paternal rule over *them* is no longer possible. The task that lies ahead for Odysseus, securing a new regime in Ithaca over which Telemachus will preside, would be made immeasurably more complicated if hundreds of men believe "they accomplished the same journey as [Odysseus] did." Odysseus knows his own responsibility for the disaster, because his narrative, "stripped as it is of any mention of the gods," corrects his earlier attribution of responsibility to Zeus (9.551–55). Blaming Zeus shows the measures Odysseus is willing to take "in order to cover up his own responsibility" (84); narrating the Laestrygonian disaster in a neutral manner shows what he learned of his own responsibility.

"The Laestrygonian disaster alters Odysseus" (84). As Benardete turns to this second and more important consequence of the replacement of the ideal by the feasible, he notes that the changes in Odysseus are forced on him as "democratic concessions": he addresses his men as friends for the first time; he shares the stag he shot; he divides his forty-four men into two equal groups and puts Eurylochus in charge of one; he conducts a lottery to determine which group will investigate the island that turns out to be Circe's. Two additional changes, however, are chosen. One is a matter of speech. For the first time he tells the names of some of his crew: Eurylochus, Polites, and "he ends his stay at Circe's . . . naming the nobody Elpenor." And the deed of the altered Odysseus? When Eurylochus returns to report that all the other men had disappeared, "Odysseus decides to rescue them," saying, "A mighty necessity is upon me." The mighty necessity marks an alteration of the first order: "This is the first time Odysseus does anything that does not involve his own advantage. He risks his life for his 'evil' companions and trusts that those he leaves behind, with the unreliable Eurylochus, will not desert him."

To always point to centers seems like cheating, like taking unfair advantage of an author's care in modulating his voice and leading his reader to things carefully constructed for private tutoring, special treasures that won't bear shouting. But Benardete pointed to centers in Homer, and one of the centers he isolated is the Circe episode (as he points out here). His own account of the Circe episode—of what the mighty necessity, the alteration in Odysseus, led to—begins at the complex center of his book, the first of two central paragraphs twinned at the center of "Nature," the section twinned with "Hades" at the center of the central chapter "Odysseus's Own Story."[7]

---

7. *The Bow and the Lyre* has nine chapters, and the central chapter, "Odysseus's Own Story," has four subchapters, "Nature" and "Hades" being the central pair. These two subchapters are also the tenth and eleventh of twenty subchapters.

The second of his two central paragraphs deals with the consequence of Odysseus's risking his life for his men: "This completely just and daring action, with its implicit recognition of what he shares with his fellow human beings, is instantly rewarded." The reward is a gift of the gods: "Hermes reveals to him that things have natures. From every point of view, both intrinsically and extrinsically, this revelation is the peak of the *Odyssey*." It can be no accident that here at the center and peak where the words can be assumed to be most studied, Benardete chose, for the fundamental insight of reason, its indispensable step into philosophy and the rational account of the order of things, words that Leo Strauss used for reason's fundamental opposite: *reveals, revelation*. Why he did so is clear. Odysseus is telling his own story after seven years with Calypso, the "Concealer" (37), years spent shaping the way he would tell the tale of his odyssey to a man like Alcinous—and *he* attributes his insight to Hermes. And Homer shapes the tale *he* tells to have the word nature, *phusis*, be used only once, right here. Benardete defers to Odysseus, to Homer, to Strauss, and calls reason's fundamental and comprehensive conclusion a "revelation." Benardete shows the necessary connection between philosophy and political philosophy in his first words about philosophy.

Before describing the actual event at the peak, Benardete shows just why, intrinsically and extrinsically, it is the peak. Intrinsically, within the *Odyssey*, Benardete finds two aspects to the peak. First, with respect to the human as such, "[i]t comes after a series of encounters with men who illustrated the character of the bestial in the composition of man and thereby exposed the conditions of political life" (84). The peak follows full exposure of the bestial conditions of political life to a thinker leading a journey home; but the peak itself is attained at the moment of exposure to a different aspect of the human fully articulated in what Odysseus relates as his encounters after the Circe

---

Where chapters have subchapters, they constitute the whole of the chapter; the book therefore consists of twenty-two units if the chapters without subchapters are added to the subchapters. Benardete placed an endnote on centers (note 127) at the center of "Nature," appended to "the shape [Odysseus] gave to his story" (85). The Circe episode, which Benardete is treating here, is the central or fifth in the story Odysseus shaped, "Odysseus's account of his nine adventures." But Hades is central "in Homer's account of Odysseus's eleven adventures." It is appropriate then that Benardete twins "Hades" with "Nature" at his center. The formal fitness of Benardete's twinned centering of "Nature" and "Hades" mirrors substantive fitness: "Nature" and "Hades" deal respectively with philosophy and political philosophy in their essential connectedness.

episode: "only various forms of the divine—Hades, Sirens, Scylla and Charybdis, and the cattle of the Sun." The peak itself contains a new aspect of the bestial: "[t]he swine Odysseus's men become complete the series" of the bestial. And the divine? It must be present at the peak and can only be—Circe being not yet encountered—Odysseus's act to save his men. His "just and daring action, with its implicit recognition of what he shares with his fellow human beings," experienced as such, known as such, seems to be the tripping point for the revelation: to be human is to be a bestial/divine mix and to be that mix essentially; to be a human being is to do what the human must do given what it is, given the forms of bestiality/divinity in its—nature. The human is what it is and not some other thing; to be human is to act out a nature, to be an instance of the kind human. From this peak of insight into nature, Benardete looks back to an event in the *Odyssey* that Homer has already related concerning the bestial/divine split. "Odysseus's narrative thus shares in his own experiences at sea after he left Calypso. He had then chosen first the divine and last the bestial" (84–85). That sequence of choices occurs within the fundamental choice Odysseus has already made at Calypso's, "his choice of home and mortality." That particular divine/bestial split related earlier by Homer "turns out to have been anticipated in the shape [Odysseus] gives to his story." The peak event is thus illuminated by pondering an event that Homer chose to tell earlier but that chronologically fell later. Folded within the complex layering of sequences lies the total chronology of the odyssey to philosophy and to political philosophy. Unfolded into its chief events it reads: the post-Troy understanding of Troy or of morality; the odyssey to philosophy itself that peaks with the Circe episode; seven years with the Concealer on what amounts to the Isle of the Blest; the choice of home and mortality that dictates taking the raft home or descending home; storms within that choice that dictate choosing first the divine and last the bestial; and actually telling the whole shaped tale when a fit audience is found, in this case a wise king.[8]

The nature of the human is one aspect of the revelation of the *moly* that makes that revelation the peak of the *Odyssey* intrinsically. Benardete shows a second aspect. "At the same time [Odysseus's] story contains versions of both 'Nestor' and 'Menelaus.'" These names stand for views of the whole

---

8. Benardete laid out Homer's presentation of the sequence of choices of divine and bestial consequent on the storm at sea (choices that followed the basic choice, the philosopher Odysseus's choice of home and mortality), on the extremely dense pages 40–43, pages that the peak helps interpret, as do pages 51 and 148.

26

that Benardete already discussed because Homer put them too earlier in his story. Telemachus journeyed to Pylos and Sparta early in the *Odyssey* to inquire of Nestor and Menelaus what they knew about his father, and here at the peak Benardete summarizes what he heard: Nestor interpreted the whole by trying "to fit everything . . . into a pattern of divine justice." Menelaus came close to "suggesting a comprehensive understanding of becoming, which Helen had deepened with her suggestion of the inscrutable heart behind all appearances."[9] Hermes' revelation is the peak also because it attempts to understand what Nestor and Menelaus and Helen attempted to understand: an order to the whole. Compared with these earlier efforts, "Hermes' showing of the nature of the *moly*, however, seems to be of a different order." The peak attains a literally different order, an order of the whole construed rationally as an order of natures instanced in the *moly*. The revelation of this order "lets Odysseus share in the knowledge the gods have without his having to share in their being." In the pleasing humor of these final words of his central paragraphs, Benardete voices Odysseus's insight into the choiceworthiness of human being over the ageless and deathless nonbeing of divinity. This choiceworthiness is not obvious to all. Benardete had made the words of Nestor's son, "All men need gods" (17), a running theme with respect to Odysseus. Does *he*? He doesn't: he can share in their knowledge without having to share in their being. He does: knowing the conditions of political life, the divine and the bestial in the human, he will learn that choosing the divine/bestial makes it his destiny to establish belief and not knowledge.

And externally? Benardete shows in his next paragraph that Hermes' revelation that things have natures is the peak of the *Odyssey* from an external point of view: he jumps to Aristotle's *Politics* and shows how its account of human nature contains the most basic elements of Odysseus's discoveries. "Odysseus's adventures so far seem to have unfolded as if they were meant to illustrate Aristotle" (85). But the Aristotelian elements in Odysseus's experiences "are not grounded in an Aristotelian understanding of nature." This seems to mean not only that they occurred prior to the discovery of nature as the means to that discovery but also that the peak insight needed a train of thinkers to arrive at the full view implied within it. Benardete again summarizes Odysseus's experiences with the Laestrygonians and the Cyclops and concludes that "[i]t now seems that the way to the discovery of nature"— the way that led eventually to Aristotle—"has been decisively prepared for"

---

9. Benardete entitled his chapter on these views "Pattern and Will," dividing it into two subchapters, "Nestor" and "Helen and Menelaus."

by two events: "on the one hand, by the unsupported human effort to reach the Laestrygonians," the inquirer's effort of a second sailing that abandons the ideal and replaces it with the feasible. And on the other hand, "by Odysseus's uncompelled choice to be just." Again, the mighty necessity moving Odysseus to his act of rescue is affirmed as indispensable: philanthropy not only belongs to philosophy, it is present at its beginning as a precondition of its beginning at all. Benardete does not often repeat himself. But here, having brought in Aristotle to glimpse the whole sweep of the Greek understanding of nature from Homer to Aristotle, he repeats himself on the mighty necessity presupposed in the attainment of philosophy: love of the human as human is a precondition of the self-knowledge that brings insight into nature.

Having proven the peak intrinsically and extrinsically, Benardete can ponder Hermes' revelation. The decisive matter is to understand the *moly* as the "antidote" to Circe's enchantment. It is not a magic potion or charm; its name carries no special powers. "What Hermes does with the *moly* is to show Odysseus its nature (*phusis*)" (86).[10] "It was black in its root, and its flower like milk; the gods call it *moly*, but it is hard for mortal men to dig up, but the gods can do everything." The revelation lies wholly in the showing: "the gods' power arises from the knowledge of its nature." Odysseus, having dug up what it is hard for mortal men to dig up, comes to know what the gods know, and that knowledge is power, power initially to resist enchantment. But knowing how to resist enchantment implies knowing how to enchant. Knowing what the gods know, Odysseus takes on the power of the gods.

Armed with knowledge, Odysseus is proof against Circe's particular enchantment, "transforming a man into a pig, with its head, voice, bristles, and build, but the mind (*noos*) remains as it was before." Benardete repeats his odd word *build*: Odysseus's "knowledge, then, is the knowledge that the mind of man belongs together with his build. They are together as much as the root and flower of the *moly*." Man is mind and build. What is *build*? It must be what is transformable into piggishness, that element of the human

---

10. Who is Hermes? As Odysseus comes near the house of Circe, he appears as "Hermes of the golden staff" (10.277–78), messenger of the gods, but in the act of giving Odysseus the antidote and explaining its nature, he is "Argeïphontes," friend of thieves (10.302). And Hermes was the teacher of Autolycus, Odysseus's grandfather on his mother's side, a man "who surpassed all men in stealing and in swearing oaths for the god Hermes himself had endowed him" (*Odyssey* 19.395–96). See Norman O. Brown, *Hermes the Thief: The Evolution of a Myth* (New York: Vintage Books, 1990), 8.

that can be corrupted into swine-like bestiality while mind remains mind. Expanding it into the other forms of the bestial that Odysseus has experienced and naming it platonically, *build* must be appetite and spirit, elements of soul that can dominate the soul and press mind into their service. Odysseus is that rarity whose experiences allow his mind to understand his build, how he's built, and thereby win control over the potentially bestial in himself: "'There is in your breast,' Circe tells Odysseus, 'a mind that does not admit of enchantment'" (10.329). If his knowledge gives his mind power over his build, it could also give his mind potential power over the build of all others ruled by build while imagining they're ruled by mind.

Benardete reflects on what "Homer was the first, as far as we know, to have come to" understand (87), the "philosophic principle" of unity according to which a *kosmos* of composite order accessible to mind underlies what is visible to the eye; to that, Homer "gave the name 'nature.'" "The unity that logos discovers can be sounded"—it can be plumbed and spoken—"but never without ambiguity." Did Homer go further? Did he understand the unities to be causes, as "Socrates seems to have proposed" (note 134)? Benardete answers in his note that "[i]n Homer, only the first step has been taken." His text agrees: "It is unclear whether Odysseus extends the principle beyond this one insight, but he does have it confirmed" (87). The confirmation occurs later, in Hades, and becomes a permanent part of Odysseus's understanding of human nature. In this anticipatory look into Hades, Benardete indicates one of its key features. "In Hades, he learns, there are recognizable images of men and women, but, with the exception of Teiresias, they have no mind." Only the wise man survives in Hades with his mind, only he has an afterlife as more than an image of his shape. Benardete notes that to escape Polyphemus Odysseus claimed to be nothing but mind; now, however, having been shown the *moly*, he knows himself better. In addition, with Circe he sees his men "in an unrecognizable form but with their minds intact." Combining these insights, Odysseus learns that no man is immortal, no man carries the unity of shape and mind into Hades, although the wise live on differently, still teaching. Therefore, years later, he is immune to Calypso's offer to make him deathless and ageless because he knows it "cannot be genuine." The revelation of the *moly*, knowledge of the unity of bestial and divine in human nature, gives mortal Odysseus immunity to the charms of both Circe and Calypso; he cannot be made swine-like, and he cannot believe he is more than he is.

Who is Odysseus then? He is the man named by his grandfather, Autolycus, Wolf Himself, and Benardete showed that the root of his name is *anger* and that Homer used the verb *odussomai* only for divine anger except when Autolycus named Odysseus (43–44). But Odysseus also named himself, calling himself *outis*, No One, in order to escape from Polyphemus's cave, and Benardete showed how *ou tis* implies *mē tis* and therefore that the name Odysseus gave himself rings of anonymous mind (*mētis*) (3, 77–79). The human mind of Odysseus, coming to know itself in the duality pictured in his names, discovers nature.

Through Circe's domestication of his men, Odysseus learns the possibility of a "city of pigs," a bestialization of man that followed his democratizing his rule. By quoting Plato's *Republic* Benardete prepares Homer's portrayal of the key step in the odyssey to philosophy. The theme of bestiality, he says, "culminates twice, first among the Laestrygonians and then with Circe's swine." The latter however points to an insight of a different order; it points, Benardete says, guarding his words, "to a humanity that, though it belongs to man as man, is not open to every man, since what he is necessarily he is not necessarily unless he knows that that is what he is necessarily." And who knows *that*? Odysseus only and only after he sees the bestiality of fully domesticated man. Only he—and only then—comes to know that it belongs to man to know who he is. Democracy "points" to philosophy; all varieties of what man necessarily is can flourish in the freedom and permissiveness of democracy, but more than that, its domestication, pressed to the full, alone makes possible that rarest variety that comes to know what man necessarily is. The step into philosophy is the philosopher learning his difference.

Odysseus the knower is unique: "Without that knowledge [of what man necessarily is] he can be enchanted and made subject to perfect rule." Does that imply that *with* that knowledge one could duplicate Circe's enchantment, perfect rule? This question takes us deeper into the *Republic*, to its very center, where Socrates announces the precondition of perfect rule, that philosophers become kings or kings philosophers. Indicating that this is what Odysseus— a king who has become a philosopher—is pondering, Benardete asks: just how "tight" is this connection between doing and knowing, justice and knowledge? Is it as tight as the connection between "ignorance and bestiality," the tightness of mutual implication? "The insight might be implicit in the action," Benardete answers, the deed of rescuing his men may imply revelation of the *moly*, "but the action is not guided by the insight" (88)—as Odysseus narrated it, the insight succeeded the action. So the next question must be: "Is the necessity Odysseus acknowledges he is under to rescue his men ultimately the same as the knowledge of the necessity of the togetherness of looks and mind?"[11] That *mighty necessity* to act, was that *already* knowledge? Are justice and knowledge so tightly connected that at the upmost peak they are the same? If they are, then the precise knowledge Benardete describes, the necessary togetherness of looks and mind and the act that led to it, are one event split by the poet into two. The peak with its mighty necessity and its revelation of the *moly* would then be an instance of "the plot of poetic dialectic" (xiii). The connection between justice and knowledge would then be so tight that *as knower* Odysseus *must* rescue his men. If this is so, the philosopher *must* rule, stoop to rule.

The next paragraph assumes this connection and indicates how action and knowledge are together. Guarding his words, Benardete says this: "If man cannot live except politically, he must live with men who, if they do not know what constitutes man, must have a version of the knowledge of what constitutes man that does not preserve, however much it may reflect, the nature of man" (88). Odysseus is a solitary in the independence of his mind, but as a man he cannot live except politically; coming to know what constitutes man and having to live with those who cannot know, he knows he must offer them a version of his knowledge that reflects it without simply baring its harming truth. The justice of Odysseus's rescue of his men includes doing himself justice; his act for others is also a self-interested act, the self-preservation of the wise man through teaching a version of what he knows in order for him to be able to live politically. Odysseus rescues his men in order to rule them through a teaching, and that teaching effects rule for the sake of what he knows. Benardete states the indispensable element in that rule: "Homer indicates that a most powerful version of that knowledge is summed up in the word 'Hades.'"

"Hades" is the next section of Benardete's book, the second half of its center, its first half being "Nature." But here Benardete brings Hades forward, treating it out of order so as to explain how Hades is connected to nature as a teaching that is a version of a knowing; Odysseus's teaching will be a version of Odysseus's knowing. "'Hades splits body and soul apart in a peculiar way: the soul retains the looks of the body, and the mind vanishes entirely." This split indicates the unreality of Hades, but Benardete's point here is to indicate the function of Hades as a teaching. First, "Hades distinguishes man from everything else. Men go to Hades, all other animals just die." Hades allows humans to believe that a cardinal difference elevates them above all

---

11. "Looks" in this sentence is a synonym for the more usual "human shape" (e.g., 87, 92).

other animals. Second, "[t]his distinctiveness of man, whether exaggerated or not, imposes on man certain constraints" of which Benardete mentions the prohibition on cannibalism. Belief in Hades both elevates man and directs his behavior. Compelled by what he knows to act on behalf of those with whom he must live and who can never be knowers, Odysseus acts to elevate and restrain through belief. "Hades is a negative determination of man, and, as such, a lawful equivalent of Odysseus's knowledge of his nature." Odysseus knows and acts out of knowledge; he will teach those with whom he lives to believe in Hades and thereby to act out of belief-imposed constraints, to act lawfully. The invisibility of Hades "seems to displace the invisible bond in the nature of man" known to Odysseus. "Hades, therefore, is not a deduction from the knowledge of that bond." It is not knowledge implied by knowledge but a poetic version of knowledge fit for believers led by Elpenor. Elpenor, *hope*, shows how necessary Hades is for him and how unnecessary for Odysseus: he "has to remind Odysseus to bury him and threaten him with punishment if he does not."

Benardete begins his next paragraph asserting that "Odysseus's knowledge of nature does not go beyond the knowledge of man in general" (88). It does not extend to the knowledge of maleness and femaleness, of Circe, say, as Benardete's next sentences show: his knowledge "does not protect him against the possibility that if he sleeps with Circe she may unman him (*anēnōr*). A difference seems to be implied between the intelligible *eidos* of human being (*anthrōpos*) and the visible species (*eidos*) of man (*anēr*) and woman (*gunē*)." Are there intelligible *eidē* of manliness and womanliness? Benardete is poised on the edge of an immensity. Circe is a goddess of a woman. Could she put her womanliness into the service of her masculine mind and do to Odysseus what Ischomachos's wife did to Ischomachos? What does Odysseus know of maleness and femaleness as such? What does Homer know? Benardete looks to the event: "If Odysseus is naked, he is helpless against Circe unless she first swears an oath not to harm him in some other way." Being naked, Benardete suggests, probably means both "to be without clothes and to be unarmed." Does Odysseus need to be armed? Not if Circe is right: "Circe understands sexual love as a way of their shedding their mutual distrust." But Odysseus doesn't trust her: he "is told that she would still have an advantage over him." What advantage? Instead of pursuing the possibility of intrinsic female advantage, Benardete looks to male weakness: "[t]here is in man some capacity to resist, a strength of soul or whatever we choose to call it, that can be lost or diminished regardless of knowledge." What is it in man that could be lost or diminished in the face of woman, rather than added or augmented as Circe may be suggesting? "It seems to comprehend more than the shame and the weakness that, in the case of men, might be thought to accompany sex." Instead of trying to identify that losable more Benardete ends by contrasting Circe: "as a goddess and a daughter of the sun, Circe has nothing to lose and nothing to hide." Can that be true of womanliness in the face of manliness—can she risk being wholly transparent to maleness? Poised on the brink of the question of manliness and womanliness, with access to the resources of the *Odyssey* and its divinization of so many females, most particularly wise, warlike Athena, Benardete lets the issue go.[12]

The Bow and the Lyre limits the knowledge of nature attained by Homer's Odysseus to "the knowledge of man in general" (88).[13] But Benardete's 1984 commentary on Plato's *Theaetetus* showed that Homer himself claimed a knowledge of nature as a whole. In *Theaetetus* Socrates makes Homer the great general standing at the head of the large army (*Theaetetus* 153a) that constitutes the tradition of Greek wisdom that holds that "all things . . . come to be from locomotion and motion and mutual mixing; for nothing ever is, but (everything) always becomes" (152d). As Socrates there goes on to say,

> all the wise in succession, except Parmenides, converge, Protagoras and Heraclitus, and Empedocles, as well as the tip-top poets of each kind of poetry, Epicharmus of comedy and Homer of tragedy. Homer with the line "Ocean and Mother Tethys, the becoming (genesis) of gods" has said that everything is the offspring of flowing and motion.[14]

Benardete's commentary on *Theaetetus* exposes Socrates' penetration of the exotericism Homer originated, describing it this way: the "veiled speech of Homer[,] 'Both Oceanus and mother Tethys, the *genesis* of gods' . . . says,

---

12. Benardete's footnote at this point acknowledges that Odysseus's unmanning may refer to sleep, not sex. His views on Penelope are not encouraging about the divinization of womanliness. See note 18 below.

13. Benardete says that Odysseus's "story contains versions of both 'Nestor' and 'Menelaus'" (85; on Menelaus see 86), that is, of the two previous attempts in the *Odyssey* to give an account of the whole. But he does not seem to elaborate an Odyssean account of nature as a whole, of human kind within a totality of kinds.

14. *Theaetetus* 152e; *Iliad* 14.302. See *Theaetetus* 180d on the inadvisability of doing what Protagoras did in openly revealing this truth about things to everyone.

according to Socrates, that all things are the offspring of flowing and motion, whereas it seems to say that the gods have their origin in a male and a female god, who did not themselves become."[15] Homer then, the first author whose writings have come down to us, is the first to convey a process ontology, a totality of becoming, and to veil it in a poetic theology of ostensibly immortal beings. But that originating Homeric achievement attains, in Socrates, something far more important than mere explicitness because Socrates sees that "the principle of everything is a something, permanent, comprehensive, that gives its own character to everything"; the whole tradition of Greek ontology from Homer onward is gathered into a Socratic culmination. But if "only now with Socrates can the truth be brought entirely into the light," that light must include its own veiling because if Socrates has just told Theaetetus "the secret of the wise," their secret is that they never "said what they meant." Wise Socrates will poetize his insight regarding the permanence of kinds into a theology of ostensibly permanent entities. This history of Greek ontology and poetic theology with its origin in Homer and its peak in Socrates seems not to enter *The Bow and the Lyre*; there, Benardete is content to follow Odysseus as he moves from the original discovery of nature in human nature to the discovery of the necessary theological-political program to shelter it.

After letting the great issue of manliness and womanliness fall, Benardete follows Odysseus's narrative into an epoch-making theological point. After Circe swears her oath and they make love, Odysseus falls into a distress that Circe cannot figure out. Odysseus shares with his fellow humans something she lacks; he pities them, she does not. She takes pity only after she sees each man clasp Odysseus's hand and hears the house ring with lamentations of longing. "This is an extraordinary thing; a god learns from a man" (89). The extraordinariness of her learning lies in its being an event in the history of religion: gods from now on pity humans and act on their pity. Like Hades, the gods' pity represents a historic advance in religion, in what a god is. Benardete wonders what might have happened had Circe not sworn her oath and learned pity: perhaps Odysseus, having attained a paradise of knowing and enjoying, "might have been dehumanized...might have suffered another form of enchantment.... Perhaps he no longer would have had the heart or manliness to resist a version of Calypso's temptation." Had he not learned that he could teach a god pity, perhaps he would have chosen to live forever on an Island of the Blest and never descended to humans. What Odysseus

---

15. *The Being of the Beautiful: Plato's "Theaetetus," "Sophist," and "Statesman"* (Chicago: University of Chicago Press, 1984), 1.105.

learned at the peak, his entry into philosophy, would have been historically useless had he not taught a god to pity; having for the first time done something just and daring, not involving his own advantage, he teaches the gods to be like him.

When Odysseus returns to bring the rest of his crew to Circe's, he uses an image for his men that turns them into domestic animals joyfully dependent on him. Eurylochus shatters that image of perfect rule, shrewd Eurylochus who charges that it was by Odysseus's wickedness that their comrades perished in Polyphemus's cave. "This charge," Benardete comments, "which casually attributes criminality to the desire to know, is too close to the truth to be answered effectively" (90). Benardete's final paragraph in "Nature" begins: "The discovery of nature is clearly linked with the problem of rule." Rule by Odysseus was once so natural, so sovereign and gentle that he took over rule in Ithaca long before his father Laertes, himself a good ruler, had died.[16] Now however, now that war and return have changed his men, now that a new generation of young Ithacans strive to replace an Odysseus thought lost and to usurp Telemachus's right to rule, now the discoverer of nature will have to establish rule that is new in two ways. One way accommodates the Elpenors with Hades, and the other way is intimated here by Odysseus's failure with Eurylochus. For "Odysseus ultimately loses out to Eurylochus" on the Island of the Sun, and here at Circe's he loses control as his men demand to return home after a year. "The obstacle Eurylochus represents points directly to the suitors." Odysseus learns from his failure with Eurylochus that successful rule by those he will put in place, Telemachus and his associates, depends upon an act of political establishment that will hold in memory the wickedness of those who opposed it and the virtue of those who established it: *all* the suitors must die and die for moral reasons.

"Hades"

"Hades can be said to be the most potent symbol" of the Olympian gods (91). In "Hades," that section twinned at the center with "Nature," Benardete shows Odysseus learning Hades' potency and therewith perhaps his hardest lesson, what he must teach. "Odysseus is about to enter upon his fate" as he draws the logical implications of his discovery of nature. Having learned that humans have a nature, act out a nature, he learns that he must teach humans

---

16. Athena appearing as Mentes betrayed the fist behind that gentle rule: "so terribly did [Mentes's father] love" Odysseus that he gave him the deadly poison for his arrows that he so insistently sought (1.260–64).

a potent supernatural. A philosopher must become a political philosopher with a theological-political teaching. In Hades Odysseus learns the two main elements of his fate. One, involving his justice, concerns Ithaca and the establishment there of the order of succession that will institutionalize wise rule in the absence of the wise man. The other, involving his piety, concerns leaving home for his final journey to establish Hades and the Olympian gods among a people who do not know them. "The discovery of nature is clearly linked with the problem of rule" (90), and in "Hades" Benardete shows Odysseus learning the two dimensions of the problem of rule plus their solutions. The center of *The Bow and the Lyre* shows philosophy generating political philosophy.

The second paragraph of "Hades" is particularly eloquent and deep as Benardete conveys Odysseus's despair at this next stage of his learning. For this is the Odysseus who just gained a stage of enlightenment that cannot but bring the deepest exhilaration—a year with Circe. Now, however, he hits a limitation on enlightenment, a limit on its power that seems to render it worthless. Benardete suggests that the problem is perpetual: "The difficulty we have in understanding Hades" is one Odysseus faced. But he solved it: if he despairs on learning that he must go to Hades he recovers slowly as he learns from Elpenor and Teiresias. Benardete introduced Elpenor at the end of "Nature" as "the man of hope…the youngest and least equipped with either brains or brawn" (90). He now reports Odysseus's telling of "the mischance of Elpenor" (91). "In the *Odyssey*, no soul goes to Hades before Elpenor's does, and Odysseus himself never speaks in this way again." But Homer does: "It is Homer who bears witness to Hades. It is the only one of Odysseus's tales that Homer retells" (92). And Hades is the only heading Benardete uses twice, for when Homer tells of the souls of the suitors going to Hades, Benardete gives that event too the title "Hades" (146–50).

"Odysseus himself," Benardete says, "seems to believe the soul to be no more than the fact of breathing…and the soul as something separable and in itself merely the hope of the foolish 'man of hope' Elpenor." By contrasting Homer and Odysseus on their view of Hades, Benardete is able to explain Odysseus's despair: it would "arise from his being told, after he had realized the necessary togetherness of human shape and human mind, that the gods can separate them." Odysseus learns that the gods have the power to do what cannot be done, separate or seem to separate the constituent elements of human nature, which can exist only together. But the gods grant a benefit too: "in the case of Teiresias" they can "put them together again apart from life and away from the light of the sun." The gods permit the wise man a singular future as the only human whose active mind persists in the afterlife.

Odysseus's despair, as Benardete displays it across this section, is the despair of the rational man at the power of the irrational. The power of the gods is the power of imaginary beings over an imaginary entity that those most lacking in brains believe goes down to Hades. Attaining insight into human nature Odysseus sees the power the gods have over human nature because of the way it rules the Elpenors. One of the lessons showing Odysseus the power of the gods comes at the end of his journey to Hades: he sees the Kimmerian people, "upon whom the sun never shines either when it is rising or when it is setting," a literally benighted people of literally no enlightenment, but a living people. "To be alive is not the same as to see the light of the sun.... Night belongs to the gods" (92). And there will always be Night, and Night will always carry its invisible powers into the Day in the needs of the Elpenors. Homer depicts his Odysseus learning the unwelcome lesson that Nietzsche, millennia later, knew would be least welcome to the newly liberated free minds of the modern Enlightenment to whom he addressed his books: the power of religion. Homer will show a despairing Odysseus learning to tap that power—the very lesson Nietzsche learned and had to teach while fearing that it came too early, too soon after the liberation from God.

In Hades, Odysseus's first two encounters and his last are especially instructive. From Elpenor, the first, he "learns about the divine duty he owes to the least important of men" (92). Elpenor fell to his death at Circe's and arrives in Hades before Odysseus. He adds to the account of his death that Odysseus has already given "that a god had doomed him.... Odysseus attributed it to a lack of brains" (93). Dim Elpenor and wise Teiresias, encountered second, each assign Odysseus a task. Elpenor asks "that his armor be buried with him, a tomb (*sēma*) be built near the seashore, and an oar be fixed on top with which he used to row when he was alive." Elpenor "wants to be known to people in the future as a somebody, even if he is not a name to them. They will know who he was from what he did. It is not much, but it is something." "[F]rom Teiresias [Odysseus] learns his future" (92), for Teiresias tells him that after killing the suitors he was fated to one more labor: "you must take up your well-shaped oar and go on a journey" (11.121). Elpenor's oar on top of his tomb "cannot be misunderstood" (93), but the oar Teiresias instructs Odysseus to carry must be misunderstood: Odysseus's journey will take him to a people who do not know the sea and do not salt their food; they do not know of ships or oars. The clear sign (*sēma*) to Odysseus that he has reached his goal will be when a traveler meets him and, on seeing the oar Teiresias has told him to carry on his shoulder, says he is carrying a winnowing fan.

When he hears his oar called a winnowing fan, "Odysseus is to fix the oar in the ground and make a sacrifice to Poseidon." In order to perform the massive sacrifice Teiresias describes, Odysseus will have to persuade the strangers among whom he has arrived to provide the animals for sacrifice. He will have to make a persuasive speech. Teiresias does not give him his words, but Benardete starts him off: "'There is a god,' he will say, 'who presides over something you cannot see.'" That unseen god is potent Hades presiding over the unseen afterworld. The sacrifice is to Poseidon, inseparable from his brothers, Hades and Zeus, and the avenging god whom Odysseus offended by blinding his beloved son Polyphemus. To make a sacrifice to Poseidon among those who do not know the sea and to tell of unseen Hades is to introduce the Olympian gods to those still ignorant of them. Wise Teiresias instructs the knower that he must journey to establish belief in gods in whom he himself has learned disbelief.

After starting Odysseus's speech on an invisible god, Benardete reverts to the setting for Odysseus's tale, Phaeacia and its wise king: "Odysseus, who was chosen to bring home to the Phaeacians that the gods have ceased to be manifest to them and are essentially invisible, is destined to extend the Olympian gods into a region where the sign of their being will cease to point to their being." Odysseus's task is historic. It is previewed in the "practice run" (50) of what he is effecting among the Phaeacians by telling his odyssey to their wise king: the knower of nature, passing on his knowledge to a wise ruler, shows himself destined to be a radical reformer in religion, replacing the visible gods with invisible Olympians; the gods disappear into words, into a veil of words. Odysseus "will break the connection with the cosmic gods that still lingers, in the element of metonymy, among the Olympian gods. The oar will be a sign with a displaced significance. That significance will be of a radically new kind" (93). Odysseus effects his revolution in religion through poetry: "the poetry implicit in the word for winnowing fan (*athērēloigos*)—it is literally a 'chaff-destroyer'—does not offer a way to explain the oar." The oar as a sign on Elpenor's tomb stands unmistakably for Poseidon, lord of the sea, and for the sailor buried under it. The oar stuck in the ground among those who do not know the sea will come to stand for Hades of the winnowing fan, symbolizing the separation of the good from the bad by an avenging justice in the afterworld. Only later does Benardete state the scope of Odysseus's theological-political labor: misreading the oar as a winnowing fan "does not just hold among a people who do not know the sea; the effect of that misreading will spread everywhere and put everyone in fear and trembling" (106). The topic has there become the fate of the Phaeacians after Alcinous heard Odysseus's story, accepted it, and commissioned a ship to take him home. Zeus tempers Poseidon's excessive appetite for punishing them for benefiting Odysseus, but Benardete is clear, he is ruthless, in stating the core of the new religion: "The essence of this new relation [between gods and men] will be one of terror" (105). The terror will be inescapable, for the new religion teaches that man is "completely porous for the gods. The gods . . . can get in anywhere, and there is no place to hide" (57). At the center of Benardete's book the only living mind among the dead instructs Odysseus on a second journey to establish invisible moral gods who will terrorize everyone everywhere. As his book moves through its second half, that journey is a constant background and frequent foreground until its last sentence announces that the hard lesson has been learned.[17]

Teiresias, the wise man whose mind lives on, tells Odysseus his far future by assigning him his journey with the oar. He tells him his nearer future as well, what he must do at Ithaca before he sets out on his final journey. Benardete devotes the center of his "Hades" section to that task, having changed the order in which Teiresias presented the tasks. He approaches the center with a paragraph on its theme, the establishment of the new regime at Ithaca whereby the wise ruler secures the succession of wise rule through the generations of inevitably less wise that follow him. Teiresias informs him of the

> troubles in your household,
> insolent men, who are eating away your livelihood
> and courting your godlike wife and offering gifts to win her.
> You may punish the violences of these men, when you come
> home. (11.115–18)

---

17. Among the riches of the second half of his book is Benardete's demonstration that corresponding to the withdrawal of the gods into potent invisibility is the internalization of guilt and the consequent fear of deserved punishment: the invisible Olympian brothers require a new understanding of the soul as well.

As Benardete says, "The violent acts of which Teiresias speaks . . . are one: Antinous hits Odysseus with a stool" (94). This is "another sign," one that "requires the killing of 108 suitors in order that there be a requital for it." The central paragraph of "Hades" investigates what "Teiresias intended" with the sign of Odysseus being hit by a stool; it investigates "[t]he apparent disproportion between the crime of the suitors and their punishment."

The suitors sue for the hand of Penelope, the queen they regard as widowed by the death of absent Odysseus: they are aspirants to rule following the tradition of legitimate succession, presuming only that they get rid of Telemachus.[18] Benardete speaks of Odysseus's "vengeance" and wonders why the suitors' "last-minute proposal should not be accepted, that they pay back what they ate and drank plus damages."[19] He concludes that "they must be punished for the thought that lay behind their gobbling up of his goods." That thought treated him as no longer alive, and "[n]ot to be alive would mean to them to be helpless"—it did not mean descended to Hades. "The suitors do not believe in Hades" (95). In place of Hades, the suitors threaten

---

18. On one matter of great seriousness, Benardete seems to me to be serially mistaken: Penelope. He ridicules her for being merely and excessively pious, for lacking hardness, being dissolvable into mere water. Penelope can be spared this unbecoming sport by considering that the suitor Amphimedon, dead and in Hades, "puts Penelope squarely in the center of the conspiracy against the suitors" (149) and "assumes that Penelope was in on it from the start" (96). Benardete thinks Amphimedon is mistaken, but he's not. Eva Brann recognized Penelope's acuteness and resolve: "When does Penelope recognize Odysseus? At first sight, of course." *Homeric Moments: Clues to Delight in Reading the* Odyssey (Philadelphia: Paul Dry Books, 2002), 274. Brann provides exegetical proof from the beautiful precision of Penelope's words to Odysseus (274–84). Recognizing her disguised husband, she tells him of her own guile in tricking the suitors into believing she was weaving a shroud for Laertes; she tells him a "dream" that conveys to him her recognition of him while also conveying her knowledge of the need for utter secrecy; and she sets up the contest of the bow in order to arm him for the fight. Very instructive with respect to Penelope's guile is John J. Winkler, "Penelope's Cunning and Homer's," *The Constraints of Desire: The Anthropology of Sex and Gender in Ancient Greece* (New York: Routledge, 1989), 129–61. See also Benjamin Haller, "The Gates of Horn and Ivory in *Odyssey* 19: Penelope's Call for Deeds Not Words," *Classical Philology* 104 (2009): 397–417.

19. Benardete attributes this proposal to Amphinomus, the best of the suitors, the one Penelope liked best and who warned Odysseus; it was actually made by Eurymachos, the leader, with Antinous, of the suitors (94).

to send wrongdoers to "the bogeyman King Echetus." Echetus lacks Hades' potency: he "is a kind of pre-Olympian Hades who sets no limits on mortals." This deficiency in punishment points to something still more significant:

> the suitors never speak at all of men as mortals…[they] do not believe that men are constituted by the contrariety of the pair immortal (*athanatos*) and mortal (*thnētos*). They therefore do not acknowledge 'mortal' as the marked term of that pair, with "Hades" and all it entails standing behind it.

Just what "Hades" entails ends the paragraph: "The vengeance with which Elpenor, a nobody, threatens Odysseus if he does not bury him, presupposes that though dead he is not helpless. He is something."[20]

Benardete did not quite say what Teiresias intended: the founding of a new religion. All the suitors, aspiring rulers of the old order, must die in order to wipe out memory of the old religion, which did not know how to set limits on mortals by threatening proper punishment. The paragraph of "Hades" that Benardete made central considers the cost of founding the religion of which Hades is the most potent symbol by setting the cost, 108 suitors, against the gain, the potency of Hades: a nobody can threaten a somebody from Hades. Odysseus had to kill all 108 suitors in order to arm the gods with Hades or to give power to the vengeance of the nobodies by making the gods agents of punishment. The "slave revolt in morality" is the work not of slaves or masters but of the wise poet.

Why give power to the nobodies? Because the coming order will necessarily be more democratic, ruled not by a wise man but by Telemachus and

---

20. In the central section of the chapter "Nonfated Things," Benardete identifies Homer's positive way for every human to be a something. Disguised as a beggar, Odysseus is challenged at the door to his palace by Irus, a real beggar. Odysseus beats him up, knocking him out—saving him from the coming killing. Odysseus "tells him in effect that he was punished for affecting to be the prince of beggars and strangers" (127). Odysseus made a number of such boasts and challenges to prove himself a superior inferior: to a beggar, a swineherd, a suitor, a slave woman. Benardete concludes: "The dignity of the human, to which everyone seems entitled, shows up together with the pride of Odysseus, to which no one else can lay claim; and everyone is punished who does not acknowledge the coincidence of the class characteristic of man with the highest representative of man. No body (οὐτιδανός) is No One (οὔ τις)" (128). Everyone is a somebody because each is a member of the same species as Odysseus.

his associates. The associate Homer makes most prominent is you, Eumaeus, "noble swineherd" and "leader of men," Homer's sole addressee within the poem, addressed as "you" some fifteen times. Homer spoke literally in calling him "noble swineherd": he was of royal birth but slavish nature, loyally tending the pigs of a master absent for twenty years, happy to condemn the freedom-at-all-cost sought by his Phoenician nurse willing to win freedom for herself by yielding him up to her deliverers. To address Eumaeus as "leader of men" "indicates that the *Odyssey* is primarily for him" (124), a leader of pigs. A more democratic order needs Olympian gods: the strength of rulers not themselves strong must be fortified by more powerful agents.

But doesn't this make the killing of all 108 suitors an act of mere calculation and not the act of justice that Homer himself, plus the gods and Penelope and Telemachus and all the others, say it is? The central paragraph of the central section of "Nonfated Things," "The Slave Girls," faces the possibility that Odysseus acted out of pure calculation: "The more Odysseus seems calculating, however, the more terrible he becomes ... we are not being overly squeamish if we find Odysseus repulsive because he can bring himself to realize an argument" (126). And Benardete blinks. He acts to restore Odysseus's morality by taking seriously all that "evidence" against a "cold-blooded Odysseus," evidence tracing his actions to his heart, to righteous indignation at suitors made wicked and blameworthy. Benardete's blink at a repulsive Odysseus serves a purpose, or proves calculating: "This reinterpretation is not meant to make us feel any better about Odysseus, but rather to bring into relief the unblinking gaze of Homer, who would in this way be distinguishing the bow from the lyre." Using the very title of his book, Benardete intimates that Odysseus's killing bow is sung as the instrument of right by the sweet lyre of an unblinking, calculating mind. The succession requires the cold-blooded killing of all the noble heirs of the old regime and requires as well allowing the gratuitous indecency of hanging the slave girls as an act of cleansing vengeance performed by the new rulers. Homer beautifies the repulsive calculation of necessity in the character he authored; he needs his moral decency intact if he is to be honored forever as the founding father of the political order we enjoy by the grace of wise Zeus.[21]

---

21. Benardete ends his book on the unrecognizability of Odysseus as the killer of the suitors: Penelope attributes the killing to the just gods; Laertes finds it the very proof that they exist. Overcoming the need to be recognized for what he really is and did frees Odysseus to submit to his fate; *now* he should know his destiny (152).

Benardete finds Odysseus's discovery of what Hades really is in the line that opens and closes the Circe episode: "There is no possibility of accomplishment for those who weep and mourn" (97). In Hades everyone weeps and mourns. "Nonaccomplishment characterizes Hades." The nonaccomplishment is of a particular kind: "Hades is dominated by the demand for the satisfaction of right.... What never dies is ungrounded or senseless expectation." Self-knowledge enabled Odysseus to recognize the power of the demand for the satisfaction of right: his own desire for revenge on Polyphemus taught him "the great strain the will is under to reinterpret necessity as right" (75). Yielding to that strain built and sustains Hades. What Odysseus sees last in Hades he takes "as a sign that he will not see [Hades] again" (97). What he sees last is Herakles. Part of what Herakles in Hades illustrates is "the unreality of Hades": Herakles in Hades is as real as the carving on his golden shoulder strap, for "Heracles himself (*autos*) is among the gods" (98). Herakles made a god means that what Herakles in Hades illustrates most crucially is "the absence of the good." For who is Herakles to Odysseus? Benardete tells his reader now what Homer withheld for later: Herakles murdered Odysseus's friend Iphitus, who gave him the bow with which he will slay the suitors. Herakles is a murderer who killed Odysseus's friend in his own home when Iphitus was there as his houseguest (21.11–41). "The gods reward injustice with immortality." "Perhaps he fears he would have seen Iphitus"—with these words of bitter eloquence Benardete ends "Hades," explaining why curious Odysseus left in "green fear." "This is the low point of Odysseus's narrative," perhaps the lowest point possible, for the unreal gods welcome to their number a real criminal, allowing him to escape Hades for Olympus and real immortal glory. Odysseus can accept the amorality of nature, but the immorality of the gods, their rewarding criminality with immortality, is harder. Still, Teiresias knows that that is the cure Odysseus must swallow.

Who then is Teiresias, that underworld instructor? The only living mind in Hades is the wise man who alone has an afterlife as himself, as a mind teaching the rare living visitor to arrive in Hades with his mind intact that he still has a task to perform. Teiresias is Homer's acknowledgment that he too was favored by a teacher among the dead. When he too journeyed to the underworld he too learned from a wise predecessor, living on in wise words, that he had a task to perform after understanding human nature. There is a long tradition of wisdom stretching back in time, Homer suggests through his Teiresias, a tradition from which he learned and to which he contributed by composing the *Odyssey*.

Who then is Homer? A singer in the epic tradition, he is, he suggests, the current nameholder for nameless wisdom passed on from wise to wise and modified or advanced as necessity dictates. As a teacher on the gods set in motion by "Teiresias," Homer teaches a wisdom about the gods that causes the visible gods whom all revere because of their evident power to fade in the brilliant light of invisible Olympians better able to work the necessary effects on human nature, better able in their invisibility to be constantly present to encourage and to judge. Being a singer in the epic tradition, he knows the power of song to mesmerize and stamp whole populations. Being Homer, he knows how to bend that tradition to new, more moral ends enforced by angry Poseidon and invisible Hades and ruled over by wise Zeus and wise Athena, the wisdom born from Zeus's very head; and he knows how to embed in the already existing exoteric form of epic verse esoteric truths to inform and instruct those like himself. With his *Odyssey* Homer became the Teiresias of aftertime; those who visit him after his death by entering the underworld of his *Odyssey* find him a mind alive, a mind with counsel for the aspiring wise on the necessity of a second journey, of aspiring to rule through words put up of the gods.

Benardete visited Homer there, but he began his book on Homer by saying he found Plato in Homer and wondered if his finding was "forced and willful" (xi). Did Plato read Homer as Benardete read Homer, as his Teiresias?

How Did Plato Read Homer?

The evidence that Plato read Homer as Benardete read Homer is, by necessity, indirect. Socrates' attack on Homer in Plato's *Republic* is not counterevidence because the *Republic* shows that Socrates too learned that it was his destiny to establish belief and not knowledge—and to establish those beliefs, the authority of Homer had to be broken. Socrates did not have to kill 108 suitors, he had to kill Homer, seem to kill Homer. I confine myself to three examples that show Plato reading Homer as Benardete did.[22]

Plato gave most of his dialogues a time and place in Socrates's life, a chronological setting that allows them to be arranged along the timeline of Socrates' life. If the dialogues are treated as wholes, the youngest Socrates

---

22. For additional examples and expansions of these three, see my *How Philosophy Became Socratic: A Study of Plato's "Protagoras," "Charmides," and "Republic"* (Chicago: University of Chicago Press, 2010).

appears in *Protagoras*.[23] The chronologically first speech in Plato's corpus is therefore the question put to Socrates by a fellow citizen: "From where, Socrates, are you appearing?" The citizen answers his own question because he believes that he knows Socrates well enough to conclude that he must be appearing from an erotic pursuit of Alcibiades, a now unlawful pursuit given that Alcibiades' first growth of beard is showing. Acknowledging the light-hearted charge that he is a criminal, Socrates defends himself with his first speech on Plato's stage: "Don't you praise Homer, who says that the most charming age is that of the early beard?" Homer says that of the Hermes who appeared to Odysseus at the moment when mighty necessity moved him to rescue his men from Circe's enchantment, the Hermes who revealed to Odysseus the nature of the *moly*. Plato therefore arranged that the first words spoken by his Socrates answer both the question of his origins and a criminal charge—and Socrates' first words praise Homer for Odysseus's encounter with Hermes, for the act of revelation at the peak of the *Odyssey*. A more awesome opening to the Platonic corpus is scarcely imaginable. From where, Socrates, are you appearing? From an understanding of nature on the way to delivering my people from enchantment.

Did Plato mean to imply, then, that Socrates is a new Odysseus? Plato set *Charmides* in late May 429, about four years after *Protagoras*, on the day after Socrates returned home from his two-and-a-half- or three-year absence with the Athenian army besieging rebel Potidaea. Socrates says he returns different, having learned in his absence a new teaching on the soul, a teaching that is a medicine that can heal the sickness of the head troubling Charmides. The medicine takes the form of "incantations" taught to Socrates, he says, by a doctor of Zalmoxis, the god of the Getae, who believe he is the only God. Who is this returning Socrates now come home after a long absence and announcing that he brings a new teaching on god and the soul? Plato leads his reader to the proper understanding by referring to the *Odyssey* four times, openly and not at all openly. Each of the four references refers to a separate recognition scene in the *Odyssey* where the returned Odysseus masked as a beggar is recognized as himself. Plato put all four in the proper order from the first recognition by Telemachus to the last by old Dolius, with the most prominent being Penelope's recognition conveyed to Odysseus through a dream she reports. Plato therefore allows his Homer-trained audience to

---

23. Within the dialogues *Phaedo*, *Parmenides*, and the *Symposium*, Plato gave his readers glimpses of a younger Socrates on the way to his mature thought, a maturity first shown in his confrontation with the man thought the wisest of his time, Protagoras.

recognize the Socrates of *Charmides* as a new Odysseus returning after a long absence to save his people with a new teaching on god and the soul.

But why does *Charmides* contain no syllable of the promised incantations? Plato set the *Republic* in early June 429, a week or two after *Charmides*: the *Republic* reports the healing incantations that the returned Odysseus promised but left unspoken in *Charmides*. The *Republic* is Socrates' report in Athens of a private conversation he held last night in the Piraeus, at the place and time that the Athenians were publicly introducing a new goddess in hopes of deliverance from the plague. Today Socrates narrates in Athens for all to hear the genuine teaching of deliverance, his own new teaching on god and the soul—and on what a philosopher should be believed to be. Plato intimates most beautifully that a new Odysseus teaches the new beliefs: he allows Odysseus's name to be spoken only twice, at other times explicitly avoiding his name as when referring to "the wisest of men."[24] Socrates first names Odysseus near the beginning, when he refers to Autolycus, Wolf Himself, Odysseus's grandfather on his mother's side, who gave him his name. He cites Homer's description of Autolycus as surpassing all men "in stealing and in swearing oaths," disreputable qualities that help Socrates seem to dismiss his argument's conclusion that the just man is the best thief (334b–c)—qualities of Autolycus, passed on to his grandson, that slowly become apparent as characteristic of the justice of the wise man. Socrates next names Odysseus at the very end, when the soul of Odysseus is the last to choose a new life in the closing myth of the *Republic*, the myth that helps establish Plato's new, post-Homeric Hades. Recovered from the love of honor, the soul of Odysseus spends a long time searching among the available lives, at last finding the one it sought, "the life of a private man who minds his own business." The *Republic* teaches that the most private of men who most minds his own business is the philosopher: the soul of Odysseus chose as its next life the life of Socrates, the returned Odysseus of *Charmides* and the *Republic*. By having Socrates name Odysseus only at the *Republic*'s opening and close and only in reference to a forebear and a successor, Plato indicates that Socrates too had his Teiresias, his forebear in the succession of wisdom: wise Homer. And Plato acknowledges thereby that he too will have a successor among souls that choose their new lives partly by reading him, by entering the underworld of

---

24. *Republic* 390a. Plato there seems to criticize Odysseus for making the pleasures of eating and drinking "the finest of all things." But Odysseus's words actually refer to the setting for what he regards as the truly finest thing, the feast of listening to a wise poet.

his writings: Plato too acknowledges that he too knows that his successor must kill all 108 suitors.[25]

From Homer to Nietzsche

Roberto Calasso said, "Every doctrine of progress is refuted by the existence of the *Iliad*."[26] No, the *Odyssey* progressed beyond the *Iliad*. And Plato's Socrates, Benardete indicates, progressed beyond the *Odyssey* both in philosophy, taking the idea as cause, and in political philosophy, teaching morally stricter gods and a morally stricter Hades. Benardete shows that Homer anticipated that next step in religion with his Theoclymenus, "he who hearkens to gods" (119). His is a "mind so possessed by the gods that it can 'see' what no one else can." "[H]e embodies the future rule of the prophet, who will be the sole intermediary between gods and men once the gods have completed their withdrawal" (120). Delivering his lamentation like a "quasi-Biblical prophecy," he "belongs to another story." Theoclymenus is, says Benardete in the most electric theological judgment in his book, "a deduction of an argument." Homer teaches with his Theoclymenus the natural history of religion as the inexorable logic of religion.[27]

Knowing the logic of religion and standing within the Homeric tradition, Plato's Socrates is the truly free mind who introduces quasi-biblical reforms: he reforms the gods in the Theoclymenean direction, making them more moral and moving toward a monotheism with a Good ruling from beyond being; and he correspondingly alters the soul by taming the thumotic element Homer watered and making the soul immortal; and he alters Hades by increasing its terror and sweetening its hope.

---

25. In his book on the *Republic*, published five years before he completed *The Bow and the Lyre*, Benardete refused to set wise Plato in the stream of supplanted Teiresiases. Instead, he works to make it seem that Plato's Socrates is a mind alive but with no predecessors: in his last paragraph he says of the fateful choice by the soul of Odysseus, "In the myth of Er no one chooses [the life of philosophy] ...Socrates himself seems never to have been Odysseus. His *daimonion*, he said, was probably unique." *Socrates' Second Sailing: On Plato's* Republic (Chicago: University of Chicago Press, 1989), 29.

26. Roberto Calasso, *The Marriage of Cadmus and Harmony*, trans. Tim Parks (New York: Knopf, 1993), 106.

27. Leo Strauss traced that logic or genealogy of religion in "Reason and Revelation," reprinted in Heinrich Meier, *Leo Strauss and the Theologico-Political Problem* (Cambridge: Cambridge University Press, 2006), 141–80.

Is there progress beyond Socrates, Odyssean Socrates with quasi-biblical advances? Nietzsche closed his first supplement to *Human, All Too Human, Assorted Opinions and Maxims*, with an entry called *Descent to Hades*. It begins: "I too have been to the underworld, like Odysseus, and will be there many times again; and I have not sacrificed only rams to be able to talk with the dead, but have not spared my own blood as well."[28] Nietzsche consulted the alive minds among the dead, eight thinkers in four pairs, "who did not refuse themselves to me the sacrificer," Plato among them, paired with Rousseau. "Whatever I say, resolve, cogitate for myself and others: upon these eight I fix my eyes and see theirs fixed on me." In his mature works, those eyes fixed on him, the new visitor to Hades, descended to that underworld from a radically transformed present, argued for the necessity of progress in both philosophy and political philosophy, in knowing the world as will to power and nothing else and in celebrating that world partly through the god-creating instinct.

---

28. *Human, All Too Human: A Book for Free Spirits*, Vol. II, part 1, *Assorted Opinions and Maxims*, aph. 408, trans. R. J. Hollingdale (Cambridge: Cambridge University Press, 1986), 299.

Chapter Four

Parmenides' Truth

John Blanchard

Seth Benardete begins "The First Crisis in First Philosophy" with a curious and exoteric sounding sentence: "Virtually everyone knows that Aristotle sometimes lies."[1] He claims that this is due to Aristotle's selectivity in writing, which leaves out of account those things that do not suit his scheme. That scheme, of course, is Aristotle's unfolding of the as yet incomplete discovery of cause by his predecessors, at the beginning of the *Metaphysics*. Although Aristotle says those earlier thinkers were somehow compelled by the truth itself,[2] his disclosure of their philosophical progress conforms to his own view that wisdom is the theoretical knowledge of cause, and this conviction apparently entitles him to hold back certain aspects of what some of them may have said (Parmenides' mind is not mentioned, whereas Parmenides' Eros is).[3] Aristotle's recounting of philosophy's truth-driven march forward might seem to describe something almost providential, were we not made aware that this history results from a dissembling. His "likely arrangement" calls to mind words of Parmenides' goddess which describe her story of mortal opinions.[4] To Benardete, the fact that this plausible ordering suddenly spawns the perplexities about being in Book II of the *Metaphysics* signals the crisis of first philosophy, for Aristotle has not established the

---

Originally presented at the conference on "The Thought of Seth Benardete," Howard University, April 2005.

1. "The First Crisis in First Philosophy," *Graduate Faculty Philosophy Journal* 18, no. 1 (1995): 237–48, reprinted in *The Argument of the Action*, eds. Ronna Burger and Michael Davis (Chicago: University of Chicago Press, 2000), 3–14.
2. Aristotle *Metaphysics* 984b10.
3. Perhaps this is Aristotle's version of the Muses telling lies like the truth.
4. Parmenides, fragment DK B8.60, *diakosmon eoikota* and cf. B8.52. References to the fragments follow the convention of Diels-Kranz in *Die Fragmente der Vorsokratiker* (6th ed.); for example, B1.28 refers to fragment 1, line 28.

field of first philosophy in his review of the pre-Socratic's incipient knowledge of cause, but has only suggested what still needs to be known, i.e., being. Aristotle's prevarication reveals itself through his non-problematic disclosure of the four causes, through which representation being comes to show itself as the problem.

Benardete explains that an interrogatory lay concealed within the resoluteness of Aristotle's story of the four causes, in the guise of formal cause. Among the categorial predicates, he points out, formal cause is both the only one of the four causes to appear, and the only predicate that doubles as a question, rather than an answer. Its question—What is?—includes in its very formulation just that which it is about. Accordingly, being lurks within the four causes (to borrow Benardete's verb) and remains immanent as the underlying question of formal cause. He reflects on this disclosure of that which is as a question as follows: "To ask about being is to acknowledge belatedly that it has come to light as a question about which one asks questions."[5] The primacy of Aristotle's first philosophy is thus brought into question by Benardete's recognition of the underlying persistence of the question of being. The seventeen questions that come to the surface in Book Beta (perhaps, as a first recognition of what is not first for us) serve *prima facie* to deprive his first philosophy of whatever ordinal claim it has to being first. And these questions, Benardete implies, could not have been fashioned without Aristotle's rather Procrustean depiction of wisdom as the theoretical knowledge of cause. Being, as being already there as a question, again somehow always comes to be a problem. Aristotle's somewhat deferred introduction of the perplexity about being—a question that already underlies the entire range of possible answers —then makes us wonder where we are to begin. In finally, or belatedly, coming to acknowledge the prescient question of being concealed in his ordering of the pre-Socratic's incomplete answers, it is likely that Aristotle has also been compelled by the truth.

If Aristotle's first philosophy cannot really be first, because his uncovering of the questions about being only comes about through his artful compilation of this seemingly non-problematic narrative tale, it also cannot be first because the perplexity of being has preceded even his inquiry about it as the question already there about which one inquires. His deceptive version of his forerunners' advancement of wisdom is that kind of selective ordering that Benardete calls lying. Parmenides' goddess, when referring to the paradox of her own speech at the beginning of the poem's third section on mortal opin-

---

5. "The First Crisis in First Philosophy," 3.

ions, also says, listen "to the deceitful ordering of my words."[6] Perhaps she is a little more honest. Yet Benardete suggests that the lie of Aristotle's artifice leads to the emergence of the problems about being, which reveals the crisis of first philosophy. One truth, apparently, that emerges in Aristotle's report of the route to first philosophy is that his account has not been the route to what is first at all. In a way, the way up and the way down are not the same.

Accordingly, Benardete divines the way to what is first through a detour. That is, he considers theology, Aristotle's synonym for first philosophy, and leads us through it back (*via* Plato) toward *the* beginning, to the beings as first disclosed by Hesiod, although Hesiod's myth about the gods is not actually his own, but properly belongs to the Muses. As virtually everyone knows, the Muses told Hesiod that they can speak lies like the truth and can utter the truth whenever they wish. Prior to philosophy, we learn, poetry already had separated lies from the truth and again rejoined them—had recognized the distinction between a tantalizing eros and artful making (or, the insertion of non-being into being). Yet, poetry cannot really be first, either, as Benardete reveals, for it also comes after the beginning, "...when the speaking about the speaking about things has become part of the speaking."[7] The beginning, he notes, must be that about which the first speaking is, and it is this, presumably, about which the Muses speak. However, our capacity to discern the truth of the Muses' account is helplessly dependent upon their own awareness of their intention to tell the truth or not, and it is also entirely dependent upon the poet Hesiod, who himself may (or may not) have imitated their intention, just as he chose to imitate their speech (but needn't have). That is, we stand at a double remove from the beginning, from direct acquaintance with what is first. Yet, this seems our only way.

The mythopoetic intention to tell the truth and its resultant form—either indirect narrative or direct, esoteric imitation—limit our capacity to gain access to what is first. They also incorporate the possibility of lying. This seems to apply to Aristotle's account of first philosophy no less than to Hesiod's imitation of the Muses *via* direct speech in the *Theogony*, for in either (and perhaps every) case intention driven selectivity is at work. However, this obstacle is also the way. Our effort to get at what is first, indeed, must engage the meaning of this limit. Benardete concludes later that, "The recovery of the beings is through the meaning of the beings, for our deepest illusion is that we know the beings

---

6. Cf. Parmenides, fragment DK B8.52, *kosmon emōn epeōn apatēlon.*

7. "The First Crisis in First Philosophy," 4.

as they are in themselves."[8] The dispelling of this illusion complicates the way of truth. Benardete points out that just after Hesiod's story of the birth of Aphrodite his account introduces gods—"Strife, *Philotēs*, Deception, Speeches (*Logoi*) and Lies"—whose effects had previously shown up in the story, and the same sequence had occurred when he told the story of the Muses. "The gods apparently come after what they really are."[9]

What this tells against, however, is the purported meaning of Hesiod's argument, for, as Benardete claims, the story Hesiod reports is evidence against his very argument. "We are forced to use Hesiod against Hesiod in order to understand Hesiod,"[10] he says, and it is necessary to do so in order to get at the meaning of the beings. (This may stand as a prelude to understanding Parmenides.) Thus, although we were told at the beginning there were lies and there was truth, which seemingly were as separate as sea from earth or night from day, they were not really separated. For since the Muses were not themselves there at the beginning, they could not directly know about the separation of lies and truth. The lie of Hesiod's argument suggests that the separation of lies from truth is merely a lie like the truth that the Muses tell. What the Muses' story does, apparently, is indulge us in our belief in the kinship of right and truth; it panders to our conviction that our belief that perjury is punishable is related to our belief in truth as knowledge of the right and just.[11] The Muses' intention to so indulge us gives the lie to such beliefs, just as Aristotle's story of the gradual disclosure of the knowledge of cause dissembles that way as the discovery of the problems of being. We no more know the beings apart from their meaning than we know that lie and truth are apart. The way up and the way down, if there is no way at all, is apparently the same.

Yet, there remains an account of the way to being, another ancient account, along which there are said to be very many signs. That account is the one that is attributed to Parmenides' poem. It compellingly tells of a jour-

---

8. Ibid., 11.

9. Ibid., 11.

10. Ibid., 11.

11. Ibid., 11–12. "The belief that we know the beings apart from meaning is on a par with our belief that lie and truth are apart. We believe they are apart, say the Muses, because we believe in right: as Horkos, who punishes men when they perjure themselves, is the brother of Speeches and Lies, so Nereus, or Truth, is not forgetful (*lēthetai*) of right and knows the just things and mild counsels. The Muses indulge us in those beliefs while they tell a story that gives the lie to those beliefs."

ney beyond the beaten path of mortals, to a goddess who tells the truth, which, she says, is the way of being. Only being is, and what is not cannot be thought or spoken. This truth she speaks denies that Parmenides exists, or that there could even be a journey, or a poem, or a poet, or reader, or audience. It is an impossible truth, made more so, seemingly, by her promise to teach about mortal opinions as well as truth. Her argument not only vitiates our experience, it utterly denies all phenomenality—multiplicity, coming to be or perishing, motion, change of any kind, time—for these rely on what is not, which is not and cannot be. Her binary logic forces apart what is and what is not, only to reject the latter, almost as soon as she has logically distinguished it, for it needs must not be.[12] The most extensive single fragment we still have of Parmenides' poem (B8) begins by mentioning the signs along the way of this one story (*mythos*): "...that what-is is ungenerated and imperishable | whole, single-limbed, steadfast, and complete."[13] These signs form part of the goddess's argument, which now, as always, abidingly commands our attention. Yet, despite the claims of this argument, Parmenides' poem obviously cannot be telling the truth, at least not in the way that we think it does. That is, virtually everyone knows that Parmenides lies, sometimes, if not always. We trust our own experience as the primary sign to what is, rejecting her dogma.

Its apparent monism aside, there are, indeed, many signs in Parmenides' poem, and some of them, as Benardete suggests about Hesiod, may force us to use Parmenides' argument against Parmenides in order to understand Parmenides. Yet, just as if we were to try to begin in one version of Zeno's dichotomy paradox, we do not seem capable of taking a first step unless we can show that it is possible to begin with his poem itself. This proves difficult, however, even though we seemingly must get a hold of it somehow in order to think it or talk about it at all. What we claim to possess of Parmenides' poem is rendered impossible by the argument that it contains. The poem could not have been written without coming to be at some time, but coming to be is not allowed and there are no phenomena nor motions nor changes nor time. Surely it is ironic, then, and perhaps more so than in the case of any other pre-Socratic thinker, that only fragments of the text from Parmenides' poem have been preserved, since its own argument declares that any such fragments cannot be. Strictly speaking, no fragment can be *qua* frag-

---

12. B2.5, *Parmenides of Elea: Fragments*, trans. David Gallop (Toronto: University of Toronto Press, 1991), 55.

13. B8.3–4, ibid., 65.

ment. The cunning Parmenidean thesis would have it that what we take to exist now as his poem's nineteen remaining pieces are done in by their apparent multiplicity. What truly is cannot admit of plurality without also admitting of contradiction, for were it not all one, but manifold in some way, what is would have to be separated from itself by what is not, though what is not is not and cannot be. Being must be continuous and all of a kind, despite so many phenomenal appearances to the contrary. Parmenides' poem asserts that only being is, but if so, the poem itself cannot be.

This predicament in Parmenides' thinking is apparently not feigned. What we do call the "poem" which communicates this self-denying argument is itself an artifact that almost perished,[14] although the argument in it declares that "perishing is unheard of" (B8.21).[15] The poem's existing text seems to depend upon our belief in division and in destruction, for it now consists of a concatenation of remnants. Yet it also explicitly claims that such things as division and destruction are not. This set of fragments is also *prima facie* incomplete, despite another claim of its argument that, "it is not right for what-is to be incomplete" (B8.32).[16] What perdures of Parmenides' poem then, whose original wholeness we accept perhaps only from hearsay, is kept from being a whole by what obviously "is not": its gaps, holes, lacunae, missing parts and transitions. These noted absences betray yet another claim by the goddess in the poem about what is, that "[it] is all continuous, for what-is is in contact with what-is" (B8.25).[17] Parmenides' now fragmentary poem seems to flaunt its own betrayal by conjoining "what-is" and "what-is not" in its literary form, and against its own reasoning, as if to confirm, paradoxically, the goddess's disdain of uncritical mortals. Moreover, the poem's existing fragments have, in fact, remained available to us only because some mortals, and principally Simplicius, considered them worth preserving, yet the goddess in the poem denigrates the opinions of mortals as bearing no true trust. Should we assume that such clear contradictions and discrepancies are just signs of some natural tension between the material text of the poem and what it says and means? Are they problems overlooked by Parmenides, or not seen by him? Or do they point toward a possible Parmenidean insight embedded in the poem and which has perhaps been heightened by its subsequent

---

14. Stewart Umphrey, "The Parmenidean Critique of Physics" (unpublished paper), 9.

15. B8.21, *Parmenides: A Text with Translation, Commentary, and Critical Essays*, trans. Leonardo Tarán (Princeton: Princeton University Press, 1965), 85.

16. B8.32, *Parmenides* (Gallop), 69.

17. B8.25, ibid., 69.

fragmentation? Certainly such inconsistencies can arouse our suspicion. We also encounter perplexity, because what we need to trust and rely on, in claiming to know or experience this poem, appears contrary somehow to what its argument asserts, yet we are not about to deny our experience.

Parmenides' words, like the journey they initially describe, seem to carry our thinking up and away. Yet his poem presents an irresolvable conundrum to our mortal understanding, for the unfolding of its appealingly logical argument proves intractable, and it draws us to the dilemma that only an experience-denying *logos* discovers the necessity of being. We are both drawn toward that reasoning for necessary being and repelled by its apparent annihilation of phenomenal being. Parmenides' *logos*, then, cannot be understood quite as one initially thinks it can, for we cannot accept that our experience can so readily be ignored. The goddess's revelation of being's singular truth apparently requires something else in order to comprehend it, regardless of whether our mortal belief in all the other phenomenal appearances is dismissed, but this would seem to beg the question. Everyone has, no doubt, always ignored the goddess's instruction to follow only the one route of thinking: its truth entails that we cannot go on, but we go on.

The trajectory Benardete traces in the pursuit of the beginning or what is first or the first beings—from Aristotle's selective lying to the intentional lies like the truth put forth by the Muses in Hesiod—shows us both about the making of lies that can function to conceal the truth, and about the disabling of them through the way thinking can turn an argument against itself in order to understand its meaning. Nevertheless, we sense that Parmenides lies, both in the manner of Aristotle, whose story of the route to the truth of being cannot be the way, and also in the manner of the Muses, for Parmenides' goddess claims her teaching is the truth, but such truth is unapproachable for us mortals and remains distant by her inscrutable intention. For getting at the truth, the unveilings in Parmenides' poem, both literal and allegorical, too often are of no avail. We are left wandering double-headed. If a separation between lie and truth cannot be known to be, but there is only a lie like the truth that plays on the fallibilities of human belief, we stand as helpless as Parmenides' youth before the goddess, in need of learning the truth and that we have mortal opinions. As a way to the truth of being Parmenides' poem first unveils a path of obstacles, a path described as "backward-turning" (B6.9).

The route to the goddess is a many-voiced (*polyphēmos*) way, filled with sights and sounds and motion (phenomenal signs of the sort the goddess says later are not) and nearly everything, except the youth (*kouros*) who is carried along in a chariot pulled by mares and accompanied by the daughters of the sun, is female. This route he travels leads from the house of Night to the light, but the way is obstructed by the gates of the house of Night, which are guarded by much-avenging Justice. She is persuaded by the gentle words of the accompanying maidens to open the gates, which swing wide to let this zetetic entourage pass. The youth's narrative account of his journey thus far is quite like Hesiod's narrative of his encounter with the Muses, for it yields a report of what the goddess said as a direct speech to him. Hesiod had also reported what the Muses said as their direct speech. Their claim to know how to tell lies like the truth, as was noted, seems to entirely confound any mortal belief as to whether they are speaking the truth or lying. Whatever truth they do utter depends upon their wish to tell the truth, and thus what they say could well be false. Truth-telling, by the Muses' own admission, is preceded by the awareness of intention. Have they also chosen to utter true things to Hesiod about their power to make duplicitous speeches? Hesiod's decision to imitate their speaking to him, rather than to describe what they said in his own narrative voice, models the paradox of interpreting their meaning. Hesiod, like the Muses, reveals the truth *via* his intention, since he can control how and whether to say or to refrain from saying the truth in his account. He is positioned to be able to craft his report of their report any way he wants, which doubles the possibility that what he reports could be otherwise. Were the goddess in Parmenides' poem to exercise such power over the truth as the Muses claim to do, against which possibility stands only our sanguine belief in divine veracity, the steadfast truth of her account would similarly remain beyond our ken. The poet Parmenides, no less than Hesiod, ably hints that behind the speech the youth represents as that of a goddess lies a range of possibility for disclosing the intention and the plan of his work.

We are told by the youth that upon receiving him, and taking his right hand in her hand, the goddess spoke to him.[18] Thereafter, that is, after she begins speaking, the youth remains silent, and her direct speech is all that we seem to hear. The goddess first declares that the youth should learn all things, "Both the steadfast heart of persuasive truth | and the beliefs of mortals, in which there is no true trust."[19] All things (*panta*) turns out to be two things, truth and mortal opinions, which pair cannot be together, despite her saying them together and pointing them out as yoked in her comprehensive account. Although the way of opinion is proscribed, the goddess claims nevertheless

---

18. See B1.22–23.

19. B1.29–30, *Parmenides* (Gallop), 53.

that the youth shall learn that such opinions (*ta dokounta*), in passing through all things completely, had to be entirely acceptable (*dokimos*), that they were destined (*krēn*) to have genuine existence (*einai*).[20] She declares that what should be learned (*puthesthai*) is the mortally unthinkable duality of truth and opinions that makes up her account of all things. But this union seems to present an irreconcilable conjunction, for the second conjunct cannot be for mortal thought. Evidently, she can have things both ways, but he can only have them one way; the way of truth which discloses being to mind, for opinion lacks true trust. Such disclosure ensures that what is will always emerge as a question. The words of the goddess spoken in the proem clearly function to inform the youth about the meaning of his journey, which has been to receive this instruction, paradoxical as it may be. The sign that this has been done is his rendering of her words as direct speech. He produces a double account within his one account. The youth's silence before her teaching is not a silence in his telling, for her direct speech is part of what he continues to narrate. The goddess's speech is subsumed by his earlier narrative and is ultimately part of it. What she says directly is something that the youth is also reporting, as her direct speech to him. The whole of the poem comes together at this seam that combines the youth's first-person report of his experience with his recital of the goddess's account, which he has modeled in his narration to be an imitation of her direct address. Since his story envelops hers, the goddess's teaching about the truth of being is not coextensive with Parmenides' teaching.

The distinction between the youth's narrative and the goddess's speech marks a less well known divide in the poem than that between Truth (*Alētheia*) and Opinion (*Doxa*), which is frequently assumed to fully comprehend Parmenides' thought. These "parts" convey the teaching of the goddess, encompassing all of the extant fragments of the poem except the first. Parmenides' poetic proem (fragment B1) describes the youth's journey and the goddess's reception of him, including her first speaking about his need to learn all things: persuasive truth and the opinions of mortals. The proem's final lines offer a clue as to how the subsequent parts might be fitted together, for the goddess suggests that the youth shall learn that mortal opinions "had to have genuine existence, permeating all things completely."[21] Only thinking can

---

20. B1.31–32, based on Benardete's translation, from his class on Parmenides in Spring 2000. Cf. "'Night and Day...': Parmenides," in *The Archaeology of the Soul*, eds. Ronna Burger and Michael Davis (Chicago: University of Chicago Press, 2012), 210.

21. B1.31–32, *Parmenides* (Gallop), 53.

comprehend this prospect, linking what is with our illusory way of thinking that we know the beings. Benardete's earlier comment about Hesiod fits here, that "our deepest illusion is that we know the beings as they are in themselves."[22] The proem's hypothetical setting has the effect of liberating the dogma of the goddess's *Alētheia* and the poetical reasoning of the *Doxa* because its poetic function, at least in part, is to try to show how they can go together. Without the setting the two halves seem to split apart. The trail of many commentators has been to wander into this divide. It has long seemed that the task of trying to bring the two parts of the poem together presents *the* difficulty in interpreting Parmenides' thought, and thus it would seem necessary to try to take the setting into account. Nowhere does this requirement seem to have been taken more seriously than in the dialogues of Plato.

Parmenides' poem is always something that we divide in trying to comprehend it, and it resists our efforts to coherently fit its parts together. We can easily distinguish its three-part structure—the setting or proem, Truth (*Alētheia*) and Opinion (*Doxa*)—and we also discern the youth's narrative and the goddess's speech, the realms of Night and Day, the decision between being and non-being (B8.16), the poet and his poem, his intention and its words. We note that the sameness of being and thinking (B3, B8.34) puts together what seems to be apart. The goddess's *logos* about being combines thinking (*noein*), being (*on*), and truth (*alētheia*), yet these are not really apart from one another. We mortals are told that we must learn that we cannot make such an articulation, for the stricture of her command to avoid the way of "is not" declares that it is "a path wholly unlearnable."[23] What she calls truth represents the one of being as an impossible two, being and non-being, and the latter one cannot be. In terms of her speech we cannot even exist, for her critical reasoning rejects any and all distinctions, nor can we understand anything, without going "off road" and thus impossibly embracing that which is unthinkable and unspeakable and must not be. Her speech seems most fundamentally to concern itself with illuminating our thinking. The impossibilities she discloses in thinking being are truth's unconcealing of being to mind.

Thinking puts together and separates. This description of thinking's double act is not unfamiliar to students of Benardete, for like the goddess's disclosure of being (*estin*) as what is always present, the dividing and coupling of thinking seems always present in his thought. Parmenides' truth always appears to be a double construal, for it is both a part and the whole of Parmenides'

---

22. "The First Crisis in First Philosophy," 11.

23. B2.5–6, *Parmenides* (Gallop), 55.

poem, yet it cannot completely account for his thinking. His goddess's *logos* of the togetherness of being and thinking unfolds the truth of the sameness of being and thinking, yet the truth of this sameness belies the intentional duality of both being and thinking, which divides as the necessary pairing of conjoining and the necessary parting of disjoining. The conjoint presence of being (*estin*) with whatever is and its disjoint separation from whatever is not (*ouk estin*) are the twoness that thinking gathers together in learning all things. Being binds together mind and that which is, though these are necessarily apart whenever opinion goes along any other road. Thinking cannot go this way, the way apart, for it was fated to be (B6.1),[24] but it goes on.

Plato's Socrates expresses his shame before Parmenides when he recollects him in the *Theaetetus*, and he refuses to consider the thesis that all is one and at rest, saying that he had not understood what Parmenides was saying or what he thought when he spoke.[25] Socrates may be speaking prudently, or dissembling before Theodorus, but he disavows having knowledge of Parmenides' reasoning or his meaning. His comment forms one of the earliest members in the continuing series of opinions about Parmenides. The fact that being nevertheless promptly emerges in the *Theaetetus*, despite Socrates' refusal to look at it directly, seems to confirm that same fact about it that Benardete points out about Aristotle's likely story of the knowledge of cause: despite the lie that looks like the truth, being surfaces as a question which we must ask about.

Parmenides' truth sometimes looks to us like lies, which we cannot accept as we think it is to be understood. It seems that Parmenides' truth rejects us, by a reasoning that denies the phenomenal world, ourselves included. But if that truth is like a lie to us in the manner which Aristotle lies, through which emerges by necessity the perplexity of being that must be, then we may be in line to become beautifully perplexed.

Seth Benardete's insights seem, at times, almost like the goddess's revelation to the youth in the poem, for we are apparently shown all things, both the way things are and the way we experience them. If the beautiful is, as Benardete defines it, the impossible togetherness of the necessarily apart,[26] then the beautiful has no better paradigm than Parmenides' poem. Its weaving

---

24. B6.1 begins by asserting that speaking (*legein*) and thinking (*noein*) are fated (*krēn*) to be.

25. Plato *Theaetetus* 183e ff.

26. *The Being of the Beautiful: Plato's "Theaetetus," "Sophist," and "Statesman"* (Chicago: University of Chicago Press, 1984), xlvi.

together of what is and what is not defies the necessity it establishes by its own argument, while nonetheless showing forth its dazzling and compelling vision that thinking must both put together and take apart. Nietzsche writes of what the Greeks prayed in praise of the beautiful, which in itself presents the Parmenidean problem of thinking's impossible togetherness with being: "Everything beautiful, twice and even three times!"[27]

---

27. Friedrich Nietzsche, *The Gay Science*, §339, *Vita femina*, trans. Walter Kaufmann (New York: Vintage Books, 1974), 271.

Chapter Five

Parmenides: The Envelope of Socrates' Second Sailing

Olivia Delgado de Torres

Seth Benardete, in "Plato's *Parmenides*: A Sketch," one of his last essays, writes: "*Parmenides* is the envelope of Socrates' second sailing."[1] And, I would add, Book 5, the "women's" book of Plato's *Republic*, is the unexpected place for the appearance of the truth of Parmenides' early prediction about Socrates, made long ago. Part of the difficulty in understanding *Parmenides* is its uncharacteristic looks, one of which is that Socrates is not terribly Socratic. It turns out, however, that young Socrates there is not so much pre-Socratic as pre-Parmenidean, for when we see him at his most characteristic, *Republic* V, he will be practicing the exercise on those things Parmenides recommended, but as variations on a theme by Aristophanes.[2]

In *Parmenides*, Socrates is at the beginning of his life in philosophy. He is young, and although well-mannered, the sheer insolence of youth prompts him to tell Parmenides that Zeno's book is just another way in which Zeno assimilates himself to his teacher.

Originally presented at the conference on "The Thought of Seth Benardete," Howard University, April 2005. We were especially grateful to have Olivia's contribution when, while preparing this collection for publication, we received the sad news of her untimely death. Olivia Balfour Maldonado Delgado de Torres died in Santa Fe, April 18, 2014. We thank Alex Priou for his review of the essay and helpful suggestions.

1. "Plato's *Parmenides*: A Sketch," 229 (cited hereafter as "Sketch"), in *The Archaeology of the Soul*, eds. Ronna Burger and Michael Davis (South Bend: St. Augustine's Press, 2012).

2. *Parmenides* begins with an immediate reference to the *Republic* in the person of Adeimantus as meeter and greeter of foreign visitors (*xenodokountes*, 419a), a distinction he believes is one of the goods of the city to be enjoyed by those to whom in truth it belongs. In contrast to *Republic*, Glaucon is here silent throughout.

To overtranslate shamelessly, the Greek goes something like this (128a4–6): "I've figured out (*manthanō*)," said Socrates, "O Parmenides, that Zeno here (*hode*) wishes to make himself a kinsman in the same household (*ōkeiōsthai*) not only by a different [mark of] love for you (*tē allē sou philia*), but also by his writings (*sungrammati*)."[3] The verb Socrates uses about Zeno has as its root *oikos*, house: it is Socrates' polite metaphor for the relation between Parmenides and Zeno, both physical and philosophical. Yet, it strikingly suggests that the activity between teacher and pupil makes a kind of family out of those unrelated by blood.[4] The idiomatic sense Socrates intends, of course, merely means to be like. Thus, the literal meaning cannot be more than allusive, if household and family are not to take on an uncommonly ugly look.

How Socrates figured out the connection requires the reader to work back. Socrates has *first* read Parmenides' poems (128a8–b1), but the reader, always behind, finds this out in the dialogue only *after* Socrates has heard Zeno's book, which the reader, of course, never does. Zeno and Parmenides have both come to Athens, where they stay at Pythodorus's house, on the occasion of the Great Panathenaea (127a8–b1, 127b6–c1), and they have come, not to present Parmenides' poems but to bring for the first time Zeno's writings (127c3–4). Socrates knows first Parmenides' work, and if he has heard Zeno's work, he has heard it from someone else without knowing its true author (128d6–e1). Having read Parmenides, Socrates would be curious to know why Parmenides comes to Athens, not to read his own work, but on behalf of another's. What enables him to connect the dual presence of the philosophers and their work is a bit of gossip within the dialogue, by Pythodorus to Antiphon, that Socrates has heard outside the dialogue (the same place and time when he read Parmenides' poems), that is to say, *before* the dialogue begins, *before* he goes to Pythodorus's house in the Kerameikos, outside the city walls. Pythodorus's aside (127b5), coming at the beginning of his narration, is first for the benefit of Antiphon, and then for the reader in the same position as any listeners to Kephalus, who might not otherwise understand the impudence of Socrates'

---

3. If MS B²T is correct, the infinitive is a perfect middle that denotes a present condition. H. W. Smyth, *Greek Grammar* (Cambridge: Harvard University Press, 1956), sect. 1946. Since the verb shows the reduplication of past action (*ōmega iota* subscript) and yet signifies that action is present in its results, along with its middle voice of self-interest, it very neatly images the past and present relation of Zeno, the *paidika*, to Parmenides. Whether MS B, T, or Proclus is correct, still all the verbs convey the sense of present condition.

4. Aristophanes *Clouds* 175–79, 870–73, 1464–67.

address to Parmenides.[5] Presumably it is unnecessary, however, for those listening to Antiphon: his half-brothers, Adeimantus and Glaucon (who perhaps have heard him practicing), Kephalus and his fellow Klazomenians who are "very philosophic" (*mala philosophoi*) (126b7).

Pythodorus, after describing the good looks of both men at their advanced ages, with a twenty-five-year difference between them, tells Antiphon that it is said that Zeno had been (and understood, still is) Parmenides' favorite (*paidika*, 127b5–6).[6] Socrates, through his understanding of the love of beautiful young boys and its link with philosophy, solves a puzzle in logic posed by the works of the two visitors. Zeno has written in a certain way, the same as Parmenides, says Socrates (128a6 ff.), but with a change, designed to gull us (*eksapatan*) into believing he is saying something different. "You . . . say the all is one (*Su men . . . hen phēs einai to pan*), . . . this one here in turn says the not-many is (*hode de au ou polla phēsin einai*)." Socrates has figured out from Parmenides' poem that the other of the other of one leg of a pair of contraries is its logical equivalent: the one (*hen*) is logically equivalent to the not-many (*ou polla*).[7] Zeno writes the many is not, Parmenides the one is; therefore, Zeno is Parmenides' favored pupil, and the one most like him. Socrates concludes: "And thus either [of the two] (*hekateron*) speaks so that nothing (*mēden*) of the same has been said, [but] those speaking seem [to mean] pretty nearly the same (*skhedon ti legontas tauta*), [and] over [the heads of] the rest of us the things being said appear to us."

Socrates is nothing if not sharp; he has after all seen the same in two things that appeared different in speech. He thinks, however, the appearance is a calculated attempt to mislead everyone. Addressing himself to Parmenides, Socrates accuses Zeno to his face of his intention to deceive, while simultaneously revealing its failure, since Socrates himself is not deceived,

---

5. Line 127b5–6 could easily be excised without disturbing Pythodorus's description of Zeno and Parmenides or Antiphon's narrative, which he resumes in his own voice, as *para tō Pythodōrō* indicates (127b6–c1). Benardete remarks: "Athenaeus found it most wicked of Plato, particularly because there was no pressing need, to mention that Zeno was said to have been the beloved of Parmenides" ("Sketch," 231).

6. *auton paidika tou Parmenidou gegonenai*: the verb is a perfect infinitive, denoting a present condition; cf. note 3 above.

7. *Parmenides: A Text with Translation, Commentary, and Critical Essays*, trans. Leonardo Tarán (Princeton: Princeton University Press, 1965), fragment 2.3, 5.

or at least not after questioning Zeno. To recognize the intention to deceive is to be deceived no longer.[8]

Zeno, handsome (*kharienta idein*), tall, and a reflection of his own paradox of the moving arrow at rest, is depicted in the dialogue as forever approaching forty years of age (127b4–5).[9] He is not offended by Socrates' impudence, but rather gives him a compliment that does not flatter, as he likens him to a standout in its category: a young, frisky, Laconian bitch, the shrewdest animal for swiftly running its prey to ground. Even when Socrates was young, it required a shift in genus and gender to render his looks and manner: after all, good strong feet, a big nose with flaring nostrils *is* the beauty of the best of the Laconian breed, the Alopekid hunting dog.[10] Zeno tells Socrates that, although he has chased down and tracked the one *logos* of the Eleatics in its two guises, he has not entirely scented (*ou pantakhou esthēsai*) the truth of Zeno's book.

Zeno, in contrast to the indirect address Socrates practiced on him, by speaking to Parmenides while pointing to him, addresses Socrates directly and with emphasis.[11] His answer perfectly illustrates Socrates' complaint about saying differently two things that seem to be nearly the same. Following the example of Socrates in his speech (127e8–9), Zeno in *his* speech allows the book to become the subject of a verb, an agent, as it were, with intentions (128a2–3, 128c2–d6). Later, when he comes to speak of the book's origin and birth, he uses the passive voice, which allows him to preserve the book as subject by shifting the focus of action to the book and away from himself, author and subject, all the while saying the same thing.[12]

---

8. Parmenides, fragment 8.50–52. For a modern variation on the problem, cf. Douglas Hofstadter, *Gödel, Escher, Bach* (New York: Basic Books, 1979), 17 ff.

9. Aristotle *Physics* 239a23–b9, 239b30–33.

10. The breed of dog is a pun on the name of the deme from which Socrates came, Alopeke. See *Gorgias* 495d1–7; Pindar, fragment 95, C. M. Bowra, *Pindari Carmina* (Oxford: Oxford University Press, 1968); Xenophon *Cynegeticus* 3.1–2; *Symposium* 5.4–7. For Socrates' looks, see Plato *Theaetetus* 143e6–9; *Symposium* 174a3–9, 209b10–c2, 215a4–b6, 219e5–220c1, 221b1–4; Xenophon *Symposium* 4.18–19; Aristophanes *Clouds* 362–63.

11. In 20 lines (128b7–e3), Zeno addresses Socrates by name as "you"—*su*, in the nominative case, or *se*, in the accusative case—seven times.

12. The Greek is striking and calls attention to itself: it is in the indirect mode, making translation awkward, and encouraging translators to ignore the passive voice and render it active. A good guess would be that, at most, not more than one translates

He could have simply said, "I wrote the book when young and rivalrous." Instead he says, "The book was written through a love of victory (*philonikian*) by my being young." Socrates, he says, has mistaken an accidental cause (*ta sumbebēkota*) for the book's real intention, which is the truth: it is a sort of auxiliary to Parmenides' *logos* against those supporters of the many who attacked it by making a comedy of it. Socrates, he says, thinks the book is written by an older man wanting honor (*philotimian*), and this is his error. Zeno suggests that both love of victory and love of honor are accidents of age, and distinguishable one from the other only by reference to age: youthful love of victory can be mistaken for elderly love of honor. The distinction is almost too subtle, and we are immediately sympathetic to Socrates in his error. Who would not think that a work brought to Athens for the first time, shepherded by its father and grandfather, so to speak, was not a new book? If the author is middle-aged, so too the tone of the book, reflecting its author, if not its own age. Thus, Zeno's book did not strike Socrates as young, even though it may well be the same age as he. The truth is, it is an old book, written by a young man. On its own the book reveals nothing of its age except an accident that can be misread, but its age, once revealed by the author, is its instant rejuvenation, and the author along with it.[13] Nevertheless, Zeno seems to confess that had the book been written when he was older, Socrates' assessment of its pompous air would not have been a misreading when he says, "And yet, just as I said, you have made [a] likeness not badly" (128e3–4).[14]

In order to point out Socrates' error, Zeno must clarify the book's birth, and the delay in its announcement. The book, Zeno explains, was no sooner written than it was stolen, preventing any consideration of whether or not to bring it into the light (*eis to phōs*), i.e., to publish it: Zeno's explanation of his book's origin is further proof of its auxiliary status to Parmenides' one. Zeno considers that someone else's sharing the arguments of his book, perhaps even quoting them as her own, constitutes theft. This is consonant with the hypothesis that Parmenides calls *his* own: the one of the first hypothesis which has nothing but oneness, not even being, and thus allows nothing of itself to

---

the Greek as written.

13. Plato's image of Zeno's book that reveals nothing of its age is like Parmenides' poem (fragment 1.24).

14. Mick Jagger of The Rolling Stones, a group which started out not only in rivalry with The Beatles but "in sympathy for the devil," is the perfect example of what Zeno means: when older, Jagger was seized by a mad desire for the honor of knighthood, much to the disgust of Keith Richards, his bandmate.

be shared (136a4–142a8). For the strictly one, any participation in its unity by others must be stealing.

Despite Socrates' suspicions, the shift Zeno makes is not simply a trick amounting to no change. Socrates, all unawares, first animated the book. Zeno draws the consequences, giving the book the appearance of a life of its own: it is a subject, so to speak, with wants and intentions and airs. Indeed the book reveals its notion of justice: as an ally to a friend and lover against the comedy-makers, it gives back not simply the same laughter it receives but more, its victory an overkill by ridicule (128d1–6). Accordingly, the book's behavior illustrates Zeno's definition of youthful love of victory.

Zeno makes use of another shift when first he tells Socrates he has understood what the book as a whole wants beautifully (*kalōs sunēkas*), but after correcting the error, tells him, "And yet, just as I said, you have made [a] likeness not badly" (*ou kakōs apēkasas*). The misreading of an accident of age by a very young man has made Socrates' understanding of the book as a whole shift from beautiful to not bad. Zeno's language suggests that so long as Socrates stuck to putting together (*sunēkas*) the many *logoi*, his understanding was beautiful, encompassing the whole book and its intention. When he attempts, however, to put together the *logoi* with the intention of their author, he succeeds to a likeness (*apēkasas*) that comes to sight as possibly beautiful only by the repudiation of its useless badness.[15] Zeno had already given Socrates an example of such a likeness in his image of him as the Alopekid pup. Zeno is the first to hint to Socrates at the possibility of redefining the beautiful in terms of the good. Seen up close, this shift of focus is not unlike the exercise (*gymnasia*) Parmenides says Zeno practiced in the book, looking not only at whether the many is or is not, but also its opposite, the one, both in relation to themselves and each other (136a4–b1).

Socrates, the frisky little whelp, though still eager to lead the chase, is made to heel, as he tells Zeno he accepts and believes it is as he says (*All' apodekhomai . . . kai hēgoumai hōs legeis ekhein*).[16] His subsequent speech is a series of ten conditionals, whose logical structure loosely follows the model of Zeno's hypothetical arguments. Each conditional is a putting forward of a

---

15. *Apeikazō* (to copy) and *suniēmi* (to bring together) resemble each other in the aorist: *apēkasas, sunēkas*.

16. The *alla* is assentient: "Agreement is presented not as self-evident, but as wrung from the speaker *malgré lui*. *Alla* then points the contrast between the assent given and the considerations which have militated against the giving of it" J. D. Denniston, *The Greek Particles* (Oxford: Oxford University Press, 1966), 16.

premise, the *protasis*, to be answered by the *apodosis*, a giving back or return to the *protasis*. In this speech, however, the possibility or impossibility of each *protasis* is not determined by a real *apodosis*, but by Socrates' capacity for wonder, whose limits are the uncommon prodigious monster, on the one hand, and the ordinary commonplace, on the other. Parmenides, in his demonstration of the *gymnasia*, will show Socrates that the ordinary is anything but commonplace, indeed rather strange (*atopon*, 156d1), while the monstrous (*teras*) is not unnatural (153b8–a4).

As Pythodorus confesses to Antiphon, Socrates' speech causes him some anxious moments. He is sensitive to the impudent tone of Socrates' challenge to his elders: "Amaze me, if you can!" And he supposes both Zeno and Parmenides to be annoyed at every word. Although Pythodorus will turn out to be wrong, he declines to edit that from his account. He reports his erroneous reading of the two men in opposition to his description of their behavior (*autos men ... tous de*, 130a3ff.): they very much applied their mind to Socrates, and looking toward each other, they smiled frequently as though admiring him. Pythodorus's error lies in his inability to comprehend the pleasure Zeno and Parmenides together share about Socrates but which does not include him, and the one mind each focuses on him (*autō prosekhein ton noun*). Not until Parmenides speaks can Pythodorus confirm that their mutual pleasure was indeed admiration of Socrates.

Socrates pauses in his address to Zeno, and Parmenides, mimicking Zeno's earlier behavior, answers for him. He tells Socrates he is worthy of admiration. The word he uses to qualify Socrates' motion toward the *logoi* (*hōs axios ei agasthai tēs hormēs tēs epi tous logous*), and will again use later (135d3), is a substantive commonly given as a name to hunting dogs: *hormē*.[17] Zeno and Parmenides not only answer Socrates in one another's places, they are of the same mind about his looks.

Parmenides runs through four categories of things for which he asks Socrates whether or not there are *eidē*. Whereas Socrates believes there are *eidē* of likeness, one and many, as well as of the just, the beautiful and the good, he is perplexed about man, fire and water. About the fourth category, however, the laughable, paltry and worthless things like hair, mud and dirt, Socrates is firm: they *are* just as we *see* them, and to suspect there is some *eidos* of them would be too out of place (*mē lian ē atopon*).

Parmenides, the eldest, discerns the crux of the matter: Socrates is afraid of the laughably ugly:

---

17. Xenophon *Cynegeticus* 7.5.9.

"For you are still (*eti*) young," said Parmenides, "O Socrates, and not yet (*oupō*) has philosophy taken hold of you as it will yet (*eti*) take hold, in my opinion, whenever you will slight none of them. But now, you still (*eti*) look to the opinions of human beings (*anthrōpōn*) on account of your age" (130e1–4).

Parmenides predicts that philosophy will have taken hold of Socrates when hair, mud and dirt no longer put him to flight because that will be the sign he is no longer in the grip of human opinion. Having weathered the comedy the many made of his *logos* of the one, Parmenides, now twenty-seven years in advance of Aristophanes' play, tries to prepare Socrates for the comedy that will be made of him.[18]

More close questioning by Parmenides uncovers *aporiai* engendered by Socrates' insistence on the two separations: of the ideas among themselves and apart from us. The biggest perplexity, Parmenides says, is that an unpersuaded disputant compels the ideas to be unknowable by humans because they belong to a realm apart from us; even more uncanny (*deinoteron*) is the consequence that the gods, because they are apart, for all their precise eidetic knowledge have no knowledge of us or the human things. The last wrings from Socrates an admission of wonder of the sort he emphasized in his first speech: "Too exceedingly wondrous (*alla mē lian...thaumastōs*)," he said, "the argument [would be], if someone will deprive the god of [the ability] to know."

Parmenides continues: "Concerning what will you make philosophy? In what direction will you turn, these things being unknown?" And Socrates answers, "Not at all [do] I seem to myself to perceive [where] in the present."

More effectively than Zeno, Parmenides has brought a frisky Socrates to halt. The *aporia* complete, Socrates has neither a way out nor a direction in which to turn to do philosophy. Parmenides tells him the reason:

"For [too] early," he said, "before having exercised [yourself], O Socrates, you are taking in hand to mark off for yourself something both beautiful and just and good and each one of the *eidē*. For I had [it] in mind not long ago listening to you conversing over there with Aristotle here present.[19] Know well now (*men oun*)

18. Aristophanes' *Clouds* debuts in 423 BC. Socrates is in his forties and Plato is five years old. See *Apology* 18b4–c8.

19. Both R. E. Allen and Emile Chambry translate *prōēn* as either yesterday (which *khthes* is, strictly speaking), or as the other day: *l'autre jour*. Both cases make a

that the impulse (*hormē*) that impels you towards the *logoi* is beautiful, even divine, but pull back [on] yourself, and exercise more by means of that which is supposed to be worthless (*akhrēstou*) and called by the many idle chatter (*adoleskhias*) while you are still young. If not, the truth will escape you."[20]

This is Parmenides' second mention of Socrates' hunting dog virtue, and because his headlong dash in pursuit of the *logoi* is so all of a piece, Parmenides makes cognate both the verb and the substantive of Socrates' motion (the impulse that impels him). Before going on to rein in the virtue, however, Parmenides assures Socrates the impulse is beautiful, even divine in its pursuit of the beings. And yet, Parmenides recommends Socrates first practice marking off the things commonly deemed worthless. He encourages Socrates to tumble into the abyss of nonsense he so fears (130d5–9), or else the truth will run away from him. Parmenides thus suggests that truth is most hidden in the things common opinion deems worthless, for he has heard Socrates say the worthlessness of hair, mud and dirt requires no *eidos* because they are just as we see them. He sees no benefit in having their paltry being present to sight, and so does not realize that the illusion there is nothing hidden, no doubling or image in these things, is precisely due to common opinion. Socrates implies, on the other hand, that for the beautiful, the just and the good, since they are important for us, there must be appearance and illusion in what we have of them; these then, require *eidē* to show what they are in themselves. Parmenides, however, sees in the double motion of Socrates' headlong dash to the *eidē* and away from the laughably paltry, the future mirror of the flight of truth away from him.

---

larger time interval in the visit to Pythodorus by Socrates and his friends. While it is possible they made repeated visits to Pythodorus's house over a two-day period, what seems more important is to see that Parmenides, the eldest of the group with the longest sense of time, intends to convey that it happened not long ago, or very recently, i.e., earlier in the day, which could only be yesterday *if* Socrates is allowed to make the day a larger time interval by combining day and night into one (131b1–6). But the day of "earlier in the day" that *proēn* means is the *daylight* of the day that is both night and day (Parmenides, fragment 8.53–54). R. E. Allen, *Plato's* Parmenides (Minneapolis: University of Minnesota Press, 1983), 13; and Emile Chambry, *Platon, Oeuvres Complètes* (Paris: Garnier Frères, 1960), t.3, 484.

20. *Men oun* is transitional: "Often the *men* clause sums up and rounds off the old topic, while the *de* clause introduces a new one" Denniston, 472.

In hindsight, of course, *after* reading *Parmenides*, there are glimpses of Socrates heeding Parmenides. In *Hippias Major*, he wrings from Hippias, an expert on beauty who is himself beautiful, the agreement that more than one made of gold, a ladle made of the proverbially worthless fig wood is more beautiful, being more appropriate to stir the favorite Athenian dish of pea soup cooked in a smooth, round earthenware pot, which is nothing more than mud (*pēlos*) made beautiful (290e3–291c5). In *Symposium*, Socrates is at his most hubristic, and makes himself beautiful to go to handsome Agathon's victory party by taking a bath, washing off all the dirt (*rupos*), and putting on shoes (174a3–9).

The verb *adoleskhō* means to talk to one's fill, and it is in *Republic* that Socrates gets to practice this idle chatter (*adoleskhia*) Parmenides recommended. Belly empty, defrauded of the fancy dinner and all-night festival promised by Polemarchus, Socrates is sated instead with speeches (328a6–8, 352b3, 354a10–b4). In *Parmenides*, Socrates insisted there is no *eidos* for hair, mud and dirt, but in *Republic*, Adeimantus accuses him of attempting to rob them of the whole *eidos* of the *logos* (*eidos holon ou to elekhiston ekkleptein tou logou*, 449c2–3), which is the entire argument about the sharing of women and children. He insists it is not the least part of the *logos* because on it rests the big, or rather the whole burden of whether the regime they are making comes into being correctly or not. The communism had been suggested, apparently innocently enough, by Socrates in faithful adherence to the commonplace truth of the old saying that "Friends have all things in common," as he attempts to fashion a guardian class. He has by that point, of course, been shown by Parmenides how uncommonly strange the ordinary can be, and so it comes as no surprise that out of this clichéd notion of friendship, he will innovate the radically uncommon practice of sharing women and children.

In *Parmenides*, when young Socrates asks Parmenides for a demonstration of his hypothesis, the latter initially declines, saying it is a great deal of work for a man his age. After having been petitioned by the company, Parmenides finally consents, and freely confesses he chooses the youngest as respondent to give himself less work: the youngest will give the least trouble; he will not lie but will answer what he thinks, and that will allow the oldest to rest (*anapaula*) during the answers (137b6–8). In other words, what the youngest will answer is already familiar to him, and the familiar affords rest. Parmenides lies, of course, as he proceeds to contradict his old man's plea for rest, and instead makes the exercise more work. Before beginning the exercise, he points out to his listeners his fear to navigate such a sea of *logoi* at such an age (137a5–6); at the end, his demonstration is a feat of stamina to rival even the youngest.[21] The price of demonstration in deed is contradiction in speech.

Parmenides, when he first meets Socrates, is a little older than Socrates in *Republic*.[22] In *Republic*, Adeimantus noticed that Socrates slid away from filling in the details of the communism earlier in Book Four (423e4–424a2). Socrates, however, never admits his attempted theft of the argument is due to age. He also denies it is fear of ridicule (*gelōta ophlein*), for that is childish (*paidikon gar touto ge*, 451a1–2), an insight he can only have gained from hearing the older Zeno describe his youthful reaction to the comedy they made of his lover's poem when he too was young and Parmenides' favorite (*paidika*), and from Parmenides' calling attention to the connection between Socrates' age and his fear of the laughably ugly. Yet if Socrates, who narrates *Republic*, presents himself, nearing Parmenides' age, yet practicing the exercise Parmenides recommended be done when young, the irresistible conclusion is that Socrates is still young.[23]

Socrates' denial in *Republic* of old age as the cause of his faint-heartedness is accompanied, however, by a confession of measured respect for the magnitude of the task; he intends to instill the same in his listeners. He says it means stirring up many arguments going back as if to a new beginning for the regime.[24] He likens the many arguments to a swarm or flock (*esmon*),

---

21. Benardete remarks: "Parmenides' request for a partner in order that he may rest between his questions and answers is somewhat spurious: most of the length of the exercise is due to Parmenides' need to explain his inferences. Were it not for Aristoteles, it would be less than half as long; cf. for example, 138a2 with the conclusion at 138b5–6." "Sketch," 237 n. 4. On average, however, Aristoteles keeps pace: he asks twice as many questions in the first part (I, II), which is twice as long, while asking half as many questions in the second part (III–IX), which is half as long. The portrait of Aristoteles lies in what questions he asks.

22. Parmenides is sixty-five (127b3), Socrates close to sixty in 411 BC, when the conversation of the *Republic* takes place; cf. Allan Bloom, trans., *The Republic of Plato* (New York: Basic Books, 1991), 440 n. 3.

23. The same holds true for Parmenides, as he demonstrates by the exercise (141b1–c4). Socrates' poetic conceit of himself as still young and frisky is the same as Parmenides' image of himself as the *kouros* in his poem (fragment 1.24). Pheidippides uses precisely this penchant of the old to be ever young in order to support his argument in favor of father-beating: *dis paides hoi gerontes* (*Clouds* 1417).

24. In *Parmenides* (133b4–c1), Parmenides says the possibility of persuading someone who disputes the existence of the ideas and their knowability depends upon two

which, when he saw them, he passed by, ignoring them so they wouldn't give a lot of trouble (*okhlon*).[25] The same thing that allows Socrates to take no notice of the arguments also hides the absence of *the* argument: the commonplace about friends that the proverb illustrates. The pre-Parmenidean Socrates, who in youth disdained the commonplace, after his encounter with the Father of Being, follows it literally in *Republic*, taking advantage of the proverbial as the accepted, or that which is taken for granted and so goes without saying. The consequence is, of course, as Adeimantus finally realizes, no argument is required (*kai lēsein oiēthēnai eipōn auto phaulōs*, 449c3–4). Adeimantus finds this an old man's sneaky attempt to make work easier for himself.

For the next seventy lines after Adeimantus' charge (449c2–451c1), Socrates treats us to what Pythodorus mercifully spared us by three and a half lines in *Parmenides* (136e5–8). Otherwise, we would have endured at least four speeches begging Parmenides, and each of his refusals, followed by his ultimate consent, surely at least seventy lines. But after all, Socrates is narrating *Republic*, and so we see him, appropriately enough at the beginning of the woman's book, being coaxed, cajoled and finally seduced into allowing himself to be persuaded to satisfy the company's demands.

Socrates says his avoidance of handling the sharing of women is fear of straying from the truth and falling down, dragging friends with him. The result would be a mistake, a trip-up about that which one should least be mistaken (*ha hēkista dei sphallesthai*). If what would seem to be most one's own, viz., one's wife, is to be shared, has one not indeed mistaken another's for one's own?[26] Such a trip-up, Socrates implies, is the same as being mistaken about the beautiful and good and just in lawful usage (*nomimos*). The man who unwittingly misleads friends about such things is like a man guilty of the involuntary homicide of his friends.

Socrates relents, only to discover that the woman drama (*nomos*) is out of order, incorrigibly, for it comes after it was necessary; and yet although out

---

conditions: (1) that the disputant is not without a good nature and much experience; (2) that he be willing to follow the demonstration from a long way back. Socrates' two interlocutors, Adeimantus and Glaucon, seem to fill the second and part of the first, but cannot be experienced since they are young.

25. Cf. the song and counter-song by the Young Girl and the First Old Woman in Aristophanes' *Ecclesiazousai* (884–89), which, according to the young girl, although *okhlos*, is *terpnon ti kai kōmōdikon*.

26. Parmenides makes a point about beginning with one's own, cf. 137a7–b4.

of order, its place is not incorrect: it comes after the man drama is completed, and is the start of what will turn out to be a self-contained detour, consisting of Books Five through Seven (543c4–6), the most philosophical stretch of *Republic*. A suspension of the order of necessity allows for a correction of that order for the sake of the best.

Socrates asserts to Glaucon that for human beings by nature and education as they have described the guardians, there is no other correct possession and use of women and children than communism, and he repeats Parmenides' very words with substantive and cognate verb (*hormēn, hormēsamen*, 451c6–7). Only then do we realize that the impulse Parmenides characterized as both beautiful and divine driving young Socrates to the speeches is at work in *Republic*, in the speeches about sharing guardian women (452b6). Socrates, the old dog and *quondam* Alopekid puppy of *Parmenides*, is still frisking about at the head of the pack of *Republic*'s guardian dogs. It is his match to Parmenides' image of himself as a prize-winning race horse.

In *Republic* V, Socrates, having reined himself in his drive toward the *logoi*, takes the plunge Parmenides recommended, into a sea of nonsense, dragging his friends right along. It is here that Socrates shows signs of being touched by Parmenidean genetics: the son who resembles his midwife mother braves three great waves of laughter (*kuma*), to show off three unripe fruits of his womb (*kuēma*):[27] the equality of education of guardian men and women, the communism of women and children, and the philosopher-king. At last, Socrates is no longer afraid of hair, mud and dirt, for the crux of his argument for the equal education of guardian women turns on Praxagora's suggestion in Aristophanes' *Ecclesiazousai* that the equality between the sexes in the title to rule is not grounded in the ability to grow a beard.[28] Accordingly, Socrates argues the difference between men and women with respect to soul is no more essential than the difference between bald men and men with hair (454c).

Parmenides' lesson that laughter is no bar to reason[29] emboldens Socrates to follow the *logos* of Parmenides' *gymnasia* literally, and make guardian women, clothed only in their civic virtue, strip naked to exercise. Only among the guardians can uncovering the mother's nakedness be more an exercise in *theōria* than shamelessness. The communism of guardian women becomes Socrates' comic, if deadly accurate, paradigm for eidetic sharing by which Parmenides had perplexed him. Guardian women do indeed belong to the

---

27. Parmenides, fragments 17, 18; Tarán, 263–66; *Theaetetus* 149a1 ff., esp. 149a8–9.

28. *Ecclesiazousai* debuts 392 BC, seven years after Socrates' death.

29. "Sketch," 232.

guardian men (454e4) but as a whole, not individually, for no guardian woman belongs to any guardian man. But some guardian men, the best, have more access to more women individually, and so more access to the class as a whole than others. The logical companion to this argument Socrates allows to glide by in silence: the communism of women is equally communism of men.

By jumping into a sea of laughter, Socrates triumphs over those who made a comedy of him, and recalls Arion's leap into the sea, fully clothed in poet's robes, to escape his would-be assassins.[30] Socrates invokes him when taking on the first wave of laughter (453d9). Arion's miraculous escape seems due to his poetic art, which must have charmed Apollo, the god of music, and apparently even the dolphin that bore him safely to shore. Socrates' three waves, or fetuses, are the philosophic equivalent of Arion's swim from Taenerus to Tarentum, thanks to Plato. If the dolphin is Apollo's gift to Arion, in appreciation of his shrill song (*nomos*), so too the invisible dolphin Plato is Apollo's gift to Socrates' *nomos*, the woman drama of *Republic* V.

---

30. Herodotus 1.24.

Chapter Six

Preface to Seth Benardete,
Socrates and Plato: The Dialectics of Eros

Heinrich Meier

Seth Benardete died on November 14, 2001. Thirteen years earlier he came to Germany for the first time to give a lecture at the Carl Friedrich von Siemens Foundation with the title "Sun, Line, and Cave: On Plato's *Republic*." That splendid evening formed the prelude of an extraordinary relation that developed between the philosopher from New York and the Carl Friedrich von Siemens Foundation. And the visit in November 1988 was the beginning of a great friendship that linked me with Seth Benardete. The rich yield of the institutional relation includes the outstanding lectures that Benardete worked out for the program of the Foundation in the '90s: 1993, "On Plato's *Symposium*"; 1994, "The *Odyssey* Seen Through Plato's Eyes"; and 1999, "Socrates and Plato: The Dialectics of Eros." But in particular two important works, on Homer's *Odyssey* and Plato's *Laws*, should be mentioned here, which he wrote and completed as a Carl Friedrich von Siemens Fellow in Munich in 1994 and 1998, respectively. They would be his last books. Our friendship grew, was tested, and was deepened in innumerable conversations, day-long and night-long, and in a series of common projects as well as in investigations of shared interest, which in the meantime have found expression in various publications. In August 2001 we reached an agreement about two future lectures. For the international symposium "Living Issues in the Thought of Leo Strauss," which took place at the Foundation in June 2002, Benardete promised a contribution on "The Quarrel Between Philosophy and Poetry," in which he intended not only to draw upon his decades-long

Originally published in German as Heinrich Meier's Preface to Seth Benardete, *Socrates and Plato: The Dialectics of Eros*, bilingual edition, with German translation by Wiebke Meier (Munich: Carl Friedrich von Siemens Stiftung, 2002), translated into English for this volume by Robert Berman.

engagement with the matter from the perspective of the ancient authors, but beyond that, to delve into Nietzsche, Heidegger, and Hölderlin. And for the special lecture series *Der Tod im Leben*, to be held at the Carl Friedrich von Siemens Foundation in the summer of 2003, he declared himself ready to take on the theme "Philosophy as the Practice of Dying and Being Dead," as a complement to his masterful lecture from 1999 on eros.

On the occasion of the first anniversary of the death of Seth Benardete, the Foundation is publishing the lecture he wrote for the special series *Über die Liebe*, in a bilingual edition. It thus honors one of the first two Carl Friedrich von Siemens Fellows the Foundation invited to Munich ten years ago, and makes the English original of the text, until now unpublished, available to interested readers throughout the world. I reproduce in what follows, without any alteration, my Introduction to the final lecture Seth Benardete gave in Germany in remembrance of the evening of July 1, 1999 in Nymphenburg:

Ladies and Gentlemen,

In political philosophy and in the engagement with the power of eros all roads lead to Plato. Here I am thinking not only of the broad royal roads of tradition, on which we meet up with the theories, concepts, and images inspired by Plato, which were transformed, reformulated, or misunderstood in a long, diverse, and entangled reception, acquired their form in opposition to him, and even then still maintained reference to Plato where they knew nothing, or wanted to know nothing, about him. I am thinking likewise about the paths that soar along the solitary heights and the wandering tracks that end in a thicket. They too remain in the Platonic topography, their problems are connected with the stock of problems and material the Platonic dialogues articulate, their questions point us to Plato, or they make it seem advisable that we avail ourselves of the possibilities provided by Platonic dialectics—the intertwining of *synkrisis* and *diakrisis*, Platonic collection and division—in order to clarify these questions, to pursue them further, if not to answer them.

Let me almost randomly call a few things to mind and take up a few questions that arose in the first six lectures of our series, *Über die Liebe*, or in the discussions, sometimes conducted very intensively, that we experienced here. Is love an anthropological universal, in other words, stated succinctly, is it part of human nature, which gets realized in the most diverse social and adverse historical conditions? And if that is so, can minimal conditions be specified that have to be fulfilled so that so-called "romantic love" can be actualized? In a rigid system of social control and channeling, such as arranged marriage, do even a couple dozen individual possibilities for choice suffice for such an actualization? In light of such anthropological considerations, how should one take a diagnosis of the present that makes plain to us a history of decline and confronts us with an all-encompassing and controlling fate, in which love is standardized, serially multiplied, de-individualized, more and more suppressed if not made to disappear entirely? Is such a far-reaching, wide-ranging makeover, such a fundamental technical transformation of love imaginable that it can be increasingly and lastingly decoupled from the physical presence of the lovers? Should we expect an immanent "world-night" *also* in matters of love?, one must ask. In light of this dark prognosis, is it any more than an indemonstrable act of faith to hope for a magical reversal, to wait with serenity until the point at which the historical process, fatefully unfolding, will open a new free space for human love, because it goes beyond or around man, no longer paying attention to him? Or do metaphysical speculations of this type miss the power of eros just as much, only in another direction, as two hundred years ago hopes for the perfecting, for the civilizing and domesticating of love, for "a paradise of love for all," failed to recognize the power of eros? The "heaven on earth" dreamt of, which became a landscape of Hades, was the talk of the opening night of the series. Let us turn to sunnier climes. In the paintings of the "Fêtes galantes" we encountered the sentence, "Eros is always directed to the beautiful things," translated into an image whereby the archaic savagery in the pictures of Rubens, Titian, and Watteau is not fully concealed. Why do the presentations of these courtship parties have recourse to statues of the gods? Does love need a rhetoric of enchantment, is it dependent on superhuman, divine models? How can the lover win over the beloved to a mutual "You must change your life," affecting both? And how can he secure his own love for himself? Not only and not primarily that of the beloved? Is an "unconscious, complete contentment," which rests upon something like a "magnetic joining together" and allows two human beings at times to have the feeling "of being one human being," sustainable? Can love persevere in speechlessness? Can it unfold at all in speechlessness? And how do things stand with the cognitive elements of love? Do they provide a new quality to that which develops out of deeper, more elementary feeling? Do they lead to an ascent? Is love in need, for its ascent, not so much of enchantment as of knowledge? Does love above all else permit insight into the happiness that arises from what cannot be at our disposal? Is it precisely love that leads to knowledge of the good that is to be found in the fact that not everything is an object of human production, not everything can be man-made, invented, manufactured, mastered?

In my welcoming speech for Gerhard Neumann's sixty-fifth birthday, I spoke a week ago about the fact that for me two presuppositions always stood clearly in mind for the realization of the long-cherished project to arrange a special series, *Über die Liebe*. The first presupposition I mentioned: to find the right partner in every respect for the conceptual preparation and implementation of the series as well as the later publication of the book.[1] The other presupposition I did not mention, in order to save it for tonight. It consisted, as you will have already guessed, in acquiring the most competent speaker for the contribution about Plato. The best expert on the Platonic corpus and the most eminent philosophic interpreter of Plato I know among the living is Seth Benardete, whom I want to welcome warmly. In him I greet a great scholar, who has been connected with the Carl Friedrich von Siemens Foundation for years in a special way, and I welcome him as a good friend.

When Seth Benardete, Professor of Classics at New York University and Professor of Philosophy at the New School for Social Research in New York, spoke to us in November 1988 about Plato's *Republic*, this was his first lecture in front of a German audience and his first visit to Germany at all. His second lecture in Germany likewise took place in Nymphenburg. In June 1993 he presented here for the first time his interpretation of the Platonic *Symposium*. If when he first lectured in Germany eleven years ago he was still an unknown, an inside tip for a very few, the publication of his second evening's lecture at the Foundation received broad national and international attention and developed in the meantime into the "best-seller" of our *Themes* series. A few weeks ago the second revised and expanded edition of the volume appeared in 9,000–13,000 copies.[2] And at his third lecture about Plato in this hall television is a

---

1. The book, which contains eight of the nine lectures of the series as well as a long introductory essay and an epilogue by the two editors, appeared in December 2000 as Volume 8 of the *Veröffentlichungen der Carl Friedrich von Siemens Stiftung*. Heinrich Meier and Gerhard Neuman (eds.): *Über die Liebe. Ein Symposion.* München, Piper Verlag, 2000. Fourth edition, 2009.

2. *On Plato's "Symposium"—Über Platons "Symposion."* München, Carl Friedrich von Siemens Stiftung, 1994 (Reihe "Themen," Bd. 57). Second, revised edition 1999. Benardete's English text from the bilingual publication is incorporated in his essay collection, *The Argument of the Action*, eds. Ronna Burger and Michael Davis (Chicago and London: University of Chicago Press, 2000), 167–85. It is also reprinted in *Plato's "Symposium,"* a translation by Seth Benardete with commentaries by Allan Bloom and Seth Benardete (Chicago and London: University of Chicago Press, 2001), 173–99. A Chinese translation of Benardete's lecture and my introduction in the "Themen" volume of 1994 was published in 2000.

guest tonight, so that an even greater circle beyond Munich can participate in the dialogue Benardete is conducting with Plato.[3]

When in 1993–94 the Foundation awarded the first Carl Friedrich von Siemens Fellowships in order to single out scholars who gave outstanding lectures in the program of the Foundation and enable them to do concentrated work in Munich on an opus, Seth Benardete was one of the two Fellows, along with Hans-Martin Gauger, to whom the invitation was extended. During his stay in Munich from January until August 1994, Benardete wrote a major book on the *Odyssey* and, as a bonus, a long paper on Plato's *Lysis*.[4] The book on the *Odyssey*, which came into being from the first line to the last footnote in Munich, appeared in 1997 under the title *The Bow and the Lyre: A Platonic Reading of the Odyssey*. During his second stay in Munich, from September to December of last year, once again as a Carl Friedrich von Siemens Fellow, he completed his most recent and until now most extensive work, a commentary on Plato's *Laws* with the title *Plato's Song and Dance: On the "Laws."*[5]

If in political philosophy and in reflection on eros all roads lead to Plato, this has its substantive reason in the fact that, for Platonic philosophizing, political philosophy and eros are not just particular matters among others, they do not constitute narrowly circumscribed fields of work or branches that can be cut off, but rather, they lead into the center of the philosophic movement itself. The Socratic turn designates the turn to political philosophy, and the sole "expert knowledge" Socrates explicitly claims for himself concerns the things of love. Political philosophy is the Socratic way to the self-knowledge of the philosopher, and the confrontation with love culminates in the determination of his nature. As little, therefore, as political philosophy is reserved for the works that are immediately occupied with political subjects, such as the *Statesman*, the *Republic*, or the *Laws*, just as little can the treatment of eros be limited to the *Symposium* or the *Phaedrus*. Political philosophy and eros concern the whole of Platonic philosophy. Whoever wants to speak on *Socrates and Plato: The Dialectics of Eros* must have in view the whole of Platonic philosophy and have a command over the thirty-five dialogues that have come down to us as Platonic. For Seth Benardete, both are true. His seven

---

3. The Tele-Akademie of Südwest Television broadcast their recording of the lecture of July 1, 1999 in a 45-minute program on January 28, 2001. The program was repeated several times and also broadcast by other television stations.

4. The paper is published in *The Argument of the Action*, 198–230.

5. The book appeared under the title—requested by the Press—*Plato's "Laws": The Discovery of Being* (Chicago and London, University of Chicago Press, 2000).

books to date on Plato offer interpretations of the *Laws*, *Republic*, *Gorgias* and *Phaedrus*, *Philebus*, *Theaetetus*, *Sophist*, and *Statesman*, in the case of the last four dialogues mentioned, accompanied by careful translations. In addition to his book of 1984, Benardete had already devoted a long essay in 1963 to the *Statesman*, and then in 1996 a further paper, which counts among his most important.[6] In it he interprets the concluding dialogue of the trilogy as Plato's most radical dialogue, as a dialogue that, like no other, provides a glimpse into Plato's workshop. In addition to the books come papers, among others, on the *Timaeus*, *Phaedo*, *Charmides*, *Lysis*, *Symposium*, *Protagoras*, *Cratylus*, *Laches*, which, along with work on Hesiod, the *Iliad*, Aeschylus, Sophocles, Euripides and Greek tragedy, will become available at the beginning of the coming year collected in a comprehensive volume under the title, *The Argument of the Action*.[7]

In conclusion, let me mention another difficulty concerning this evening's theme, which at the same time has become highly important for the distinctive profile of our speaker. It is not only that eros and political philosophy concern the whole of Platonic philosophy. They are also not given to us as subjects of a "Platonic teaching." What we hear about them we perceive out of the mouths of Platonic characters, who direct themselves to concrete addressees and speak in the particular concrete situation of a dialogue, which in turn is embedded in, or narrated under, concrete external circumstances. Benardete has paid great attention to the distinction between the doctrinal and dialogic levels, the intertwining of speech and action, the interplay of universal and particular, out of which a new theoretical argument emerges, and like no one before he has made consideration of the literary form, the poetic framework, and the events of the dialogue fruitful for philosophic interpretation. Thus also the programmatic title of the collection, *The Argument of the Action*. That he demands much of his readers and audience with his complex, highly differentiated approach is familiar from their own experience to many in this room. Let us say it openly: Benardete is the most demanding interpreter of Plato conceivable. But whoever engages him seriously will be richly rewarded. He will be led to think for himself and in the best case moved to wonder. To that wonder which is the beginning of philosophy.

---

6. "The Plan of the *Statesman*" in *Metis. Revue d'anthropologie du monde grec ancien*, VII, 1–2, 1992, recte: 1996: 25–47; reprinted in *The Argument of the Action*, 354–75.

7. *The Argument of the Action* was published in 2000; see note 2 above.

Chapter Seven

The Thumotic and the Erotic Soul:
Seth Benardete on Platonic Psychology

Ronna Burger

Sparkling-wreathed, O deathless Aphrodite...
But you, O blest,
a smile on your immortal face,
asked what was wrong this time, why
was I calling this time,
what did I most want to happen to me
in my raging heart. "Whom shall I sweet talk this time
and lead back to your love? Who, Sappho,
is doing you wrong?"...
Come to me now once more, and free me from jagged
sorrow, and make what my heart is
longing for, happen. You yourself
fight alongside me.[1]

I. The Dual Principles of Platonic Psychology

In her ode to the goddess Aphrodite, Sappho gives expression to her "raging heart," suffering from the experience of unrequited love. Summoned by the poet, Aphrodite comes down from heaven to ask Sappho who has committed an injustice against her and in the end Sappho seeks the promise of the goddess to be her ally in war. In this poem, Seth Benardete

Reprinted, with slight revisions by the author, from *Interpretation* 32, no. 1 (2004): 57–76. Originally presented at the conference on "The Philosophy of Seth Benardete," New School University, December 2002.

1. Sappho, fragment 1, "Ode to Aphrodite," trans. Peter Bing and Rip Cohen, in *Games of Venus* (London and New York: Routledge, 1991), 71–72.

comments, love is understood "in terms of right and Aphrodite as a goddess of revenge. The issues of justice and love are presented together, and there is no suggestion that they could be separated once Sappho asks a god to alleviate her suffering." Benardete discerned in the poem what he took to be the two fundamental principles of Platonic psychology: "Eros and moral indignation seem to be alternative grounds for what constitutes the nature of man."[2]

These comments on Sappho's ode appear in the Epilogue to Benardete's study of the *Phaedrus* and *Gorgias*. In the *Phaedrus*, he observes, Socrates acknowledges the experiential truth of Sappho's coupling of justice and love through his image of the war chariot of the soul, but he also suggests how it would be possible to uncouple them. "The result of such an uncoupling," he goes on, "can be seen in the *Gorgias*, where Socrates anatomizes the will to punish and its appearance of rationality."[3] Benardete was working out both possibilities in pairing his reading of Plato's two dialogues on rhetoric. The art of speaking, which consists in the adjustment of speeches to souls, necessarily takes a two-fold form, reflecting the two fundamental and irreducible principles of psychology: in connection with the longing for justice, which can inspire moral indignation, punitive rhetoric, in connection with love of the beautiful, erotic rhetoric. But the two are not of equal rank: one turns out to be "spurious rhetoric," which is nothing but "a phantom image of justice," while "genuine rhetoric is the science of eros."[4] Benardete indicates their respective status by the title of his book, *The Rhetoric of Morality and Philosophy*.

The nature of the soul reflected in these two forms of rhetoric shows up in the two distinct forms of idealization displayed by the longing for justice, on the one hand, and the love of the beautiful, on the other. The dual principles of psychology bring in their wake, as a consequence, a two-fold theology—of punitive gods, who enforce justice, and beautiful gods, who inspire eros. The two kinds are paradigmatically represented by the gods Benardete singled out as the special creations of the poets, Hades and Eros. With Hades as the setting of the *Protagoras* and Eros as the subject of the *Symposium*, those two dialogues, Benardete proposes, exhibit the theological dimension of the *Gorgias* and *Phaedrus*, with which they are

---

2. *The Rhetoric of Morality and Philosophy: Plato's "Gorgias" and "Phaedrus"* (Chicago: University of Chicago Press, 1991), 195.

3. *The Rhetoric of Morality and Philosophy*, 195.

4. *The Rhetoric of Morality and Philosophy*, 2.

thereby paired.[5] Now Hades, as Benardete shows through his reading of the *Republic* as well as the *Protagoras*, "is nothing but a name for the city," and the god Eros, on Benardete's reading of the *Phaedrus*, is nothing but "the manifold of human erotic natures."[6] In the gods of the poets—the higher beings we fear and those we look up to in admiration—Benardete found "the prefiguration of the problematic unity of a Platonic psychology."[7]

Precisely as such a prefiguration, the gods point to that same "problematic unity" in being itself, more specifically, in the relation of the just and the beautiful: the theology implied by the principles of Platonic psychology is the pointer to ontology. If philosophy always aims at an understanding of being or the beings as a whole, it has, in Benardete's beautifully paradoxical formula, an "eccentric core," which is political philosophy;[8] but what links political philosophy to first philosophy is the understanding of the human soul. Benardete formulates this relation in reflections on Leo Strauss, on the occasion of a memorial speech. It is a conclusion he draws from his interpretation of Strauss's *Natural Right and History* as a study of modern political philosophy's "successive dismantling of the disparate wholeness of the soul."[9] The remark he goes on to make in that context—"Plato's psychology was Strauss's way to Plato's ideas"— seems even more obviously applicable to his own thought.

If psychology is the way to the ideas, Strauss's way into Platonic psychology, Benardete observes, was through the *Republic*; but no Platonic dialogue, he adds, yields a complete theory of the soul.[10] Socrates introduces his

---

5.   *The Rhetoric of Morality and Philosophy*, 3.

6.   *Socrates and Plato: The Dialectics of Eros* (Munich: Carl Friedrich von Siemens Stiftung, 2002), reprinted in *The Archaeology of the Soul*, eds. Ronna Burger and Michael Davis (South Bend: St. Augustine's Press, 2012), 247, 259.

7.   *The Rhetoric of Morality and Philosophy*, 2.

8.   "Memorial Speech for Leo Strauss" (manuscript, 1974), published in *The Archaeology of the Soul*, 375, and "Leo Strauss' *The City and Man*," reprinted in *The Archaeology of the Soul*, 362.

9.   "Memorial Speech for Leo Strauss," *The Archaeology of the Soul*, 376.

10. The *Republic* itself, Benardete notes, reveals the tension between the political and the natural relation of *thumos* and eros, and it does so by the action that accompanies its argument. "Memorial Speech for Leo Strauss," *The Archaeology of the Soul*, 376. Does he mean that the surface argument spells out the political relation of *thumos* and eros, while the natural relation between them is suggested by the

psychology in the *Republic* with a warning to his companions—which is Plato's warning to his readers: the present path they are following, in their search for justice, cannot lead to a precise account of the soul, but a longer and harder road would be required (435d). Socrates suggests one way to interpret that longer and harder road when he later expresses his hesitancy to discuss the good—the final end that every soul pursues and for the sake of which it does everything (504a-505a, 505e). But since every Platonic dialogue seems to offer its own unique way into the human soul, perhaps the longer and harder road would in fact require putting together all those partial and distorted paths, or understanding why they cannot be put together. Benardete, who traveled far on that longer and harder road in the course of his life's work, seems to have come to the conclusion that Plato's plurality of ways into the human soul are all variants on two fundamental and irreducible modes, the thumotic and the erotic, determined by two central experiences, the will to justice and love of the beautiful.

The template of the thumotic soul is worked out in Book IV of the *Republic*, where Socrates addresses the question whether the class structure of the city has a perfect match in the structure of the individual soul.[11] The template of the erotic soul is furnished by the chariot image of the soul, which Socrates presents in the "mythic hymn" to Eros he delivers in the *Phaedrus*. The two accounts are typically assumed to be roughly the same; each articulates, after all, a tripartite psychology—the Platonic theory, scholars argue, that marks an advance on the supposedly earlier treatment of the unitary soul, soul as essentially mind, with no place for the passions.[12]

The *Republic* and the *Phaedrus* may each present a tripartite analysis of the human soul; but each account is colored, of course, by the unique role it

---

action of the dialogue? The first, that would mean, belongs to the "best city in speech," the second to what Benardete came to call the "dialogic city." Cf. *Socrates' Second Sailing: On Plato's* Republic (Chicago: University of Chicago Press, 1989), 137, 140.

11. That template is filled out, Benardete demonstrates, by the sequence of three interlocutors in the *Gorgias*, where rationality of some sort is represented by Gorgias's praise of his art of rhetoric, spiritedness by Polus's display of the will to punish, and desire by Callicles' advocacy of hedonism. *The Rhetoric of Morality and Philosophy*, see especially 91–92.

12. See, for example, G. M. A. Grube, *Plato's Thought* (London: Methuen and Co., 1935; Reprint, Boston: Beacon Press, 1958), 131, 133 or Nicholas Smith, ed., *Plato: Critical Assessments* Vol. III (London and New York: Routledge, 1998), viii.

plays in its particular context. Benardete set out, on that assumption, to uncover the distinctive understanding of the soul caught in the grip of erotic passion in contrast with the soul consumed by moral indignation; yet he was able to accomplish that task precisely because of his recognition of the common way both accounts work, which undercuts the standard view of each. The fixed structure of the tripartite soul, in its two versions, is the official Platonic doctrine that emerges from the speeches of the *Republic* and the *Phaedrus*; by uncovering the deeds that give rise to those speeches, Benardete's reading sets that rigid structure in motion. What he discovers is a dynamic process of shifting self-division, or self-multiplication, through which the soul structures itself. In the case of the soul suffering moral indignation, that self-structuring is the deed of *thumos*; for the soul aroused by the beautiful, it is the product of eros. These deeds contain the key to an understanding of the passions of the soul and the ideas with which they are linked. Each account thus proves to be a striking model in miniature of what Benardete came to call "the argument of the action."[13]

II. The Thumotic Soul

The city that provides the model for the soul in *Republic* IV has been constructed out of three classes: the money-making class, the guardians, and the "perfect guardians" or rulers. About that highest class we know almost nothing at this stage of the argument, and most importantly, nothing about the philosopher playing such a role. This city has been found to be just insofar as each of the three classes in it does its own thing. To find out whether justice means the same thing in the individual, we have to determine if there are three corresponding forms (*eidē*) in the soul (435b). We would have expected to hear of "parts" of the soul, but there is no talk of parts because, as we shall see, there is no whole.[14]

A construction of the soul parallel to the class structure of the city requires three steps. The first separates desire and reason so absolutely that neither has any trace of the other and they are essentially in conflict with each other. To accomplish this absolute separation, Socrates holds our psychic experience up to the law of non-contradiction—the first time, scholars say,

---

13. "Strauss on Plato," *The Argument of the Action*, eds. Ronna Burger and Michael Davis (Chicago: University of Chicago Press, 2009), see especially 409.

14. The term "part" (*meros*) appears for the first time only when the psychology becomes the basis for an account of the virtues (*Republic* 442b–c).

this fundamental principle is articulated: since the same thing is not willing to do or suffer opposites in the same respect in relation to the same at the same time, any appearance of such opposition psychologically means it is not the experience of a single subject (436b).[15]

To make desire itself free from any internal contradiction, Socrates must assign to each appetite a syntax, as Benardete puts it, which yokes it to a precisely specified object—much thirst for much drink, little thirst for little drink, while thirst itself is the desire for drink itself, drink that is not hot or cold, much or little, or, most importantly, good. Desire, according to this analysis, has nothing of that natural orientation to the good Socrates will later ascribe to it (cf. 505e). To make the separation between the rational and the desiderative, Benardete observes, Socrates "must disprove himself—he who seems to insist everywhere that all men desire the goods (438a3–4)."[16]

If the soul of the thirsty person wants nothing but to drink, anything that pulls it back from drinking when thirsty, Socrates reasons, must be something other than that which drives it like a beast toward drinking (439a-b). Out of nowhere desire is bestialized. With just as little justification, Socrates asks whether it is not calculation that prohibits, restraining the irrational craving of diseased appetite. But why, Socrates should have been asked, must desire always lead forward and reason pull back? Couldn't desire in some cases pull us back in repulsion and reason urge us forward? Why indeed should desire necessarily be diseased, not to mention bestial? And why should reason have no other function than to restrain desire?

To apply the law of non-contradiction to the soul, Socrates appeals to the image of the archer: we must say he does nothing as a whole, but one hand pushes the bow, the other pulls. Of course, Benardete reasons, those opposite motions yield one result, so if desire and reason are like the two hands, they are in fact bound together from the start, aiming at the good as their target.[17] But at the moment Socrates reaches a conclusion that altogether denies such a possibility: that by which the soul calculates is entirely other than that by which it feels passionate love (*eran*) and hunger and thirst and the flutter of other irrational desires (439d). With no argument at all, Socrates slips eros into the class of desire, of which hunger and thirst were the exemplars. Like

---

15. It is an abstraction of mathematics—the spinning top whose axis is perfectly at rest—that provides the model, Benardete notes, for the soul turned into an "idea." *Socrates' Second Sailing*, 95.

16. *Socrates' Second Sailing*, 94.

17. *Socrates' Second Sailing*, 137, 140.

all the appetites, it has no rationality of its own, and stands over against a reason that has no desire of its own. Eros as desire for the good, which has philosophy as its core, is on this account utterly incomprehensible (cf. *Symposium* 203e–204b).

Once desire and reason have been so radically divorced, the task remains of separating spiritedness, or *thumos*, from each in turn. The immediate response of Glaucon, whose character is manly and erotic at once (cf. 357a, 402d–403c), is to assume the natural unity of *thumos* and desire. Socrates sets out to disprove such a possibility on the basis of a story he has heard. A certain Leontius was on his way up from the Piraeus when he became aware of corpses lying at the place of public execution. As intensely as he desired to look on the scene, he turned himself away just as intensely in disgust.

> And for a while he fought and covered his face, but finally overcome by his desire, he dragged open his eyes, ran toward the corpses, and said, "Here they are for you, O miserable wretches, get your fill of the beautiful sight. (439e–440a)[18]

The anecdote is supposed to illustrate the cut between *thumos* and desire. Desire was illustrated originally by thirst and hunger and Leontius's case looks as if it fits that model when he commands his eyes to satiate themselves. Their feast is a "beautiful spectacle"; but that is only the sarcastic voice of anger speaking. Baffled by the nature of the strange desire that is supposed to be moving Leontius, commentators have debated whether it is to be understood as some kind of perverse sexual appetite.[19]

As is so often the case, Benardete's eye was captured by a detail that commonly goes unnoticed, though once brought into one's field of vision, makes the whole picture look entirely different: the corpses Leontius wants to gaze upon lie at the site of public execution. This impulse can be attributed to the faculty of desire, Benardete observes, only because "language decides the issue before Socrates can be asked the right question: what is the desire to see the corpses of publicly executed criminals?"[20] What is moving Leontius is the desire to see justice done. But this impulse fills him at the same time with

---

18. Benardete's translation, *Socrates' Second Sailing*, 99.

19. See, for example, John Cooper, "Plato's Theory of Human Motivation," in *Plato: Critical Assessments* Vol. III, 33–35, 41, or Julia Annas, *An Introduction to Plato's Republic* (Oxford: Oxford University Press, 1981), 127–28.

20. *Socrates' Second Sailing*, 99.

shame. Leontius, the spectator, not the agent of punishment, must find something disgraceful in the pleasure of vicarious revenge he anticipates; he addresses his eyes, Benardete notes, with a comic word that expresses contempt (*kakodaimones*). But the shame Leontius exhibits goes deeper: he wants to see justice done because it is something noble or beautiful, but punitive justice appears before him in all its ugliness and ignobility. His psychological conflict is the response to a contradiction within the just, in its relation to the beautiful.[21]

Leontius' angry self-rebuke is presumably the expression of his *thumos*; but his desire to see justice done, which is the target of his anger, belongs no less to the spirited part of the soul. The story of Leontius is in fact an illustration of *thumos* in conflict with itself. It has been turned into an illustration of *thumos* warring against desire by a series of poetic tropes. By a double metaphor the demand for justice becomes the desire for a certain sight, and that in turn becomes bodily hunger; then by a double synecdoche, the eyes that stand in for the desire to see become a stomach to be filled; finally, through personification, Leontius treats his eyes as an independent subject with a will of their own. The "cannibalistic eye," as Benardete puts it so vividly, is "a belly hungry for a beautiful sight." And it is only anger that could have created this independent living being in order to satisfy its needs while remaining innocent itself.[22]

Anger, Glaucon agrees after hearing the story of Leontius, sometimes wars against desire as something alien; but the possibility that *thumos* could ever ally itself with desire is something he suddenly finds shocking. The obvious case is the lover who finds his unrequited love unfair; but the denial of that possibility, Benardete notes, reflects the presupposition of the *Republic* as a whole, "that justice and love are wholly separate and never interfere with one another."[23]

---

21. Benardete's reading of Socrates' exchange with Polus in the *Gorgias* is an extended reflection on this contradiction within the just and the psychological conflict it engenders. Cf. *Socrates' Second Sailing*, 99, and *The Rhetoric of Morality and Philosophy*, especially 54–55. See also Benardete's reference to the Athenian Stranger on the tension between the just and the beautiful (*Laws* 859d2–860c3), in connection with *Republic* 443e5, in *Socrates' Second Sailing*, 102. Cf. Robert Berman, "The Socratic Principle and the Problem of Punishment," Section II, in this volume.

22. *Socrates' Second Sailing*, 99.

23. *Socrates' Second Sailing*, 100. The way "the justified indignation about injustice

Whatever the occasion might be, what makes *thumos* boil up, Socrates reasons, is the belief that one is suffering unjustly. In such a condition, *thumos* allies itself with what is believed just and persists in the fight for it until it accomplishes its will or else meets with death—unless it is called back by *logos*, like a dog called back by the shepherd (440c–d). What Socrates has in fact described is the attachment of *thumos* to its own sense of injustice, which can lead to self-destruction if not restrained by an opposing *logos*. But the familiarity of the image of the watchdog—from which Socrates had deduced the possibility of the guardian nature (376a–c)—is enough to convince Glaucon that Socrates has demonstrated the natural allegiance of spiritedness with reason. In speaking of this allegiance, Socrates introduces a new designation—the *thumoeides*. Benardete uncovers here, as he so often does, the argument conveyed through language itself. The *thumoeides*, as its suffix indicates, is only *like thumos*: it is always playing at being the natural impulse of anger. By a kind of pun, at the same time, its name suggests that the *thumoeides* has a role to play in the formation of *eidē*. Now we understand why Socrates asked originally whether the three classes in the city have a counterpart, not in three parts, but in three *eidē* in the soul: the *thumoeides* is in the midst of constructing those forms, whose atomistic independence and absence of internal contradiction seem to reflect the character, on one understanding at least, of the *eidē* as such. The *thumoeides*, in Benardete's words, is "the spirit of eideticization."[24] The two features of the *thumoeides*—in its connection with anger and with the "ideas"—first show up together in Thrasymachus (336b and 340c–341a). Benardete credits Strauss with the discovery of this two-fold significance: having learned from Alfarabi about Thrasymachus's ability to play the city in its anger, he went on to connect that with Thrasymachus's insistence on the artisan in the precise sense, who never errs.[25]

If the structure of the soul is to map perfectly onto the class structure of the city, a cut must still be made between the *thumoeides* and the calculating part of the soul. To accomplish this, Socrates appeals to Homer's portrait of Odysseus in a moment of inner conflict: "He struck his breast and rebuked

shifts insensibly into the unjustified indignation about unrequited love" is, Strauss once suggested, "perhaps the deepest secret of spiritedness." "The Origins of Political Science and the Problem of Socrates," eds. David Bolotin, Christopher Bruell, and Thomas Pangle, *Interpretation* 23, no. 2 (1996): 192–93.

24. *Socrates' Second Sailing*, 100, cf. 56.

25. "Leo Strauss' *The City and Man*," *The Archaeology of the Soul*, 365.

his heart" (*Odyssey* 20.17–18).[26] Odysseus is lying on the floor at night in his own home, disguised as a beggar, watching the slave girls laughing and cavorting as they go to sleep with the suitors. *Thumos* was aroused in his breast, Homer tells us, and his heart growled, like a bitch guarding her babies at the sight of a stranger. Homer's image seems to have inspired Socrates' description of the nature of the guardians as spirited and philosophic at once—like a watch dog that discriminates solely on the basis of what is familiar or strange, which is supposed to exhibit its character as a lover of learning, that is, a lover of wisdom (376a–c)! With this "evidently forced solution," Benardete remarks, *thumos* "has made the philosophic nature in its own image."[27]

Just as he is about to jump up and kill the women, Odysseus holds himself back, remembering his bigger plan to confront the suitors. When Socrates cited the same passage in *Republic* III (390d), he included the next line: "Endure, heart! You once put up with something even more disgraceful" (*kunteron*, literally, "more doglike"). Odysseus gets control of his anger back home by recalling one of the most terrible moments on his journey—watching the Cyclops seize two of his companions, dash them to the ground, cut them up, and devour them. At that moment, as Odysseus himself later describes it, his *thumos* was possessed by a sense of helplessness. When the Cyclops lay down to sleep, however, he formed a plan in his *thumos* to stab him with his sword; but another *thumos* then held him back, as he realized the impossibility of escaping from the Cyclops' cave, blocked by a rock too large to move (*Odyssey* 9.299). In that situation, Odysseus tells his heart as he watches the laughing slave girls, you endured until wisdom (*mētis*) found a way out of the cave (20.22–24). Odysseus connects wisdom (*mētis*) with "no one" (*mē tis*), the name he gave himself in his encounter with the Cyclops: his profound pun, which lies at the heart of Benardete's reading of the *Odyssey*, points to the anonymity of mind and raises the question of the relation between reason and anger in Odysseus's motivation.[28]

---

26. The line that was cited in *Republic* III to illustrate the virtue of patient endurance (390d), and is now supposed to show how Homer has made [*pepoiēken*] that which calculates about better and worse rebuke the irrationally spirited element in the soul, as if one thing against an other (*hōs heteron heterō*, 441b), is used in the *Phaedo* to support the claim that the unitary soul can oppose the feelings of the body (94b–c).

27. *Socrates' Second Sailing*, 57.

28. See *Odyssey* 9.366, 407–14, and Benardete, *The Bow and the Lyre: A Platonic Reading of the* Odyssey (Lanham, Md.: Rowman & Littlefield, 1997), 74–79, 124–28.

At the moment he reacts to the slave girls, in any case, Odysseus seems to be moved by the passion of anger; and if it is rationality that holds him back, it is a purely instrumental sort, which, by means of beating and rebuking, restrains spiritedness only to help it achieve its own end. If this inner struggle of *thumos* with itself looks like two independent agents in conflict, it is by the silent poetry Odysseus uses to get control: identifying his "self" with the calculation that holds him back, he treats his passion for revenge as something alien, projecting it onto his body. More specifically, he identifies his passion for revenge by a synecdoche with his heart, and then personifies his heart so it becomes an agent with a will of its own, which can be exhorted to behave in the desired manner.

Homer, we realize, has provided the model for the soul in its thumotic mode, of which the Leontius story looks like Plato's invented variant. Of course, the Homeric passage is a depiction of self-mastery, whereas the story of Leontius is one of self-defeat. Odysseus's anger is firmly directed outward and his conflict is simply about when to act. Leontius, on the other hand, is torn apart inside as a result of his sudden awareness that the beautiful and the just do not always coincide; his moral indignation toward others, consequently, has taken on a punitive form turned against himself.

Socrates does not call attention to the complex nature of the thumotic soul as he has disclosed it in deed. Looking back, instead, on his speeches, he breathes a sigh of relief that he has somehow made it through these troubled waters and demonstrated the tripartite structure of the soul in perfect correspondence with the class structure of the city. He can now draw a conclusion on the basis of that political paradigm: justice in the soul must be the condition that obtains when each of the three forms does its proper work, while injustice is faction or disease in the soul. The question that set the whole inquiry in motion—whether being just is truly in our self-interest—now seems to Socrates' interlocutors ridiculous even to ask, if justice is nothing but the inner order of the healthy soul. Socrates has, apparently, overcome the skeptical doubts of his companions—the *Republic* should end right here; but whether health of soul has been adequately represented is another question.

The speeches of *Republic* IV have confirmed the *eidos* of justice as the proper order of the tripartite soul and the parallel city. But that order has been produced by justice as a passion of the soul—the passion to see the guilty punished. If we follow Benardete's lead and look to the action behind the speeches, we realize it was *thumos* that was responsible for the bestialization

91

of desire; and it was *thumos* that reduced reason to calculation, with no end of its own. In following the argument of this action, one performs what Benardete calls an "eidetic analysis."[29] In the course of that analysis, the spurious character of the *eidē*, in all their fixity and complete separation from one another, is replaced by the fluid structure of an "indeterminate dyad":[30] *thumos* first melds itself with reason in order to detach desire as the other, then it gets fused with desire in order to detach reason as the other. Behind three separate parts of the soul lies the dynamic relation between thumotic desire and thumotic reason.

Justice as health of soul is supposed to be the inner order that obtains when spiritedness allies itself with calculation in order to suppress desire; but that is an inner order that cannot belong to the philosopher, in whom desire and reason are inseparable and *thumos* seems to have no place.[31] The argument of the action of *Republic* IV discloses the essential limits of the thumotic soul; what lies beyond those limits is the erotic soul, which belongs above all to the philosopher.

III. The Erotic Soul

The erotic soul is the subject of the account Socrates presents in the *Phaedrus*, in the last of the dialogue's three speeches on eros. In this "palinode" or recantation, Socrates sets out to purify himself from his previous condemnation of eros, delivered in competition with the original written speech by the rhetorician Lysias. Lysias represented a sober non-lover seeking

---

29. The soul analysis belongs to the whole *Republic* as "an eidetic analysis of the beautiful, the good, and the just insofar as they contribute to the understanding of the just." *Socrates' Second Sailing*, 5.

30. On Benardete's notion of the "indeterminate dyad," see, for example, "The Plan of Plato's *Statesman*," in *The Argument of the Action*, 371–72.

31. That, at least, is what Plato seems to imply when he has a variety of figures— from Callicles to Crito—accuse Socrates of being unable or unwilling to stand up and defend himself against injustice. The Athenian Stranger imagines the speech of a legislator who exhorts every man to be thumoeidetic as well as gentle, since it is not possible to escape from incurable injustices other than by defending oneself and punishing, which no soul can do without noble *thumos* (*Laws* 731b–e). The Stranger seems to be preparing the ground, Benardete comments, for "the enigma of book 9: how a Socratic principle can be the foundation of criminal law." *Plato's "Laws": The Discovery of Being* (Chicago: University of Chicago Press, 2000), 157.

to persuade a beloved against granting his favors to the mad lover; Socrates' revision, while retaining the argument of the non-lover, reveals him to be a seductive lover in disguise. Moved now by shame at giving voice to that argument, and fear of the god Eros, Socrates promises to establish the divine madness of eros as the source of our greatest blessings in life.

To demonstrate this, Socrates must provide an account of the nature of the soul, divine and human. The starting point (*archē*) is the proof that soul is ever-moving self-motion (*Phaedrus* 245c). Socrates seems to leave that principle behind when he turns to the *idea* of the soul, which should exhibit its structure.[32] In place, however, of a "divine and long narration" about the *idea*, Socrates offers a "shorter and human" likeness of the soul—the famous image of the chariot team, composed of a pair of winged horses and charioteer (246a). The story that unfolds turns on the relation between the two "motions" of this psychic chariot team: on the one hand, an ascent to the region beyond the heavens where the pure beings are to be seen, on the other, the advance of the lover toward union with the beloved. The wings of the soul are responsible for lifting it upward, the horses for pulling the chariot-team of the lover into the presence of the beloved—or rather, that one of the horses who is obstreperous and hard to control. This unruly horse makes it difficult to remain aloft, contemplating the hyperuranian beings; but without his persistent demands to advance toward the beloved, the upward journey would not be initiated at all. As Benardete here and so often observed, the way is the obstacle. The wings of the soul, he explains, "do not convey the soul straight up; instead the horizontal motion of the horses interferes with such an ascent. A resolution of the two motions leads to a skewed ascent."[33]

This skewed ascent is the path the human chariot-team follows in the company of a god, one of the eleven Olympian gods—Hestia, the twelfth, stays at home. But in whatever divine troop it follows, no soul can enter into the figure of a human being unless it has caught a glimpse of the beings, however momentary and partial. Mind, according to this speech, looks like the defining feature of the human. The extent of our vision of the beings determines a typology of human beings, which Socrates articulates in a ranking of nine classes. How, we wonder, are those nine cognitive types to be put together with the eleven erotic types, determined by the Olympian god each of us fol-

---

32. On Benardete's understanding of the general tension between principle and structure, see *Socrates' Second Sailing*, 126 and "On Plato's *Sophist*," *The Argument of the Action*, 345.

33. "Socrates and Plato: The Dialectics of Eros," *The Archaeology of the Soul*, 257.

lows? Benardete alerts us to the puzzle of the speech as a whole by calling attention to this sign of the gap between the passion of soul and mind; what bridges that gap is the beautiful.

Our rationality, which is supposed to define us as human, consists, according to Socrates, in our capacity to collect many perceptions into one form, which is a recollection of our hyperuranian vision. But there is one experience in particular that has the power to elicit this recollection: while all the other beings, like justice or moderation, have only obscure likenesses here on earth, beauty alone reveals itself to us in all its resplendence. The visibly beautiful, in the appearance of the beloved as an Olympian god, awakens the memory of the truly beautiful. Erotic madness is just this experience, in Benardete's words, of "being reminded of the non-discursive beautiful itself by the sight of a phantom image of it."[34]

As Socrates describes this experience, the soul that is uncorrupted, when it comes upon the sight of a "divine-like face or some *idea* of the body," is filled with awe and reveres the beautiful one like a god (251a). A stream of beauty flows into the lover's eyes and warms him, watering the hard and choked passages from which the wings can then begin to grow. The torturous prickings of desire—Socrates likens the experience to teething—fill the lover's soul with terrible pangs, which can only be relieved, momentarily, by the sight of the beloved. This reception of the beautiful is a universal experience; but everyone undergoes it in a distinctive way. Each lover looks for the traces in his own nature of the god he follows, then seeks a beloved who instantiates the type; and when he finds him, Socrates adds, he molds him into that model. "The response to the beautiful," Benardete remarks, "is shaped by a prior form of soul that depends not on the beings but on the gods.... Accordingly, there is a forced fitting of the beloved into a previously fashioned image."[35]

The lover falls in love, literally, "at first sight." But the vision of the beloved does not alone satisfy his longing. He cannot help but yearn for the requital of his love. There is no reason, however, that the beloved should respond at first sight, if at all. The problem was first indicated by Lysias' non-lover, who blamed the lover for his unjustified appeal to justice, as if his passion brought with it the right to be loved in return (*Phaedrus* 233d–234a). The lover's effort to draw the beloved to himself can only be accomplished by fashioning an image in speech that will be persuasive to the beloved: he

---

34. *The Rhetoric of Morality and Philosophy*, 154; cf. "Socrates and Plato: The Dialectics of Eros," *The Archaeology of the Soul*, 258.

35. *The Rhetoric of Morality and Philosophy*, 154.

needs to replace by speech the beautiful vision that aroused his love without any need for speeches. This task marks the moment when the seemingly disparate topics of the dialogue—eros and rhetoric—intersect. The lover's construction of an image in speech exemplifies the practice of erotic rhetoric, and it contains, as Benardete explores it, the key to the structure of the soul.

It is no accident, then, that Socrates puts the image of the chariot-team to work only at the last stage of his speech—in describing the capture of the beloved. The need for the "capture" of the beloved is especially striking when Socrates begins to speak at just this point of the blessings that will come to "the one befriended" from his "mad friend" because of eros (253c), invoking the natural reciprocity of friendship. Socrates now recalls the beginning of his speech, which distinguished in the human chariot-team, as opposed to the divine, one horse that is "beautiful and good" (*kalos k'agathos*)—the ordinary term for a "gentleman"—from the other, who is just the contrary; but it is only at this point that Socrates is prepared to explain what that difference consists in and how it shows up in our erotic experience. The one horse, we now learn, is well-articulated, high-necked with an aquiline nose, white in color with dark eyes, a lover of honor with moderation and shame, a companion of true opinion, obedient to command and *logos* alone; the other is crooked and heavy, jumbled together at random, thick-necked and snub-nosed, dark in color with bloodshot eyes, a companion of hubris and pride, scarcely obedient to the whip and spurs (253d–e). As is so often the case, one small detail, almost always overlooked, caught Benardete's eye: a snub-nosed horse? The black horse is Socrates![36]

The erotic soul as a whole, it seems, is contained in the black horse alone. Who, then, or what are the white horse and the charioteer? Benardete addresses this question by tracing the lover's interaction with the beloved through all its twists and turns. While the black horse, filled with longing, clenches the bit and pulls the team shamelessly toward the beloved, his partner, controlled by shame, is dragged forward against his will. Despite all his resistance, the charioteer at the same time is brought face to face with the beautiful one, and the sight awakens his memory of beauty itself; as a result, he falls back in reverence, inadvertently yanking the reins so violently that the whole mouth of the black horse is covered with blood (254b–d). After enduring this painful experience time after

---

36. See *Theaetetus* 148e, 209c; cf. *Republic* 474d. If the snub nose weren't enough, the "randomly ordered" character of the black horse (*eikē sumpephorēmenos*, 253e) echoes Socrates' description in the *Phaedo* of his own way of inquiry, which he mixes up at random (*eikē phurō*, 97b).

time, the obstreperous horse is finally humbled. His suffering is the condition, it seems, for the paradoxical identity of madness with moderation that distinguishes divine eros from human.

Once the beloved, meanwhile, has admitted the tamed lover into intimate association, the stream of beauty that originally flowed from him into the eyes of the lover begins to overflow from the lover; like a wind or an echo bouncing off a surface, it rebounds into the beautiful one and waters the ducts from which the wings begin to grow. Now he is possessed by the phantom image of love, which he believes to be friendship. Filled with perplexity, he sees himself in his lover as in a mirror but is not aware of what it is with which he is falling in love. He is responding in fact to the model the lover has constructed in speech, which, as Benardete puts it, "renders the lover to the beloved in a joint version of their common nature. The beloved moves in pursuit of an illusory other who is in truth himself. He undergoes self-motion through his self-ignorance." If the lover constructs this image irrationally, Benardete continues, "his self-representation takes on the conventional disguise of an Olympian god; if he does it rationally, he is Socrates, and whatever god he fashions for the beloved is a necessary means for a shared ascent to the hyperuranian beings (cf. 256e1)."[37]

It is in the plot of this story that Benardete uncovers the genesis of the tripartite erotic soul. The black horse is eros itself, the white horse nothing but the beautiful image he constructs with which the beloved falls in love. "The lover," Benardete explains, "tries to pair the beloved with himself in his own soul. The white horse is this inserted self as other; it is perfectly obedient. That which does the insertion is the black horse, which thus comes to light as either hubris or madness."[38] Benardete focuses on the genesis of the white horse from the black and says little about the charioteer. The black horse, it seems, if he is Socratic eros, should already contain mind and desire in himself. How, then, should one interpret the detachment of the charioteer? If his only role were pulling back on the reins—like the calculating part of the soul in *Republic* IV— he would look like a product of the black horse splitting off from himself the force of restraint that humbles him. But the charioteer is also the subject who sees the hyperuranian beings and his pulling back on the reins seems to be just the unintended consequence of his falling back in awe when he is reminded of the beautiful itself by the sight of the beloved.

The action that produces the structure of the erotic soul is at the same

---

37. *The Rhetoric of Morality and Philosophy*, 151.

38. *The Rhetoric of Morality and Philosophy*, 154.

time, Benardete demonstrates, that which generates the sequence of speeches on eros. The written speech of Lysias, ascribed to the non-lover who boasts of his sanity and sobriety, comes to light as the representation of the perfectly controlled charioteer. At the same time, Socrates' first speech shows itself to be the white horse by which he tried to draw Phaedrus toward himself; but that means it is the product of the black horse, which must be Socrates' mythic hymn to eros, in which the structure of the whole is being disclosed.[39] This model should be applicable, not just to the speeches on eros, but to the Platonic dialogues more generally, if the *Phaedrus*, as Benardete maintains, is the passkey to all of them. The written work as a perfect whole, Benardete suggests, is always a white horse, which "reflects the interlocutor back to himself in a form he can follow and aspire to." That is a beautified image projected by the black horse at the core of every dialogue, which is the erotic impulse of Socratic philosophy. The dialogue thus imitates the double movement of eros, which, as Benardete summarizes it, "splits into the motion of ascent and the motion of self-motion. These two motions are always split and always paired. The motion of ascent is the motion of Socratic ignorance; the motion of self-motion is the motion of self-ignorance."[40]

IV. Ontological Psychology

The *Republic* and the *Phaedrus* display the human soul in action, structuring itself in distinct ways moved by the experience of moral indignation or erotic madness. The model for the thumotic soul is the class structure of the city; the model for the erotic soul is an Olympian god. The erotic soul of the human being can be understood, it seems, only in light of its divine counterpart; the thumotic soul is human-all-too-human. Each account presents what appears to be a fixed tripartite structure; but Platonic psychology comes to light in each case only through the action responsible for producing that structure. That action, however, is not the same in both cases. The thumotic soul constructs its inner order by projecting any conflicting impulses within itself onto something external; the erotic soul acquires an inner order by incorporating the other into the self. *Thumos* divides the self through an action that turns its punitive impulse inward. But eros, too—this is perhaps a great surprise—seems to involve some kind of self-punishment, however inadvertent; it is the internal taming of the erotic soul, more precisely, of the black horse,

---

39. *The Rhetoric of Morality and Philosophy*, 150.
40. *The Rhetoric of Morality and Philosophy*, 154.

that allows for the paradox of divine madness as moderation.[41]

The common theme of Platonic psychology is, one might say, the idealism that shows up in the longing for perfect justice and the city that would embody it no less than in the worshipping of the beloved like a god. But the two are not of equal rank. Eros, Benardete asserts, "presents an individual whole superior in both its individuality and idealism to the whole of the city and its laws."[42] Their ranking is determined, ultimately, by the relation of each to rationality: "The individuality of the will and the wholeness of eros seem to be in competition," as Benardete puts it, "for the hand of reason."[43] The difficulty of the choice is indicated by the two structures of the self involved in love and punishment. While the internal division of a better and worse self in the case of punishment exhibits the mere "appearance of rationality," the construction of the white horse by the black looks no less irrational. If Socrates finds that "eros is naturally superior to the will despite the fact that the illusion of the self against the self seems not to differ very much from the illusion of the erotic ideal,"[44] it can only be because of his understanding of philosophy as an "erotic art." The experience of falling in love is the counterpart of the will to punish the guilty; but erotic passion results, however mysteriously, in the soul's ascent to the vision of the beings, while there seems to be no equivalent to that for the thumotic soul. Or could one say the counterpart is the construction of the best city in speech? It is, in any case, only the soul in its erotic mode that shows what it means for the good to be that which every soul divines and for the sake of which it does everything (cf. *Republic* 505e).

Benardete moved with imagination and precision, humor and depth, along the road from Plato's psychology to Plato's ideas. In one of the last pieces he wrote, on Plato's *Parmenides*, he examined how the aged Parmenides sets the very young Socrates on his life's project. To express his reluctance to perform the laborious logical exercise that is apparently required for this purpose, Parmenides borrows Ibycus's image of a race horse compelled to enter the competition in his old age:

---

41. *Socrates' Second Sailing*, 94, and "Socrates and Plato: the Dialectics of Eros," *The Archaeology of the Soul*, 256.

42. *The Rhetoric of Morality and Philosophy*, 153.

43. *The Rhetoric of Morality and Philosophy*, 195.

44. *The Rhetoric of Morality and Philosophy*, 195.

Once more Eros, under darkened
lids, fixing me with his melting gaze,
drives me with every kind of spell into the
tangled nets of Kypris.
And yes, I tremble at his coming,
As a horse who's borne the yoke and won the prize, but aging now,
When hitched to the speeding chariot, goes to the race against his will.[45]

Eros, Benardete comments, stands for the beautiful, while Aphrodite, born from the castrated genitals of Ouranos, is connected to the just; Ibycus's poem makes a claim, through these gods, about the effects of the beautiful and the just on the human soul. The task to which Parmenides is urging Socrates, Benardete concludes, is "to learn how to replace the gods with the ideas and incorporate them into an ontological psychology."[46]

Benardete points out one way into this project in the preface to his commentary on the *Laws*, when he calls to mind the *Minos*, which begins with Socrates' claim that "Law wants to be the discovery of what is" and ends with the question of how the good legislator makes the soul better. While the *Laws* makes explicit the connection between the legal system and psychology, the primary purpose of his study of the dialogue, Benardete asserts, "is to try to uncover its concealed ontological dimension and explain why it is concealed and how it comes to light."[47] Benardete suggests another application of ontological psychology in his interpretation of the *Timaeus*, which turns on the parallel between Timaeus's likely story of the universe and the *Republic*'s account of the city through the soul. Speaking on the dialogue in a conference on "The Philosophy of Leo Strauss" in 1999, Benardete begins with a response he once received from Strauss to an earlier paper. The *Timaeus*, Strauss claims, had always been sealed for him with "seven to the seventh seals," but he did see two things clearly: "Timaeus's account of the human soul is in agreement with Socrates' imprecise and political understanding of the soul in the *Republic*, and Timaeus's denial of eros to the original constitution of man is a necessary consequence of that agreement."[48]

---

45. Ibycus, fragment 287, trans. Peter Bing and Rip Cohen, in *Games of Venus*.

46. "Plato's *Parmenides*: A Sketch," *The Archaeology of the Soul*, 238.

47. *Plato's "Laws": The Discovery of Being*, xi–xii.

48. "Strauss on Plato," *The Argument of the Action*, 376.

Benardete makes the project of ontological psychology an explicit, and central, theme of his late work on the *Parmenides*, the *Timaeus*, and the *Laws*. But if the core of ontological psychology concerns the nature of desire and spiritedness in their respective connection to the beautiful and the just, the relation of those ideas to the good and of the psychological passions to reason, this is a project in which Benardete was deeply immersed in his philosophic work all along.

Chapter Eight

Seth Benardete's Second Sailing: On the Spirit of Ideas

Michael Davis

In twelve books, six translations, and over fifty scholarly articles Seth Benardete wrote with unsurpassed breadth and depth on Homer, Hesiod, Pindar, Herodotus, Aeschylus, Sophocles, Euripides, Heraclitus, Parmenides, Aristotle, Cicero, Horace, Apuleius, and twenty Platonic dialogues.[1] His thought comprehends the whole of antiquity to which his writings provide a guide of incalculable worth. Still, of his books, six are commentaries on Platonic dialogues, one is a collection of twenty essays—eleven of which are on Plato, and another is an edition of Leo Strauss's commentary on Plato's *Symposium*. And Benardete himself traces to Plato two of his other books—on Herodotus and on the *Odyssey*—and his influential interpretation of Sophocles' *Oedipus Tyrannus*. Accordingly, it does not seem unjust to say of him what he said of Leo Strauss—that for Seth Benardete "what philosophy is seems to be inseparable from the question of how to read Plato."[2] And for Benardete, as for Plato, "[n]o matter how remote from philosophy a question may appear to be . . . the argument always turns around and points to philosophy,"[3] for

---

Reprinted from *The Political Science Reviewer* 32 (2003): 8–35. Originally presented at the conference on "The Philosophy of Seth Benardete," New School University, December 2002.

1. See "Works by Seth Benardete" at the end of this volume.
2. "Strauss on Plato," *The Argument of the Action*, eds. Ronna Burger and Michael Davis (Chicago: University of Chicago Press, 2000), 407.
3. *Socrates and Plato: The Dialectics of Eros* (Munich: Carl Friedrich von Siemens Stiftung, 1999), reprinted in *The Archaeology of the Soul*, eds. Ronna Burger and Michael Davis (South Bend: St. Augustine's Press, 2012), 246.

Philosophy comprehends the apparent manifold of things and the single truth of their meaning. More precisely the one thing needful for man is latent in everything men say, do, and experience. There is a coincidence in philosophy and only in philosophy of the understanding of all human things with the human good.[4]

To turn to Benardete's Plato, then, is to turn to his understanding of all human things and of the human good.

Now, the conventional opinion (never simply to be despised, for it is no mean part of philosophy) is that of Platonic dialogues, the most comprehensive is the *Republic*; Books 5–7 are certainly the *locus classicus* for the discussion of the good and the idea of the good. It therefore may not be altogether arbitrary to approach Benardete's thought by way of his *Socrates' Second Sailing—On Plato's* Republic, especially given Benardete's view that "political philosophy is the eccentric core of philosophy."[5] It is the eccentric core of philosophy because in making manifest the problem inherent in the surface of things and only in the surface of things, it brings us to the heart of things.

I.

To turn to Benardete on the *Republic* means first to pass through Leo Strauss, for Benardete himself tells us that *Socrates' Second Sailing* "began as a review of Leo Strauss's *The City and Man*"[6]—a review in which there is no clear attempt to distinguish Strauss's understanding from Benardete's own or to be narrowly critical of it. The review is an example of what Benardete calls "hermeneutical moderation"; it involves "surrender[ing] to authority while fighting all the way."[7] This means following your nose without losing your head and requires having the courage to "look before you leap" while at the same time bearing in mind that "he who hesitates is lost."[8] Benardete reads Strauss as he reads Plato, governed by the prudential hermeneutical

---

4. "Socrates and Plato: The Dialectics of Eros," *The Archaeology of the Soul*, 247.

5. "Leo Strauss' *The City and Man*," *The Political Science Reviewer* 8 (1978): 5, reprinted in *The Archaeology of the Soul*, 362.

6. *Socrates' Second Sailing: On Plato's* Republic (Chicago: University of Chicago Press, 1989), ix.

7. "Interpreting Plato's *Charmides*," *The Argument of the Action*, 243.

8. See "Plato's *Laches*: A Question of Definition," *The Argument of the Action*, 266.

principle (grounded in experience) that he will find nothing simply wrong and that, accordingly, it is always to the good not to presume fully to have understood where an argument is headed. Benardete discovers the double movement of thought, either from or to first principles, in the "fundamental change in Strauss' way of approaching the ancients" who "are no longer the beginning from which, they are now the beginning to which [Strauss] goes."[9] In the language of the *Republic*, in *The City and Man* the ancients are like *eidē* rather than *ideai*—they do not so much provide us with answers as lead us into certain questions.[10]

Like Strauss, Benardete "calls one's attention to the resemblance between an 'idea' [*eidos*] and the collection of Plato's dialogues, each of which looks like both an individual member and a species of the same genus."[11] This, in turn, means that for Benardete, as for Strauss, understanding the ideas of the *Republic* is inseparable from understanding their presentation—a theme that Benardete argues becomes progressively more prominent in *The City and Man*.[12] Of course, this means that to understand the *Republic* one must understand the concrete situation in which its argument comes to be—this is the argument of its action. The way to dialectic (*dialegesthai*) runs through conversation (*dialegesthai*).[13] This, a common theme of Strauss and Benardete, guarantees, in turn, that every Platonic dialogue will leave something important out, for

> Every Platonic dialogue is a whole; every Platonic dialogue deals with a part of the whole apart from the whole. The apartness of the part makes possible the appearance of its wholeness. It is through this abstraction from something essential to the understanding of the part as part that each dialogue can appear whole. That the impossible is the price for wholeness is less shocking

9. *Natural Right and History* "goes forward from the pre-Socratics to Burke"; *The City and Man* "goes back from Aristotle through Plato to Thucydides." "Leo Strauss' *The City and Man*," *The Archaeology of the Soul*, 359.

10. See *Republic* 595a–c and *Socrates' Second Sailing*, 215–16.

11. See "Leo Strauss' *The City and Man*," *The Archaeology of the Soul*, 362, as well as "Socrates and Plato: The Dialectics of Eros," *The Archaeology of the Soul*, 259–60.

12. See "Leo Strauss' *The City and Man*," *The Archaeology of the Soul*, 361.

13. See *The Rhetoric of Morality and Philosophy* (Chicago: The University of Chicago Press, 1991), 155; and "Socrates and Plato: The Dialectics of Eros," *The Archaeology of the Soul*, 251.

than that it is the price for understanding as well; but it ceases to be shocking once one realizes that the wholeness of a dialogue is essentially a function of its being an instrument of communication, and that through the impossible Plato merely reproduces the conditions in which we stand initially in regard to anything.[14]

But the way we stand toward things is governed by what Socrates calls the good. In *Socrates' Second Sailing*, echoing what he had said about the dialogic form eleven years earlier in his review of Strauss, Benardete has this to say about the good:

> No being . . . can come to light before us as something to be known unless it is detachable from the whole to which it belongs. The good, as our interest, makes for this detachability and hence for partial knowledge. This is obvious enough. Socrates, however, claims that the cause of the detachment of the beings from the whole is the cause of the attachment of the beings as parts to the whole. The good makes possible both the apartness of the beings from and the participation of the beings in the whole. (156)

That in the end the two questions—dialogic form and the good—are the same proves to be one of Benardete's distinctive themes.

The question of presentation images the question of appearance; hermeneutics thus shadows phenomenology and prepares the way for another of the great themes of the *Republic*—the relation of poetry to philosophy. These questions lead both Benardete and Strauss to *thumos*—spirit, for in human beings *thumos* shows itself in relation to the impossible—both in its construction of impossible ideals as "indispensable means for understanding"[15] and in its inevitable resentment in the face of their impossibility. The artificial wholeness of the products of poetry is in its way willfully impossible—Oedipus is too good to be true. By unwittingly employing these products to guide us in our lives (Benardete reminds us that "the poets are the *unacknowledged* legislators of mankind"[16]), we all but guarantee that we will experience a disproportion between their beautiful purity and the reality they claim

---

14. "Leo Strauss' *The City and Man*," *The Archaeology of the Soul*, 363.

15. "Leo Strauss' *The City and Man*," *The Archaeology of the Soul*, 364.

16. *Socrates' Second Sailing*, 223.

to render. And when our *thumos* gets hold of this disproportion, even it will be rendered impossibly ideal. It may be that "the idea of justice is the delusion of *thumos*,"[17] but so is the "polished statue" of the perfectly unjust man that Glaucon sets over against it in *Republic*, Book 2. The product of this poetizing is the world insofar as it is constituted by shadows or images—the *polis*; hence Socrates cannot defend perfect justice without placing it in a perfect city. But his real intent is to show that and why the city that would support such perfect justice is impossible. The *Republic* is thus the greatest critique of political idealism ever written. Were it not for its being narrated, it would have the form of a tragedy, an idealized version of the self-destruction of a pure ideal (and even if its actual form is more like the *Iliad*, Homer may well be the greatest of the tragic poets[18]). But Plato also means for us to see that what we come to see is absolutely dependent upon our having at first failed to see.

II.

What does it mean that Benardete calls his book *Socrates' Second Sailing—On Plato's* Republic? The title playfully calls our attention to the fact that Socrates makes a second sailing on Plato's *Republic*. The *Republic* itself is a ship, but the ship is the idealized city.[19] A book, a writing, like the city, involves idealizing.[20] Socrates' second sailing will be a way at once to overcome and to make use of the poetic idealizing of *thumos*—a way not accidentally rendered in a poetic image.

In the first sentence Benardete tells us that "second sailing" is a phrase Plato has his teacher Socrates use in the *Phaedo*. Immediately thereafter in a footnote he refers us to his own student, Ronna Burger, for a "more detailed analysis."[21] Her book, *The* Phaedo: *A Platonic Labyrinth*, has as its announced goal to call into question the status of the theory of ideas and the immortality of the soul as the "twin pillars of Platonic philosophy."[22] For Benardete, something like this is true as well of the *Republic*. The cave image will "reveal Hades for

---

17. "Leo Strauss' *The City and Man*," *The Archaeology of the Soul*, 367.

18. See *Republic* 595b–c, as well as Aristotle *On Poetics* 1451a23 and 1460a5, 19.

19. See *Socrates' Second Sailing*, 145.

20. See *The Rhetoric of Morality and Philosophy*, 155–60.

21. *Socrates' Second Sailing*, 1.

22. Ronna Burger, *The* Phaedo: *A Platonic Labyrinth* (South Bend: St. Augustine's Press, 1999), 1–2.

what it really is"—"the city,"[23] while at the same time revealing that "wisdom is an idol of the cave,"[24] the ideas are the shadows on the wall taken as predicates floating free from their subjects, and everyone but Socrates is a conventional Platonist. Benardete's second sailing, like that of Socrates, involves taking passage on a book written by a student. It involves understanding in general the consequences of the partiality of one's beginning—looking ahead so as to anticipate the future necessity to look back and correct what one is about to do. It means knowing one will not finish the job—there are always students. Of course Burger's book was written some five years earlier than *Socrates' Second Sailing*. This image, like all images, is something of a lie.

According to Benardete, Socrates' account in the *Phaedo* of his second sailing (his first second sailing) arises out of Cebes' unease at the tension between the good of the soul's separation from body and the necessity of soul's conjunction with body. Socrates interprets the good of the soul in terms of the tension between teleological and mechanical causation. At first it seems as though the detachment of the soul required for knowledge may be at odds with the selfish longing of the soul to realize its own good. But then one sees that the detached precision, presumably characteristic of mathematics, cannot really provide an adequate causal account of things. It is not even very precise, for it cannot distinguish between the two which is the effect of division and the two which is the effect of addition. To give an account of the world means to say how its separate things hang together. But Socrates sees that putting things together and separating them is really not a matter of mechanical causation; it is a matter of mind. On occasion hydrogen atoms, aces, and planets may all come in pairs. Pairing and parting are thus occasional—not a question of distance but of intent. Accordingly, if we are to say why things are as they are, we must make mind the cause that intends the separate parts of a whole. We need a teleology. Yet, if mind is at once the cause of the togetherness and of the apartness of the parts, it is the source of an "order" indifferent to whether they are together or apart. Such a mind will not assuage Cebes' fears, for

> Mind now orders things but it does not order them for the good. Mind is now the sole cause, but it is not rational.... [Mind] splits between purposive and configurative rationality. The pattern of things is not the same as the goodness of things....[25]

---

23. "Socrates and Plato: The Dialectics of Eros," *The Archaeology of the Soul*, 247.

24. *Socrates' Second Sailing*, 179.

25. *Socrates' Second Sailing*, 2.

This tension between mechanical and teleological causation gets reproduced within mind. We *desire* to understand. Understanding itself demands disinterested detachment. Yet our interest is what singles out for us what we find interesting. Neither mind as configurative nor mind as purposive can think mind together. The one would keep the two functions of mind, order and goodness, simultaneously apart and together; the other does not put things together at all.[26]

Socrates saw that mind cannot be the cause of the being apart and being together of things without also being the cause of the good.

> But if the good is at the end of a series because it depends on nothing else, the series might fall away with no loss to the good; and if the good is distributed along the series, it is necessary to know the entire series before the good can be ascribed to anything in the series. Final cause seems to be a necessary principle whose application is impossible.[27]

A non-teleological account cannot make sense of why the convicted Socrates has not taken his muscles and bones to Megara rather than remaining in Athens to await execution. A teleological account founders on the fact that both Socrates and the Athenians have it in mind for him to remain, but they do so for opposite reasons. "The grounds for Socrates' being in prison seem to be overdetermined and incoherent."[28]

The true and the good must be and cannot be together. This shows up, not accidentally, as a series of problematic dyads in the *Republic*: praying and seeing, paying back debts and truth-telling, Thrasymachus's art in the precise sense and Thrasymachus's anger, philosopher and king, to name only a few. Socrates' second sailing is meant to be a way to unify these dyads without forcing the issue. "Second sailing" means taking to the oars when the wind fails—turning to oneself rather than to something alien as a source of motion. In the *Phaedo* it means discovering that the tension between configurative reason and purposive reason, pattern and goodness, can be ameliorated once we learn how to resist the power of patterns to blind us to their own incompleteness and polish up our understanding of what is good. It is possible to

---

26. Compare *The Tragedy and Comedy of Life: Plato's "Philebus"* (Chicago: University of Chicago Press, 1993), 92–93.

27. *Socrates' Second Sailing*, 2.

28. *Socrates' Second Sailing*, 3.

understand the apparent conflict between the Athenians' good intention and Socrates' good intention once one sees that

> [t]he bits and pieces of the good that show up in opinion are not as bits and pieces what they are in the whole truly articulated by mind. These bits and pieces are the speeches or opinions of things to which Socrates has recourse after the possibility of looking at things directly has foundered on the problem of causality. These fragmentary speeches parade as wholes or *eidē* and Socrates saw it as the proper task of philosophy to proceed from them to the true *eidē*. I call this procedure eidetic analysis. It is designed to replace teleology without giving up on either mind or good.[29]

Eidetic analysis involves first being taken in by a false whole, then discovering that it is a false whole, and finally coming to see what the hidden source of its attraction really is.[30] Were Plato always straight with us, the first stage would reveal to us a powerful pattern in a burst of insight; in the second, we would unravel the thread of an argument that would take us somewhere we never expected to go; and in the third we would retrace our steps and discover why we ended up where we ended up. But Plato never lets Socrates play straight with us.

> Disinterest will always take the first discovery for the final dis- covery; interest will shape the discovery itself. If the smugness of disinterest is to be avoided no less than the reinforcement of pre- judice, discovery, it seems, must involve a displacement of what one starts out to discover.[31]

Accordingly "a burstlike argument...rarely decides an issue," and in a fila- ment-like argument "new premises are being smuggled in or terms are being continually deformed until...we feel trapped rather than convinced."[32] It is this very feeling of being trapped that turns us around; our surprise at where we are makes us wonder how we could have got there and gives us the incen-

---

29. *Socrates' Second Sailing*, 4.

30. Compare with "On Plato's *Symposium*" and "On Plato's *Phaedo*," *The Argument of the Action*, 180–81 and 281–84.

31. *Socrates' Second Sailing*, 44.

32. *Socrates' Second Sailing*, 4–5.

tive to learn why we had to. For example, truth-telling and paying back debts, which seem first quite arbitrarily joined, slowly reveal themselves to be a necessary pair. And the beautiful and the good break apart unexpectedly when we ask whether it is important for each of them to be real.

> Parting and pairing . . . make it impossible for any argument to run smoothly, for it is the unexpected break and the unexpected join in arguments that constitute the way of eidetic analysis.[33]

A final example: In the Introduction of *Socrates' Second Sailing*, after the general account of eidetic analysis (which presumably has something to do with the being of things), Benardete moves abruptly to the characteristics of Platonic argument (which presumably have to do with the presentation of the being of things). Benardete makes this break because "eidetic analysis does not lend itself to presentation apart from its dialogic practice."[34] Eidetic analysis reveals itself only in examples of itself. But, since as we already know Plato merely reproduces in his dialogues the way in which we stand toward things, Benardete's break shows itself unexpectedly to be a join, and his Introduction proves to be an example of what it is about.

III.

The *Republic* surprises us by literally joining together in one word two things we expect to be very far apart. *Thumos* (anger or spirit) and *eidos* (form, look, or idea) are compounded in the word *thumoeides* (spirit-like, or having the form or look of spirit); on virtually any account it is a word at the heart of the political teaching of the *Republic*. Socrates makes spiritedness the cause of courage (375a), and the extended argument of Books 2–10 of the *Republic* begins when "Glaucon, being, in fact, always most courageous with regard to everything" (357a), demands that Socrates defend justice in itself as sufficient for human happiness, even though Socrates has just placed it among those things good for themselves and for their consequences. The argument that runs from Books 2–4 gets its direction when Glaucon angrily intervenes to demand meat after Socrates has attempted to satisfy him with the "true city"—the city of pigs. Meat is, of course, only a symbol of his

---

33. *Socrates' Second Sailing*, 5. See also "Leo Strauss' *The City and Man*," *The Archaeology of the Soul*, 374.

34. *Socrates' Second Sailing*, 4.

dissatisfaction; he also wants utensils, tables, and couches—Glaucon demands that eating provide him with ritual significance as well as animal satisfaction. This rebellion leads, in turn, to men like Glaucon being put into the army or police force—the guardian class—which is to be characterized by the strange combination of the gentleness of philosophy and the harshness of *thumos*. Their education is the story of Books 2–3; as it is finally not possible to police the police with other police, *the* issue of politics becomes the gentling of *thumos* through education. In Book 4 *thumos* proves to be the principle that accounts for the unity both of the city and of the soul. And in Books 8–9 it seems to be the principle underlying Socrates' account of the "history" of the falling away from the best regime—i.e., his account of defective regimes. The principle of oligarchy is not so much love of wealth as the desire to be honored for wealth. Democracy is rooted not simply in a devotion to the freedom to do whatever one wishes but rather in a more moralistic attachment to permissiveness pursued not out of desire but out of *thumos*. The tyrant, Socrates informs us, does what we all dream about; yet when we dream we do not really get the object of our desire—our hunger is not satisfied by dreams of eating a steak. Rather, the satisfaction of desire always has two objects—its immediate goal and the satisfaction that comes from the fact of achieving the goal. The satisfaction of dreams has to be the latter, and upon inspection, it turns out to be grounded in *thumos*. The key to the tyrant is that he is eros *personified* (573b)—not the various particular desires but desire as such, a great winged drone. This eros is not a description of longing but of some *thing* to be longed for. Without any additional context eros simply turns into a desire not to have one's desires thwarted—a desire for victory or freedom. Eros personified is *thumos*. In all of these ways, *thumos* is central to the teaching of the *Republic*. What is not yet clear, and what is perhaps the most distinctive feature of Benardete's interpretation in *Socrates' Second Sailing* is that, although the word itself is literally absent, *thumos* is equally central to understanding Books 5–7 of the *Republic*—the "theoretical" books. Benardete has thought through what is only hinted at in *The City and Man* when Strauss uses the goddess Nike as an image for a Platonic idea.[35]

Thumos, the thumoeidetic, and philosophy enter the *Republic* together in the middle of Book 2 (375a–c). The city Glaucon has just liberated from necessity needs men of a special nature to guard it—men with the nature of dogs, or perhaps puppies. Socrates characterizes the soul of the warrior as

---

35. Leo Strauss, *The City and Man* (Chicago: University of Chicago Press, 1964), 120.

thumoeidēs—a word compounded from *thumos* and the suffix *eides*, which is cognate with *eidos*. In Homer *thumos* may mean anger, heart, or even soul, but by Plato's time it is dying out of the language and is normally applied to horses. As Plato seems to be reviving it here in order to label a part of the soul, the "part" it names must previously either have had no name or have been named differently. The label, then, must have seemed as strange to the Greeks as it does to us. The suffix *eides* everywhere else in Plato means "like" or "having the form of "—Benardete cites as his example the sphere-like men of Aristophanes' speech in the *Symposium*; we perhaps ought to remember them as the creatures with "big ideas" who assaulted heaven. *Thumoeides* thus means having the form of *thumos* or *thumos*-like. The guardians will therefore have a nature that participates in *thumos* and is like *thumos* but is not itself *thumos*. Socrates tells Glaucon "that *thumos* is unbeatable and unconquerable, and when it is present every soul is fearless and undefeatable in the face of everything" (375a–b). As Benardete points out,

> [*t*]*humos*, it seems, never shows itself as itself in anyone; its pres-
> ence in soul makes the soul like it but not the same as it. The lan-
> guage is surely the language of the "ideas"....[36]

Socrates goes on to lament that they need a nature at once gentle and with a great *thumos*, but since the mixture of the gentle and the thumoeidetic seems impossible, the good guardian seems impossible. However, Socrates immediately chides himself for having too easily given up on their previous image (*eikōn*)—the dog. This chiding is itself playfully rooted in a thumoeidetic unwillingness to acknowledge necessity and admit defeat. That their whole mode of inquiry is saturated with the thumoeidetic is borne out by the remarkably forced argument that follows. This argument turns on the iden-tification of the philosophic with loving what one knows and hating what one does not know, which, in turn, requires that we perversely take philosophy as love of learning (*philomathes*) to be equivalent to knowing what is dear or loved (*mathein ta phila*). As Benardete points out, "It seems that *thumos* itself, in its refusal to admit defeat, has taken part in this evidently forced solution."[37]

The solution is even more problematic than we have indicated. All of the privatives that characterize *thumos* in Socrates' account are ambiguous in their meanings. *Aphobos*, for example, may mean fearless in the sense of not having

---

36. *Socrates' Second Sailing*, 56.
37. *Socrates' Second Sailing*, 57.

fear or in the sense of not causing fear. *Amachos* may mean "against whom no one fights," but it may also mean "without fight." *Thumos* thus already contains within itself the problematic double nature that Socrates will claim to discover when he seeks to join it to philosophy. And even were this not the case, since Socrates' forced argument has just supposedly proven that philosophy itself means being harsh to enemies and loving friends, it remains unclear why he needs the *thumoeidetic* nature at all. To establish the necessity to mix the two, Socrates has to ignore the fact that they are each already mixed. In the case of *thumos*, this means ignoring the fact that a privative may point not only to opposition but to a certain indifference as well, and therefore may be itself compatible with gentleness. Being without fear need not mean being ferocious. Aristotle, after all, makes *thumos* the part of the soul responsible for *philia*—friendship.[38]

Philosophy and *thumos* enter the argument of the *Republic* at the same time and each in a particularly equivocal way that requires Socrates to force them into univocal forms before he can do anything with them. Underneath this example of a filament-like argument that doesn't play straight with us lies a real double suggestion: first, that there is something more willful about philosophy and thinking generally than we are initially inclined to think and second, that there is something more philosophic about *the* political passion. In addition, just prior to a discussion of the relation between poetry and truth, we are told that the philosophic willfulness of *thumos* has something to do with making and holding on to images. In compounding *thumos* and *eidos* to form *to thumoeides*, Socrates has shown us in a single burst the double problem of the whole dialogue, for the *Republic* is concerned not only with philosophy as a condition for politics but also with politics as a condition for philosophy.

IV.

The most extended explicit treatment of *thumos* in the *Republic* is in Book 4. The argument after Book 2 is generated from Glaucon's self-hatred; he "who is most courageous in everything" cannot help despising himself for being so slavish as to desire to rule absolutely unopposed. Accordingly he angrily demands that Socrates praise justice so extravagantly as to redirect his desire and dissipate his anger at himself. This demand takes the form of a challenge. Glaucon creates poetic representations of the goodness of the life of injustice and the badness of the life of justice and dares Socrates to

---

38. See *Politics* 1327b35–41.

gainsay them. Socrates' response takes three books in which he first establishes a city with a tripartite class structure and virtues appropriate to the parts and then must read off *eidē* in the soul parallel to these classes and with parallel virtues. Since everything depends on the success of the parallelism, it is something of a surprise that Socrates begins by admitting that their way of handling the matter will guarantee imprecision (435d). This is especially puzzling since almost immediately thereafter he calls for them to agree more precisely in order to avoid disputes in their argument (436c). In pursuit of this precision Socrates introduces a version of the principle of non-contradiction that allows him to distinguish three elements of soul: the calculating, the desiring, and the thumoeidetic. Now, as Benardete points out, the minimal condition for establishing a parallel between the classes (*genē*) of the city and the *eidē* of soul is that "*eidos* must have the rare meaning of part."[39] A division of the soul in thought thus becomes a division of the soul in fact. Socrates goes so far in his precision that the unity of the "I" that desires with the "I" that thinks and the "I" that gets angry is utterly obscured and "threatens at any moment to disintegrate the self."[40]

> An analysis of soul, if done imprecisely, leads to a proliferation of ideas, for it takes its bearings by language. Speech, because it admits of greater precision than fact, produces greater imprecision about facts.[41]

Socrates' use of the principle of non-contradiction to establish the separation of a desiring part and a calculating part of soul is an ideal example of this loss of precision through over-precision. The argument is complicated, but in general it involves the successive purification of thirst until it is not thirst for any particular drink but "thirst itself neither of much or little, nor good or bad, nor *in a word* [emphasis mine] of any sort but thirst itself alone for drink itself" (439a). The language is the language of Platonic *eidē*, and the argument here in its way a paradigm for their generation. Once Socrates has distilled thirst into its pure eidetic form (that is, into the form in which it appears in *logos* and only in *logos*), given the law of non-contradiction, he can say that whenever something opposes it, it must be other than it. And since calculation often opposes desires it must itself be other than desires (we note in passing

---

39. *Socrates' Second Sailing*, 91.
40. *Socrates' Second Sailing*, 94.
41. *Socrates' Second Sailing*, 96.

that with this move Socrates seems to have defined *philo-sophia* out of existence). One also notices that had Socrates not tacitly pushed the argument to *desire* itself, it would be hard to see why thirst itself might not be opposed by another desire—someone overcome by sexual desire might well forego quenching his thirst.

The extremely willful character of the argument becomes clearer in the sequel—the Leontius story—where Socrates claims to separate *thumos* from the other parts of soul. Ironically, precisely where he appears to part *thumos* from thinking, he pairs them. Benardete cites the story in full; here is his translation:

> Leontius the son of Aglaion was going up from the Piraeus near the North Wall on the outside; he noticed corpses lying by the place of the public executioner; and simultaneously he desired to see and in turn was disgusted and turned himself away, and for a while he fought and covered his face, but finally, overcome by his desire, he dragged open his eyes, ran toward the corpses, and said, "Here they are for you, O miserable wretches, get your fill of the beautiful sight." (439e7–440a3)

The story is supposedly meant to prove that the thumoeidetic, in opposing desire, must necessarily be other than and apart from desire. But it is a strange proof. Isn't the desire to see the corpses of executed criminals already a rather peculiar desire? One might understand it as a species of antinomian curiosity, or perhaps it is fueled by the spirit of righteous indignation, but the thirst for knowledge and blood-thirst seem only metaphorically akin to thirst. This is the only part of his proof of the separate parts of soul that Socrates presents as a story—a poetic image. Even granting that we are dealing with a desire, Leontius behaves strangely. He speaks with contempt to his eyes and attributes the desire to them. And then he claims to punish them by giving in to them. If, as Socrates says here, "the *logos* signifies that anger (*orgē*) opposes the desires," it does so by creating a scapegoat; it personifies the eyes—gives them a will of their own—so that it can then go on to attribute guilt to them.[42]

---

42. For interesting parallels to this account of anger see Benardete's *The Bow and the Lyre: A Platonic Reading of the* Odyssey (Lanham, Md.: Rowman and Littlefield, 1997), 124–28; see also "Sophocles' *Oedipus Tyrannus*" and "On Greek Tragedy," *The Argument of the Action*, 77–80 and 126–35.

The Leontius story is meant to show us how *thumos*, by imposing a structure on a situation, interprets as simple something really much more complex; in this regard generates a burst-like argument. *Thumos* generates a pattern having to do with desire that justifies itself as the opponent of desire. This, in turn, has some bearing on the previous argument separating desire and calculation. It too was *thumos* at work. In making the shorter, simpler way of dividing the soul possible, *thumos* is the reason for the imprecision of the argument even as it makes the argument possible in the first place. Benardete puts it this way:

> Anger generates syntax; it needs to understand things eidetically, for it knows nothing of nature or the body. It would thus find no difficulty if the soul were thirsty (cf. 621a3), for it is hungry for revenge and satiable without its feeding on any other food than that which it supplies for itself. *Thumoeides*, then, means not only that anger is always angerlike, but that it is the spirit of eideticization.[43]

Close to the end of Part II of *Socrates' Second Sailing,* Benardete says that "the thumoeidetic analysis of soul attends only to the labels of things."[44] Eidetic analysis has become thumoeidetic analysis. But "the thumoeidetic, which is the driving force behind eidetic analysis, does not let itself be understood eidetically. Access to it lies through experience and anecdote."[45]

There is, therefore, an alliance between *thumos* and *logismos*—calculation. But it is not the one Socrates first seems to indicate. It cannot be the case that *thumos* never sides with desire—the behavior of any two-year-old child is sufficient proof to the contrary, as one of Glaucon's own examples even suggests (441a). Rather, *thumos* rationalizes; it imposes an order or structure. Accordingly, it cannot simply side with desire because as soon as it does, desire is no longer simply natural desire. Rather than being aimed at something particular, its object now takes on the character of an *eidos*. *Thumos* is in a way the desire of nouns rather than things; it is appropriately accompanied by oaths (440c). The connection between *thumos* and thinking is confirmed when Socrates first tells Glaucon that he has beautifully understood the necessity of the separation of *thumos* from desire but wonders whether he is also aware of how different it must be from the calculating part. The verb Allan Bloom translates

43. *Socrates' Second Sailing*, 100.
44. *Socrates' Second Sailing*, 104.
45. *Socrates' Second Sailing*, 101.

here as "to be aware" and could be rendered "take to heart" or "ponder" is *enthumeomai*—literally, "to have in one's *thumos*" (440d–e). *Thumos* here must mean something like "mind."

Socrates has shown two things: the role of *thumos* in generating *eidē* and the moralism and anti-desire character of *thumos*. "Morality," says Benardete, "is the animation of the mathematician's abstractions."[46] *Thumos* is the common root of morality and abstraction and, accordingly, in its way, also a common root of politics and philosophy. "The coincidence of philosophy and political power thus seems to represent the coincidence of philosophy and political philosophy in Socrates' thinking."[47]

The purpose of the overly precise division of soul was to match its three *eidē* with the three *genē* of the city; this was to be the means to finally answer Glaucon's question about the goodness of justice. The problem with Socrates' explicit procedure is that justice did not appear *within* the city they constructed but was rather "rolling around at [their] feet" (432d); it belongs to them as members of their community, the dialogic city, in their act of founding a city in speech. For it to be of the same sort *in* the soul, justice would have to be *outside* the soul. Accordingly, it would require that we separate ourselves from ourselves and treat ourselves as objects to be admired or condemned, but this is just the moralistic movement of *thumos* in the Leontius story. Justice depends on our ability to project ourselves beyond ourselves. Whether it is Socrates' twice-used example of Odysseus smiting his breast and personifying his heart so as to exhort it (390d, 441b), Leontius's blame of his eyes, or, most important, Glaucon's imaginative projection of the souls of the just man and the unjust man, every such projection in the *Republic* depends, in turn, on something like poetry. Polemarchus virtually begins the dialogue by sending his slave to order Socrates and Glaucon to stop—thwarting their ascent to Athens—and, in what must be a playful spirit, threatens them with force if they disobey. Thrasymachus is the next to threaten Socrates; he bursts into the argument of Book 1 "just as though he were a wild beast" (336b). *Thumos* always seems to involve playacting, poetic projection, or personification. Benardete remarks of it that the "word *thumoeides* itself…, to say nothing of Thrasymachus, implies that it is always pretending more or less."[48]

---

46. *Socrates' Second Sailing*, 11.
47. *Socrates' Second Sailing*, 152.
48. *Socrates' Second Sailing*, 102.

Socrates' real project in Books 2–4 is not to answer Glaucon's question so much as to show why he asked it as he did. Glaucon's understanding of the soul as a thing wholly independent of and detachable from body and of which it makes sense to say it can have a being totally apart from any seeming is already a product of the *thumos* that he demands be satisfied. Glaucon does in his question what Leontius does in his address to his eyes. Glaucon had to make the "real self" into an invisible thing beyond the body in order to make his appeal to pure satisfaction plausible, an appeal that bears the thumoeidetic stamp of implacable insistence on purity. Without his realizing it then, Glaucon's rejection of justice is rooted in justice; he has a tyrannical longing for justice. Socrates shows that it is the way of *thumos* to satisfy itself by projecting itself outside of itself. In doing so it has two allies: the city and poetry. Glaucon purifies the city in speech to satisfy a longing not really for unlimited pleasures but to be in control. His longing shows itself as the demand for the isolated purity of the just soul that is simply the extension of the ordinary political understanding of the soul as a fully responsible agent answerable to the law. The vehicle for this purification is poetry, the way of which Benardete once described as follows:

> Poetics: the other is the same only through the other, i.e., *mimēsis*, and hence *katharsis*. It is poetry that keeps the other away from the same and hence washes it away. I.e., *diaeresis* is dialectics is the philosopher's way.[49]

Given the way poetry and politics conspire to maintain the reality of the projections of *thumos*—the shadows on the cave wall—it is not surprising that poetry should be treated so harshly in the city in speech of the *Republic*, for if poetry is to wash away the distinctions between its version of the world and the reality of the world, its power will have to be invisible. If the founders of the best city are the "poets of the best and most beautiful tragedy possible" (*Laws* 817b), there can be no poets in the city to compete with the reality they project.[50] Sealing off the cave so that there is no reality to compete with the images on the wall requires that there be no hint within the cave of what it means to make an image. Thumoeidetic analysis attends only to the labels of things.[51]

---

49. Private correspondence, August 10, 2001.

50. See Benardete, *Plato's "Laws": The Discovery of Being* (Chicago: The University of Chicago Press, 2000), 216–23.

51. See *Socrates' Second Sailing*, 104.

V.

Why thumoeidetic analysis is both a necessity for philosophy and a danger for philosophy becomes clear in Socrates' account in Book 10 of the ancient quarrel or difference between philosophy and poetry (607b). To oversimplify considerably, complete human happiness requires perfect justice, understood as the reality of the Greek compound that denotes a gentleman—*kalos k'agathos*. Justice is the coincidence of the beautiful (the most powerful and yet least visible version of which is the conventionally moral) and the real good. This would require the obliteration of the difference between philosophy and poetry, which the whole of the *Republic* shows to be impossible. For philosophers to become kings—that philosophers have rule (*archē*)—would require that they be idealized or poeticized—presented as though their activity could stand by itself. But philosophy is never a beginning (*archē*). It never comes first because it exists only as a reflection on the errors of one's way.[52] It is a second sailing in which what seemed to be a source of power altogether outside of us is seen in fact to originate within us. For philosophy to rule would mean for something essentially parasitical or second to be transformed into something independent or first. But the distorted version of philosophy in the city in speech of the *Republic* is what philosophy looks like when such a transformation is effected. Real philosophy is at least three steps removed from this idealized version. It is not even represented in the dialogue of Socrates and the others in the Piraeus as they construct a city in speech. Whether it may be found in Socrates' narration remains a question.

That Book 10 of the *Republic* begins with a critique of poetry and ends with a poem suggests that either the critique is not simply what it seems or the myth of Er is meant to be a new kind of poetry. In a way both are true. Socrates cannot simply dispense with poetry. He repeatedly mentions its charm and his examples of the ancient quarrel always involve poets deprecating philosophy, never the reverse. In criticizing it for the unreality of its images, he seems to leave open the possibility of making images while knowing them to be images. Also, the structure of the myth of Er has two distinctive features (the column of light and the whorls) that are very hard to put together. In the middle of the myth Socrates provides an interpretation of the choice of lives by which he makes clear that poetry requires *sullogizein* and praises this "thinking together" as the best life. Accordingly, Socratic poetry seems to have a double nature; it presents a puzzling surface that pro-

---

52. See *Socrates' Second Sailing*, 105.

vokes thought (in this way it is like the city in speech), and, as much as possible, it presents the life of thought as the best life (in this way it is like the dialogic city).

Socrates' critical account of poetry itself has the problematic unity of Socratic poetry, for Socrates begins by telling Glaucon that, upon reflection—*enthumētheis*—they were right in the way they treated poetry in founding the city. His choice of words reminds us that the underlying issue is *thumos*. There follows a complicated passage based on a pun.[53] Socrates hesitates to attack Homer but says they must honor the truth more. Glaucon agrees. Socrates then says, "Listen, or rather, answer," and Glaucon says, "Ask" (595c). This "ask" is the imperative *erōta*; if the accent is shifted from the penult to the antepenult (and of course accents were not yet written in Plato's Greek), it becomes the accusative of eros. It would then be not simply an innocuous response on Glaucon's part but an answer to the question asked at 595b. There Socrates announces that the poets' imitations maim the thoughts of those who hear them unless they possess as a drug knowledge of what these imitations really are, and Glaucon then asks what Socrates means. Glaucon's *erōta* at 595c then becomes his answer to his own question at 595b—eros is the source of the maiming of which we require knowledge as a cure. Poetry will prove to be its result. The erotic is therefore not simply at odds with the thumoeidetic.

The meaning of this reading becomes clearer in the sequel. Socrates asserts that all imitation *wants to be* is what it imitates—the real. He then chastens Glaucon and invites him to answer. Then he says that in answering they will use their usual method of setting an *eidos* over a many that they know to be a one but without knowing how they know. *Eidos* here thus grounds a question. Socrates then changes terminology; artisans are said to look to the *idea* to know what to imitate signaling that by a combination of habit and unconscious longing, what was first meant to be a tool of analysis (an *eidos*) has been turned into a being in its own right (an *idea*).

> That the posited *eidos* could be the same as the *idea* of the craftsman seems impossible, for the *eidos* is initially a question—"What is that which makes every couch a couch?"—and the *idea* is an answer to which the couchmaker has complete access.[54]

---

53. See also *Cratylus* 398c–d and "Socrates and Plato: The Dialectics of Eros," *The Archaeology of the Soul*, 258.

54. *Socrates' Second Sailing*, 216.

This, then, is the truth of Glaucon's *erōta*. Behind our own backs out of a longing we do not even acknowledge, we all make types of the true reality. This process is at the heart of Socrates' critique of poetry and the poets—not that we do it, but that we do not know we do it.

Socrates attacks the poets as makers in ways that are manifestly inadequate. They are placed at a remove of three from the truth—a painter imitates a couch made by an artisan, who, in turn, imitates the *idea* of a couch made by god. Poets are like men who use mirrors to make images of the things of our world, things themselves mere images of the true world. What it means that the objects of poetic imitation are treated as artifacts and how one is to make sense of the traditional subjects of the poets—the gods, Heaven, Hades—as objects mirrored by the poets are two problems by themselves sufficient to make us wonder about this account of poetry. What then might Socrates have in mind by attacking the poets as imitators of artifacts? An artifact is always linked to some need. Couches are for reclining, tables for eating. But in the hands of the poets something happens to these artifacts. Not accidentally, Socrates uses images of couches and tables—the very examples Glaucon had used in Book 2 to register his contempt for life in the city of pigs. Socrates therefore suggests that the poets altogether conventionalize what is natural; they are like the oligarchs "third from the king" (597e), for both are concerned with *nomisma*—conventional value or money. The poets are like shadow painters and puppeteers (602d; cf. 514b); they are the ones who hold up the artifacts that cast shadows on the walls of the cave. Poetry is dangerous because it attaches us to the cave—to the conventions of our world. It paints images based on the way we always polish up reality—images that become so perfect as to threaten to replace the reality they imitate. Poetry is especially dangerous, for it could seal off the cave from the light of nature precisely because it seems so powerfully anti-conventional. "Poetry stands outside the city but not outside the cave."[55] The example of such a danger in the *Republic* is Glaucon's demand of Socrates at the beginning of Book 2. Here in Book 10 we are given a more general example; the movement from *eidos* to *idea* is a movement into the cave disguised as a movement out of the cave.

All poetry attaches us to the cave without our realizing that it does so; tragedy goes yet one step further. Tragic poetry takes a conventional virtue like courage and shows that when you try to be fully courageous you turn into a monster. In showing us how the shadows that we believe to be real are self-

---

55. *Socrates' Second Sailing*, 218.

contradictory, tragedy threatens us with despair. This is what Glaucon has experienced before the *Republic* begins. If what the poet praises were really praiseworthy, he would do it and not simply talk about it. Tragedy shows us why the poet does not do it but without diminishing our sense that it is *the* thing worth doing. The tragic poet presents the action of the tragic figure as *kalon*—beautiful or noble. All poetry thus threatens to seal the cave; tragedy threatens to seal the cave and then tell us that living in it is unbearable—"Not to be born surpasses every *logos*," say the chorus of the *Oedipus at Colonus* (1224–25). Socrates means us to see that tragedy can do this only because it is still using the standards of the cave/city to find the cave/city wanting. By not making their own activity thematic, the tragic poets let stand the view that the idealizing of human life that we are witnessing is the only reality there is. The *Republic* itself has something of this character (when he turns from the painter to draw conclusions about the poet at 605a, Socrates calls it an antistrophe) but not simply, for Socrates indicates that the proper use of their argument against poetry is as an epode—a song to be sung after the rest of the poem to remind us of the dangers of falling in love. Socratic poetry has as its purpose to present an idealized second sailing.

Socrates uses as an example of the danger of poetry the man in mourning for his son who wails in private but not in public. His suppression of grief is the *kalon* acting to overrule his connection to the real. Like a table or a fork it enables him to put a natural feeling at a distance. This is somehow what it means to be human. That grief is felt at all is a sign that education to the *kalon* is never completely successful. (Earlier, it was pleasure, strangely enough, that provided a natural access to the good—a sure sense of the discrepancy between what we are told is good and what we somehow cannot deny to be good that allows us to begin to ascend from what is conventionally held to be good to what is really good.) We all distinguish between what we do in public and what we do when alone, by ourselves. This is morality; it is perhaps hypocritical but not for that reason altogether bad. Poetry—idealizing—in some sense makes this possible; it gives us an image of our best selves to which we can strive to live up.[56] But it also reveals to us our inner selves and so brings out what morality, *engendered by poetry*, has been at great pains to suppress. Given what it is, poetry cannot help idealizing this too. It shows us Achilles' weeping and makes us admire him for it. This is simply a version of what we all do when, for example, we rehearse to ourselves perceived slights and injustices to ourselves. Repeatedly going over them in our

---

56. See *The Rhetoric of Morality and Philosophy*, 132–54.

minds, we generate dramas with ourselves starring as victims. This process gradually pushes us further and further from reality as we polish ourselves up as heroes of our personal tragedies. Losing ourselves in this way is particularly dangerous, for it leads us to think we are no longer under the influence of conventional behavior when in fact we are becoming progressively more conventional with each celebration of the injury to ourselves. Socrates is surely not simply serious about being able to dispense with poetry; on the other hand he is deadly serious about the way it tends to displace reality and the good in the name of the *kalon*.

> The family resemblance between the experience of tragedy and the Leontius story suggests that poetry tends to establish the spurious alliance between reason and spiritedness. Imitation transforms the cannibalistic eye of Leontius into the innocent eye of the spectator, so that he believes he is taking in through reason what he is absorbing into his heart.... The lovers of poetry are enchanted by the poetry and praise the poet. They split the pleasant from the good (cf. 607e1–2). Through this dissociation they believe they are with the poet and are with the poem. Philosophy does not dissociate; there is for it no artifact apart from the artificer. Socrates tells his own story.[57]

VI.

Socrates' Second Sailing is an extraordinary dissection of the structure of Plato's *Republic* into its proper parts. The problem is established in Book 1. Books 2–4 are concerned with the *kalon* (the beautiful) in its connection to the idealizing impulse of *thumos* that is at the heart of political life but also at the heart of human thought. Books 5–7 are concerned with the good and are meant to make clear that the perfect is at odds with the good, for the good is what is beyond being and serves to make us dissatisfied with our idea of the good, which is in fact one version or another of the beautiful. Elsewhere Benardete calls this the "teleology of evil." "The *Republic* begins as a story of a thwarted ascent"[58] because philosophy must always have the character of a thwarted ascent (or, since Benardete surely intends the pun, a thwarted assent—i.e., affirmation); the whole plot of

---

57. *Socrates' Second Sailing*, 222.

58. *Socrates' Second Sailing*, 9.

the *Republic* imitates this movement. The last part of the dialogue, Books 8–10, is concerned with justice. The just is always experienced as the unjust—what is unfair. It is the felt discrepancy between the beautiful and the good—here induced by the experience of the movement from Books 2–4 to Books 5–7. Properly understood, this is our privileged access to the good. "Political philosophy is the eccentric core of philosophy."

Philosophy is necessarily a second sailing. All thinking involves pairing and parting—putting things together and separating them. At first this seems to be dialectics—what Benardete calls the way of eidetic analysis—and, while his extended account of it in *Socrates' Second Sailing* is certainly rich and complex, if this were all there were to it, it would remain fairly conventional. But Benardete sees that when the way of eidetic analysis is altogether smooth, it is really thumoeidetic analysis, and we unwittingly discover in the world only what we have put there. It is therefore the "*unexpected* break and the *unexpected* join in arguments that constitutes the way of eidetic analysis [emphasis mine]."[59] This means that it is not really possible to give a structural account of the *Republic*, for this would require taming the unpredictable so as to make it altogether conventional. One could give such an account of the *Republic* only if the city in speech it presents were itself possible. And for that we would have to be able to make philosophers, but, as Benardete liked to say, philosophers are like mushrooms; it is their nature to pop up unexpectedly. To give an account of this popping up would be like illustrating a misprint. Thinking may begin thumoeidetically by imposing a purified structure on the world in an unexpected burst of insight, but it must then follow the equally unpredictable ways in which this structure unravels. This is the reason why Aristotle makes *muthos*, plot or story, the most important part of tragedy.[60] Genuine thinking is a second sailing that we must make repeatedly whenever we are tempted to think we have found our way straight through a problem. In the end philosophy must be a self-consciously playful version of the thumoeidetic, which is itself always only a playful version of *thumos*. If philosophy once gives in to the temptation to take itself so seriously that upon seeing itself "undeservedly spattered with mud" (536c) it becomes indignant, it will have substituted the *idea* of philosophy for philosophy, and because "[p]hilosophy is not an *idea* to which one looks and in light of which one makes oneself,"[61] it will have ceased to be philosophy. A philosophic argument must then finally be an argument

---

59. *Socrates' Second Sailing*, 5.

60. See *On Poetics* 1450a.

61. *Socrates' Second Sailing*, 222.

of the action. In a concluding note to a reprinting of his doctoral dissertation Benardete indicated that he did not always know of this relation between plot and structure.

> [U]nder the influence of modern poetry, I believed that the discernment of a symbolic pattern was enough to show the poet's hand, even though the pattern could not be grounded in any plausible sequence of actions.... By reading Homer too poetically, I did not read him poetically enough.[62]

Benardete made similarly self-critical remarks about the development of his interpretation of *Oedipus Tyrannus*, and his revisions of his understandings of Herodotus and of Plato's *Theaetetus*, *Sophist*, and *Statesman*. All of this suggests that, like Socrates, he underwent a second sailing in his own thought. Lest we too quickly poeticize this Benardetean "turn," however, it must be said that early Benardete does not always look so different from late Benardete in this regard. No doubt he changed his mind about things, but he was playful from the beginning. He seemed always to have had an uncanny sense for the unexpected break and the unexpected join. This makes one suspect that, although Benardete may have playfully submitted to the necessity to present it otherwise, second sailing is not so much an event in the life of thought as the way of thought itself.

---

62. *Achilles and Hector: The Homeric Hero*, ed. Ronna Burger, Preface by Michael Davis (South Bend: St. Augustine's Press, 2005), 135.

Chapter Nine

The Socratic Principle
and the Problem of Punishment

Robert Berman

Neither the opinion of the many nor [the Stranger's] own is consonant with the law. The common opinion is that everything just
is beautiful, and his own opinion is that no one is willingly bad.
The Socratic principle the Stranger endorses cancels criminal
law; the common opinion…shatters on the necessity for punishment…. Experientially, regardless of what the many may maintain
in speech, punishment simply drives a wedge between the beautiful and the just, and however irrational it may be to deny
Socrates' thesis, the city cannot afford to let everyone off who
mistakenly commits a crime and send him back to Socrates'
"reflectory" until he has learned his lesson.

We did not know that criminal law could be as funny as it must
be perplexing if Socratic ignorance is at its core.[1]

Abolitionism about punishment is the thesis that there is no justification
for criminal punishment and *a fortiori* for the criminal law. Socratic abolitionism would be that unique version of abolitionism that follows from the specif-

---

Based on a talk originally presented at the conference on "The Thought of Seth Benardete," Howard University, April 2005.

1. *Plato's "Laws": The Discovery of Being* (Chicago: University of Chicago Press,
   2000), 260–61, 268. These are some of the issues I was looking forward to exploring
   with Benardete in a discussion devoted to the subject of law, which was slated to be
   the last of our conversations for *Encounters and Reflections: Conversations with Seth
   Benardete*, ed. Ronna Burger (Chicago: University of Chicago Press, 2002). Regret-
   tably, that anticipated meeting never occurred, and I am as uncertain now about
   how it might have gone as I was then in keen expectation.

ically Socratic principle—no one commits a criminal wrong voluntarily —
based on the premises that everyone wants what is truly his own good, but,
since what goes around comes around, doing wrong to another ultimately
brings harm to oneself, so it could only be done out of ignorance.[2] The Socratic
principle puts the justification of punishment into question as radically as possible, and education looks like its necessary replacement, either through the
city's law or its rival, Socratic philosophy. But the Platonic dialogues explore
several other options, in particular, two models that maintain punishment
while reinterpreting it as educational or therapeutic, as well as a conception
of restitution or corrective justice meant to be a substitute for punishment. In
Book Nine of Plato's *Laws*, the Athenian Stranger, having previously explored
the prospects for the law-bred educational alternative to punishment, seems
to endorse the Socratic principle, while attempting to reconcile it with crime,
punishment, and the criminal law.[3] It looks like a rather quixotic attempt, rife
with inconsistency. Or is there a sense in which, even if the Socratic principle
does entail abolitionism, it is only a station en route to the reestablishment of
criminal law and punishment as a political necessity, which political philosophy
must recognize?

I. The Socratic Principle and Socratic Abolitionism

Punishment is an essentially reactive practice. Legal punishment in particular is, as one might put it in Hegelian terms, doubly mediated: it presupposes both the substantive criminal law that defines what counts as a crime
and the actual criminal transgression of the law. Not only does the principle
of justifiable punishment hold that there can be no crime without law (*nulla
poena sine lege*), but there must be a criminal violation of the law as well. Pun-

---

2. The version of the argument that Socrates presents in the *Apology* is examined
   in Section I below. See also the connection David Daube suggests between the
   Socratic principle and Jesus's prayer in the New Testament: "Father, forgive them,
   for they know not what they do." *The Deed and the Doer in the Bible: David Daube's
   Gifford Lectures*, Volume 1 (West Conshohocken, Pa.: Templeton Foundation
   Press, 2008), 86.

3. See Lorraine Smith Pangle's discussion, in "Moral and Criminal Responsibility
   in Plato's *Laws*," *The American Political Science Review* 103, no. 3 (August 2009):
   456–73. On the challenge to the Socratic principle by the Mosaic penal legislation,
   see Thomas Pangle, "The Hebrew Bible's Challenge to Political Philosophy: Some
   Introductory Reflections," *Political Philosophy and the Human Soul*, eds. Michael
   Palmer and Thomas Pangle (Lanham, Md.: Rowman & Littlefield, 1995), 76.

ishment is a response to the pre-established fact of criminal guilt, and this criminality has its conditions in turn.

First, there is an act requirement—the agent must have actually done something that counts as a criminal violation. Furthermore, at least paradigmatically, there are no victimless crimes: if crimes are acts of injustice, they produce victims of injustice. But for criminal actions to produce victims of injustice, they must cause more than merely damage or injury to property or person of others: the injury must be of a certain kind—in modern-day moral and legal parlance, harms, i.e., injuries that could be understood as violations of rights or, if these are further distinguished, as setbacks to fundamental interests deserving of protection. Finally, another eidetic division must be acknowledged to be at work on the side of the agent of injustice. If he has committed a crime, his act of transgression must involve more than merely a behavioral breach; there is also an ineradicable requirement concerning his "state of mind," which includes not only his knowledge of the law, but also the deliberateness of his action and his intention in acting as he does. Crime, in short, requires both wrongdoing and culpability. This does not immediately implicate the distinction between the criminal act and the criminal nature of the agent—between doing and being unjust—nor does it, therefore, lead directly to the entrance of the broader issue of virtue. It does, however, necessarily require as a condition of criminality and the punitive response a specific kind of psychic or mental state (*mens rea*).[4]

In his analysis of Plato's *Gorgias*, Benardete examines the complex problem raised by this set of requirements.[5] The problem arises, for one thing, from the relation between the wrongful injury or harm to a victim and the intention of the agent. Someone can intend to wrong another, and thus act unjustly, but the intended victim might be invulnerable to being harmed in that way. Or a benefit can be conferred unjustly, if the good for the recipient results from a malicious intention ultimately to produce harm to the recipient of the immediate benefit or to harm a third party by providing the benefit. Once effect is split from intention, the very idea of crime already carries with

---

4. Cf. J. S. Mill, *On Liberty*, ch. 4 (Indianapolis: Hackett Publishing, 1978); George Fletcher, *Basic Concepts of Criminal Law*, ch. 5 (Oxford: Oxford University Press, 1998). See the discussion in connection with notes 5, 15, and 23 below.

5. See *The Rhetoric of Morality and Philosophy: Plato's "Gorgias" and "Phaedrus"* (Chicago: University of Chicago Press, 1991), 25–26, and *Gorgias* 457e–458b. Benardete briefly reminds the reader of this problem in his analysis of the Athenian Stranger's treatment of criminal law (*Plato's "Laws,"* 267).

it the distinction, in Platonic terms, between the good and the just.[6] The problem increases in complexity when one takes into consideration the experience of the victim. Injuries received do not necessarily indicate an act of crime just because they are perceived as such by the victim, who may impute a malicious will where there is no such thing at work. In fact, a real benefit not recognized as such by the recipient might be falsely experienced as a slight rising to the level of injustice. In his exchange with Gorgias, Socrates announces that he is the kind of man who would with pleasure refute another, if he spoke something untrue, but would with just as much pleasure be refuted by another, considering it a greater benefit to be relieved of something bad in himself. He would appreciate gaining his own advantage as the recipient of *elenchus*— in being, as the term connotes, convicted or punished; and if Gorgias is like him—and unlike Polus—he will not misconstrue Socrates' refutation as an injustice against him, but as the greatest benefit (*Gorgias* 457e–458b).

It might be thought that the justifiability of punishment depends solely on whether the subject to be punished satisfies the requirements for his action to count as criminal. Satisfaction of those requirements, however, is only a necessary condition for the justification of punishment—it leaves open the question of the justifiability of the practice of punishment itself. Abolitionism from this point of view considers punishment, insofar as it deliberately causes harm, to be itself an act of criminal wrongdoing, no more justified than the crime to which it reacts. This is the message of Menninger's title, *The Crime of Punishment*:[7] two wrongs simply do not make a right and that's the end of it. Thus, it turns out that arguing for the abolition of punishment can take two distinct forms—either rejecting the practice of punishment itself, or denying the justification of punishment on the grounds that, although the practice of punishment is above reproach even if it at times miscarries, the requirements for criminality have not been satisfied.

To address the question of Socratic abolitionism, consequently, one has first to determine the basis for his opposition to punishment. 1) Is Socrates an abolitionist because of an opposition to punishment based on its very nature as a harm-causing and hence essentially criminal practice? Or rather, 2) does he accept that punishment in and of itself is a justifiable practice, opposing it instead on the grounds that the conditions of criminality that

---

6. And further consideration of the psychology of punishment reveals that the problem of the relation between the just and the beautiful is lurking close by. See the discussion in connection with note 12 below.

7. Karl Menninger, *The Crime of Punishment* (New York: Viking Press, 1966).

would justify the penal practice are not satisfied? And in the latter case, a further question arises: 2a) Do those conditions remain unsatisfied de facto, i.e., as a matter of fact in particular cases, or 2b) are they unsatisfiable in principle?[8] A perusal of the Platonic dialogues shows Socrates offering arguments in support of abolitionism of each of these diverse types, in different contexts.

As part of his defense speech in the *Apology*, in his second argument with Meletus (25c–26a), Socrates initially looks as if he is arguing as a de facto abolitionist of the second type. In that context, he argues to the conclusion that he himself ought not be punished for the reason that he has not, in his particular case, satisfied the set of conditions, necessary and sufficient, that any candidate for punishment by the city must satisfy if his punishment is to be justifiable: it is permissible for the city, and perhaps even incumbent upon it, to punish a person if but only if he voluntarily, i.e., knowingly and intentionally, does injustice to another.

While Socrates insists that he does not deserve to be punished for the crimes of which he has been accused and for which he is on trial, he does not stop at arguing that his particular case fails to meet the necessary requirement for permissible punishment. The argument Socrates offers to Meletus implies, rather, that it is not possible for him or for anyone else, under any circumstances, to meet the set of requirements he lays down for criminality and thus for justifiable punishment. For his argument includes, as the decisive premise, the Socratic principle meant to characterize all human motivation: it is not possible for anyone voluntarily, i.e., knowingly and intentionally, to do injustice to another without also voluntarily bringing harm to himself, and since in principle no one is capable of doing that, because everyone aims only at what he believes to be for his own good, it is not possible for an agent to commit injustice voluntarily and so fulfill the conditions required for culpable wrongdoing. If everyone does deliberately only what he believes to be for his own good, and doing harm to another entails the karma-like blowback of harming oneself in the process, any wrongdoing one commits, however harmful in its effect, must be involuntary, hence not criminal. Acts that cause harm

---

8. This distinction between in principle and de facto can have no place in abolitionism based on the nature of the practice of punishment itself, where its unjustifiability is held to be an essential feature, not a bug of the practice. Abolitionism based on the satisfaction of criminality conditions, in contrast, has to accommodate the distinction between the real possibility of de facto cases in which an agent does actually satisfy those conditions, so that punishment is permissible, and the denial in principle of this possibility.

to another—or in the case of suicide, to oneself—if they are guided by false opinion about the good, are not crimes and so not justifiably subject to punishment. Socrates expresses no objection here to letting criminal laws remain on the books, but his principled abolitionist argument denying the possibility of criminality guarantees that the penal code will be buried in the dust of desuetude; the conditions of application of the criminal laws can never be present, because the requirements of criminal guilt not only are not, but cannot possibly be satisfied.

Within the dramatic chronology of the dialogues, the question of the justifiability of punishment had already come up in Socrates' conversation with Euthyphro, who seeks to define the holy in such a way that he can justify his intention to see his father punished to the full extent of the law. His proposal that the holy is what is dear-to-god evokes Socrates' initial criticism of potential self-contradiction: prosecuting his father might be dear to Zeus, but it would be hated by the god's father, Kronos, and hence holy and unholy at once. Euthyphro tries to save his definition by appealing to the fact that all gods agree about one thing: anyone who acts unjustly must be punished. Of course, Socrates adds, so would all humans. If gods, like humans, dispute about anything, it must be about whether someone has done injustice; for there is no one, Socrates has Euthyphro affirm, who would dispute that someone who does injustice must pay the penalty (8b–e). An abolitionist who denied the possibility of criminality might grant this prescriptive claim about the relation between criminal guilt and punishment, but at the same time define what it is to act unjustly in such a way that no one would turn out to be a punishable agent. And he could do so either strictly enough for it to turn out that the agent in each particular case could not justifiably be punished for his misdeeds; or he could define unjust action so strictly, by setting the culpability bar so high, as Socrates does in his argument with Meletus, that in principle there could never be a criminally guilty agent. Either way, such a stance would still not be an endorsement of abolitionism based on the very essence of the practice of punishment itself. It would thus maintain a modicum of harmony with Euthyphro and the city, in its commitment to the permissibility of the practice provided the criminality conditions are satisfied, while denying that there are or could be cases that would warrant the meting out of punishment.

That possibility of harmony appears to be put into question, however, in the *Crito*. Sitting in prison with his old companion, Socrates tries to articulate the principles that are supposedly to guide his decision whether to acquiesce in the capital sentence of the Athenian court (49c–e). He begins by laying down the premise that doing injustice is inevitably bad as well as shameful for the one who acts unjustly, hence that one should never do injustice in response to injustice. Nor, Socrates adds—claiming merely to repeat the point in different terms—should one ever do bad in response to being treated badly. But this means that punishment, insofar as it involves doing bad, can never be condoned. No conversation is possible, Socrates observes for Crito's consideration, between those who disagree on these principles. But Socrates has just put forward in effect a claim that underwrites principled abolitionism of the first type, which the city must reject: the city cannot do away with criminal law, which requires the permissibility of punishing, of doing bad or harming as a legitimate reaction to those who do bad to the city. Of course, Socrates has obtained Crito's agreement to the claim of principled abolitionism based on the very nature of punishment by appealing to a completely unsupported, and presumably false premise—that there is no difference between doing bad and doing injustice. This certainly casts doubt on the claim of principled abolitionism that considers punishment unjustifiable even if the conditions of criminal guilt are or can be satisfied; yet proceeding on this questionable basis has enabled Socrates to highlight by the sharpest contrast the assumption that underlies the practice necessary to political life and thus his own conflict with it.

II. Non-Punitive Alternatives to Punishment: Education, Medicine and Restitution or Corrective Justice

From the principled abolitionist argument of the second type that Socrates presents to Meletus at his trial, which undermines the city's justification for subjecting him to punishment, he draws a further conclusion: if he has corrupted his fellow citizens, since it is not voluntary or intended, but brought about out of ignorance, instead of punishing him the city should teach him (*Apology* 26a). If virtue is knowledge, ultimately of one's own good, and vice ignorance, anyone who does wrong must be misled by a false opinion about his own good. Given this internalist premise of the motivational efficacy of belief and knowledge, someone armed with knowledge of what is truly in his own best interest could not possibly commit injustice. Is there an education to such knowledge that could serve as a, or the, fitting alternative to punishment? Insofar as the city's law is intended to mold the citizens to virtue, it carries with it an implicit claim to furnish such an education. Yet the need for a criminal code that seems to be recognized by every city suggests the impossibility of the law being entirely successful in its formative pedagogical task.[9] If it turned out that the only possibility for education to prudence, or knowledge of one's own good, was through Socratic philosophy, the question would still remain whether it could ever function as a realistic alternative in the city to the role of criminal law with its threats of punishment.

In contrast to the idea of education as a genuine alternative to punishment, the Platonic dialogues explore two other models meant not to supplant punishment, but rather to cover over its real nature by reinterpreting it. The rhetorician Gorgias puts forward a medical model, which is simply euphemistic—an attempt to gussy up the ugly reality of presumptively just punishment by construing it as the doctor's benevolent healing response to a curable disease.[10] Despite or rather because of its attempted beautification of punishment—what Benardete might call its hypocoristic intent[11]—the medical model reveals something important about the human soul. By highlighting the need to present punishment as a therapeutic practice, it raises the question of what exactly accounts for the ignoble character of punishment, which the rhetorician wants to mask. Punishment, for one thing, calls attention to defectiveness, more specifically, to the lack of virtue that, if present, would have made punishment superfluous. But what the rhetorician especially wants to hide with his euphemistic talk is the shameful or ugly character of punishment itself, which has a two-fold focus: it includes, not only the indignity the criminal undergoes, slavishly, at the hand of the punisher, but also the hedonistic relish that the punisher might take in fulfilling his own anger-based desire for a guilty pleasure.[12] The *Republic* story of Leontius's self-rebuke vividly illustrates this two-fold focus.[13]

---

9. See the discussion in connection with note 17 below, on the Stranger's reluctant introduction of criminal law in Book IX of the *Laws*.

10. See *Gorgias* 456a–c, 464a–465c, 478d–479c, and Benardete, *The Rhetoric of Morality and Philosophy*, 56–57.

11. See *Socrates' Second Sailing: On Plato's* Republic (Chicago: University of Chicago Press, 1989), 138.

12. See Benardete, *The Rhetoric of Morality and Philosophy*, 54, 58–59, and *Plato's "Laws,"* 260. The Athenian Stranger analyzes the tension of the just with the beautiful, which punishment brings to light, as an inconsistency in the views of the many, who at the same time think of the just as necessarily beautiful or noble (*Laws* 859d–860b).

13. See *Republic* 439e–440a and Benardete, *Plato's "Laws,"* 263. Cf. Ronna Burger, "The Thumotic and the Erotic Soul," in this volume.

Plato puts into the mouth of the Sophist Protagoras another euphemistic remodeling of punishment, this time as education (see *Protagoras* 323d–324d). Unlike the idea of education as a replacement for punishment, the Sophist's makeover re-interprets punishment itself as a matter of giving lessons to one who is in need of them. If it is to preserve the notion of punishment as a reactive attitude mediated by the perceived injustice to which it is a response, the Sophist's education model, like the rhetorician's medical model, must instantiate the formal structure of punishment, again in Hegelian terms, as the negation of a negation. Some kind of defectiveness motivates and justifies the drive for its own elimination. Medicine presupposes disease, which the healing therapy is designed to eliminate in restoring the patient to health; education presupposes the learner's ignorance, which the teacher's lesson is designed to overcome.

Both the medical model and the sophistic education model, however, rest on premises incompatible with any plausible justification of punishment as such. Punishment presumes the moral guilt that should satisfy the conditions of accountability. But the doctor must abstract from blaming the patient for bringing about his own disease; and it looks as if the teacher has to ignore the question of the student's responsibility for his ignorance, whether it takes the form of false opinion or simply lack of knowledge, since it is the epistemic defect alone that calls forth the need for education in the first place. This raises the question—to which we will return in the end—of the possibility of negligence, i.e., liability for ignorance, as a basis for criminal law and of punishment consistent with the Socratic principle.

Whatever problems it poses, the education model, like the therapeutic model, construes punishment as in some way rational: in each case the aim is to provide a needed compensation for a lack. Both models are supposed to exhibit the instrumental rationality of choosing optimal means to achieve a benefit. Punishment construed as medical treatment should cure a disease of the soul. Punishment as education is supposed to advance the good that comes with knowing how crime brings pain and harm to the criminal: it intends to teach the criminal to hate and thus to avoid crime. It offers a hedonistic calculus, by which to compute costs and benefits for one's own good. Correction through education, like medical therapy, is forward looking, with an eye towards future benefit (see *Protagoras* 324a–b). Punishment as such, however, is most naturally justified retributively, as a matter of meting out just deserts for injustice already done. The primary argument against the retributive conception, which expresses the essential character of punishment, is its irrationality. Even if it vindicates right by acknowledging wrong as wrong and reacting accordingly, punishment as retribution and vindication of right is a defective means to achieve future benefit; it neither deters nor rehabilitates, nor does it in any other way reduce or eliminate the evil of criminally produced injustice. The attempt to reconstruct punitive practices as therapeutic or educational thus only discloses the most questionable character of punishment. What remains missing from these models, however, becomes especially obvious when one further alternative to punishment is brought into view.

This alternative is the practice Aristotle designates "corrective justice," defined by its demand for penalties of restitution or compensation as the proper response to unjust loss or gain (see *Nicomachean Ethics* V.4). This is meant, not as a euphemistic attempt to maintain punishment, but rather as a replacement for it; for, while punishment is primarily focused on making the criminal suffer for his crime, and only secondarily on the victim and his family or community, corrective justice makes its sole concern the loss to the victim, who must be made whole again. The impossibility of this solution, in any strict application, is most obvious in the case of homicide—as Benardete notes in utter deadpan, it would require the legislator to effect a resurrection.[14]

The difficulties with corrective justice, however, have deeper roots in the nature of the soul, already showing through the cosmetic veneer of the medical and education models. If restitution of the victim were a sufficient substitute for punishment, it would have to handle the victim's felt experience of injustice among the putative harms calling for compensation. But in some cases, these are experiences based on false opinion, with "no support in the real":[15] the Gorgiases, Poluses, and Callicleses of the world can experience the suffering of any injury, however severe or slight—indeed, even possibly the bestowal of a real benefit—as the height of injustice. But are there not also cases in which the claim to have experienced genuine injustice is justified? In such cases, the perpetrator who inflicts the harm might be willing to write off the demand for compensation as part of "the cost of doing business"; but what the victim wants that will be adequate to make him whole is payment for a violation of right, demanding a pound of flesh as evidence of the perpetrator's deserved suffering. Involuntary harms could perhaps be resolved purely through an objective scheme of compensation insinuating no culpability, as long as both parties presupposed mutual recognition of the other's good will. But even then something seems to be

14. Benardete, *Plato's "Laws,"* 266.
15. Benardete, *Plato's "Laws,"* 267.

lacking, as the Stranger suggests in the *Laws* when he proposes rules of exile, especially in cases of unintended killing, wounding, and maiming, which assume the victim's righteous anger in response to the perpetrator's assumed ill will. There is a desire, which must have some satisfaction, to see justice done, either on the part of the victim or his relatives—at least the law makes sure there is such a desire on the part of the relatives.[16] The Stranger's legislation covering such cases implies that the ordinary understanding of justice and injustice cannot be eradicated, as the model of corrective justice attempts to do. The price of treating corrective justice as the whole of justice is the denial of the reality of the passions of the soul, which demand assurance that the harm-causing agent receives his just deserts.

III. The Stranger's Reconciliation Project

The Gorgianic rhetorical and Protagorean sophistic gambits fail to carry off the project of maintaining punishment even as they euphemistically present it as medical treatment or giving lessons, while the reductive strategy of corrective justice proves unable to ignore the experiences of the soul moved by the desire to see justice done. The only political alternative that an abolitionist could endorse seems to be that implied by Socrates' proposal in the *Apology*, namely, a law-mediated education designed to overcome the ignorance that is, according to the Socratic principle, the source of all criminal wrongdoing. In Plato's *Laws*, the legal code the Stranger builds up in the course of the first eight books, with all its regulations and "preludes" in speech, is meant to explore the possibility of the city's law fulfilling this educational function. Hence the Stranger announces his turn to criminal law at the beginning of Book IX with the greatest reluctance:

> It is indeed in a certain way shameful even to legislate all the things we are now about to lay down, in a city such as this, which we claim will be well administered and correctly equipped in every way for the practice of virtue. (853b)

Yet, the inevitable failure of the law in its aim to eliminate crime by molding the character of the citizens is indicated by the Stranger's explanation of the need to continue the task at hand. He and his interlocutors are not like the ancient lawgivers, legislating for heroes who were children of the gods;

---

16. See *Laws* 864e–871e, 876e–877c, 881d and Benardete, *Plato's "Laws,"* 272–73.

they are humans legislating for the seed of humans, and they must be prepared for some citizens who are "tough nuts to crack."[17]

The Stranger embarks on his account of criminal law and punishment while explicitly embracing the Socratic principle, yet apparently refusing to admit the conclusion Socrates draws from that principle (860c–861a).[18] He insists, on Socratic grounds, that any commission of so-called injustice is involuntary, and so, strictly speaking, not injustice at all, at any rate, certainly not the kind of criminal injustice that would trigger the practice of punishment. How, then, can he nonetheless propose penal laws and punishments, which presuppose the existence of criminals to whom moral guilt can be justifiably imputed (860c–861a)? The Stranger himself addresses the question, not whether punishment as such is ever justified, but how he is going to be able to differentiate degrees of severity in punishing crime if he admits no distinction between voluntary and involuntary injustice as its basis. He promises to find another way to divide classes of crime, which will justify differential punishment (861d).

It might be thought, at first glance, that the Stranger only appears to be caught in a tangle of inconsistencies. Perhaps he endorses a more limited Socratic principle, consistent with the defensible claim that at least some injustice is voluntary, thus making room for imputing the kind of criminal culpability necessary to justify the practice of punishment. Yet the Stranger wholeheartedly endorses the Socratic principle without restriction—at least initially. Only initially, however; for as his account proceeds, he begins to whittle away at it, slice by slice. In the course of doing so, he brings to light simultaneously both the limits of the Socratic educational alternative to punishment and the essential character of political life as a whole with all the exigencies it entails.

---

17. See *Laws* 853b–d; cf. 880e and Benardete, *Plato's "Laws,"* 254. In fact, the criminal law proves not to be simply a later development that follows after the failure of law in its function of rendering citizens virtuous; rather, its threats play a part from the beginning in molding the citizens. Benardete finds here an explanation for why the civil law is not taken up until Book XI of the *Laws*, after the treatment of criminal law: "The criminal law keeps intact the innocence of the law-abiding, which they themselves are led to believe education supports all by itself.... What was presented to us as the experiential deviation from the law proves to be the precondition for the law" (253–54).

18. See Benardete, *Plato's "Laws,"* 267–68.

When the Stranger began the task of legislating in Book IV of the *Laws*, he argued for the need to correct the tyrannical nature of law, evident in all actual cities, by the use of persuasive or instructive preludes for the law. He explains by proposing an analogy with the way a slave doctor treats a slave in contrast with a free doctor's treatment of a patient who is free: the slave doctor acquires his art by following the orders of his masters and relying in practice on experience, not by following nature as the free doctors do, learning from and teaching their students. A slave doctor handles his slave patient by giving orders, like a tyrant, whereas the free doctor investigates the disease from the beginning, or from the principle (*ex archēs*), in dialogue with his free patient, teaching him as much as possible, and not giving orders until he has persuaded him (720a–e). The Stranger recalls this analogy in the discussion of criminal law in Book IX, when confronting the problem of how punishments are to be differentiated proportionate to crimes: a free doctor treating a free patient would engage in dialogue with him, "almost philosophizing," in the attempt to grasp the disease from its beginning, or from its principle, taking into consideration "the whole nature of bodies." If one of the slave doctors, who practice by experience without *logos*, were to hear this, he would ridicule the free doctor: "Idiot! You're not doctoring the sick man, you're practically educating him, as if what he needed were to become a doctor, rather than healthy (857c–e)!"

The Stranger is open to his interlocutor's thought that the slave doctor's view might be correct; but, he adds, should one not consider that anyone who goes through laws in the way they are doing is educating citizens, not legislating (857e)? In their conversation, at any rate, they can afford to proceed in the manner of the free doctor: it is their examination of criminal law, in particular, that raises fundamental questions about the nature of the human soul. But the city cannot dispense with the slave doctor's view—one does not cure the sick patient by teaching him.[19] The Socratic principle, if it entailed the reduction of political life to education, would be dangerously blinkered: it would be altogether mistaken in assuming the harmony of the city and philosophy. Adherence to that principle leaves one unable to recognize, in the first place, the grounds for the inevitable failure of the educational function of law and the unavoidability of criminality, hence the need for criminal law and punishment.

---

19. See Benardete, *Plato's "Laws,"* 282. Cf. Aristotle *Nicomachean Ethics* 1105b9–19 and Ronna Burger, *Aristotle's Dialogue with Socrates: On the "Nicomachean Ethics"* (Chicago: University of Chicago Press, 2008), 55–56.

After beginning with his endorsement of the Socratic principle—no one does wrong voluntarily—the Stranger proceeds to separate injury or harm (*blabē*), referring to the effect of an action on a victim, from injustice, understood as a condition of the soul of the agent. The harm done should be compensated as far as possible, as a form of restitution or corrective justice; the psychic condition of injustice is a disease, which should be cured, if possible, but if incurable, the individual is better off dead (861e–863a). The Stranger's interlocutor is ready to accept the distinction between injury or harm and injustice, but he is understandably confused about how it is related to the question of a division between the voluntary and the involuntary. The Stranger enters into an elaborate psychological account in response.

He begins by distinguishing three sources of error in the soul: anger, desire, and ignorance (863b–864c).[20] Ignorance in turn is subjected to a further analysis: it can be simple, just a lack of information, or double, a lack of information accompanied by a false belief in one's wisdom, and that double state is in turn divided between a condition of weakness, which is the source of childish or senile errors, and a condition of strength, which is the source of "great and nonmusic errors."[21] The double state of ignorance, believing falsely that one knows what one does not, is the condition Socrates aims to address in conversation with an individual whose opinions he subjects to examination.[22] But a state of ignorance hidden beneath a false pretense to wisdom, in the case of a subject with strength is, as Benardete makes clear, a perfect characterization of the city.

Once the Stranger has articulated a five-fold classification of crimes based on his analysis of the soul, he finally returns to his initial promise to make a division in two in order to justify differential treatment in the punitive law. But the basis for that dyadic division comes as a surprise: the class of actions done through force and in the open is set over against those done in darkness and with deceit (864c). The Stranger makes no explicit claim about how this division is supposed to be related to the psychology he has articulated;[23] but

---

20. See Benardete, *Plato's "Laws,"* 267–71.

21. The Stranger combines, as Benardete puts it, "a version of the soul that we know best from the *Republic* with an account of ignorance that we know from the *Philebus* (48a–50a)" (*Plato's "Laws,"* 268).

22. See especially Plato's *Sophist* 230a–e.

23. The Stranger presents his dialogue partners—or Plato presents his readers—with a multilayered task of addressing these questions: How is the analysis of the soul related to the initial separation of harm to the victim from injustice in the

when he goes on to propose punishments for various crimes, the division between actions taken out in the open and those done in secret seems to map onto the distinction between crimes motivated by anger in contrast with desire. And in the punishments proposed, desire for pleasure is always treated more harshly than anger: the city, it seems, cannot afford to suppress anger as it does pleasure.

Given the Socratic principle with which he began, we might have expected the Stranger to reduce his whole account of criminality to ignorance. In fact, the crimes the Stranger takes up in Book IX are traced largely to anger or desire, while he appeals to ignorance primarily, if not exclusively, in the discussion of impiety in its various forms, to which he turns in Book X. The Stranger proposes that if one commits an impious act based on an atheistic opinion, unless one has first developed a theology that can pass dialectical muster, one is subject to punishment for impiety and cannot claim exculpatory ignorance about the gods as a defense. Ignorance about the gods does not indemnify the careless or negligent atheist against the criminal charge.[24] And yet, it looks as if anyone who endorses the Socratic principle, as the Stranger does, cannot countenance the possibility of culpable ignorance. The treatment of impiety here reflects, and even seems to be the culmination of, the strategy the Stranger has been following all along. In the course of developing his account of criminal law, he has been conducting a number of legislative experiments, which bring to the surface inconsistencies that serve as tests of the limits of the Socratic principle; they are probes used to discover just where the tangent borders of philosophy and the city press against one another.

IV. The Socratic Principle
and the Possibility of Culpable Ignorance

Both law and morality operate with a distinction between exculpatory and culpable ignorance.[25] In contrast, such a distinction seems to be excluded

---

agent's soul? How, within the analysis of the soul, are the passions as sources of error related to ignorance? And how, finally, is that analysis related to the division of open vs. secret actions? As Benardete concludes, with the remark cited in the epigraph to this paper: "We did not know that criminal law could be as funny as it must be perplexing if Socratic ignorance is at its core" (*Plato's "Laws,"* 268).

24. In Book X, Benardete observes, the Stranger "handles atheism as a form of *doxosophia*, not to be excused by a plea of ignorance" (*Plato's "Laws,"* 270).

25. Consider Aristotle's distinction, in Book III of the *Nicomachean Ethics*, between

by the Socratic principle, which Socrates invokes in order to replace crime, criminal law, and punishment with education. One can do wrong to another without intending to, either simply through accident, which tells us nothing about the psychology of the agent, or, more importantly, through error.[26] In the case of error, according to the Socratic principle, an agent is engaged in a pursuit of the good, but it is guided by false opinion. Harm can be the intended result of unjust actions only if done voluntarily; but since that would require knowledge, which is lacking in the case of wrongs committed through accident or error, they cannot, strictly speaking, be harms and thus cannot be injustices. Those, on the other hand, who know what their own good requires and entails cannot do injustice voluntarily; hence, injustice, punishable because culpably perpetrated, is in principle not possible. If the category of voluntary in contrast to involuntary wrongdoing is the exhaustive basis for determining culpability, which underwrites the punitive model, then there can be no culpable ignorance.

Two considerations suggest, however, that even Socrates should be both willing and able to make room for culpable ignorance and in doing so modify, ever so slightly, his type of abolitionism. As it turns out, Socrates himself indicates, in his discussion with Meletus in the *Apology*, that he is completely aware of the reality of culpable ignorance. For there, in his first exchange with Meletus, Socrates claims that "it takes a village"—at least to corrupt the young—and he rebukes Meletus for his negligent failure to know that the finger of blame should point, if anywhere, not to Socrates, but to himself and the city he presumes to champion, "the great sophist" (see *Apology* 24d–25c). Ignorance can thus be the basis for ascription of a kind of culpable wrongdoing; and such a wrong, though perhaps not as grave as those that are fully voluntary, should, therefore, be at least in principle punishable nonetheless. Furthermore, the education model itself, to which Socrates himself appeals as the alternative to punishment, cannot in the end exclude attributions of

---

particular ignorance—ignorance of circumstances, which allow an action to be considered involuntary—and general ignorance, for which one can be held responsible (1110b18–1111a2).

26. In his essay, "Error and Accident in the Bible," David Daube explores why, not just in the Bible but in all ancient sources, interest is concentrated exclusively on acts performed in error, while "acts performed by accident play no part in reflections on human fate and responsibility." *Biblical Law and Literature*, Collected Works of David Daube, Vol. 3, ed. Calum Carmichael (Berkeley: Robbins Collection 2003), 360.

culpable ignorance. On the contrary, every competent teacher would reject out of hand a student's argument that the low mark he received for failing to learn his lesson is unjustified on the grounds that his poor performance was due solely to his ignorance! Whether an ignorance plea is a sufficient excuse to put punishment out of play remains an open question without first determining the kind of ignorance at issue. But it seems that the very alternative of education through Socratic philosophy that Socrates invokes provides the means of limiting the Socratic principle and reopening the question of punishment in the face of harm-causing violations due to culpable ignorance.

The ground for Socratic abolitionism was supposed to be the premise that everyone wants his own good, while Socrates' plea for the educational alternative to punishment rests on the further claim that in the event of an individual's ignorance he would have every incentive to want to come to know his own good. Hence, if a person's action has the effect of bringing injury or harm to himself—as doing injustice is found to have—it must have been done out of ignorance, thus not voluntary, and therefore not punishable. What happens when the question is pushed to the level that the Stranger calls double ignorance, where one's lack of knowledge is accompanied by the false belief that one knows? This pretense to wisdom (*doxosophia*) is the only target of Socratic philosophy in its practice of examination of opinion. Is this kind of ignorance itself involuntary, and subject to the Socratic principle? If one who truly understood his own good would do everything in his power to avoid *doxosophia*, the failure to act that way would necessarily be due to ignorance about one's own good, for which one could not be held responsible. Or, does the situation change in the case of *doxosophia*, so that one can be held responsible for the false belief that one knows when one does not, or at least for not doing everything in one's power to avoid harboring such a false belief? Socrates' interactions with various interlocutors in the Platonic dialogues suggest this kind of blameworthiness: one can be at fault for a kind of negligence in avoiding the challenge of seeking to discover within oneself anything one believes one knows without truly knowing. There is no defense against the failure to seek self-knowledge of ignorance. Whether such a sin of omission should be punished in any way is another question. Perhaps the penal response is one that follows of its own accord: to live without seeking knowledge of one's own ignorance is to fail to live the one life worth living, and that is a punishment in itself.

However that may be, the Socratic principle articulated by Socrates in the *Apology* and invoked by the Stranger in the *Laws* plays a part in a larger argument showing that the alternative of philosophic education actually points back to the city's own contrary principle as its indispensable complement. A man with a perfectly ordered soul and in possession of the political art, if given the opportunity to rule, might be a bane to the city; for precisely such a philosopher-king, being in no need of law himself and minding his own business, might be dangerously indifferent to the city's need for robust criminal law to deal with those unlike himself, the non-philosophers who are defined by their potential recalcitrance to education through the law. Alternatively, he might become a busybody, seeking to overcome the distinction between philosopher and non-philosopher; in his effort to ensure that no one shirks his duty to live a life worth living, he would aim to make everyone like himself (see *Euthyphro* 3c). Yet, as the Stranger's effort in Book IX of the *Laws* shows, acceptance of the Socratic principle, which is the philosopher's premise, cannot dispense with the city's need for criminal law and punishment: a city of philosophers would be no city at all. Socrates' friendship with Crito, such as it is, cannot be the model for political life, even in a city ruled by a philosopher.

Chapter Ten

Aristotle and the Politics of Slavery: An Introduction to Aristotle's *Politics*

Patrick Goodin

Aristotle's *Politics* gives a description and analysis of political life that in a certain way is exhaustive—in any case more complete and subtle than any subsequent description or analysis. The bringing to light of the elements of the city, the critical and impartial analysis of the claims of the different parties, the exploration of the problem of justice, of the relations between liberty, nature and law: the phenomenology of political life is presented without either prejudice or lacuna. Whoever wants to orient himself in the political world, for the sake of either action or understanding, finds in Aristotle's *Politics* a complete teaching.

—Pierre Manent, *Modern Liberty and Its Discontents*

[Aristotle] will be seen as attacking the problem of man's livelihood with a radicalism of which no later writer on the subject was capable—none has ever penetrated deeper into the material organization of man's life. In effect, he posed, in all its breadth, the question of the place occupied by the economy in society.

—Karl Polanyi, *Aristotle Discovers the Economy*

The background for this paper was the author's talk on Aristotle's introduction to the study of nature in *Physics* I.1, presented at the conference on "The Thought of Seth Benardete," Howard University, April 2005.

I.

To scholars who do not admire the ethical-political wisdom of Aristotle, his account of slavery in Book I of the *Politics* is not problematic: to them Aristotle simply read a central institution of his own world into the very nature of political society as such. To scholars who do admire Aristotle's ethical-political wisdom, this same account is challenging:[1] Is it possible to reconcile slavery, as Aristotle understands it, with ethical virtue or with morality? To scholars of African descent, another question arises: How is Aristotle's account of slavery related to the legacy of its incarnation in the New World? However it is to be evaluated, Aristotle's account is, perhaps, the only formal, theoretical and systematic treatment of slavery in our tradition.[2] It is what one might call an "ontology" of slavery, as opposed to an economics, a sociology, an anthropology, or even a psychology.[3] For not only does Aristotle work out and give a metaphysical definition of the slave-by-nature, he also makes the master-slave relationship along with the male-female relationship the basic components of the household (*oikia*)—the basic unit of the *polis* or the city. The master-slave relationship not only informs the core of Aristotle's political philosophy, it also is at the core of the *polis*. If one wishes to understand an institution that has profoundly determined who we are and caused us such deep pain, one can do nothing better than confront directly Aristotle's treatment of the master-slave relationship.

What exactly is the meaning of the master-slave relationship in Aristotle's *Politics*? This question is far less easy to understand than is commonly

---

1. See, for example, Mary Nichols, "The Good Life, Slavery, and Acquisition; Aristotle's Introduction to Politics," *Interpretation* 11, no. 2 (May 1983): 171–83, and Wayne Ambler, "Aristotle on Nature and Politics: the Case of Slavery," *Political Theory* 15, no. 3 (1987): 390–410.

2. See Moses I. Finley, *Ancient Slavery and Modern Ideology*, expanded edition edited by Brent D. Shaw (Markus Wiener Publishers, 1998), 188. See also Peter Garnsey, *Ideas of Slavery from Aristotle to Augustine* (Cambridge: Cambridge University Press, 1996 and 1999), 11.

3. See Orlando Patterson, *Slavery and Social Death* (Cambridge and London: Harvard University Press, 1982), 1–34. See also Geoffrey de Ste. Croix, *Class Struggle in the Ancient Greek World* (Ithaca: Cornell University Press, 1981); Sydney Mintz and Richard Price, *An Anthropological Approach to the Afro-American Past* (Boston: Beacon Press, 1976); David Turley, *Slavery* (Oxford: Blackwell Publishers, 2000), 1–13; C.L.R. James, *The Black Jacobins: Toussaint L'Ouverture and the San Domingo Revolution* (New York: Vintage Books, 1963).

supposed, both by Aristotle's detractors and by many of his admirers. The account of this relationship and of the slave-by-nature is given in *Politics*, Book One, Chapters 4–7. However, the intelligibility of this account—and in particular the key chapter (4) in which Aristotle defines the slave-by-nature—depends decisively on understanding the intention of the *Politics* as a whole. And that is certainly not easy. This essay is devoted to developing such an understanding and examining the master-slave relationship in the light of it. To address these tasks, the remainder of this essay divides into four sections. In section II, I adduce reasons as to why the *Politics* in general and the issue of the master-slave relationship in particular are difficult to grasp. In section III, I offer an account of Aristotle's intention in the *Politics* as a whole on the basis of an analysis of Chapters 1 and 2 of Book One. In section IV, I examine the master-slave relationship in Chapters 4 through 7 with concentrated focus on Chapter 4, where Aristotle renders a full and positive account of the slave-by-nature. In the final section, I draw some conclusions about the meaning of the master-slave relationship as a whole and its relationship to political rule. I want to suggest that there is much that is useful about Aristotle's account of the master-slave relationship for us in the modern world and it should be of more than just historical interest.

II.

The *Politics* is a text neither easy to approach nor to understand, for one thing, because it is a work of political philosophy—ancient political philosophy—and there is an enormous gulf between ancient political philosophy and modern political science.[4] The distinction, as is well known, turns on the modern separation of philosophy and science, accompanying a new interpretation of nature that came about in the seventeenth and eighteenth centuries along with a new understanding of science.[5] The centrality of science and scientific knowledge to our modern conception of the world cannot be overemphasized.[6] Along with this new understanding of nature and science

---

4. See Seth Benardete, "Leo Strauss' *The City and Man*," *The Political Science Reviewer* 8 (1978): 1–2, reprinted in *The Archaeology of the Soul*, eds. Ronna Burger and Michael Davis (South Bend: St. Augustine's Press, 2012), 359–60.

5. See Leo Strauss, *On Plato's "Symposium*," edited with a forward by Seth Benardete (Chicago: University of Chicago Press, 2001), 4.

6. What science can and cannot do plays a crucial role in Aristotle's argument about natural slavery (see section IV below).

emerged a new understanding of soul, now understood entirely as mind. What used to be a part of soul, *nous*, has in modern discourse now replaced soul, which no longer has a significant role.[7] According to Aristotle, the relationship of ruling and being ruled is modeled on the relationship of soul to body. If the meaning of "soul" in Aristotle and the pre-modern tradition is not understood, then there is much about the master-slave relationship that will remain opaque.

Ancient political philosophy was guided by the question of the best *politeia*, the best regime. The question of the *politeia* concerns the organization of the *polis*. No one today talks seriously about the "*polis*" or the "political *koinōnia*." Rather, we talk about "state" and "society," "civilization" and "culture." Different terms imply very different ways of looking at the world.[8] Nor are we concerned with seeking the best regime: We already think we know what it is. Rather, we moderns most typically pose the question of how to bring it about. As Michael Davis has observed, we are theoretically ill at ease with treating the issue of the best regime as an open question.[9] Moreover, while Aristotle and the ancients spoke constantly of *arēte* or virtue, that notion, as Seth Benardete once noted, "[has] become an anachronism.... [W]e have lost a just appreciation of virtue, which only the world around us, and not poetry alone, can supply."[10] These and other problems create what I call a tremendous *dianoetic* distance between us and Aristotle's text so that a kind of archaeological excavation of it becomes necessary.[11]

---

7. An exception should be made for the Catholic tradition. See Descartes, *Meditations on First Philosophy*, and Richard Kennington, "The 'Teaching of Nature' in Descartes' Soul Doctrine," *The Review of Metaphysics* 26, no.1 (September 1972): 86–117, reprinted in *On Modern Origins: Essays in Early Modern Philosophy* by Richard Kennington, eds. Pamela Kraus and Frank Hunt (Lanham, Md.: Lexington Books, 2004), 161–86.

8. See Leo Strauss, *The City and Man* (Chicago: Rand McNally, 1964), 30–35. See also Pierre Manent, *The Intellectual History of Liberalism* (Princeton: Princeton University Press, 1964); and Leo Strauss, "On Classical Political Philosophy," *The Birth of Classical Political Rationalism*, ed. Thomas Pangle (Chicago: University of Chicago Press, 1989), 49–50.

9. *The Politics of Philosophy* (Lanham, Md.: Rowman and Littlefield, 1996), 1.

10. *Achilles and Hector: The Homeric Hero* (South Bend: St. Augustine's Press, 2005), 71.

11. For a fuller appreciation of the "obstacles" in our way, see Strauss's chapter, "Aristotle's Politics" in *The City and Man*. See also Seth Benardete, "Leo Strauss' *The City and Man*."

In saying that the *Politics* as a text is enormously difficult to understand, I do not refer simply to issues of textual corruption or the proper placement of Books 7 and 8.[12] It is difficult because even though it presents itself as a treatise and not as a (Platonic) dialogue, our modern notions of treatise-reading simply do not apply when it comes to understanding the principle of its division into books, or within each book the division into chapters. Nor is it easy to understand the choice of themes included and those excluded. Why is there no thematic discussion of empire? If the *Politics* was written during Aristotle's last sojourn in Athens (335/4 to 323), how could he not have before his mind the emergence and demise of the Athenian empire vis-à-vis the Persian Empire, or the emergence and the meaning of the Macedonian Empire?[13] Why would Aristotle choose to present thematically the *polis*, the political *koinōnia*, and characterize man or *anthrōpos* as a political animal or *zōon politikon*, at just the moment when it is absolutely clear that the *polis*, as he describes it, is dying out or dead? As Peter Garnsey has pointed out, "freedom and independence had been enjoyed in their fullness in the fifth and fourth centuries only by a few hegemonic *poleis* (principally Athens, Sparta and Thebes)...."[14] This must be seen as an extraordinary piece of irony, which deepens the question of Aristotle's intention in the *Politics*.

While *archē* as empire or imperial rule may be conspicuously absent from the *Politics*, *archē* as rule is the core of Aristotle's analysis. As Jacqueline De Romilly asserts, "There is no Greek word to express the idea of imperialism. There is simply one to indicate the fact of ruling over people, or to indicate the people ruled over taken as a group: that word is *archē*."[15] It just so happens that

---

12. For a fairly recent translation of the *Politics* by Peter L. Phillips Simpson and his discussion "Unity and Order of the Text," see *A Philosophical Commentary on the* Politics *of Aristotle* (Chapel Hill: University of North Carolina Press, 1997), xvii–xx.

13. This seems a particularly odd exclusion after the defeat in the battle of Chaeronea in 338 BC. "A decisive turning point in Greek history: never again would the states of Greece make foreign policy for themselves without considering, and usually following, the wishes of outside powers. This change marked the end of the Greek city-states as independent actors in international politics," according to Thomas Martin, in *Ancient Greece: From Prehistoric Times to Hellenistic Times* (New Haven: Yale University Press, 1996), 190.

14. *The Cambridge History of Greek and Roman Political Thought*, eds. Christopher Rowe and Malcolm Schofield (Cambridge: Cambridge University Press, 2006), 401.

15. *Thucydides and Athenian Imperialism*, trans. Philip Thody (Oxford: Basil Blackwell, 1963), 13. See also Lisa Kallet-Marx, *Money, Expense, and Naval Power in*

one of the two relationships out of which Aristotle constructs the household is the master-slave relationship. And the master-slave relationship turns out to be Aristotle's model for the relation of ruling (*archon*) and being ruled (*archomenon*).

Is the master-slave relationship as Aristotle analyzes it either a stand-in or an apologia for the institution of slavery that we today find so abhorrent? If so, one may well ask with Richard Kraut, "How could Aristotle have believed it? ...What led Aristotle to make this horrendous error? ...Why did he not see what is so obvious today?"[16] Rather than diminish Aristotle, many scholars shrink from a direct confrontation with his account of the master-slave relationship and the slave-by-nature in the *Politics*. And this holds true even for the most important chapter of Book 1 (4) in which Aristotle defines the *phusis* (nature) and *dunamis* (capacity) of the slave-by-nature. As Michael Davis has observed, "There is no place in contemporary discourse for speculation about natural slavery...."[17] All of this makes determining the meaning of the master-slave relationship in Aristotle's *Politics* a truly daunting task.

III.

In the first two chapters of Book 1, Aristotle indicates his intention in the *Politics* as a whole. He does so by following the opposite strategy from that of Socrates when he constructs an ideal city in speech in Book 2 of the *Republic*. There, after the brothers Glaucon and Adeimantus have reformulated the problem of justice, they challenge Socrates to show what justice really is and its power in the soul. The ideal city in speech, which Socrates constructs in response, images in its ideality the reality of every real city. In other words, the ideal city is not really an ideal city, that is, a projection of what ought to be, but rather in its structure represents the reality of every real or actual city, though it is only as the discussion goes on, in the later books of the *Republic*, that Socrates shows how "real" cities emerge. Aristotle, in contrast, begins not with the ideal city but with real cities —with what we see (*horōmen*)—and links each to an ideal. Every real city embodies in its reality a people's ideal as to what it considers good.[18] Here in Chapter 1, Aristotle draws our attention to the fact that every real *polis* is a *koinōnia* that is made

Thucydides' History 1–5.24 (Berkeley: University of California Press, 1993), 6.

16. Richard Kraut, *Aristotle: Political Philosophy* (Oxford: Oxford University Press, 2002), 277–78.

17. Davis, *The Politics of Philosophy*, 1.

18. *Politics* 1252a1–6. See also 1328a35–b3.

or instituted always in the light of some ideal. Every *polis*, so to speak, contains an element of ideality. The *polis* as the political *koinōnia* is the most sovereign *koinōnia*. It comprehends every other *koinōnia* and aims at the most sovereign good. The *polis* is both comprehensive in its scope and precise in its aim, although it is not immediately evident how it can be both. For if every *koinōnia* aims at one particular good and thereby of necessity excludes every other good, how can there be a *koinōnia* that comprehends every good and excludes none? What is the relationship between the *polis* as the most sovereign *koinōnia* aiming at the most sovereign good and the *polis* as the *koinōnia* that comprehends every other *koinōnia*? Aristotle gives an account of this in Chapter 2. We shall wait and see how he accomplishes this.

After stating the problem of political *koinōnia* as a whole in Chapter 1, Aristotle introduces four different kinds of rule and rulers—*politikon, basilikon, oikonomikon* and *despotikon*—and immediately raises a dispute as to how these are to be understood. Is the difference between them to be understood as purely quantitative, or do they differ according to *eidos*? The dispute is generally taken by commentators to be directed against Plato, or more precisely, against a passage in Plato's *Statesman*.[19] If Aristotle's critique turns on the fact that the four modes of rule differ eidetically and not quantitatively, then surely he was aware of how the *Statesman* begins, with Socrates reprimanding Theodorus for reducing an evaluation of worth to an arithmetical calculus.[20]

According to Aristotle, some people believe (*oiontai*) that the same person can be an expert in all four modes of rule. But these people, Aristotle says, do not speak beautifully (*kalōs*). He does not say here that they do not speak truly. However, when Aristotle states why these people believe (*nomizousi*) the four modes of rule are the same, then he states that they do not speak truly. They do not speak truly because they understand the difference between the four modes of rule fundamentally in terms of number, that is, as differing only quantitatively. It seems that the four modes must somehow differ in *eidos*. Otherwise, serious problems arise. If, for one thing, the difference between a family and a group of families is simply a matter of number, incest cannot be a problem. But incest is a problem for every city.

Actually, the city proves to be structurally constituted by the four-fold modality of rule Aristotle analyzes, which must be understood eidetically, but the city cannot understand itself that way. For if it did, it would have to admit

---

19. *Statesman* 259c1–4.

20. *Statesman* 257a1–b7.

that its unity is problematic and it would not be fully in control. There would have to be some limit to its authority, and this no city can ever admit. There turns out, then, to be a fundamental tension between the necessarily eidetic complexity of the city and the city's self-understanding. The city, as Aristotle indicates in Chapter 2, turns decisively both on its eidetically complex structure and on speech—more precisely, on its speech about itself.[21] What might have looked at first like a petty dispute Aristotle conducts with Plato proves to be a dispute rooted in the structure of the city and how the city understands itself. Once this is apparent, one can also see that it reflects the fundamental tension found earlier in Aristotle's initial formulation of the political *koinōnia*. How can the city aim at the most authoritative good and simultaneously comprehend every other good? The most authoritative good cannot be on a continuum with every other good.

The modes of rule introduced in chapter 1 and the understanding or misunderstanding of them turn out to determine not only the course of Book 1, but the remainder of the *Politics* as well. Chapter 2 begins this development by turning to precisely the questions that remain unanswered at the end of Chapter 1: Are these four kinds of rule comprehensive? What precisely is the relationship among them? Aristotle presents his account of the four modes of rule here in what I will call an "archaeology."[22] He begins with an account of despotic rule and proceeds through to political rule, showing how the *polis* is the comprehensive *koinōnia*, the most sovereign, and aims at the most sovereign good. At the outset of this archaeology, in his discussion of despotic rule, Aristotle generates the household out of two basic relationships: the male-female (not man-woman) relationship and the master-slave relationship. The former is for the sake of genesis, while the latter is for the sake

---

21. One is here reminded of Socrates' third definition of law in the *Minos* (315a–b): Law wants to be the discovery out of itself of that which is.

22. One may fruitfully compare this archaeology to the one contained in the first book of Thucydides' *History of the Peloponnesian War*. In order for Thucydides to use the war between Athens and Sparta to explain something about human society that will last for all time, he must somehow show that the conflict contained all the fundamental elements that make apparent the essence of man vis-à-vis the city. Insofar as he wishes to say something in the manner of an art (*ti technikon*) about the four modes of rule, Aristotle too must also suppose these four modes of rule are comprehensive. See also Lisa Kallet-Marx on Thucydides (cited in note 15), 1–20.

of preservation (*sōtēria*).[23] Most scholars do not find the first relationship problematic; the latter they find troubling and unacceptable.

Aristotle introduces the master-slave relationship as a way of characterizing ruling (*archon*) and being ruled (*archomenon*) by nature—its active and passive elements. Here Aristotle characterizes the master-slave relationship in a way that he never repeats explicitly, and in terms he never uses again in the remainder of the *Politics*. The ruler-by-nature and hence the master is he who can look ahead by means of *dianoia*. The ruled-by-nature and hence the slave is he who is able to do these things with the body. As soon as Aristotle adduces these two basic relationships, he says the barbarians mix them up, i.e., they in some sense reduce the one to the other. Aristotle insists that neither can be reduced to the other.[24] One may here legitimately wonder why Aristotle introduces the issue of the barbarian, and then proceeds to give an example of "barbarian" behavior as carried out by Greeks.[25] Who precisely is a barbarian? What exactly is it that the barbarian misses in failing to recognize *dianoia* as the distinguishing mark of the natural ruler?

It is neither self-evident nor immediately clear what Aristotle means by his initial characterization of the master-slave relationship. But he proceeds to build all the other *koinōniai* up to the *polis* out of these two basic relationships. There will not be a third. Out of many households emerges the village, understood as an extension of the household—literally, an *apoikia*, that is, a colony. The village is a group of households ruled as a household. With the village emerges kingly rule. Out of many villages emerges the *polis*, the last and final stage, and the first *koinōnia* said to be self-sufficient. It comes into being for the sake of living but is for the sake of living well. It is also this *koinōnia* that explicitly turns on the use of *logos*, which is the distinctive mark of the human being.

---

23. For useful and informative glosses on the meaning of *sōtēria*, see Aristotle, *On Poetics*, trans. Seth Benardete and Michael Davis (South Bend: St. Augustine's Press, 2002), 44. See also Emily Kearns's essay "Saving the City," in *The Greek City: From Homer to Alexander*, eds. Oswyn Murray and Simon Price (Oxford: Clarendon Press, 1990), 324–25.

24. See Benardete's discussion of the Circe episode in Book 10 of Homer's *Odyssey* in *The Rhetoric of Morality and Philosophy* (Chicago: University of Chicago Press, 1991), 196.

25. For an excellent discussion of what Aristotle may intend by introducing the issue of the barbarian, see Michael Davis, "The Tragedy of Law: Gyges in Herodotus and Plato," *The Review of Metaphysics* 53, no. 3 (March 2000): 635–55. See also Chapter 1 in his *The Politics of Philosophy*.

The *polis* as the political *koinōnia* seems to emerge seamlessly and non-problematically out of the first three *koinōniai*. However, quite a bit has been left out of our discussion here, particularly if one considers the quotations or examples Aristotle has used at each stage of his archaeology to illustrate his meaning, which when looked at carefully turn out to indicate a different and deeper account.[26] Nevertheless, what we have described so far regarding the first two chapters of the *Politics* allows us to see both the rest of Book 1 and the remainder of the whole text. Consider the following schema.

At the beginning of Chapter 3, Aristotle says that the proper parts (*moria*) of the *polis* are now evident—evident, that is, on the basis of Chapters 1 and 2! Of the four modes of rule mentioned earlier, Aristotle treats despotic rule under the rubric of *oikonomic* rule. These first two kinds of rule are the subject matter of the remainder of Book 1. The last two kinds of rule are not treated individually as were the first two. Rather, they are dealt with in conjunction with the first two. We can begin to grasp the reasoning behind Aristotle's way of proceeding by referring to a passage in Plato's *Laws* where the Athenian Stranger asserts that every regime has "two mothers, as it were," monarchy and democracy.[27] As Benardete remarks in his commentary on the passage, "they are the two principles of any city regardless of how a city has come to be constituted."[28] Monarchical rule is the rule of many households as if they were one; democratic rule is collective rule by the people themselves. When the last two modes of rule understood in this manner are combined with the first, it makes plain what Aristotle means in asserting that he has given the proper parts of the *polis*. The subject matter of Books 2 through 8 is regime analysis. In the very first chapter of Book 2, Aristotle links despotic and household rule to the other two modes, i.e., kingly rule and political rule. He does this through the question of whether citizens should share (*koinōnein*) everything, nothing, or some things and not others. For the remainder of Book 2, Aristotle explores various ways of understanding this fundamental issue. In Book 3, he discusses thematically the *polis* as composed now of citizens, and takes up the questions of who is a citizen and what is the *politeia* or regime. Books 4 through 6 are concerned with the fundamental sorts of regimes, how and why they change,

---

26. See Davis, *The Politics of Philosophy*, Chapter 1.

27. *Laws* 693d2–e3.

28. *Plato's "Laws": The Discovery of Being* (Chicago: University of Chicago Press, 2000), 114–15.

and how each is preserved or destroyed. Finally, Books 7 and 8 take up the question of the regime one would most pray for.

If the above analysis is correct, what Aristotle has adumbrated through his account of the four modes of rule is a truly comprehensive picture of any political *koinōnia*. When Aristotle articulates the six different kinds of regimes, he finds two main kinds in actual political life—oligarchy and democracy. In oligarchies the wealthy rule, and in democracies the poor. The dialectic of oligarchy and democracy puts together the last two modes of rule with the first two. Every political society will of necessity have this structure.

Let's look more closely at how Aristotle discusses the first two types of rule in the remainder of Book 1. In Chapter 3, we have a redefinition of the household. It now consists not of the male-female and master-slave relationships, but rather of free and slave. The relationship of free and slave breaks down into three sorts: master-slave, husband-wife, and father-children. To this triad, Aristotle adds a fourth—*khrēmatistikē* or money-making. He then spends the remainder of Book 1 discussing these four relations. He begins with the master-slave relationship, discusses the issue under the rubric of acquisition (Chapters 4 through 7), but does not, as one would expect, give an economic definition of the slave-by-nature. Nor does he define the free-by-nature. He then discusses every sort of acquisition (Chapters 8 through 11). Aristotle ends Book 1 with a very brief chapter on husband-wife and father-children relationships, and a final chapter wherein he takes up some general problems about all these relationships.

IV.

The master-slave relationship and its components are taken up thematically in Chapters 4 through 7. Chapter 4 is the most central and most difficult. In it, Aristotle claims to spell out the *phusis* and *dunamis* of the slave-by-nature. He begins by asserting that possession (*ktēsis*) is part of the household and the art of acquisition (*ktētikē*) is part of household management. "For without the necessary things it is impossible to live or to live well."[29] Although the issue is here framed in economic terms, Aristotle ends up with a definition of the slave-by-nature that does not conform as expected to this economic model.

---

29. *Politics* 1253b23–25.

Aristotle begins the derivation of the slave-by-nature as something that has been acquired (*ktēma*) by comparing what the household manager needs with what the practitioner of a definite art needs. They both need tools. Here Aristotle puts *poiēsis* and *praxis* side-by-side, along with the activities and tools proper to each. These are fundamentally different modes of being. As Aristotle will say, no *praxis* is ever *poiēsis* or vice versa.[30] A slave is a tool for *praxis*, and life is *praxis* not *poiēsis*. A slave is a living possession (*empsuchon ktēma*). Now Aristotle uses the strongest possible terms to assert that slaves are necessary. Assistants are tools that wield tools.

> If tools could be commanded or if they were to perceive before-hand what work is to be completed—like they assert of the statues of Daedalus or as the poet asserts the tripods of Hephaestus do, which come on their own to the gathering of the gods—so that shuttles of themselves weave, or the pick play the lyre, then master-craftsmen would not need assistants nor masters slaves.[31]

The examples Aristotle adduces to show the necessity of assistants and slaves clearly reflect the fundamental difference between *poiēsis* and *praxis*.

One might wonder if the choice of Daedalus to illustrate the use of productive tools and of Hephaestus to illustrate the use of *praxis* tools is accidental. We seem to have the following proportion:

productive tools (commanded tools) : the things of Daedalus ::
praxis tools (able to perceive beforehand) : the tripods of Hephaestus

As we know, Daedalus was an Athenian who killed his nephew—his assistant—out of jealousy and the things he is reputed to have made are strictly speaking impossible. Could there be a connection between Daedalus's criminality and the impossible objects he is supposed to have made? Could his situation be an illustration of the fundamental limits to technical production—in a sense pointing to the limits of science—and what happens when there is a desire to overcome them?[32] On the other hand, there is the lame Hephaestus, the impossible being and a defective one at that, who makes objects that deal more with meaning and right than with technical produc-

---

30. See *Nicomachean Ethics* 1140a1–8.

31. *Politics* 1253b23–1254a1.

32. See Glaucon's narration of the myth of Gyges in Plato's *Republic* 359b6–360d7.

tivity. For all his technical abilities, Hephaestus cannot correct his original condition but only compensate for his defect. In the passage in the *Iliad* to which Aristotle refers, Hephaestus makes a shield for Achilles—out of a perceived moral obligation to Thetis—on which there is an elaborate depiction of a city at war and a city at peace, every element of which Achilles understands and which satisfies his soul, while almost everyone else becomes afraid when they see the shield.[33] The congenitally defective god is able to make a shield that in terms of what it depicts perfectly satisfies Achilles. How did Hephaestus know what would please the soul of Achilles? Could Hephaestus be the prime example of the slave-by-nature? Could the slave-by-nature be the tool for the creation of meaning? In any case, on the basis of the above examples, Aristotle implies that only in the realm of legend and poetic privilege could such things happen. In real life, master craftsmen need assistants and masters need slaves. The slave is a possession of *praxis*, whose meaning consists only in its use. Life is *praxis* and slaves are necessary. According to Aristotle, this means that, at least in terms of politics, human beings need and must use other human beings.

Before Aristotle gives the final determination of the slave-by-nature, he compares the slave as a *ktēma* to a proper part (*morion*). A proper part is not only of another, but simply (*haplōs*) of another. If this is true, then the whole being of the slave is to be of another. This suggests, though, that the master must be radically incomplete and defective. The slave-by-nature, then, is by implication the sign of the necessary incompleteness of the master, and hence the master's need of the other. The same goes for the *ktēma*. So the master is master of the slave but is not simply (*haplōs*) of him. The slave, however, is not only a slave of the master but is wholly (*holōs*) of him.

Aristotle concludes the chapter by stating fully both the *phusis* and *dunamis* of the slave-by-nature. "He who while being a human being (*anthrōpos*) is not of himself but of another is a slave by nature. And an *anthrōpos* of another, though an *anthrōpos*, is a *ktēma*, and a *ktēma* is a *praktikē* tool that is separable."[34] Aristotle has now defined the slave-by-nature as a *ktēma* under the rubric of household acquiring (*ktēsis*). But why give an account of the slave as a *ktēma* under the rubric of *ktēsis* before giving an account of every sort of *ktēsis*?

---

33. Homer *Iliad* 19.12–17. See Benardete's *The Bow and the Lyre: A Platonic Reading of the* Odyssey (Lanham, Md.: Rowman and Littlefield, 1997), 91. See also his *Herodotean Inquiries* (South Bend: St. Augustine's Press, 1999), 10.

34. *Politics* 1254a14–18. While Aristotle has now defined the slave-by-nature, he has not defined the free. That he does in the *Metaphysics*, Book A, Chapter 2.

Shouldn't the account of slavery have been given as part of the account of all kinds of acquisitions? In addressing that puzzle, a comprehensive picture emerges of the meaning of the slave-by-nature.

Aristotle has gone to great lengths to distinguish between *praxis* and *poiēsis*. The slave is a tool for *praxis*, never *poiēsis*. If in all *poiēsis* there is always some definite end that one can bring about rationally, then in a sense what characterizes *praxis* is that it involves some definite end that one wishes to bring about but which one cannot bring about rationally. One never knows how things are going to turn out. The end one wishes is never guaranteed. The slave-by-nature then is a *ktēma* in a *praxis* wherein the outcome is never known with any definiteness.[35] Now let us combine this understanding of the slave-by-nature with Aristotle's definition of the master-by-nature in Chapter 2. The master is he who can see ahead by means of *dianoia*. What is the meaning of *dianoia*? Typically, it is the umbrella term that comprehends *sophia, nous, phronēsis, technē, epistēmē*, i.e., the dianoetic virtues discussed in Book 6 of the *Ethics*. It also has the meaning of intention—a certain kind of intention.[36] If the master is he who can look ahead by means of *dianoia*, then on the one hand this suggests that he who knows by means of one of the five cognitive virtues rules he who does not know. And who can rationally deny this? On the other hand, it is man who determines each of these virtues in the light of his needs. There is not and cannot be any external confirmation of the results of any of the calculations in any one of these virtues. Additionally, man must determine dianoetically who he is, what his life means, and how he should live.

Aristotle has gone out of his way to frame the problem of the slave-by-nature in an economic manner, yet he does not follow through with an economic definition. Rather, he seems to go to great lengths to avoid the language of ownership—for any talk of ownership would already imply a determinate value and one would have to ask about how it was determined. He will discuss every kind of acquisition and economics strictly after the discussion of the slave-by-nature. Talk of the labor power of the slave, combined with the conception of the slave-by-nature as an acquisition, makes the order of Aristotle's presentation especially puzzling. The suggestion seems to be that the master-slave relationship is the originary and fundamental mode of acquisition.

---

35. See *Nichomachean Ethics* 1139b9–11. There Aristotle suggests that when a *praxis* occurs, not even a god can reverse it.

36. For a particularly important and telling use of the verbal form of *dianoia*, or *dianoēthen* as intention, see Plato's *Parmenides* 128c3.

It is that mode through which we determine the currency of every other acquisitive relationship, but which itself is not economical and cannot be understood under any other relationship. One may almost be tempted to say that its pristine purity makes it a relationship that exists and can only exist in speech. In its being wholly indeterminate, it provides the template for determining every other acquisitive relation. Insofar as the slave is a proper part of and yet external to the master, while the relation between them is modeled on the soul-body relation, the heterogeneous master-slave relationship looks like a paradigm of the way human beings are generally bound to one another, and require each other in order to know who they are individually. The only possible confirmation of who one is, is through another human being. The human being who carries out the intention of another, and thus confirms the projections of that other, is by nature the slave. The master-slave relationship has its source in nothing other than the incompleteness of the master, who because of this will seek to complete himself. It is this originary incompleteness and the desire on the part of the master to remedy it that determine and define the master-slave relationship. And this relationship in turn determines all valuation.[37] The master-slave relationship is an ineradicable part of the human condition, and as Aristotle will indicate in Chapter 5, it runs the gamut from the highest to the lowest.

Only after Aristotle has given an account of the slave-by-nature does he raise the question of whether anyone of this sort actually exists. He does this in Chapter 5, along with a more thematic analysis of ruling and being ruled. We also learn here of the paradigmatic case of ruler and ruled—that is, the soul and the body, respectively. Chapter 6 is devoted to the distinction between the slave-by-nature and the slave-by-law or force. Here, Aristotle also shows that actual slavery cannot justify itself except in terms of slavery-by-nature. Finally, in Chapter 7, Aristotle declares that it is manifestly clear that there are really different kinds of rule, i.e., that the despotic and the political rule differ in kind. This means that in some fundamental sense the whole is not homogeneous but rather heterogeneous. What is the character, then, of that which knows the parts that differ in kind?

---

37. Our account of the master-slave relationship, in all its indeterminacy, fits quite well with Aristotle's account of *eudaimonia* in *Nichomachean Ethics* Book 1. See *Politics* 1328a36–b3 for a possible confirmation of our assertion.

V.

If the slave-by-nature has the character defined by the preceding discussion, such a figure is essentially distinguished from the slave-by-law, based as it is upon force. As Aristotle indicates in Chapter 6, no one can knowingly or rationally justify enslavement by force for obvious reasons. Every justification of actual enslavement must be based on some version of the slave-by-nature. And if the justification is based on anything other than on Aristotle's definition of master-by-nature, it can easily be refuted. Why, someone might legitimately ask, make the slave-by-law so prominent? I suggest the following: the slave-by-law is a sign things do not work (or always work) according to reason. Human beings can always bond together and impose their will on other human beings. One can eliminate actual slavery at a particular place and time; one can never eliminate its possibility at any time or place. Political life seems of necessity to involve a compromise between the dictates of *dianoia* and the reality of force.

Aristotle's account of the master-slave relationship holds insights as important in our time as in his. He explains, for one thing, how the master-slave is grounded in a congenital neediness, and that neediness is not only on the bodily level: the account of the master-slave relationship in terms of *dianoia* means man is needy in his very soul. The recognition of this relationship grounded in human neediness can, perhaps, serve as a moderating influence in our utopian tendencies. Furthermore, if the slave-by-nature and the slave-by-law or force can never be the same, and if enslavement always requires justification through some form of argument from the slave-by-nature, then it is always possible to be critical of any actual condition of slavery in light of this standard. At the same time, the awareness that enslavement remains possible at any time is a condition for remaining vigilant against it.

Chapter Eleven

Being and Politics:
Seth Benardete on Aristotle's *Metaphysics*

Richard Velkley

Although he will not be remembered principally as an interpreter of Aristotle, Seth Benardete was much engaged with this philosopher throughout his life of teaching and writing. He taught seven graduate seminars on texts of Aristotle between 1968 and 1993, and published remarkable essays on *De Anima* and the *Metaphysics* in the 1970s. Benardete approached Aristotle as a true Socratic who philosophizes in a Platonic manner. The central problem of philosophy is the soul, inquiry about which opens the way to the nature of being. The way to the soul, however, must be through the realm of opinion, and that means above all the political phenomena of the arts, the laws, and the gods. The soul must be the central theme of philosophy because all efforts to grasp the nature of being directly fail, as Socrates relates in the autobiographical discussion of the "two sailings" in the *Phaedo*. Indeed the elements of first philosophy or wisdom seem to be incompatible. Even so, they strangely exist together in the soul of the being that seeks wisdom. Benardete saw that Aristotle employed his own version of the Socratic-Platonic procedure of dividing and collecting those elements. The first approach to them for Socrates is to posit them as separate ideas; their appearance of separateness, however, must be abandoned in further inquiry. Similarly Aristotle seems to found wholly separate sciences of distinct subject-matters, but on closer examination one sees that the treatises contain diverging accounts of the soul, nature, and being which demand to be put together. That the task of combination is not finished by Aristotle, and is perhaps not finishable, belies the traditional view that Aristotle understands himself as attaining wisdom, and

Reprinted, with slight revisions by the author, from *The Political Science Reviewer* 34 (2005): 7–21. Originally presented at the conference on "The Philosophy of Seth Benardete," New School University, December 2002.

as proposing a metaphysics and cosmology which, "as distinguished from Plato's, is unqualifiedly separable from the quest for the best political order."[1]

Metaphysics and the Soul

Benardete notes a peculiarity of Aristotle's *Metaphysics* at the beginning of his essay "On Wisdom and Philosophy: The First Two Chapters of Aristotle's *Metaphysics* A."[2] After presenting critiques of his predecessors in the first books of his *Physics* and *De Anima*, Aristotle offers in the second books his own definitions of nature and soul. The second book of the *Metaphysics*, however, "seems to be nothing but a series of questions" (396). The inquiries of metaphysics or first philosophy lack something self-evidently prior, such as soul. "Soul is even more self-evident than nature," Benardete writes in his essay on *De Anima*. "Soul alone is in being first for us first by nature." The immediate access of the soul to itself permits a high degree of accuracy in its investigation. Yet "for all that it admits of precision it still remains an object of wonder."[3] "Nature and soul are there regardless of what anyone might say about them (*Physics* 193a3); but without perplexity there is nothing to metaphysics. Metaphysics seems to be the only science that in asking questions discovers all of its own field, and so, in completing philosophy, somehow returns philosophy to its origin in wonder" (396). If the subject-matter of metaphysics is questioning, then the soul as questioning provides the access to its field. In a sense its subject is the soul as questioning, or the soul as wondering. Accordingly, metaphysics as inquiry about the principles and causes

---

1. Leo Strauss, *The City and Man* (Chicago: The University of Chicago Press, 1964), 21. Benardete's writing on Aristotle poses a challenge to Strauss's claim that "Aristotelian philosophizing has no longer to the same degree and in the same way as Socratic philosophizing the character of ascent." On Benardete's reading, Aristotle's presentation of his thought in treatise form is a new mask under which the Socratic dialectic proceeds. See also my essay, "Prelude to First Philosophy: Seth Benardete on *De Anima*," in this volume.

2. The essay first appeared in *The Review of Metaphysics* 32, no. 2 (December 1978) and is reprinted in *The Argument of the Action*, eds. Ronna Burger and Michael Davis (Chicago: The University of Chicago Press, 2000), 396–406. Page numbers in parentheses in the text are from the reprinted version.

3. "Aristotle *De Anima* III.3–5," *The Review of Metaphysics* 28, no. 4 (June 1975): 621, reprinted in *The Archaeology of the Soul*, eds. Ronna Burger and Michael Davis (South Bend: St. Augustine Press, 2012), 279. For more discussion, see the author's essay cited in note 1 above.

of being has special regard for the being of the soul as wondering. A form of psychology centering on the being of wonder is the core of metaphysics.

In *De Anima* the soul studied with precision is not the soul as wondering, but the soul as knowing. Crucial to the account is *phantasia*, as the link between the noetic and the aesthetic as well as between thought and desire. But the discussion does not disclose what makes these linkages possible; *De Anima* lacks a causal account of the unity of the soul. The *aporia* of the *Physics*—how does the realm of unchanging form relate to nature as the realm of change?—is still its *aporia*. The precise account of soul cannot be a causal account. It shows the "that" of the powers of the soul, but only incompletely the "why." The focus of the account is on the "now": what is, or can be, actual to the soul at any moment. *Phantasia* operates in the soul nearly always, even in dreams, but wonder is a passing condition. The path to being may be through wonder as the key to the unity of the soul, yet that key is strangely not a permanent feature of the soul, found in every "now." There may be an important connection between *De Anima*'s abstraction from wonder and its abstraction from the question of causal unity. Both are central themes of the *Metaphysics*. *De Anima* comes to the threshold of first philosophy by treating the highest condition (self-thinking) of the highest part of the whole (the rational soul) but it does not pass over the threshold.

Perhaps wonder involves a special case of *phantasia*. In *De Anima* *phantasia* is the prime evidence for the peculiar double nature of the mind. Mind is receptive to the *noēton*, considered apart from the whole, but at the same time the mind is open to all beings, to the whole as such. In light of the mind's universal openness it is hard to grasp how the mind can have any distinctive nature, or how it can be anything except pure possibility. But the mind must be capable of an active initiation of thought. Knowing is negativity, insofar as the mind grasps the sensible particular not just as itself, but as an instance of noetic form, hence as other to itself. Straightening chalk lines so they can be read as pure lines of geometry entails seeing the arbitrariness of the sensible. But if intellection is only the reception of the noetic, another power must come to its aid to carry out the transformation of the sensible. *Phantasia* does this by suspending the truth-claim of the sensible and converting "I see a man" into "It seems to be a man." It allows the sensible image to be viewed just as image. This power enables the mind to be both turned toward itself and open to the whole of being. *Phantasia* can try to be complete in itself, since its dwelling on the appearance as appearance seems to free it from being, but its reading of being as only image presupposes the recognition of being. When it serves intellect, *phantasia* allows the intellect to find the noetic in the sensible, and its suspension of the given is only a step toward understanding. Yet the two actions are inseparable, and thus the rational animal is characterized by a problematic freedom. This account of *phantasia* surely has an important connection with poetry, and in the *Metaphysics* poetry is related to wonder.

But *De Anima* makes none of these connections. Outside its purview lies a deeper negativity than that of seeing the image as image, and therewith also a deeper doubleness of the mind. Poetry and philosophy address these issues as rivals; it is only fitting that the problem of doubleness should have a two-fold solution. By abstracting from such issues the account of *De Anima* proves to be, in more than one sense, less than poetic.

Freedom and Necessity

In chapter one of *Metaphysics* A the examination of opinions about wisdom and knowledge substitutes for the lack of the self-evidently prior. The first phenomena of opinion are the delight in effortless acquisition of knowledge, and admiration of those manifestly superior to ourselves in knowing. Delight and admiration share selfless freedom from calculation. But the absence of calculation and ratiocination, which characterize the arts as knowledge of causes, is a deficiency in the natural desire to know. As emerges later, philosophic wonder includes both selfless delight and the self-regarding concern with cause, and thus wonder as complex comes to light through partial perspectives on it. (By contrast Heidegger's exclusion of calculation from openness to being impoverishes the complexity of the origin of philosophy.) At first the choice of sight, as the most revelatory of the senses, and the reasoning of the arts seem wholly unrelated. Similarly the delight in seeing and knowing, which is always present and at work, is not the same as the desire to learn. "To love wisdom is not in the same sense natural" as this delight (397). The natural delight is indiscriminate, non-hierarchical, and satisfied by the noting of any differences, being only "the most satisfying filler of our idle moments." It seems that humans are either idle or laboring, with these opposites seeming to form no natural unity.

Benardete quotes from the *Politics*: "Man is by nature the political animal." Clearly this sense of the natural points away from the idle desire to know. Art and calculative reasoning are related to political life through their common conditions: speech and the division of labor. The introduction of the arts and therewith the city in the *Metaphysics* brings into view the soul as a needful being. Yet speech is dual, as both the articulation of the beings and as means of communication. It is doubtful that human communities came into being for the sharing of knowledge, even if they arose in a noncalculative way. Thus in the Socratic dialogues philosophic conversion is the rare coincidence of the two sides of speech. The duality of speech can be restated as the duality of the human as such: "As a kind (*anthrōpos*) man is political; as individual (*pantes anthrōpoi*) he desires to know" (397–98). The difference between the human as kind and the human as individual is reflected in the difference between genesis and telos in the city. Since speech is not accidentally related to knowledge, "perhaps knowledge as that which alone is truly sharable, is the ultimate ground for human society." But ultimate end and temporal origin, or the eidetic and genetic orders of being, are not the same (although poetry seeks to identify them). "The city as an association of freemen could thus be a divination of the freedom that belongs preeminently to the highest kind of wisdom" (398). Modern criticisms of the Aristotelian account of the free life of *theōria* claim that it is a mere prejudice, rooted in the vanity of an aristocratic *nomos*. But this stance willfully denies the natural force of the difference between the free and the needful, and thus supposes that human incompleteness, being an accident of circumstances, can be remedied by human self-production.

For Aristotle the duality is so basic that it is evident in sight itself, which is at once the most pleasant and the most useful of the senses. Sight more than other senses reveals wholes, and wholeness is the object of both eros and knowing. Sight as both "most needful and most delightful perhaps reflects the fact that form (*eidos*) too, is a cause" (398). The connection of sight with *eidos* may relate to its freedom, for in choosing sight most of all senses, we perfect natural desire. This account of sight runs contrary to the tragic wisdom of the poets, since the freedom of sight, our ability to turn it on or off at will, relates to its power to put the greatest distance between ourselves and whatever it brings to light. Oedipus's self-blinding seems to indicate the impossibility of such cognitive distance, as if the tragic hero always sees and so always intends to act. "To dream (*horan*) is also to see" (398). Even so, wisdom cannot be understood without art, and hence without poetry, for art is the index of the human difference. Some animals live solely by perception, and others need memory and instruction. But the human not only supplements the given with experience; it perfects experience with art. The greater admiration accorded to the expert over the experienced amateur—to the botanist over the gardener with a green thumb—attests to widespread intuition of art as the mark of human superiority. We esteem inventors more than their inventions, since utility is not the highest ground of esteem. Aristotle exaggerates the separation of experience and the arts in order to bring out the element of luxury in the arts. This exaggeration, it could be said, is reflecting the tendency of opinion to look away from possible connections between the beautiful or useless on the one hand and human neediness or incompleteness on the other. Although the arts may be a sign of human superiority, they would not exist without human incompleteness. "Man seems to be more incomplete than any other animal" (399).

Notably absent from chapter one's list of ways of knowing is prudence. Benardete observes that the unification of prudence with the other characteristics of wisdom, discussed in chapter two, remains a question. Prudence is neither art nor science, but it unmistakably arises out of the useful, such that the beauty and freedom of precise knowing are alien to it. All the same, it has a comprehensiveness of vision unavailable to any of the specialized arts. Prudence points to the central perplexity of wisdom: how to combine comprehensiveness with precision. If prudence is more closely allied to the useful than to the free, then comprehensiveness comes to light more readily from the standpoint of the useful. But the account of wisdom stresses the requirements that relate to free and precise knowing. Accordingly, it can be doubted whether wisdom thus described attains true comprehensiveness.

Art and History

Benardete follows Aristotle in taking up another aspect of the contrast between art and experience. Art grasps the universal and is therefore teachable; experience is always attached to the particular, and is deaf and dumb. Art discovers causes with universal insights which demote experience. "In its own eyes, art has no 'history'" (399). With art the mind reaches a plane above the genetic series of perception, imagination, memory and experience. One recalls Aristotle's account of the double sense of *ousia* as concrete whole and essence. Benardete notes that for experience's particularism "Socrates is accidentally man" whereas for art's universalism "Man is accidentally Socrates" (400). For Aristotle both are right and both are wrong. The *Republic* shows how the identification of justice with art in the exchange with Thrasymachus leads more directly to philosophy than the appeal to experience by Cephalus. Yet experience as "the cognitive counterpart to virtue" is closer to character. Philosophy acknowledges the claims of both art and experience, Aristotle could be saying, since in order to grasp the universal one must reason and live as a particular being, as Socrates or as Glaucon. If that is so, when art makes the turn to philosophy it can no longer ignore its own history. Aristotle introduces his account of the causes by relating the history of their discovery. Yet art and history never simply coincide, and no practitioner of an art can fully explain how he attained his insights. Even the highest science has conditions in incommunicable experiences.

Thus it is not surprising that even within the arts themselves this duality appears. The opinion that the arts more removed from need are closer to wisdom rendered mathematics and poetry supreme among the arts in early times. But apart from impracticality the two have little in common: mathematics is eminently teachable and poetry is held to be unteachable and impossible without inspiration. Both lack the knowledge of causes which originates in the useful arts. Thus the contrast of communicable art and incommunicable experience gets complicated by the other contrast of the free and the necessary. The contrasts do not coincide. The human delight in knowing can detach the universal from the origin of its discovery in need. But the arts of leisure which thereby rise above the mechanical arts do not form a true whole. The disparity of mathematics and poetry indicates the illusion of supposing that wholeness is inherent in free activity, since freedom remains divided between the teachable and the unteachable, the precise and the allusive. The free delight in knowing still exhibits features of human incompleteness. To advance toward true wholeness, thinking must return to the level of causes, hence back to the needful. But for Aristotle there is no smooth sailing in such a return. Benardete observes: "Even if poetry were irrelevant for wisdom, a wisdom that just combined the theoretical character of mathematics with the knowledge of causes the arts contain seems to be something of an oxymoron." Aristotle famously "denies the possibility of a mathematical physics" (401). That the kinds of knowledge found in mathematics, poetry, and the arts that discover causes may be uncombinable is special cause for wonder. Aristotle's text provides an occasion for wonder and thus performs an action instantiating the theme of its argument.

Benardete points to the political counterpart of this *aporia*. Political life makes possible the transformation of universal natural curiosity into the arts of leisure. Leisure is the political equivalent of the free play of the senses. But there would be no leisure without the productive arts that satisfy primary needs, and it is from the knowing of these arts that causes were first understood. The knowing for which the city exists, its telos in arts of leisure, is not the knowing that brings the city into being. Final cause and efficient cause are disjunct. Benardete remarks "the nature of the knower and the nature of knowledge seem not quite aligned with each other" (401). It is appropriate here to think of the two great achievements of modernity, mathematical natural science and liberal democracy, each of which claims to overcome that misalignment through uniting the free and the productive, or the useless and the causal. Aristotle is the skeptic, not Descartes or Kant, about whether the nature of the knower and the nature of knowledge can be brought into accord. The modern solutions rest on the claim that the object of knowledge must conform to conditions set by the knower or, very crudely put, that we know only what we make. The hope is that the mind as productive can overcome its internal divisions. By contrast Aristotle "separates the insight, to which the arts give access, of what knowledge is, from the way in which the arts apparently make over the natural to serve human needs" (401). Aristotle presses to the point of paradox the view that "the productive arts are not primarily directed to production." Thus the edifying Aristotelian claim that "art is not the conquest of nature but rather its imitation or completion" leaves unresolved the relation between origin and telos. The perfection or completion of which human nature is capable must rest on uncertainty about that relation. Here is the deeper version of the problem of *phantasia*—the relation of the noetic to the aesthetic— emerging on the level of the arts and politics, which level involves the confrontation with human neediness.

The Requirements of Wisdom

The second chapter of *Metaphysics* A takes up the diverse opinions about the wise man and compresses them into three pairs of oppositions. Benardete claims that the incoherence of these characteristics, "or at best their lack of mutual implication," preserves the truth that "no known science can satisfy all that opinion demands of wisdom" (401–02). The science fulfilling those demands would be the most comprehensive science and the most difficult science, the most precise science and the science uncovering the highest causes, the science sought for its own sake and the science of the good. All these characteristics except the concerns with causes and the good point to mathematics. Mathematics among the sciences most exemplifies the natural desire for knowledge while not indicating the content of wisdom, since mathematics does not reflect on the whole as such. Its kinship with play, as witnessed in the myth of its origin in Palamedes' games, brings forth the tension between play and seriousness (403). The beautiful of mathematics is not the good. These elements are found together in the souls of some seekers of wisdom, like Socrates, but no actual science brings them together. The nature of first philosophy can be approached only through the nature of the knower,

166

or rather through the diverse natures of knowers, whose characteristics are seldom found together in one knower. Questioning whether a science of first philosophy is possible, Benardete notes that if realized, such a science would have all its principles present to itself, and be without potentiality (403). It would possess certainty that there are four causes and no others. If Aristotle had such a science, why would he need the history of thinking about causes to establish that there are only four and that he has not overlooked a fifth? Furthermore, can knowledge of the subordinate kinds of being have the precision and completeness of the knowledge of the highest genera? Benardete asserts that "the principles of knowledge cannot but must be the same as the principles of being. Aristotle's use of *ousia* for both 'beingness' and a being places this perplexity in being itself" (404).

Knowing at the highest level would bring together contemplative knowing for its own sake and causal knowing of the good. This would be the self-knowing that knows why knowledge for its own sake is good, and that grasps the reason for the desire to know. Benardete notes that this highest knowing is foreshadowed in wonder, which oddly was not introduced at the start of *Metaphysics*, although it is the condition for the pursuit of wisdom. The reason for this postponed entrance, Benardete suggests, is that wonder is linked to poetry, which conveys a false conception of wonder. Therefore Aristotle first offers essentially true opinions about wisdom that allow him to separate philosophic from poetic wonder. I offer a related suggestion. Aristotle first discloses the problem of the conflicting requirements of philosophic wisdom before turning to poetic wisdom, which claims to have a unified account of the whole. He thereby plants the seeds of doubt about any claims to possess such wisdom, prior to bringing poetry's claim on the scene. The doubt about the poetic claims will then apply just as well to the poetic view of wonder.

Philosophy and Poetry

Aristotle is now ready to expose the two elements of wonder: it is a selfless condition related to the natural desire to know and a "certain kind of conscious neediness (*aporia*)" related to the causal thinking of the arts. The desire to know "is an indiscriminate greediness to transform the opaque into the plain (information); but wonder is the recognition of the opaque in the plain. The wonderful is that which shows the hiddenness of the unhidden. It is every 'that' which seems to be in itself a 'why?' when seeing is not believing, and the given is a question. The wonderful is a beautiful perplexity" (404). Philosophic wonder turns toward that which is closest to us and thus most "plain," namely, the soul, but discovers an opacity in it which then colors everything given. In its erotic pursuit of this perplexity, philosophy is a paradoxical combination of the self-regarding and the self-forgetting. But the ordinary desire to know is turned away from the perplexity of the soul, since it delights only in what can be made transparent. Poets, however are not wholly unlike philosophers. They wonder also at the given, but they wonder even more at what they make. Wonder is more the result than the starting-point of the poet's activity. Mythic or poetic wisdom is "the enigmatic solution to the enigmatic" (405). Poets are in error in thinking that the wonders of poetic making exceed the natural wonders of experience and thought. Perhaps the poets are liars only because they cover over a truth at the basis of their activity. If the greatest wonder is the soul itself, then surely the poets wonder at the soul, but their manner of wondering tends to obscure what is wonderful about it. Since poets do not toil they exhibit the freedom of wisdom, but poetry as a productive art serves the city as the "community of the arts of the necessary" (405). Their freedom obscures the foundation of their art in need and so obscures the nature of knowledge more than other productive arts. But even in this problematic unity of freedom and necessity, poetry is more comprehensive than other arts. Poets address the character of the whole, but they think that making is the ground of the whole, and so they conceive the gods as efficient causes. But a whole grounded in making is unintelligible, since production presupposes incompleteness and the existence of some sort of whole is a condition for incompleteness. That the poets think of the gods as needy is apparent from their claim that the gods are jealous of human seekers of wisdom. The poets therefore do not admit, or perhaps do not care, that the beings they portray as both whole and needy are contradictory.

But again, poetic wisdom is not baseless. The togetherness of freedom and necessity in the state of wonder is not simply a natural state, but a special condition of the soul. This observation could lead to the poetic conclusion that the soul is not naturally a unity. It is hard to claim that the poets are altogether wrong in this. Aristotle subtly indicates that the unity of soul described in De Anima is not the soul as such, but an abstraction. Poetry corrects that abstraction by calling to mind how rare are the high experiences which assuage the soul's normal condition of incompleteness and longing. But the poets are too impressed by their temporary triumphs and do not reflect sufficiently on the enduring causes of the soul's disunity, or what Aristotle calls the natural enslavement of human nature. Philosophy strangely finds great satisfaction in dwelling on the causes of perplexity and in resisting every alluring prospect of a solution that would gratify without altering the underlying causes. Every elevation of the human condition presupposes that we remain only human, and otherwise has no meaning. Thus for the philosophers no poetic solution of human problems can possibly be more wonderful than the enduring forces in human nature that resist poetic solutions.

The poets believe that they, or the gods as poets, make the world into a home for the soul. Poetry is the house of being. By contrast, philosophic wonder is permanently homeless. Benardete says it "induces homelessness without nostalgia" (405)[4]—a formula that evokes how the soul as thinking is both near to and distant from what it thinks about, and so exposes the connection between *phantasia* and wonder. Benardete calls *phantasia* the power of virtual distancing: the *noēton* is made just distant enough so as to be seen as part of a larger whole.[5] Thus the distance of wonder is grounded in familiarity with things, not in flight into abstraction. Poetry, too, rests on virtual distancing, but also annuls the distance of things by anthropomorphizing the whole. It reveals a kind of *phantasia* essential to being human, even so, for it allows the human to appear as a kind of whole amidst other things in the whole. It creates a larger setting for the human in which, admittedly, everything revolves around human concerns. It is easy to see why the poets regard their making as so important, since this power of imaginative self-distancing is in most human beings too artless to be very effective. Art transcends ordinary nature in order to fulfill it. Poetic invention is therefore not one of the ever-present powers of the soul in *De Anima*.

The human need for self-distancing points back, again, to human incompleteness. It is human for individuals to want their projects to have some necessary place in the whole of things, and for them to endow the particular and contingent with the aura of the universal and the necessary. This is the dark side of the beautiful of poetry, which receives no acknowledgment in the natural delight in seeing and knowing. One could call it the original negativity, the primordial difference between genesis and telos which the poets believe their making can overcome. It is the negativity that marks the human as political animal, and Aristotle shows that it is the permanent rift underlying the inquiries of first philosophy. Yet philosophic wonder is not animated by *Angst*. Benardete notes "it is neither painful nor pleasant. It neither compels nor

---

4. Benardete cites here Plato *Symposium* 203d11. The dual nature of Eros in Socrates' speech (as the child of Poros and Penia) calls for comparison with Aristotle's account of the dual nature of wonder. Both presuppose human incompleteness.

5. "Aristotle *De Anima*," *The Archaeology of the Soul*, 275.

entices. There is nothing in it to be feared from which one runs away or which roots one to the spot (like awe), nor does it have the natural attractiveness of seeing" (405). Philosophy can be seen as good, akin to the divine, and even as such immune to divine jealousy, if "the highest beings are causes only as final cause, and their causality is compatible with their being for their own sake" (406). Philosophic wonder is content with "the separation between the being of the highest beings and their being as cause." The same separation allows Aristotle to affirm that the origin of philosophy is only "accidentally at a certain stage of 'history.'" The fortunes of political life and the discoveries of philosophy cannot be identical, or even causally related in a philosophy of history. They are necessarily linked, all the same. "The cause of philosophy is the effect of the good."

Epilogue

The problem of being cannot be articulated by turning directly to being. Aristotle follows the Socratic turning to *logoi* by uncovering the elements of first philosophy in the phenomena of human opinions about experience, arts, states of soul, and their relations to wisdom. No science seems capable of meeting the demand revealed by this examination: to encompass the free and the necessary, the precise and the comprehensive, the eidetic and the genetic. Yet somehow the togetherness of these components is adumbrated in the soul as wondering. The soul's nature contains a perplexity that can seem ugly or beautiful: a certain lack of alignment between the nature of the knower and the nature of knowledge. The perplexity of soul is, however, the perplexity of being itself: the separation between the being of intelligibility and the being of causality, or between the beautiful and the good. The soul brings these together through its activity. In striving to understand the relation of *eidos*— beingness or essence as known precisely—to the coming into being of beings, the soul is the bond of being. "To figure out an insight might well be the epistemic equivalent of the union of causality and beingness" (397). The misalignment, arising first for us in political life, is not even seen by the natural pleasure in noting differences and is deeply experienced but not healed by poetry. Philosophy's careful articulation of it discloses its benefit to the soul. The philosopher understands that the rift in being exercises causality as final, not efficient, by making possible the best human life, that of inquiry. The case is not unlike that of the geometrician who grasps the cause (*aitia*) of the incommensurability of the square's diagonal: he would wonder at nothing as much as if the diagonal were to become measurable (*Metaphysics* 983a15–21).

Chapter Twelve

Prelude to First Philosophy:
Seth Benardete on *De Anima*

Richard Velkley

I.

Seth Benardete published two essays on Aristotle, both treating the nature of first philosophy.[1] The essay on *De Anima* III.3–5 reads the treatise on the soul as an implicit introduction to first philosophy, and concludes with the claim that the self-thinking of mind is the highest concern of inquiry into being, into what is. This claim, however, completes an account of *phantasia* as the bond between noetic and aesthetic soul, an account showing that *nous* without *phantasia* is impossible. The essay on *Metaphysics* A.1–2 describes how these two chapters, the explicit introduction to first philosophy, are a reflection on the knower and on knowledge, and in essence another treatise on the soul. The reflection, however, brings forward tensions and contradictions between kinds of knowing—above all, between useless precision and useful imprecision—which first philosophy or wisdom must strive, and must fail, to resolve. Just as the *De Anima* essay approaches self-thinking mind, and therewith being, through the double nature of *phantasia*, the *Metaphysics* essay approaches mind and being

Reprinted from *Epoché* 7, no. 2 (2003): 189–98.

1. "Aristotle, *De Anima* III.3–5," *The Review of Metaphysics* 28, no. 4 (June 1975): 611–22, reprinted in *The Archaeology of the Soul*, eds. Ronna Burger and Michael Davis (South Bend: St. Augustine's Press, 2012), 272–80, and "On Wisdom and Philosophy: The First Two Chapters of Aristotle's *Metaphysics* A," *The Review of Metaphysics* 32, no. 2 (December 1978): 205–15, reprinted in *The Argument of the Action*, eds. Ronna Burger and Michael Davis (Chicago: University of Chicago Press, 2000), 396–406. All numbers in parentheses in the text refer to pages in the first essay. I thank Martin Sitte for his helpful comments on this article.

through the double nature of knowledge. Each essay reflects on the feature of otherness to itself, or duality, that mind must have in order to be self-knowing. What may seem at first to be only an imperfection of mind is in truth essential to it. Aristotle's account of mind recalls the Platonic view of "the difference and the sameness of the beautiful and the good."[2] A primary aim of Benardete in these essays is to demonstrate that Aristotle practices the Socratic-Platonic way of philosophizing, in which first philosophy is inseparable from political philosophy. The following discussion, with due regard for human limitations, proposes a reading of only the earlier of the two essays. It is hoped that these thoughts will open up paths to the other essay and indeed to Benardete's approach to Greek philosophy as a whole.

I shall take the liberty to anticipate the telos of Benardete's argument. The concluding passage of the essay on *De Anima* observes that first philosophy, unlike every science, regards each kind of being as part of the whole (621–22). Every science has a specious autonomy, having an acquaintance with the "that" of its subject matter but an insufficient grasp of the "what." Each science, being ignorant of other sciences, cannot see its own subject matter in the light of what it is not. Aristotle's "physics" is, however, actually first philosophy of nature, as examining the principles of nature in the light of what they are not. And so it is that every Aristotelian treatise on a "science" quietly subverts its apparent autonomy by pointing to this larger context. "First philosophy looks like every science without ceasing to be itself." But this is precisely the nature of mind itself: it takes on the character of whatever it knows without ceasing to be itself. It remains itself by having distance on what it knows, relating the known to the whole as but a part of the whole. Mind has therefore an odd double existence, as receptive to the given part and as open to the whole. About each known thing it can think two different kinds of "whatness": what each being is in itself, and what each is as part of the whole. In thinking about the differences between the sciences, and thus in disclosing these different senses of whatness, mind discloses its peculiar power. In first philosophy the mind thinks itself.

Unlike the beings that are known or the *noēta*, the whole is not a being or a *noēton*. Aristotle is a philosopher of ontological difference. Mind alone can make this difference manifest, even if there exists, in some way, a whole of being without mind. Mind makes the whole a genuine whole. But the difference cannot be thought without the aid of *phantasia*, and *phantasia* cannot function without relating to the sensible. The ontological difference comes

---

2. "On Wisdom and Philosophy," *The Argument of the Action*, 403.

to light only through a finite sensible being, and the mind that makes the whole a genuine whole is human, or finite and sensible like the human. Benardete argues in his writings on Plato and Aristotle that this is the true Socratic understanding of mind and being. Being is a question—it is named by a question, *ti estin* (618). It is a question because the primary feature of being is that each being provokes the question how it is both itself and part of the whole. The problem of that relation is not something created by mind but inherent in the beings, although only mind brings this feature—as problem or question—to light.

Benardete accordingly denies that Aristotle departs from the Platonic understanding of philosophy as aporetic. Plato's use of dialogue to convey this understanding is mirrored in Aristotle's employment of the treatise. The Platonic dialogue form discloses the truth about its subject matter through the distorting lenses of the interlocutors, who always think in abstraction from some crucial aspect of the subject-matter. Thus Theodorus, the mathematician, misses the essential political dimension of the philosopher's nature. Thereby the dialogues show how all thinking begins with isolating some quality or thing from the true whole to which it belongs. Benardete called this the "vulgar idealism" of opinion; he saw in the necessity of beginning in such idealism the meaning of Socrates' "second sailing." The need to begin in error reflects the nature of being itself, since being is manifest both as noetic heterogeneity and as an elusive whole in which things are related. The truth of being cannot be found by an impossible factoring out of distortions introduced by the mind. There is no access to truth except through the *phantasmata* that both reveal and conceal. Dialectic uncovers the separateness and togetherness of beings by proceeding with the "thumotic" divisions of the beings that the soul, to the extent it can learn in a friendly or erotic discourse, may correct through more inquiry. The doctrine of separate ideas is the expression of this initial thumotic division of being, and every dialogue indicates that it is unsatisfactory.

Benardete reads Aristotle as using the treatise form to enact his own version of a second sailing.

> The Platonic Forms show up in the manifold of treatises Aristotle wrote, and Plato disappears from the apparent separateness of those treatises, only to show up once more in the incoherence of the principles that do not allow Aristotle's treatises on demand to be put together. It is this kind of separation and combination that

we are left to accomplish on our own when we come to Aristotle and that Plato's Socrates practices continually.[3]

For both Plato and Aristotle, the human soul alone is able to disclose the separateness and togetherness of the beings. For both, the necessity for inquiry to start in "opinion" is inseparable from the political nature of the human soul. Hence reflection on politics is the way to soul's nature, and reflection on the soul's nature is the way to first philosophy.[44] Benardete observes, however, that *De Anima* is "as silent about the virtues as it is about memory and *empeiria*," and the soul as a whole is not its theme (611). Aristotle says he will expound a knowledge of the soul outstanding in point of accuracy, but "the recalcitrance of moral matters to accuracy and finish in their treatment" results in the exclusion of such matters from the treatise. This abstraction from the moral and political—and hence from opinion—entails that the highest point of the discussion of soul, the account of self-thinking, is necessarily incomplete. To complete the transition from the account of soul to first philosophy Aristotle must return to the level of opinion, as he does in examining opinions about wisdom in the opening chapters of the *Metaphysics*.

II.

Benardete begins his treatment of *De Anima* III.3–5 with the claim that this work is not truly about the soul as such, but about the soul as experiencing the "now." Its subject is the soul as thinking pre-predicatively, not encountering error, and in unity with what it knows—with all beings. Only the soul as abstracted from time can be known precisely (611). Even so, Aristotle does not claim to have a science of this soul—he does not use any of the familiar terms

---

3. "Strauss on Plato," *The Argument of the Action*, 410.

4. What Aristotle asserts about *phantasia* and intellect in *De Anima* has to be revised in light of his accounts of opinion in other writings. Benardete shows how the opening chapters of the *Metaphysics* crucially assist in this effort, since their characterization of the diverse and conflicting requirements of wisdom reveals the partiality of the demand for precision, which dominates the discussion of the soul in *De Anima*. The demand for a precise account of soul thus proves to be a kind of opinion, a perspective that distorts the subject matter, although it is an unavoidable perspective at a certain stage of inquiry. Hence the treatise (*De Anima*) describing *phantasia* as the power which grasps how a *noēton* is either well translated or distorted by a sensible image must be read and corrected, being itself a distortion, through a use of *phantasia*.

for scientific knowledge. Precise knowledge of soul does not attain the rank of science, and whatever can be known about the soul as whole, the soul in time, is imprecise. The intent of *De Anima* is not just to show what the precise account is, but to indicate as well what it is not. The problem is made evident by the consideration that a science of the soul as whole would have to combine a physicist's account of the passions in terms of motion and a dialectician's account of them as ordinarily experienced. This unified account is unavailable, but Benardete notes what its central theme would be: the power of *phantasia*, which is a kind of motion translating acts of awareness into causes of movement. As the bond of the soul, *phantasia* is the link between the noetic and the aesthetic, and necessarily relates to both thought and desire. But what physical account, in terms of motion, can make this link intelligible (612)? Is there a physics of *phantasia*? The theme of Aristotle's *Physics* is in fact the relation of the noetic to the aesthetic, or the relation of form as essentially unchanging to nature as principle of motion (620). The Platonic *aporia* of this relation is unresolved in the Aristotelian treatises on nature, and reaches its most critical stage in the account of soul. This latter account, through disclosing how this problem inheres in being at the highest level, forms the transition from physics to metaphysics.

Phantasia is then the crucial metaphysical problem—the access to the problem of being. Just as *phantasia* is the power allowing deception and illusion, *phantasia* deceptively appears distant from the principles of being. Being's hiddenness is the self-concealing of *phantasia*. The senses as such never err, and failure to perceive is not ignorance. Error, ignorance and opinion belong to thought, which in acts of judging puts itself outside what it puts together. *Phantasia* seems at first inessential to thinking, since it merely suppresses the question of the true and the false, by framing the perceived with quotation marks, transforming "I see the man" into "It seems to be a man" (613). This suspension of truth neutralizes the negativity of thought, so that the *phantasma* seems complete in itself. But the completeness is as spurious as the separation of the question of truth from the *phantasma* (614). *Phantasia* lacks the completeness of *aesthēsis*, which makes no distinction between sensation and the sensed, since *phantasia* distinguishes between the *phantasma* and the other which it seems to be. The presupposition of *phantasia* is the recognition of being, but a recognition that does not attain the level of knowledge (614). The "as" of *phantasia* both frees it from and binds it to the "is" of being. Because it contains otherness, *phantasia* contains implicitly the point of view of the perceiver. It brings forward the lack of necessity, the arbitrariness, in that point of view. The unification of the various senses is always uncertain. Does the globe I see have to be blue, solid and heavy as well as spherical? Could it not be orange, vaporous and light?

Phantasia allows that reflection, showing that we can rearrange our sensations arbitrarily, and therewith it introduces the otherness or negativity essential to thought. Thinking does not occur in an empty noetic space, but in relation to the sensible, with *phantasia* as the link between thought and sense. In order to grasp the chalk triangle as an instance of triangularity, whereby thought uncovers the noetic in the aesthetic, *phantasia* must transform the *aisthēmata*, straightening the sides of the perceived chalk triangle. It thus exposes the arbitrariness of what is perceived. An attitude akin to doubt—the awareness of the fallibility of perception—allows perception to become intelligible. In any assertion about perception, the possibility of its negation is implicit or co-intended. To think X as Y (chalk figure as a triangle) is at the same time to think X as not Y (crooked lines as not a triangle) while cancelling the latter thought. It follows that the possibility of negation is the presupposition of non-empty speech. The structure of speech and the structure of *phantasia* are the same, since both entail the capacity for arbitrary combination.

III.

In the second part of the essay, Benardete argues that nous as inseparable from *phantasia* partakes of the incompleteness of *phantasia*. He shows that the nature of the mind is paradoxical, and that a science of mind is an oxymoron. Each sense is opaque to the objects of the other senses, but mind, by contrast, is transparent to all possible *noēta* (615). Unless all *noēta* are homogeneous, mind can have no distinctive nature limiting its receptivity, and in the reception of a *noēton* it can undergo no change that could interfere with the reception of other *noēta* (614). Indeed mind is "nothing but possible." But then how can mind initiate the apparent change of thinking? If nothing outside the mind (*noēta*) can produce a change in mind, then mind as initiating change in itself must always be thinking. Yet Aristotle does not say of mind what he says of sense, that a part of it (touch) is always at work. This perplexity of mind, Benardete notes, is the necessary complement to the perplexity of being. Just as the transparency of mind seems to imply that it is always the same and unaffected by being, so the separation of the principles of incorruptible and corruptible being raises the question of what preserves the difference between them. Is the difference incorruptible or corruptible?

Just as the incorruptible must be and cannot be related to the corruptible, mind must be and cannot be related to non-mind.

The paradox inherent in mind is manifest in and further clarified by the power of *phantasia*. It makes evident how mind must be dual in nature, as both productive and receptive. At first the duality is placed in productive mind itself (*nous poiētikos*), when it is compared to light. The light of mind conveys the *noēta*, and at the same time itself, to thinking. This seems to show how mind as knower of *noēta* is self-thinking. As such mind is eminently natural, since start and finish are the same. But the metaphor of light conceals a problem: light allows distance on the *noēton*, so that it can be thought as part of the whole, but the distance is cancelled when thinking and what is thought become the same. How can distance and identity be the effect of the same power? (Here, incidentally, Benardete through Aristotle discloses a problem in Heidegger's account of truth as unconcealment, *a-lētheia*. As Benardete comments elsewhere, Heidegger neglects the problem of the image central for both Plato and Aristotle.) Only if distance is virtual can they be reconciled: *phantasia* is the virtual distancing of the *noēton* (616). The metaphor of illumination fails to capture the interpretation of the *noēton* required for intelligibility. Productive intellect as light would convey nothing but itself to thought. Not accepting the (allegedly) Platonic separation of the noetic from the aesthetic, Aristotle illustrates the work of *phantasia* in the prime instance of the noetic, mathematical truth. Since apprehension of the noetically discrete (point, line, plane, etc.) must always relate to the indeterminate continua of motion and time, mathematical truth requires constructive demonstration (617). This is what *phantasia* provides, by constructing the drawn line that represents the pure line of the figure. But no drawn line or construction, and hence no proof, belong essentially to the truth, since the line chosen for the construction is arbitrary.

The world would not be knowable, and the mind would be enclosed in itself, if *phantasia* did not transform the *aisthēton* so it can be read as a *noēton*. But about this constructive power there is no science. What makes possible a *logos* of being has no *logos*. The relation between noetic discreteness and the infinite continuity of the sensible depends on the mind's capacity to grasp the deformations of the *noēta* in the sensible as deformations. But there are no rules to tell us which constructions of the sensible translate the *noēta* well and which pervert them.

Benardete relates this observation on Aristotle to the problem of being in Plato's *Sophist*: we do not know whether the perfect sophistry belongs to the art of the *eikon* (the precise or perspectiveless image) or that of the *phantasma* (the image proportioned to the knower's perspective) (617).

IV.

Aristotle tries to reduce the problem of arbitrariness, and restate the duality of mind, through the distinction between productive and passive intellect (*nous pathētikos*) (618). The latter is a continuum that is limited by *phantasia*. For example, *phantasia* makes marks in the continuum that are read as "ones" by productive intellect. Two ones become "two" with the help of a line drawn between them by *phantasia*. Mind must relate to something other than *noēta*, for *noēta* are always at work, and if the mind related only to these it would be always thinking (617). But that other to which mind relates must be always available to mind, since mind cannot be affected by non-mind. That "other," according to Benardete's brilliant analysis, is the passive intellect as "the matter of mind." As the "class of all beings, the universal of universals," it is the same as the being of beings (618). I explicate this as follows: the continuous or the unlimited, as the realm of the possible instantiation of *noēta*, belongs essentially to mind as the power of thinking *noēta*. Why is this so? The actualization of *noēta* in thinking presupposes a potentiality which is not the same as the *noēta* qua *noēta*, which are always at work. The potentiality instead belongs to the sensible as the realm of possible knowledge. But how does mind relate to that realm of potentiality? The relation is unthinkable, unless that realm is another form of mind. Somehow the entire realm of the aesthetic (time and motion) must be accessible to mind from the start as a realm of noetic realization. That realm, the continuous, thus has to be a form of mind: the passive intellect. The active intellect which is active in the thinking of each *noēton* does not know in advance what parts of the realm of possibility are noetically realizable. Indeed the active intellect's relation to passive intellect is in one sense constant, and in another sense sporadic. Seldom does active intellect think about passive intellect as such. In the act of thinking a *noēton*, the passive intellect or being qua being vanishes. The revealing of being is also a concealing. But the hiddenness of being is not solely for us, for being as such is hidden. "The perplexity of thought reveals the perplexity of the thing." Things are such that revealing something about them always brings forward more questions. Thus things have a relation to mind even in their elusiveness to our knowing. In a wonderful formulation, Benardete writes that "questioning is the active privation of mind. Questioning is to mind what motion is to form, the being at work of the possible as possible.

Knowledge of knowledge and knowledge of ignorance constitute evanescently passive intellect" (618). In inquiry passive intellect comes into view and does not vanish. It is no longer mere condition but actively present to thought. What then comes into view is being as the realm of the possible as possible. As exposing our ignorance of being, the passive intellect is the ground of knowledge of ignorance. Decisive here is the point that the being of which we are ignorant is not external to all mind but a form of mind, since otherwise knowledge of our ignorance would be impossible. "Being is not thinking, but the being of beings comes close to the being of thinking" (618). The being of beings comes close to the being of thinking in the way that passive intellect comes close to active intellect.

V.

In the third and final part of the essay, Benardete relates the double nature of mind to the question of being's unity and heterogeneity, or the problem of the One and the Many. How can each being be an individual, and at the same time a participant in countless many wholes (genera)? In the case of mind the difficulty assumes a radical form, since the mind is both one being and open to all beings. The problem is already encountered on the level of aesthetic soul. Benardete calls *De Anima*'s discussion of this more baffling than any perplexity of mind (620). The aesthetic soul senses itself, and seems in its completeness to prefigure intellect's self-thinking. The aesthetic soul is the non-aesthetic *eidos* of everything aesthetic, and "seems to usurp in part the work of mind." How does aesthetic soul sense simultaneously the "nows" of the different senses?

How is the "now" of seeing recognized as the same "now" as the "now" of hearing (619)? Since each sense is receptive only to its own *aisthēton*, the recognition is not the work of any one sense. Certainly no faculty apart from the senses, one not knowing their "nows," could bring them into a synthesis. And a sixth sense would simply have its own object. Benardete then notes that there is a common root of the senses, a discriminatory power, which is like a point from which five lines radiate. The point has no dimension of its own, but is both one and five, and so employs itself several times simultaneously. In other words, the common root of the senses is both discrete (a point) and continuous (five lines). The discrete exists only as the limit within the continua; Benardete remarks that this double reference of the limit-point is the same as the double nature of the "now" of time. The use of the mathematical model shows how science is dependent on *phantasia*, which attempts to illuminate the non-mathematical by means of such models. The mathematical figure cannot, of course, accomplish the perceptive act of the soul. This is the secret, Benardete claims, of Aristotle's physics and psychology (620). It is characteristic of Aristotle's speculative sobriety that he points covertly to how the sensible eludes the grasp of the noetic, unlike Plato who declares the problem openly. An Aristotelian treatise begins with the self-evident as *archē* (in this case, the experience of the unity of sensation) and ultimately returns to it, in spite of the fact that our attempts at explanation are forced to leave behind the natural as it appears "first for us."

Turning to the self-thinking of *nous*, Benardete asks about whether and how it is parallel to the self-sensing of aesthetic soul. Does self-thinking characterize the thinking of every *noēton*, or is it only an occasional event (621)? Thinking the mind and thinking the beings cannot be identical, unless the whole is homogeneous. On the other hand, if mind does not think itself when thinking other beings, then it is not wholly mind, and not truly itself, when thinking other beings. The heterogeneity of mind and beings would seem to entail that mind thinks the beings at its own expense. Now indeed the self-thinking of mind implies heterogeneity, but one internal to mind itself. Suppose that mind were pure openness to beings, or pure possibility. Then the mind would lack any determinate nature of its own, and receptivity to itself would be impossible. The fact of self-thinking entails that the mind has actuality of some sort. In that case, however, the mind is aware of itself as an actual being, yet one whose being is openness to all beings, to all possibility. It is aware of itself as other to itself. "To be open to the whole and to be must and cannot be the same" (621). Mind is the supreme case of the togetherness of determinacy and indeterminacy characterizing all being. The heterogeneity of self-awareness and awareness of beings at first seems to reduce mind to just one more *noēton*. But thinking the determinacy or actuality of mind, the knowledge of knowledge, is instead more like knowledge of ignorance: awareness of the possible as possible.

Benardete proposes that mind's self-thinking might be like a pleasure, a condition that accompanies and completes each thought, while not being the same as that thought. The sustaining of such pleasure is first philosophy (621). In that case, however, first philosophy is not the simple identity of thinking with itself, but rather the thinking of necessary difference, mind's otherness to itself. Aristotle is properly cautious about suggesting openly that the highest condition in the whole involves difference rather than identity or simplicity. It is natural for the human kind to think that the happiest condition would be the resolution of problems in a state of simple unity and wholeness. But the difference in being that is related to countless forms of perplexity in human life is also the source of the highest pleasure when understood as the necessary condition for the activity of mind. Evil is necessary for the being of mind, and thus of the good. As separate from the beings, thinking about itself simply and not about the possibility of beings, the activity of mind would lack content and meaning. Active intellect without passive intellect and *phantasia* cannot get off the ground. The self-thinking of mind—a human philosophizing which is also the genuine attainment of wisdom—is supremely satisfying because it affords the highest insight into the necessarily non-simple structure of being as a whole. How this insight is both necessary and hard for our enslaved nature is the common inquiry of political philosophy and first philosophy.

Chapter Thirteen

Empire as Wasteland,
or Seth Benardete with Ronald Syme

Holly Haynes

Fellini's *La Dolce Vita* ends with a party at a rich man's house. Marcello, the protagonist, announces that he has given up newspaper reporting and is now in publicity. For the right sum, he can make anybody look like somebody. The man's ex-wife performs a striptease, two drag queens dressed as show-girls begin to dance, and there appears to be plenty of liquor; but no one takes much notice. In fact no one can think of anything amusing to do, despite the luxury with which they are surrounded. Drunk, Marcello humiliates an even drunker girl by riding on her back as if she were a donkey, and covering her with feathers. The rich man returns and throws them all out, after which they wander down to the beach to look at a monstrous fish that has just been caught. Marcello notices a very young girl he had met earlier in the film, who calls out to him; but he cannot hear her and will not approach her across the small rivulet of water that separates them. Instead he shrugs, waves, and turns to join a woman from his group who has returned for him.

These scenes, and indeed the film itself, are in many ways an apt metaphor for the tenor of early Imperial literature, which often expresses itself in terms of irony, nostalgia, excess and spectacle. Fellini's fish, unrecognizable in shape, regards the revelers with a cold, lifeless eye—just one—like a camera lens that deadens whatever comes within its range. It is inhuman, incomprehensible to those who look back. The power of the camera in this film is supremely destructive: its ability to confer immortality also turns everything into a representation, and the whole of life becomes a psychological prison that admits no plural perspective and therefore no possibility of self-reflection. The only self-reflective character—a German—ends up

---

The author presented a talk on Vergil's *Aeneid* and Tacitus at the conference on "The Thought of Seth Benardete," Howard University, April 2005.

killing both his children and himself. As the paparazzi surround his wife, in the moments before she is told about the tragedy, she smiles and asks, "Are you mistaking me for an actress?"

Seth Benardete and I had several conversations in which we talked about Roman Imperial literature in the light of themes in this film, beginning with my intuition that *La Dolce Vita* is a much truer representation of Petronius's *Satyricon* than Fellini's film of the same name. There are two particular memories I have when I reflect on these conversations. The first is of his revelation to me that after he had read Ronald Syme's *Tacitus*, he had written to Syme announcing: "Now I understand that Tacitus is the truth of Vergil."[1] The second is of a recollection by a colleague, after Benardete's death, that he had once been completely mystified by an offhand reference Benardete had once made to the "zero at the center of the *Aeneid*." What did I think he had meant by this? These two anecdotes illustrate an important strand of Benardete's understanding of Roman Imperial literature as a representation of Plato's vision of tyranny; in other words, not simply tyranny in the classical sense of the term, or as a particular form of ancient government, but as a condition of the soul that wrecks itself and everything around it. He was interested in my observation about *La Dolce Vita* because it spoke to his own thought that just as Aeneas (who I believe is the "zero") wishes he were dead before the *Aeneid* even really gets going, the changes Octavian instigated spelled the destruction of the Imperial government from its inception. Like Marcello's world of dead desire, Rome in the Imperial period was already a walking ghost, dead, like the father in one of Freud's dream cases, without realizing it.[2] In this paper, I work out some of the ways in which Imperial authors represented their own visions of Rome's living death.

---

1. Of course I immediately wanted to know if Syme had responded, but Benardete cheerfully said no, that he was sure Syme had thought he was quite crazy!

2. Sigmund Freud, "Formulations Regarding the Two Principles of Mental Functioning" (1911), in *The Standard Edition of the Complete Psychological Works* Vol. 12, ed. and trans. J. Strachey (London: Hogarth Press, 1953–74), 225. If we follow the analogy of Rome as the dead father, the observations of Jacques Lacan on the effects of the father's "not-knowing" become interesting for an analysis of the constitution of the Imperial subject ("son"), but beyond my scope here. See "The Subversion of the Subject and the Dialectic of Desire in the Freudian Unconscious," in *Écrits: A Selection*, trans. Alan Sheridan (New York: W. W. Norton, 1977), 292–325.

I. Tacitus

Calgacus, the Briton leader in Tacitus's *Agricola*, succinctly summarizes the devastation caused by Roman Imperial expansion. His enigmatic rhetoric also introduces the ideological problem it poses for authors who write as its subjects: "They call stealing, butchering and rapine 'imperium' by false names, and 'peace' where they make a wasteland" (*auferre trucidare rapere falsis nominibus imperium atque ubi solitudinem faciunt pacem appellant*, 30.5).[3] It might seem to make more sense for Calgacus to say "They call [these crimes] by the *false name imperium.*" But the implication of the plural *falsis nominibus* together with the singular *imperium* is that *imperium* is both a whole and a sum of parts. As a whole it represents Rome's body of knowledge about itself, an ideological concept that splinters into many other names that Calgacus says are false. He

---

3. Antonio Negri and Michael Hardt interestingly misquote Tacitus when they use the second part of this passage as the epigraph to the first chapter, "World Order," of *Empire* (Cambridge: Harvard University Press, 2000), 3. Their translation is "They make a slaughter and they call it peace," which bypasses both the problem of the original connections Tacitus makes and his emphasis on the element of language that grounds Imperial crimes (*falsis nominibus*). As I argue, the concept of slaughter embodied in Tacitus's expression "plundering, butchering and stealing," however, is associated with "empire," while "peace" brings devastation of a different kind—*solitudo*—connoting emptiness and the hollowing out of human experience. Hardt and Negri do not discuss their use of the epigraph directly, but their misquote celebrates the notion of the coming of a new age of empire in which a borderless, shifting, global network of relations will make possible a new *emancipation* of the human subject, although they see the current stage of that process as still marked by violence and oppression. Their theorizing of this new world order is at least in part a midwifing of new possibilities for the subject to recognize its own power and agency; in other words, the opposite of empire as force that evacuates the subject. In their Preface, they describe this global network as sharing a grounding concept of older forms of empire in its existence as "an order that effectively suspends history and thereby fixes the existing state of affairs for eternity.... In other words, empire presents its rule not as a transitory moment in the movement of history, but as a regime with no temporal boundaries and in this sense outside of history or at the end of history." But this formulation surely echoes Jupiter's prophecy about the Roman people in Vergil's *Aeneid*: "I place upon them no boundaries of fortunes or time: I have given them *imperium* without end" (1.278–79), whose problematics I discuss below. Hardt's and Negri's project celebrates the coming of a utopian ideal of empire, but cannot shake the tyrannical associations of borderlessness that the Imperial authors understood so well.

does not specifically enumerate what these other names are, only what a barbarian about to lose everything calls them. But this barbarian is a character in a Roman text, speaking Latin.[4] In this moment Tacitus makes the Roman language itself a devastation, and Calgacus a stand-in for the Imperial Roman subject whose speech itself deprives him of agency. The words that collectively make up *imperium* are missing, and their stand-ins signify ruin in infinitives that make the language of devastation inexorably eternal. *Pax* comes up not as one of the names of *imperium*, but instead in connection with *solitudo*. Merely speaking Latin makes of both the Imperial subject and the external world a *solitudo* that Imperial discourse bodies forth in images, like the beautiful ones with which *La Dolce Vita* bombards Marcello and us, but that finally dissolve in the dead eye of the unrecognizable sea-creature. In identifying Imperial ideology, embodied in the term *pax*, as a wasteland, Calgacus confronts the Roman reader with a vision of the self-annihilation that accompanies Rome's particular capacity to subjugate others.

One way to understand Tacitus as the "truth" of Vergil would be to see the content of his work as the historical instantiation of Vergil's poetic visions, and hear his language as the poetic echo of Vergil's historical intuition. Benardete's interpretation of the *Aeneid* might be briefly summarized as "the text's destruction is built into itself."[5] Thus Tacitus's often-impossible Latin, ironic vision, and overall sense of doom would indeed seem to capture the essence of Benardete's Vergil. Even more than these features of his prose, however, Tacitus's understanding of the principate as a form of government that evacuates language grasps in historical terms the imploding poetic force of the *Aeneid*. For Tacitus, the tyranny of the principate inheres in the force it exerts on the language of its subjects, so that subjectivity itself is an expression of coercion. This takes place not only under the "bad" *principes* like Nero and Domitian, where speech is dangerous, but from the very inception of the Imperial government under a man who decides to name himself after an abstraction. Tyranny has to do with making language into an image of itself, and the subject of speech therefore a ghost.

---

4. I have argued elsewhere that with the use of *nominibus* as opposed to *vocabulis* or *verbis* Tacitus calls attention to Calgacus's discourse as both Roman and barbarian. See Holly Haynes, "Tacitus' Dangerous Word," *Classical Antiquity* 23, no. 1 (April 2004): 33–61.

5. Seth Benardete, "*Aeneid*," in *The Archaeology of the Soul*, eds. Ronna Burger and Michael Davis (Chicago: University of Chicago Press, 2012), 300.

"Augustus" etymologically connotes the concept of "increasing" and its corollary "authorizing." By choosing this title Octavian installs himself in the signifying system as a point of origin that nevertheless has no fixed place: there must be some reference point from which to measure increase, but this point is contingent. This identity is fashioned through abstraction, substantiating itself via a series of other titular abstractions: *tribuncia potestas*; *pater patriae*; *primus inter pares*. Thus Octavian's "subjects" became such not by an act of usurpation of power on his part, but because of a rearrangement of power effected through language. The true coup—the true violence—comes through a rearrangement on the symbolic level that effaces itself in such a way as to assign subjects their place and make them believe they want to take it. There is no evidence of much overt negotiation between Augustus and the senate about the level and scope of his powers; rather, this negotiation seems to have taken place through unspoken agreement that he would propose and they would ratify. The rupturing of "Republican" language—meaning the language people spoke before the introduction of Octavian's new name and powers—leads to a split in its speakers between a self-identification through the "old" way of speaking and whatever identity might emerge through speaking this new language. But this new identity cannot announce itself in any direct way, since the changes in the language do not announce themselves as different from anything that had gone before.

II. Vergil

The theme, language, and title character of the *Aeneid* all represent the hollowing-out of Imperial subjectivity. It remained for Tacitus to explicate the metaphors of the poem through historical events. We could say that Vergil folds the evacuating force of the principate into the center of his poem, and Tacitus draws it back out. In what follows, I will trace some moments of the *Aeneid* that particularly show how *solitudo* and tyranny are commensurate in the Imperial world; then link Vergil's vision to Horace and Petronius. In this way I hope to show, in a preliminary way, the genealogy of Tacitus's Vergilian "truth."

At *Aeneid* 6.853, Anchises cautions the future Roman about the nature of *imperium*: "You, Roman, be mindful to rule peoples with *imperium*—these will be your arts—, and to impose law upon peace; to spare the subjugated and fight down the arrogant" (*tu regere imperio populos, Romane, memento / [hae tibi erunt artes], pacique imponere morem, / parcere subiectis et debellare superbos.*) If this comprises the Roman ideal, first Aeneas and then the Romans themselves fall far short of it—at least if we are to judge by the killing of Turnus

186

and Calgacus's assessment of Roman activity as murder and rapine. The reality of *imperium* lies somewhere in between. Anchises creates a stirring image, but he does not elaborate upon the problems that attend vast-scale acquisition of territories and peoples. His declaration consists of a chiasmus in which *regere imperio populos* corresponds with *debellare superbos*, and *paci imponere morem* with *parcere subiectis*. To rule others with Imperial power entails beating down those arrogant enough to put up a fight; mercy consists of subjecting them to law and peace. The chiasmus dresses the fundamental violence of Imperial power in a rhetoric of diplomacy, but the double meaning of *subiectis*—civil and military—makes Anchises' meaning clear.[6] Neither represents the absolute truth of *imperium*, but the two together represent in microcosm the problem of the *Aeneid*, which in turn represents that of Roman identity during the early part of the Empire.

The successful violation of others implies a domestic truth that is also less than desirable: the Romans' own subjugation to one master.[7] In his depiction of Lucius Junius Brutus, Caesar, and Pompey, Anchises suggests this eventuality: Brutus has an "arrogant spirit" (*animamque superbam*, 6.817) and receives the "savage axes" (*saevasque securis*, 6.819); he condemns his treacherous sons to death "for beautiful *libertas*" (*pulchra pro libertate*, 6.821), but his motives are "love of the fatherland and a huge lust for fame" (*vincet amor patriae laudumque immensa cupido*, 6.823). The reference to the fatherland is anachronistic—in Brutus's time the Romans had not coalesced into what could be described as a *patria*. However, Brutus's desire for fame implies a vision of the future that includes the time when *amor patriae* will be possible.

---

6. For the double sense of *subicere*, see Livy 26.49, 31.29, 37.53–54; but never Cicero. For the juxtaposition of justice and subjugation, see also Horace 1.12.51–56: *tu secundo / Caesare regnes. / ille seu Parthos Latio imminentis / egerit iusto domitos triumpho, / sive subiectos Orientis orae / Seras et Indos* ("With Caesar as your vice-regent may you rule. Whether he will have led the Parthians who threaten Latium, conquered by a just triumph, or the subjugated Chinese and Indias of the Eastern shore..."). Although the translation of *subiectos* is contested, some commentators wish to read "lying next to." Cf. R. G. M. Nisbet and Margaret Hubbard, *A Commentary on Horace: Odes, Book I* (Oxford: Oxford University Press, 1989), *ad loc.* Coming as it does directly after *domitos*, however, "subjugated" seems to make the most sense.

7. Cf. Pliny *Panegyricus* 32.2, "He has joined with reciprocal lines of communication the east and west in order that all peoples may learn in turn what they produce and what they require, and that they may grasp how much more advantageous it is, for those who serve a discordant liberty, that there be one person whom they serve."

Amor patriae according to Anchises is therefore the corollary of Brutus's private ambitions, an observation that casts some suspicion upon the definition of *libertas*. Indeed, Brutus has several of the characteristics we might expect Anchises to apply to the Tarquinian kings, but instead *he* looks like the tyrant—even Superbus's epithet is transferred to him—whereas they receive no description at all.[8]

The idea of *patria* becomes significant in the descriptions of future Romans that Anchises interposes between Brutus and Caesar/Pompey: "But look at the Decii and Drusi far off, and savage Torquatus of the axe, and Camillus bringing back the standards" (824–25). The names represent two of the most important stages of Roman relations with outsiders. The Decii, father and son, died gloriously in the Samnite War, one front of the Social War which erupted after the death of Marcus Livius Drusus. Following in his father's footsteps, Drusus had agitated for Latin emancipation; he also introduced ideas for jury reform to combat widespread corruption in the law courts. In calling Aeneas's attention to them, Anchises presents two facets of the Latin struggle for independence, the military and the civil. The war ended sooner rather than later because the Romans conceded citizenship rights; henceforth *patria* could more properly be said to exist: in the communal interest that the different Italian peoples had in Rome, and vice-versa. Even more importantly, the Social War saw the rise of Sulla, the power of the dictatorship, and the possibility of rule by one man.

The names of the Decii and Drusi recall the coalescence of Rome's national identity, the bloodshed it cost, and the price the Romans paid in terms of their own *libertas*. Torquatus and Camillus represent a previous stage in Roman history—the Gallic invasion—when Rome very nearly ceased to exist as any kind of political identity. Anchises sandwiches the Decii and Drusi between the instant of foundation, which already displays the fault line of Roman politics, and the early wars with Gaul, which herald the Imperial expansions to come. He therefore takes the reader from the problem of leadership, instantly posed by the expulsion of the kings, to the inception of Roman Imperial success. In between comes the later vehicle for that success. Finally, Anchises depicts the war between Caesar and Pompey. The anachrony of his list creates another chiasmus in which Brutus corresponds to Caesar/Pompey, and the Decii/Drusi to Torquatus/Camillus; in other words, group (A) comprises the leaders who begin and end the Republic, and (B) the

---

8. Cf. James E. G. Zetzel, "Rome and its Traditions," in *The Cambridge Companion to Vergil*, ed. Charles Martindale (Cambridge: Cambridge University Press, 1997), 198.

people who made the history of the Republic. Caesar and Pompey remain nameless—Anchises only refers to them as *socer* and *gener*—as if they represent forces larger than the named people whose exploits make up the prior historical narrative, or as if by the time they take the stage, the Republic has gathered irreversible momentum from the time of its birth toward an inevitable conclusion. They also carry in their wake the geography of Empire: "The father-in-law coming down from the Alps and the citadel of Monaco; the son-in-law marshalled with and from the hostile East!" (830–31).

The sense here is that everything is over before it has even begun; the final member of the parade, the doomed Marcellus, only reinforces this impression. Anchises' narrative acts as an extension of Aeneas's own weary exclamation to the Sybil before he enters the Underworld: "I have anticipated everything and have gone through everything with myself in my mind" (6.105). This seems bizarre, taken in conjunction with our first encounter with him, in which he wishes to die (1.92), and later the wonder he expresses to his father that anyone would wish to be born: "'O father, must we believe that some souls go from here high up to heaven, and then return to sluggish bodies? What dread desire for light do the wretched have?'" (6.721). Aeneas thinks he knows everything, and thinks it better never to be born.

Anchises begins his response with an explanation of the migration of souls: after punishment some stay in Elysium because their faults become thoroughly expunged. Others—presumably those whose souls are still not pure—are recalled by the god to drink from the river Lethe and be reborn in human form. Immediately following the depiction of the latter, Anchises begins the list of famous Romans. The implication is that to be born is good because one can be born Roman. But, just as Anchises suggests that the founder of the Republic has tyrannical qualities, so to be born Roman is also to be born criminal. Later, on the shield of Aeneas, we will see Catiline and Cato in the positions of these two kinds of souls: In Tartarus Vulcan has depicted Catiline "hanging on a rock and trembling at the faces of the Furies; and [he has depicted] set-apart pious ones—Cato giving the laws to these" (669–70). According to Anchises' logic of metempsychosis, it is Catiline's soul that will be born again, whereas Cato's and those of the "pious" (*pios*) occupy the never-never land of Elysium (hence "set-apart," *secretos*). "Republic" looks like a dream that was never anything but the founding fiction of imperialism, the desire for which exists in individuals and the state alike.[9] The city is the man, and vice-versa.

---

9. Cf. Benardete, "*Aeneid*," *The Archaeology of the Soul*, 300.

Aeneas's assertion that he knows everything mirrors the response that Vergil would have expected from his Roman reader. The stories about Rome's founding were not new in themselves, and we can imagine that the Roman reader felt quite familiar with Vergil's material; what would be new was his telling of it. But the *Aeneid* is quite often spectacularly boring, most of all because its hero is incomprehensible as a character. That he both wishes to die before anything in the narrative gets going, and marvels, just before his re-entry from the Underworld to the greatest part of his mission, that anyone would want to be born at all, means that Vergil asks us to look at his world through the eyes of a cipher—a characterless character whose perception and behavior provides no internal logic to the narrative. In this sense, the text is more like a series of juxtaposed paintings or tableaux that convey meaning without causality. Fellini explores this principle in *La Dolce Vita*, a plotless narrative that consists of a series of scenes loosely connected by the protagonist's involvement in each, and by the theme of the omnipresent *paparazzi* who turn each action into a still-life. In the *Aeneid*, it is Aeneas's shield that represents the freeze-frame quality of the whole narrative.[10] In comparing it to that of Achilles in the *Iliad*, Lessing remarks that Achilles' does not resemble a painting, because Homer describes it as a work in progress: "Thus, here too he has made use of that admirable artistic device: transforming what is coexistent in his subject into what is consecutive, and thereby making the living picture of an action out of the tedious painting of an object. We do not see the shield, but the divine master as he is making it."[11]

By contrast, the description of Aeneas's shield comes after Vulcan has finished with it and Aeneas has marveled at it: "By its eternal 'here is' and 'there is,' 'close by stands' and 'not far off we see,' the description becomes so cold and tedious that all the poetic beauty which a Vergil could give it was required to keep it from becoming intolerable" (96). Lessing's astute critique misses only one factor: Vergil was surely not unaware of what he was doing. Upon the shield he makes pictures of Roman history which become a delight-

---

10. Cf. Gordon Williams's description of Aeneas's journey through the Underworld, which seems to me paradigmatic of the journey as a whole: "It is as if a series of set scenes were passing before Aeneas's eyes rather than that he were making a journey in a region with a defined geography. The verbal signals insist on a journey, but the intellectual organization suggests more the vivid incoherence of a dream." *Technique and Ideas in the* Aeneid (New Haven: Yale University Press), 53.

11. *Laocoön: An Essay on the Limits of Painting and Poetry*, trans. Edward Allen McCormick (Baltimore: Johns Hopkins University Press, 1984), 95.

ful spectacle for Aeneas, which the latter cannot understand because they do not tell him a story but dumbly show him images whose relation to one another is uncertain.[12] Vergil allies the reader with Aeneas when at one point he says *videres* ("you would see...," 676), but he also gives "you" the opportunity to understand what Aeneas has not. Seduced by the pictures, Aeneas forgets what he saw in the Underworld and learned from his father: that criminal souls are the ones that undergo metempsychosis. Vergil introduces "you" at the same moment as he introduces the image of Augustus at Actium; immediately prior to it is that of Catiline and Cato in Tartarus, as if Catiline were waiting to be reborn into Augustus while Cato looked after the pious in a far-away place. Aeneas does not understand this, but "you" either might or might not, depending on whether you look back from the picture of Actium that Vergil has set in front of you and read it against the wisdom of Anchises in the Underworld. Either way, Aeneas is the hero of the poem, not you; it is his knowledge that supplies the foundation of the Roman nation. What Vergil can give you, if you read him attentively, is a self-critical distance, not an answer to the problems.

Another way to put this is briefly to compare Aeneas to Achilles. Through the course of the *Iliad*, Achilles comes to understand his own nature, and his need of the gods if he is to succeed. There is an arc to his character, a *pathei mathos*. Aeneas already knows he needs the gods, he is *pius* by nature. Though he suffers many things, as we are told in 1.5, he arrives at no self-knowledge by the end of the poem—his anger at Turnus marks a change, but not a self-conscious one. In the character of Aeneas, we locate a phenomenon of the poem as a whole: plotwise, it goes nowhere. Although it includes a mass of information and detail, little of it is relevant to the overall goal: indeed, Vergil draws out thematic elements, such as the episode at Carthage, and collapses those that most contribute to the action.[13] When Aeneas visits Tarchon at 10.148–156, for example, he gains the ally without whom he could not win his battle. Yet Vergil narrates the incident speedily,

---

12. But compare Philip R. Hardie's analysis in *Virgil's* Aeneid: *Cosmos and Imperium* (Oxford: Oxford University Press, 1986), 346–65. However, Hardie relies almost entirely upon the actual events of Roman history to make narrative sense of the shield—i.e., projects onto the shield a narrative cast retrospectively upon random historical events. On the problem of narrative coherence on the shield, see Zetzel, "Rome and its Traditions," in *The Cambridge Companion to Vergil*, 200–201.

13. For an overview of narrative problems and intricacies in the poem, see Don Fowler, "Virgilian Narrative: Storytelling," in *The Cambridge Companion to Vergil*, 259–70.

in indirect statement: "He went over for the king his name and his birth; what he was seeking and what he himself was bringing; what arms Mezentius was procuring for himself, and the violent heart of Turnus he explained; reminds what fidelity there is in human affairs and mingles prayers. Scarcely was there a delay. Tarchon joined forces and struck a treaty..." (149–54).

This list which comprises both Aeneas's speech and the series of actions around it, reads more like annalistic history than epic poetry. The history of Rome depicted on the shield and the list of famous Romans in the Underworld share this quality, which displays events without providing an explanation for their existence and therefore contributes to a sense of timelessness, or lack of forward movement in time. With causality absent, one cannot know how to sort the pictures or elements into their correct progressions; Aeneas does not know, and he does not care: "Such things on the shield of Vulcan, the gift of his mother, he marveled at, and ignorant of the events he delighted in the image..." (8.730).[14] The dysfunctionality of time is a prevalent theme both in the *Aeneid* and Imperial literature generally, and gives some important clues as to how the concept of "history" was construed in the early Empire.[15] If, in the *Aeneid*, we lack the important links that would bind the elements of the plot meaningfully for us, what we do have is a wealth of thematic material. This makes a painting of the whole text, as in Lessing's description of the shield. One could remove a book at random and not have the omission make any difference to the plot; but to do so in terms of theme would be impossible. The "plot" therefore takes place in an eternal present in which the only interchangeable elements are place and name.

Anachronism defines Aeneas's and the Trojans' journey, and therefore character. At the end of Book 3, Aeneas narrates how, on Polyphemus's island, they meet a survivor from Ulysses' sojourn there who warns them to escape quickly. Taking him with them, they sail round the south coast of Sicily.

---

14. Cf. Aristotle on the man who does not know the original of what is represented, and who will therefore enjoy its manner of representation, but not learn anything from it. *Poetics* 1448b.

15. For a detailed literary and sociological study of Roman concepts of time, see D. C. Feeney, *Caesar's Calendar: Ancient Time and the Beginnings of History. Sather Classical Lectures,* 65 (Berkeley: University of California Press, 2007), who has important arguments about Vergil's and Tacitus's contributions to our understanding of time in the early Imperial period, and whose focus on time as a cognitive tool wielded for ideological purposes has influenced my own thinking about the connections between these two authors.

Aeneas lists the towns they pass, briefly describing each; when he comes to Acragas, he calls it "the producer, formerly, of great-hearted horses" (*magnanimum quondam generator equorum*, 3.704). *Quondam* tells us that Greece is history. At the same time, the Cyclopes still inhabit their mythic island. In Vergil's world, when Greece is gone, monsters remain. The monsters reappear in Book 5, in the form of the ships captained by the Trojans in the funeral games for Anchises: Mnestheus takes the "Leviathan," and is destined to found the Memmian *gens*; Gyas the "Chimaera"; Sergestus, founder of the Sergian *domus*, the "Centaur"; and Cloanthus, founder of the Cluentian *genus*, the "Scylla." What is Vergil trying to tell the Romans about themselves?

When the Trojans reach Circe's island, they do not stop because they cannot repeat this part of the *Odyssey*. For Odysseus, the adventure with Circe meant discovering the difference between man and beast, which entailed understanding the properties of the natural world in the form of the moly plant. In this place, Odysseus discovers philosophy; and he discovers what it is to be human. But Aeneas and his men are denied this knowledge as Neptune keeps them off the shore: "But lest the pious Trojans suffer these monstrous things, carried to the port, or undergo the terrible shores, Neptune filled their sails with favorable winds, gave them an escape, and carried them past the seething shallows" (7.21–24). Pious but not wise, the Trojans are already beasts. Anchises tells Aeneas as much when he enumerates the three skills the Romans will not possess: philosophy, rhetoric, and the imitative arts: "Others will hammer out bronze that breathes and yields to the touch (indeed I believe it), they will draw out of marble faces that live; they will plead cases better, trace out the movement of the sky with the pointer, and speak of the rising stars..." (6.847–50).[16] When Anchises chooses sculpture to describe the deficiency of the imitative arts, he emphasizes the ability others have to make their creations look alive—living and breathing. In other words, non-Roman image-makers will have the ability to create three-dimensional

---

16. Various philosophical tenets can be identified in the *Aeneid*, but it is difficult to interpret from them a unified system. Susanna Braund suggests as much, but concludes that the lack of such a philosophical system demonstrates Vergil's allegiance to Roman Imperial ideology, in which the individual was not educated to become a "free thinker" but to reflect "upon his role as an individual in the state." See "Virgil and the Cosmos: Religious and Philosophical Ideas" in *The Cambridge Companion to Vergil*, 221. I argue the opposite: Vergil systematically represents the ramifications of the lack of philosophy at Rome. This is not a patriotic gesture but a profoundly melancholy reflection upon the intellectual landscape of Empire.

beings—in imitation, presumably, of the world they see around them. The Romans' world is therefore to be flat, like Aeneas himself, because without image-makers they will not perceive the difference between themselves and statues: everything will be a statue without being recognized as such.[17]

Anchises' Underworld speech splits between the philosophical and the historical. After Aeneas despairingly asks why anyone would want to be born and live again, Anchises gives him a roughly Platonic account of the transmigration of souls, and an account of Roman history. Aeneas then returns to the upper world. But Anchises' historical account sheds a less than complimentary light on the Romans, and ends with mourning for Marcellus, who, in the Underworld, represents the hope of Rome lost before it ever comes to be.[18] In the Myth of Er, Socrates rather surprisingly observes that even a citizen raised in the best city will choose the life of the tyrant the second time around, if he does not have philosophy (*Republic* 619b7–d1). Since Anchises alerts Aeneas that the Romans will not have philosophy, his speech reproduces the split that necessarily engenders the criminal choice. In Aeneas, we see the lack of awareness that characterizes the unphilosophical soul who chooses to be a tyrant: he is persuaded by his father, and unquestioningly leaves for the upper world he earlier found so suspect. His exit by the gate of false dreams confirms his lack of understanding. In this section, where Vergil creates an image of the political result of the failure of philosophy, he is consistently Platonic.[19]

From Anchises, we are to understand that for the Romans a radical split will exist between politics and the three aspects of self-expression he picks

17. On the "flatness" of Aeneas's character as expressing both the political inertia of the Augustan regime, and the self-effacing character of Augustus himself as he worked through political institutions rather than appear to seize power, see David Quint, *Epic and Empire* (Princeton: Princeton University Press, 1993), 95.

18. Dennis Feeney comments upon the lack of continuity between what he sees as a moral exhortation (Platonic philosophy) and the portrait of criminality that follows. The lack of philosophical resolution engenders the feeling of exclusion that characterizes both Aeneas, and, Feeney suggests, the audience of the poem. See "History and Revelation in Vergil's Underworld," in *Why Vergil?*, ed. Stephanie Quinn (Mundelein, Ill.: Bolchazy-Carducci, 2000), 119. However I would argue that the philosophical aspect of Anchises' speech lies not in the mish-mash of philosophical theories that Anchises advances in the first part, but in the juxtaposition of philosophy with criminality. That is, Anchises is the mouthpiece for a (lack of) Roman philosophy that turns instead toward the criminal.

19. Cf. Cicero's *De Re Publica*, in which the dream of Scipio undermines the coherence of Roman history with Platonic philosophy that the rest of the text tries to establish.

out as belonging to "others": sculpture, science, and rhetoric. Imperial authors strive to understand and articulate the ramifications of this split; they often return to images of spectacle and desert, and themes that express temporal disorientation. Vergil points the way when he has Jupiter promise Venus in Book 1 that the scope of Roman imperialism will be *imperium sine fine*, a world with no boundaries in time or space. The *Aeneid* delivers this arid space—as Lessing puts it, it took a Vergil to make it palatable—but shows through Anchises' Underworld communication with Aeneas the mental landscape that corresponds to it. Aeneas is the prototype of the Imperial subject; the exemplum of one who lives in the desert. Vergil transforms history into still-life; but still-life as spectacle, not imitation, because it portrays those in whom representation evokes no recognition.

III. Horace

In a contradictory pair of poems, *Odes* 1.12 and 29, Horace elaborates on the connection between *imperium sine fine* and the arts that the Romans lack. The first expresses in hyperbolic terms the extent of Augustus's power as Jupiter's regent on earth, with references to India and China, which had not become part of the Empire; 1.29 chides a friend for abandoning his philosophical pursuits for military ones: "Who would deny that downward-flowing rivers can climb up steep mountains and the Tiber reverse its course, when you, though you promised better things, strive to exchange for Spanish breastplates the Socratic school and books of noble Panaetius bought from everywhere?" (1.29.9–16). This poem indicates the incompatibility of philosophy and Empire, whereas 1.12 seems to extol only the virtues of Empire, with philosophy nowhere under consideration. One might attempt to explain the contradiction by noting that the *logos* of 1.12 is psychological rather than poetic, as Horace is overcome by the Imperial spirit.[20] But the culmination of 1.12 is the poet's request that Jupiter grant Augustus just triumphs and an equable rule: "Whether that one leads the Parthians in a just triumph, who threaten Latium, or the Chinese and Indians lying close to the Oriental shore, he will rule a fortunate world, in fairness, as your subordinate. You will shake Olympus with your heavy chariot; you will send your hostile thunderbolts upon the sacred groves that have been polluted" (1.12.53–60).

---

20. Hans Peter Syndikus, *Die Lyrik des Horaz. Eine Interpretation der Oden. Bd. I: Erstes und Zweites Buch* (Darmstadt: Impulse der Forschung 6, 1972), 152.

Like Anchises' description of Augustus, Horace's is part of a list of famous Romans whom he asks the Muse to help him choose for celebration. Of none of the others does he say anything about justice or piety; rather, it seems that the exploits of these men, which all have to do with the extension of Empire, lead to its ultimate expression in Augustan rule. In Augustus, justice and religion combine to make him the second-in-command of Jupiter, and legally sanctioned to conquer far-flung nations; but the nature of Jupiter changes when Horace praises him as a Roman god. In his Greek incarnation, the scope of his rule is spatially and temporally cosmic: "he who regulates the affairs of men and gods; the sea, lands, and world with the changing hours?" (*qui res hominum ac deorum, / qui mare et terras variisque mundum / temperat horis?*, 1.12.13–5). He rules nature not with justice or morality, but with a divine providence that has wisdom (Pallas) as its second-in-command. Horace repeats the combination of supreme/subordinate deity in the Roman Jupiter and Augustus, who, like Pallas, comes second to the highest divine authority; but Augustus and the god to whom he is subordinate represent conquest and punishment, not a natural order that comes about in its own time (*variisque...horis*) and the understanding thereof. Horace's Augustus/Jupiter combination fulfills Anchises' representation of the Romans as conquerors and punishers (*debellare...superbos*), not philosophers and poets.

In 1.12, Horace praises first Greeks, then Romans. The Greeks are either gods (Jupiter, Minerva, Bacchus, Diana, Apollo) or demi-gods (Hercules, Castor and Pollux). No men are praised until he comes to the Romans. The transition is made via a stanza that describes St. Elmo's fire, the natural phenomenon represented by Castor and Pollux, which seems out of place in the poem. David West interprets it as a "peaceful interlude"; Fraenkel as a reference to Augustus as a bringer of calm after the storm of war.[21] But Fraenkel admits that the connection between Augustus and the Dioscuri, and Augustus and Hercules, which is made explicit elsewhere by Horace, "will not be realized in *Odes* 1.12 unless the links between the descriptions of the various gods, heroes, and men and the subservience of all of them to a dominating idea are appreciated." Naturally, but the circular logic of this interpretation starts with the assumption of Augustus as the object of praise and refers everything back to him. There may be a more dominating idea at stake.

---

21. D. A. West, "The Bough and the Gate," in *Oxford Readings in Vergil's* Aeneid, ed. S. J. Harrison (Oxford: Oxford University Press, 1995), 58; Eduard Fraenkel, *Horace* (Oxford: Oxford University Press, 1981), 294.

The star of the Dioscuri heralds certain weather signs that sailors recognize. These are not in fact predictable, but happen *quom sic voluere* ("when they [the Dioscuri] will it," 1.12.31). The transition between Greeks and Romans therefore occurs through the medium of chance. When Horace comes to praise Romans, he has become uncertain and hesitates as to whom to praise first. The hesitation has roots in the tension between Rome's royal and Republican past, with the stanza consisting of the pairing of Romulus/Cato in the first and last lines, and Numa/Tarquin in the middle, and the Imperial future as embodied by a moral Augustus/Jupiter. In Romulus and Cato, the founding of Rome is paired with the death of the Republic; in Numa and Tarquin, the extremes of justice and injustice in regal behavior. The birth and death of pre-Imperial history act as parentheses around the kings, whose characteristics correspond to the ones we find embodied in Augustus a few stanzas later. With his transition, therefore, Horace implies that chance governs the world of both Greeks and Romans; but whereas the Greeks recognize its natural rhythms and their god works with it, the Romans impose upon it the logic of Imperial justice. This justice is born of Republican morality, represented by the choice of Republican heroes (e.g., the frugal Scaurus and Fabricius; the poor Curius and Camillus), and the justice of kings, represented by Numa (establishment of law, where in the first part of the poem there was none) and Tarquin (tyranny).

Marcellus provides the transition between Republican heroes and Augustus: "His fame grows like a tree in hidden time; the Julian star shines among the rest like the moon among lesser fires" (1.12.45–9). The Julian star recalls the star of the Dioscuri, but theirs is not "like" anything else, and it effects changes in the natural world, while the Julian one only looks good. The Greek phenomenon simply appears in the poem, as in life; the Roman one is an image. Augustus is therefore introduced as somehow not real, and the impression continues as his and Jupiter's rule become nearly one. Although Horace separates them by calling Augustus *minor*, this is only true because Augustus rules the earth while Jupiter rules Olympus. But their concerns are the same: Augustus will conquer everywhere because he is Jupiter's second, and Jupiter takes care of the morality that is Augustus's major concern. Unlike the relationship of Zeus and Pallas, in which the goddess sits next to Zeus but is completely unlike him, Augustus and Jupiter become virtually indistinguishable from one another; except for the fact that the one can effect changes on a larger scale, their method of rule is the same.

The "Julian star" refers to a comet that appeared each night of the games Octavian held four months after the death of Julius Caesar, which people interpreted as Caesar's immortalized soul. Horace makes the transition to Augustus not only via a simile. The star also metaphorically recalls the process of deification that culminates in his virtual inseparability from Jupiter in the last stanzas. In a simile, x is "like" y, but still different—e.g., the bizarre assimilation of the Julian star to the moon—; in metaphor, the star takes the place of the deification, and Augustus that of Jupiter. By the end of the poem, we see images that look real because there are no markers of their difference from non-images; but Horace has already indicated what is to come when at the beginning he calls himself a "playful echo" (*iocosa...imago*, 1.12.3–4) of Clio and, we understand, of Pindar, his model. The poem is an echo, or image, of something else; but until the last four stanzas, Horace uses metaphorical language only at the beginning, where he establishes the Pindaric tone. The similes at the end of the poem make of Augustus's family images at a second remove, with Augustus as both the ultimate signifier that has no referent, and the concealer of this development.

1.12 and 1.29 express the transition from Greece to Rome in terms of the loss of poetry and philosophy respectively. Both indicate the incompatibility of Empire with the arts that represent and illuminate the natural world, while 1.12 in particular emphasizes the imagistic quality of Empire that results from this loss. The perception of this era as a kind of freeze-frame is based on a perception of history that both Horace and Vergil represent as anachronistic, the problem epitomized by the demand made by Juno that the Trojans give up their name and language and mingle with the native Italian stock. In 3.3, for example, Horace's Juno makes Rome's Imperial success directly dependent upon the punishment of Troy, thereby collapsing history along with the Greek role in effecting this mythic event. After describing the sack of Troy, she says: "From this time forth (*protinus*) I shall relinquish my grave anger and shall give up to Mars the hated grandson whom the Trojan priestess bore..." (3.3.30–3). *Protinus* makes the coming of Romulus contemporaneous with the fall of Troy—it is as if Greece's conquest of Troy were directly responsible for Rome's conquest of Greece, along with the rest of the world.

In this "Roman" ode, Horace delineates the Imperial themes of 1.12 and 29 more clearly, as he shows in his overt reworking of a major event in Book 12 of the *Aeneid*. Whereas 1.12 echoes the list of heroes in Book 6, 3.3 follows more deliberately in Vergil's footsteps. For both poets, the Romans suffer an identity crisis. Their Trojan lineage gives them the gloss of culture, whereas the Italian stock with which it mingles provides the moral qualities—*pietas, frugalitas, fides, ius, castitas*—that they credit as the backbone of Empire. But as we see from both Vergil and Horace, the Trojan side snatches defeat from the jaws of victory: its history is over before it has even begun. Aeneas brings his *penates* from the Homeric world, but does not graft Homeric space onto Italian space. Greek culture goes underground along with the loss of the Trojan name and language, but in the resulting Roman race—a hybrid—the lack of the arts is concealed by the fantasy of a Greek past. It is this fantasy that Vergil and Horace represent through temporal anomaly, which leads to the vision of history as a series of panels, or pictures.

Vergil's Jupiter expresses the freeze-frame quality of Roman history in his famous promise to Venus: "I place (*pono*) upon them no boundaries of fortunes or time: I have given (*dedi*) them *imperium* without end" (1.278–9). In a boundless universe, there is no necessary interaction between things; no reason for any activity to take place in the way that it does. The shift from the present *pono* to the perfect *dedi* implies that the infinite setting for all the events in the *Aeneid* has already been put in place—they all unfold in a universe without causality. This suspicion is confirmed by Jupiter's complaint at the beginning of Book 10 that nothing is turning out the way he had intended: "'Great sky-dwellers, why have you changed your decision, competing now, with such opposing wills? I had denied that Italy make war on the Trojans. Why this conflict, against my orders?'" (10.6–9). The *imperium sine fine* that Jupiter has given the Romans is apparently greater than his own power to organize events.

With Anchises' announcement about what will and will not constitute Roman virtue, Vergil juxtaposes the split between politics and the arts with a perception of time Augustus more or less invents to create his Rome. The *Aeneid* is an open invitation to later writers to consider the consequences of this split for their own position within the Imperial system. He creates an anxiety of influence in which not he, but Augustus, is the "strong poet." When Calgacus calls the Roman mental landscape a "wasteland," he expresses through the voice of an outsider a view that Tacitus learned from Vergil, but through him Tacitus also represents for us only the space whose inside an outsider could not possibly represent. In Aeneas, Vergil makes a cipher through whom we perceive the problems that give Imperial space its peculiar, undelineated character; later authors understand and represent with varying degrees of ability their experience of what that space is like inside.

IV. Petronius

In the middle of the extant portion of Petronius's *Satyricon*, the protagonist, Encolpius, enters a picture gallery after an angry rampage around town. He sees depictions of various mortals who, though loved by the gods, suffered less than desirable fates: Ganymede snatched away by Zeus; Hylas ravished by the nymph; Hyacinth accidentally killed by Apollo. Each mortal suffers worse than the last, but Encolpius interprets the paintings through his own experience, bemoaning the fact that the gods were allowed to enjoy their beloveds free of rivals, whereas he himself has lost his young boyfriend to a treacherous companion. It was for this reason that he had been roaming the town, looking for fights with people and eventually having his sword taken from him by a passing soldier. He comes to the picture gallery in a calmer frame of mind, but the paintings stir his sense of injustice again: "Among which faces of painted lovers I cried out as if in a wasteland: 'So love after all touches even the gods. Jupiter did not find in his heaven what he was looking for, and ready to do wrong on earth he nevertheless did no injury to anyone...'" (83.4).

Encolpius's reaction is a parody of Aeneas's understanding of art. Standing in front of paintings in a gallery, he is like Aeneas at the temple of Juno; but he interprets them according to his own understanding of justice, not sympathy. In this sense his reaction reflects Aeneas's as he catches sight of Pallas's belt on Turnus. Aeneas follows up his interpretation of the belt with the irrational act of violence with which the poem ends and which renders every other act in the poem ambiguous; similarly, Encolpius adduces nonsensical reasons to justify the violent behavior of the gods: Jupiter did no one any harm, the nymph would never have harmed Hylas if she had known Hercules was coming for him, Apollo turned Hyacinth into a flower after killing him. This passage takes a jab at the function of art, both in its content (Encolpius's selfish reaction to the paintings) and form (its allusion to Vergil). The number of representations Encolpius sees do not create for him a plenitude—of meaning, experience, emotion—but rather a "wasteland," *solitudo*, that causes him to bemoan the only injustice he sees: he cannot get away with the same injustices as the gods. Petronius's picture gallery represents in visual terms the poetic wasteland of the *Aeneid*, which produces in the reader the sense that the story it recounts was over before it began, defined by its allusion to, but utter difference from, other stories. Both Vergil and Petronius link this experience with the notion of justice as the arbitrary exercise of power; thus, both suggest a rather bleak prospect for the artist. Yet the *Aeneid* and the *Satyricon* have been received, each in its own way, as enormously rich and influential texts. This tension between the wasteland that they describe and the representation of their own experience in it gives us an idea of the tensions at large in Imperial politics and ideology.

After Encolpius's viewing of the paintings, he encounters another character, Eumolpus, who tells him a ribald autobiographical story about a boy he once seduced. The boy turned the tables on him by demanding more sex than Eumolpus could give; in the end, Eumolpus was the one who threatened to tell the boy's father. This story contrasts human eros with the divine eros represented by the paintings. In his account of the paintings, Encolpius links eros with justice and punishment, and envies the gods for their ability to love—which also implies harm—with impunity. Encolpius's own love story is a tangled non-narrative, in which the lover makes one scene after another, but never fully realizes his goal of possessing Giton. Eumolpus's story cheers him up a good deal (*erectus his sermonibus*, 88.1), because he recognizes in it what he craves: the beloved both loved and threatened with punishment. In his story of the boy of Pergamum, Eumolpus combines Encolpius and the gods in the picture gallery in his own person.

If Encolpius's interpretation of the paintings parodies Vergil's representation of art, Eumolpus's story parodies the paintings. The prerogatives of divine eros become human, and degenerate into a dirty joke. Immediately thereafter, Encolpius asks for an account of the decline of painting. Eumolpus delivers a lecture about how love of money has led to the disappearance of philosophy and art; then, noticing that a painting of the fall of Troy has captured Encolpius's attention, he declaims a longish section of a poem on that subject, about the death of Laocoön. Eumolpus's lecture and poem juxtapose the current state of affairs with the story that accounts for their inception: imperial Rome and ancient Troy. It appears that while he has been talking, Encolpius's attention has wandered from the one to the other. It is a Freudian slip and suggests the truth of Eumolpus's account: the destruction of Troy, not money, destroyed Rome. His subsequent narration in poetic form of the events depicted vividly recalls Book 2 of the *Aeneid*, not, as has often been argued, to show off Petronius's own sense of "literary belatedness," but as an original interpretation of a major theme in the Vergilian text.[22] Eumolpus's suggestion that money ruined Rome is undercut by the similarities between

---

22. Catherine Connors, *Petronius the Poet: Verse and Literary Tradition in the* Satyricon (Cambridge: Cambridge University Press, 1998), 93.

his lecture and Anchises' speech in Book 6; its importance becomes clear at the very end of the extant text, when Eumolpus, Encolpius and Giton find themselves in the country of fortune-seekers, crows, and corpses; that is, they have come to Hades, and money, the fruit of Empire, keeps them there.

The *Satyricon* thoroughly examines the fundamental premise of the *Aeneid* both by imitation and parody. Although the structure of the whole is lost, it is possible to reproduce partially a significant element of it, which consists of the Iliadic story of the sack of Troy (Eumolpus's poem) and the wanderings of Odysseus (the boat journey and encounter with Circe). The *Satyricon* therefore represents both the texts represented in the *Aeneid* and the *Aeneid* itself as a separate text. This metatextuality points to some important external realities. In front of the Laocoön painting, we are once again in the temple of Juno looking, like Aeneas, at the sack of Troy; but Aeneas has no Eumolpus to tell him about what he sees. Vergil's reliefs are mute—we receive Aeneas's interpretation, but must wait for Vergil the narrator to provide all the pieces of the puzzle before we form any judgment of it. Petronius gives us the spectator Encolpius, who is also the narrator of the whole; Eumolpus as the narrator of the artwork; and the artwork itself. He suggests the complication of the relationship between representation and interpretation since his predecessor's era—more layers of imitation exaggerate the dreamlike or fictional quality of Imperial reality. Petronius's literal-minded interpretation of Vergil's freeze-frame narrative illustrates a further stage in the nightmare of Augustan political atemporality imagined by the latter: not only history but the mobility of perception have come to a standstill. The problem is also enacted at the dinner of Trimalchio, where the guests are repeatedly asked to look at the spectacle of food, yet eat nothing.[23]

We cannot know how the *Satyricon* really ended, but the end of the extant fragment puts the remaining characters in Croton, a town that parodies Rome in its obsession with seeking other people's inheritances. That Eumolpus should pose as a rich man in order to be wined and dined by hungry legacy-seekers is on the one hand a funny portrait of a phenomenon we know also from Martial and Juvenal. But Eumolpus gets himself into trouble when his ruse begins to be suspect. To ward off problems, he declares that no one will inherit his fortune unless they eat his dead body first; this will not be as hard

---

23. Tacitus describes something similar at Vitellius's visit to the battlefield at Bedriacum, *Histories* 2.70.1. The new emperor gazes greedily upon the sight, but although the corpses had been rotting there for around forty days, Tacitus makes no mention of the smell. A dead gaze, informed and enlightened by no other sense.

as it sounds, as several tribal peoples do it, and Roman generals besieging towns had often found that the inhabitants had taken to eating one another rather than surrender. The text ends with a particularly horrific depiction of the latter: soldiers entering a town where mothers hold half-eaten babies on their laps. Eumolpus wants to make a place where people metaphorically eat each other (feed on the legacies of the dead) a place where they literally do it, and he adduces as an example like himself the Roman generals who force foreign townspeople into cannibalism.[24] Croton is an Underworld which lacks all vestiges of civilization, as Eumolpus, Encolpius, and Giton are told by a man they meet before entering the town: "'You will approach a town that is like fields with plague, in which there is nothing but corpses which are torn or crows which tear them'" (116.9).

Croton is the oldest town in Italy, the three know, but they ask the man if there is anything left of it because it has been worn down by many wars. He tells them to go there if they are good-for-nothing liars, because Croton has no respect for the literary arts, eloquence, or old-fashioned mores (116.6). The ones who thrive there now are the lawyers who draft wills. In its behavior, Croton seems to be a vindication of Eumolpus's assertion that money has ruined the arts; but its history reminds us of that first arrival in Italy and the impulse to build a city there. At the end of this extant fragment, the characters terminate their journey where Aeneas did, and it is a hell that consigns the three to a perpetual fiction. The narrative of the *Satyricon* prepares for this moment in its

---

24. It has been suggested that the final speech in the extant text is delivered not by Eumolpus, but by a character named Gorgias, who appears at the end of the preceding fragment: *Gorgias paratus erat exsequi* ("Gorgias had been prepared to follow the funeral procession/follow up the argument," 141.5). Cf. Gian Biagio Conte, *The Hidden Author: An Interpretation of Petronius'* Satyricon, trans. Elaine Fantham (Berkeley: University of California Press, 1996), 135n.44, for a summary of the bibliography on this position. Conte also discusses the parallelisms between rhetoric and cookery, borrowed from Plato's *Gorgias*, that apply here: *inventio* will be needed to get the audience to "swallow" the proposition Eumolpus makes in his will. But Socrates uses the metaphor of the pastry cook in order to demonstrate how, in terms of the fitness of the soul, rhetoric is only the image of justice, just as for the body pastry baking is the image of medicine. Using Plato as a model, Petronius makes rhetoric an image that persuades people to eat not just an image of what is good for them (pastry)—this would be an ingestion of something external that damages the body—but to self-consume, or self-annihilate. At the end of the extant portion of the *Satyricon*, Petronius gives us rhetoric as the image of the image—the origin of the wasteland.

montage of scenes that allude to literary history and reveal what Petronius as external narrator understands as the political and ideological significance of his literary inheritance. The nature and form of Petronius's pastiche have been clearly and thoroughly studied; but such inquiries fall short of theorizing why such a text should exist and what its relevance within the realities of Imperial discourse might be. The cannibalism depicted in the scene of Croton is an apt metaphor for Petronius's Protean narrative, whose plot consists of fitting together representations of interpretations of other texts.[25] But this pastiche also has a plot of its own, which can be discerned in the arrangement of elements: the ostensible plot may make no sense, but, like the *Aeneid*, the internal logic of the text lies in the combination of themes.

We cannot relate the parts of the *Satyricon* to one another in terms of beginning, middle, and end; but we can preliminarily make connections between the extant portions that illuminate a possible thematic unity. If this unity is plausible, it responds to Anchises' assertion that the Romans will have no culture of their own. What we have of the text begins with Encolpius's denunciation of the state of rhetoric to a pseudo-orator, Agamemnon. In Encolpius's view, greatness in the literary arts has not been achieved since Thucydides and Hyperides—i.e., never in Rome—and the same is true of painting. For the latter he holds the Egyptians responsible, because they discovered a "short-cut of such a great art" (*tam magnae artis compendiarium invenit*, 2.9). Encolpius's addition of Egypt, almost as an afterthought, alludes to the problematic relationship between time and space that characterizes this stage of Imperial ideological development. Encolpius mentions Egypt because its corruption of painting also implies that of rhetoric. The hieroglyphic combination of painted image with written word collapses the possibilities of representation; it is a "short-cut" because the word becomes the thing. Thus Encolpius reaches both across the globe (the problems with rhetoric spread from Asia to Athens) and back into history (Egypt) to explain the intellectual blight, but the geography of his answers is indecisive and he resorts finally to a kind of "original sin" hypothesis.

For Encolpius, the Egyptian literal-mindedness is a mark of arrogance— *Aegyptiorum audacia*. But the *Satyricon* suggests just the reverse: it is Rome that has both the proliferation of representations and the dearth of intellectual imagination. When Encolpius and company visit the house of Trimalchio, they are immediately met with paintings of Trimalchio's life; the *Iliad*,

---

25. The stakes are surely higher than what Conte calls "descry[ing]...the outlines of the intellectual life of the early Empire." *The Hidden Author*, viii.

Odyssey, and gladiatorial games; and of a large dog that frightens Encolpius before he realizes it is just an image.[26] Much of the conversation at the dinner revolves around the inutility of learning, and Trimalchio declares that on his tombstone he wishes to have inscribed the fact that he never listened to a philosopher (71.12). The images in the entryway appear to mark a transition from an objective reality, however strange or confusing, to a world of radical subjective understanding, in which the narrator wonderingly hears stories and sees amazing things. In the last scene before the company encounter Trimalchio, Encolpius, with his highly-sexed companion Quartilla, peer through a keyhole at Giton and a young girl. The scene arouses them and they turn their attention to one another; that is, the eroticism of the external event prompts a similar response. At the dinner party, there are only images and stories that require subjective analysis. Outside Trimalchio's house, theft and sex are balanced by justice and religion: Encolpius and Ascyltos get into trouble over a stolen cloak, and are punished by Quartilla for not honoring Priapus. Social parameters appear to be upheld, whereas inside Trimalchio's house the (dis)order is an excess of food and money—we seem literally to enter the house of Wealth, Pluto, Hades, through a gateway of images.

The *Satyricon* illustrates, however, the illusory or fictional nature of the distinction between objective and subjective. The world that Petronius represents as outside Trimalchio's house is only a space in which we pretend that social norms and narratives apply. After Trimalchio's party, we tumble headlong into a metafictional world in which escape from representation and interpretation is impossible. The *Satyricon* represents the *Aeneid*, which represents by imitation its own difference from the *Iliad* and *Odyssey*. Petronius illustrates the difference between the Vergilian and Homeric epics by adding paintings of gladiatorial games to those of the *Iliad* and *Odyssey* on one side of Trimalchio's entryway. In the *Aeneid*, no one learns by suffering to be just or wise, as is shown by its arrangement of the Homeric poems: first comes the *Odyssey*, which in Homer's rendition sends the hero away at the end after he has made provision for the rule of his son and the end of stasis in his kingdom. In the *Aeneid*, the hero completes his journey only to cause war, at the end of which there is no return and burial of his enemy's body. The lack of burial is what makes Aeneas's violence, unlike Achilles', mere cruelty. He and Turnus become fighters of the arena, not Homer's battlefield; what we see on Trimalchio's wall are not three separate representations, but one—that of the *Aeneid*.

---

26. On Encolpius in the role of spectator/interpreter, see Niall Slater, *Reading Petronius* (Baltimore: Johns Hopkins University Press, 1990), 57f.

205

In the juxtaposition of *Iliad* and *Odyssey* with gladiatorial scenes, Petronius takes us from fiction to spectacle within the context of an image that is part of a fiction—a gesture that recalls a type of punishment made popular by Nero, in which the criminal took part in a play that ended with his death. The gladiatorial games become the emblem not only of inseparability between violence and spectacle in the Empire, but also of Empire itself as a spectacle that entails violence. Further, it is a spectacle that excludes the representational, communicative, and intellectual arts, and that Petronius ultimately depicts as funerary. At Trimalchio's party, the guests' hands are washed in wine by Ethiopian slaves of the sort who sprinkle perfume at the arena (34.4). Immediately thereafter, Trimalchio meditates upon the brevity of human life versus the longevity of wine, a silver skeleton is brought in and laid upon the table, and Trimalchio declaims a little *carpe diem* poem; whereupon a carver begins his work like a gladiator practicing to a water-organ (36.6).[27] The extravagance of action and material goods in Trimalchio's house reflects the condition of Empire: Trimalchio is a parody both of Empire, in the extraordinary rise of his fortune gained from abroad (76), and of the emperor, in the designation of his slaves as members of a *decuria*, and in the extent of his estate: "[My new suburban villa] is said to be adjoining Tarracina and Tarentum. Now I want to link up Sicily with these plots, so that when I want to go to Africa, I'd be sailing through my own boundaries" (48.2–4).

Funerals and the funerary form a running theme in the scene of Trimalchio's dinner party, which ends with Trimalchio having his will read and giving instructions for his burial. Structurally, this long episode prepares us for the civil war poem of Eumolpus and the group's subsequent adventures in Croton. Eumolpus is a pseudo-poet as Agamemnon is a pseudo-orator and Trimalchio a pseudo-philosopher: all three display (non) abilities in each of these disciplines, but Petronius accords each a dominant claim to one discipline, and thereby demarcates the major sections of the text. Agamemnon's debate on education introduces the legal troubles experienced by Encolpius and Ascyltos over a stolen tunic, as well as their culpability in defiling Quartilla's rites for Priapus, for which she exacts punishment. Trimalchio both eschews philosophy and introduces himself as a philosopher, in his explanation of a course set out like the zodiac. The dinner party scene carries a running commentary on the status of education in literature, philosophy, and oratory, and the inutility of these for the entrepreneur. Ironically, the frescoes opposite those of the *Iliad* and *Odyssey* depict Trimalchio's life, in one of

---

27. For Trimalchio's obsession with time, cf. Slater, *Reading Petronius*, 55.

which he enters Rome under the protection of Minerva, who acts as the patroness both of resource and wisdom. He holds a *caduceus*, usually the property of Mercury for conducting souls to the Underworld, while Mercury himself appears in the climax of the series, helping Trimalchio up to an official's tribunal. The frescoes imply that Trimalchio represents the new Roman, whose world is that of the image.

In the final part of the extant fragment, the poet Eumolpus first makes a speech about the decline of painting, then recites a poem about the fall of Troy. There ensues the narrative of a sea voyage, after which Eumolpus speaks about the appropriate mode and subject matter for epic poetry, and then recites his poem about the civil war. The two poems form bookends to the story of Roman history, in which on the one hand the Romans as Trojans died before being born, and on the other end up killing each other, as they killed those whom they were to become when they first arrived in Italy.[28] The decline of painting lecture leads to the fall of Troy, which looks like the truth about the corruption of Rome. This seems particularly plausible in light of the fact that Encolpius has been looking at paintings about love—*amor*—before Eumolpus's lecture, and so would be looking at its inverse—*Roma*—afterward.

In his introduction to the civil war poem, Eumolpus asserts that epic poetry should be free from the strictures of historical fact and should properly deal with divinity and prophecy (118.6). However, his own poem mostly does the reverse: it narrates many true things about Rome and Caesar, but of the gods mentions only those of the Underworld, or those put to flight by it (120–21; 124). In these sections, Dis is depicted as opening up and sending forth what is usually hidden: "Lo, [the Romans] seek my kingdom. Earth dug up yawns with their insane efforts; now the caves groan with the mountains swallowed up, and while my stone finds empty uses, the infernal shades express their hope of heaven..." (120.90–93). The greatest crime of civil war is the loss of the sacred, which is exactly what the travelers discover when they arrive in Croton, the land of cannibalism. Croton corresponds to some of the most powerful material in the preceding poem, which treats events and attitudes more or less accurately; that is, as *res gestae*, which Eumolpus had said did not constitute poetry. Croton represents the history—the actuality—of what Eumolpus has attempted to poetize, and the two together illustrate how civil war and cannibalism are the ultimate forms of imperialism.

---

28. Vergil could have had Aeneas and his men go straight to Evander, alliance, and the actual site of Rome, thereby avoiding all conflict with the Latins.

Chapter Fourteen

Review of *Achilles and Hector: The Homeric Hero*

Steven Berg

At the age of twenty-five Seth Benardete presented his Ph.D. dissertation on Homer's *Iliad* to his committee at the University of Chicago. That dissertation has now been published posthumously as a book under its original title—*Achilles and Hector: The Homeric Hero*. This is only fitting, since the work exceeds in a startling way all measures established for the assessment of the performance of doctoral candidates. It is, in fact, the first fruit of a mind of extraordinary power, capable of producing, at an age when most are idle or halting, an indispensable guide to Homer's craft and thought. In the broad field of Homer scholarship it finds its match only in the study of the *Odyssey* that the same author completed in the last years of his life.

According to the young Benardete, Homer's work is structured around two central themes: the true character of heroic virtue and the nature of the difference between the virtue of the hero or "real man" (*anēr*) and that of a human being (*anthrōpos*) in the proper or "absolute" sense (16–17). Homer uncovers the former through displaying the identity of Achilles and Hector and the latter through articulating the difference between Achilles and Odysseus.

As Benardete shows, the heroes of the *Iliad* live in the light of the distinction between *andres* and *anthrōpoi* (11–17). This distinction is dependent upon the intimacy which the heroes enjoy with the gods. They are their offspring and special care: the gods' providence extends really only to the hero and only to the hero at war; mere human beings are left to the vicissitudes of chance (15, 77–84). This providence, however, is the ground of what Ben-

Reprinted from *The Review of Metaphysics* 60, no. 2 (2006): 387–89. Page numbers in parentheses refer to *Achilles and Hector: The Homeric Hero* (South Bend: St. Augustine's Press, 2005).

ardete calls "the paradox of heroic virtue" (77): on the one hand, the providence of the gods supports heroic virtue—through the beautification of their deaths and the moral limits they set on their conduct in battle, the gods prevent the "great-spiritedness" of the heroes from degenerating into bestial cruelty and bloodthirstiness (81, 45–46); on the other hand, their intervention in the combat nullifies the operations of heroic virtue and substitutes for it something that is indistinguishable from chance (77–88). The presence of the gods makes possible and impossible the manifestation of heroic virtue.

The solution to this impasse, Benardete understands Homer to suggest (Books V–VII), appears when the gods retreat and the principle of the war is displaced from that of justice to the pursuit of immortal fame (85–88). Fame, as the object of the heroes' ambition, serves, as did the presence of the gods, to beautify the heroes' death and ennoble their bloody contest, but also allows, as the presence of the gods did not, for the means to that beauty and nobility to be the actions of the heroes themselves, unobscured by divine interference. Hector embodies this desire for immortal fame at its maximum (85).

Achilles, however, remains the fly in the ointment. For, though his retreat from the war parallels the retreat of the gods and likewise makes possible the manifestation of "the worth of each hero," the cause of his retreat is the principle of justice (93, 96): he claims rightful ascendancy over Agamemnon's ancestral authority on the basis of his natural power and pre-eminence—"the right of natural right" (29–34, 135). On this basis, Achilles rejects the plea of the embassy of the Achaeans that he re-enter the war. Untempted by fame, he insists that his virtue is honored not by men, but by Zeus, and not in its performance, but in its divine "absoluteness" (97–98). Through Achilles' insistence that he is honored as a god, Homer shows the ambition of all heroic virtue: the attempt to leave behind humanity in the ascent to divinity (65, 75–76). The whole of the *Iliad* is an "experiment in immortality" (72, 105) that displays the tragic consequences of this ambition.

Benardete shows how the progressive isolation of the hero on the way to divinity coincides with the sloughing off of the constraints of "civil shame" or the "concern with those weaker than oneself" (100–101). This abandonment of shame, however, results not in the hero's ascent beyond the human, but his descent into the sub-human monstrosity of the Cyclopes. Both Achilles and Polyphemus are without mercy and both "consult only their *thymos*." "Polyphemus is...the brute perfection of Achilles, Achilles without weakness, without Patroclus" (101–2). Patroclus proves to be the last tie to humanity that Achilles cannot break and that ultimately returns him from the monstrous to civil shame and humanity, though only after his own anger has effectively destroyed him (113–14).

It would appear then that Hector—"a civil Achilles, an Achilles who has not lost his . . . shame" (101)—embodies the solution to the problem of Achilles and thus the truth of heroic virtue. In one of the most brilliant turns in the argument of the book, however, Benardete shows how Hector's civil shame proves to be the ground of his ultimate identity with Achilles. It is this shame which, during the Trojan rout before Achilles' onslaught, makes it impossible for him to return to the city and face the ridicule of the men of Troy. It compels him to stand his ground and face death at Achilles' hands, a death which, though guaranteeing his own immortal fame, seals the doom of his city and condemns his own "Patroclus" (his wife Andromache) to slavery. Hector's shame and his thirst for immortal fame combine to cut his ties to the human with an even more effective ruthlessness than his nemesis and counterpart. Achilles and Hector are one in their Cyclopean isolation, and heroic virtue is identical to bestial vice (121–24).

The hero's ambition to become a god, according to Benardete, culminates not only in the bestial, but in the will to be a thing (51, 55–57, 113–14). The identity of arms and the man that heroic virtue posits (40–43) entails the desire to become an artifact of Hephaestus. For Homer, however, Hephaestus is not only the divine blacksmith; he is another name for fire, and fire is that to which, in their wrath (*thymos*), Achilles and Hector are most often compared (61). "The heroes burn with [Hephaestus'] fire as they wield his weapons. . . . To be his work and to work with his fire would seem to be the aim of heroic virtue" (62).

In this aspiration to the artificial and elemental, Achilles becomes "as anonymous as Odysseus" (51–52, 119–20). But Achilles' anonymity is of a wholly different order than that of Odysseus: it is the mindless anonymity of a self-canceling thymos, aspiring to a solitude so perfect that it aims to roll up the past in order to free itself from the determinations of its origins (64–65). The "namelessness" of Odysseus—he is "no one" as he cunningly declares to Polyphemus in plotting his escape from the Cyclopes' cave—is the sign of his liberation from the determinations of the ancestral not in deed, but in speech and thought: it is the anonymity of mind (30–31). The anonymity of mind proves to be the truth of the aspirations of heroic virtue. But the excellence of Odysseus does not belong to the same world as that of Achilles and the heroes (16). Though Achilles' virtue is superior to, as encompassing of, all the virtues of the other heroes, no separate measure is required to make clear its supremacy (3). In the case of Odysseus this is not so. He is singular in a way that the hero can never be. He is "an *anthrōpos* not only as opposed to the gods... but absolutely so" (16), and his humanity is exhibited not only in his powers of speech and mind, but in his rejection of the goal toward which all heroic virtue is poised: he chooses mortality over immortality—to be a human being rather than a thing (67).

Chapter Fifteen

Review of *Achilles and Hector:*
The Homeric Hero

Bryan Warnick

Seth Benardete (1930–2001) was one of the twentieth century's premiere scholars of the classical world. His prominence was largely due to his technical excellence in both ancient philosophy and classical philology, a rare combination that allowed him to become, as Harvey Mansfield has written, "Our greatest student of the relation between poetry and philosophy."[1] He wrote groundbreaking discussions of Greek literature (especially the tragedies) and the Platonic dialogues. His work culminated in his study of *The Odyssey*, *The Bow and the Lyre* (1997), a book that compared the plot of epic poetry to the development of a Platonic dialogue.

Before Benardete achieved lasting fame, however, he was a doctoral student at the University of Chicago, working with Leo Strauss and the Committee on Social Thought and developing friendships with people like Allan Bloom. The writing of his dissertation is the stuff of scholarly legend. According to the story, it developed from a pile of nonsensical notes on the *Iliad* to a work of budding genius in four weeks. This dissertation, "Achilles and Hector: The Homeric Hero," was published in *St. John's Review* in 1985, and it has now been reprinted so that we can examine for ourselves the significance of Benardete's early work.

As the title suggests, Benardete's dissertation looks at the theme of heroism in Homer, focusing on the *Iliad*. He examines the relationships between

Reprinted from *The Journal of Aesthetic Education* 40, no. 3 (Fall 2006): 115–19. Page numbers in parentheses refer to *Achilles and Hector: The Homeric Hero* (South Bend: St. Augustine's Press, 2005).

1. In a remark about Benardete's study of the *Odyssey* (on the back cover of *The Bow and the Lyre*), cited in Ronna Burger's memorial essay for Benardete. [http://www.benardetearchive.org/about_benardete/biography.html.]

the poem's smallest parts and its largest themes. The book is divided into two sections. In the first section, Benardete grapples with how the small components of the *Iliad*, the epithets and similes, work together meaningfully to inform the larger heroic themes of the epic. The second section examines Homer's view of the tragic hero through an analysis of the plot. The analytic skill exhibited in both sections is fascinating: some parts of the study are brilliant, others strained, but none are boring.

Benardete's purpose in the first section, he says, is to "vindicate the epithets" (125). This vindication is necessary because, as scholarship on the oral nature of the Homeric epics has developed, the significance of the smaller components has seemed to diminish. The epithets and similes have come to be seen as mere crutches for the oral poet; they are linguistic tools whose characteristics allow them to be plugged into Homer's unrelenting dactylic hexameter whenever a particular rhythmic pattern is needed. The poet uses the epithet of "swift-footed" Achilles, then, not so much because he particularly wants to say something meaningful about Achilles' swiftness, but because the particular rhythmic pattern of the epithet is a handy way to complete a line of poetry. The meaning of things like the epithets in any particular moment, it has seemed to many, should therefore be taken with a grain of salt. In contrast, Benardete wants to argue that each particular use of an epithet has a significant meaning that informs, and even constructs, the epic's larger themes (for Benardete's purpose, the theme of heroism).

Benardete's success in this goal is somewhat uneven, as even he later came to realize. A few of his conclusions appear rather stretched and neglect to consider the whole in the analysis of the parts. For example, Benardete looks at the Trojan epithets *megathymoi* ("great spirited") and *hippodamoi* ("tamers of horses") and finds them to be two manifestations of a constant Trojan character. One epithet is for the activities of war (*megathymoi*), the other one for peace (*hippodamoi*). But for Benardete they both say the same thing about the constantly emotional, almost animalistic nature of Homer's Trojans, who are perfectly defined by passionate warfare: "The Trojans are more readily affected than the Achaeans, who can remove their armor and be different in peace than in war: but the Trojans cannot so easily shake off their temper" (21). While certainly interesting, such an analysis neglects to take into account prominent scenes like the one in which Astyanax, Hector's son, cries at the sight of Hector dressed in his battle gear, implying that this Trojan has been disfigured and changed by war. For Hector, the leader of the Trojan army, there is a great difference between his nature at war and his nature at peace.

At other moments, however, Benardete's conclusions are keen and insightful. He looks at the epithet "swift-footed," which, he admits, seems to occur in "reckless profusion" (47). Achilles is given this epithet, as are many other characters, both human and animal. Even characters as different as Hector and Paris are assigned this description. Surely, we might think, this little phrase must not be so meaningful. Benardete argues, though, that swift-footedness is used to tie together certain groups for the purpose of comparison. The description of swiftness ties together Achilles, Hector, and Paris:

> Critics have been annoyed that Hector obtains the same simile [as Paris]...and yet the reason for the repetition is not hard to find. Both are equally swift but exultant differently. Paris, godlike in Beauty, flashing like the sun and "smiling with self-satisfaction," puts on beautiful armor; while Hector returns to the fight after being almost mortally wounded, with renewed strength. Paris is beautiful like Nireus, Hector like Ajax: even in war Paris has the glitter of peace, even in a lull Hector terrifies his son.... They stand at the two poles of heroic excellence, beauty and power, which are fused in Achilles. (49)

Through the use of the common designation "swiftness," Homer creates a group for comparison that serve to highlight differences. They are all swift, but swiftness is for one character tied to a shallow beauty, for another to an irresistible power, and for yet another to a perfect combination of both beauty and power.

Another example of Benardete's analytic skill is demonstrated in a discussion of gods and heroes. Benardete notices that similes surrounding the deaths of warriors are almost never present when the gods have withdrawn themselves from combat. When the gods are absent from the battlefield, death is only clinically described; when the gods are present, death is adorned by simile. Death does not simply come to Crethon and Orsilochus, then, when they die in the presence of gods; rather, they are compared to "two lions who, having caught sheep and cattle, are slain at last by men, and they fall like tall pines" (79). Benardete writes, "Their death appears not only as itself but as something else: doubled in the simile's reflection, it magically loses all its horror, becoming beautiful and almost pleasant" (79). He concludes that the gods "transfigure death, which is, without them unfeigned, but in their presence more poetic" (122). By looking closely at Homer's use of simile, Benardete powerfully affirms the heroes' dependency on the divine.

As a final example of Benardete's skilled reading ability, consider his analysis of the discus that Achilles awards during the funeral games of Patroclus. Homer remarks that the discus is from the city of Eetion, a place that the Achaeans and Achilles had gloriously sacked in the early stages of their expedition. Rather than letting this detail pass by, Benardete shows how the history of the discus connects deeply to Achilles' character. He points out that everything else we know about the city of Eetion—that it is the former home of Chryseis, Andromache, and the horse Pedasus, and the original location of Achilles' lyre—connects to the series of mistakes Achilles commits throughout the poem:

> The return of Chryseis provoked Agamemnon and led to his taking Briseis, who came from Lymessus near Thebes (the city of Eetion); Andromache, the wife of his enemy, stood for Patroclus in the story of Phoenix; the lyre showed us Achilles' inaction and the wasting of his virtue; the death of Pedasus, as that of Patroclus, was the death of the mortal Achilles, and the mass of iron, which he may not toss, stress again Achilles' idleness. (128)

The discus, which reminds us of Achilles' greatest exploit in sacking Eetion, also seems to embody his failures. Benardete sees this as emblematic of the tragedy of Achilles: "He must even in war, while he proves himself virtuous, collect the symbols of his future doom." He concludes that Achilles is "never apart from his destiny: the seeds of his wrath, his isolation, and his guilt were contained in the evidence of his prowess" (128).

The significance Benardete finds in seemingly meaningless details, then, is remarkable. He has a keen eye for subtle connections among different passages and for subtle difference among similar passages. He is able to catch meaning in the continual repetition and cessation of epithets and similes. For this reason alone, the book should be read by anyone with a serious interest in epic poetry. But it would also be beneficial for any student of the humanities to read, not because all of Benardete's conclusions are correct, but because he shows himself to be a model of close and careful reading. Benardete simply assumes that every piece of the *Iliad* is important and tries to connect the pieces into meaningful wholes. The results speak for themselves. Students could benefit from being exposed to this sort of engagement with a text.

Apart from helping us to understand the text of the *Iliad* and serving as a model of close reading, does Benardete's book have any larger significance? Does his reading of Homer say anything of interest about issues of human concern? I believe it does. Benardete's exercises in close reading develop his larger argument about the paradoxical nature of heroism. The Homeric hero is the embodiment of contradiction. The Homeric hero stands in a strange limbo between the gods, ordinary men, and animalistic impulse. They are driven by fate yet remain responsible for their actions. Their success depends on the gods, yet they claim glory and honor for what they do. The heroes depend on their communities for honor and prestige, yet they must also stand independent from their communities in important ways. In winning virtue, they sow the seeds of their destruction.

Benardete shows that the Homeric heroes must align themselves with multiple ideals and that these ideals cannot easily coexist. In the end of the *Iliad*, as Hector faces Achilles, they both are representatives of their heroic failures, but these are failures that are brought about by the tensions within the heroic code itself. By angrily standing apart from battle to maintain his honor, and by allowing Patroclus to enter combat in his stead, Achilles has not been sufficiently sensitive to the shame that should come from neglecting one's comrades-in-arms. Hector, in turn chooses to face Achilles rather than risk the shame of the people of Troy. In direct contrast with Achilles, Hector is *overly* wary of shame and thus forfeits the only real chance to defend Troy. Benardete writes:

> Although [Hector] cares more for Andromache than for the rest of Troy, he prefers to act rashly than to save even her; for to maintain his own self-esteem exceeds all other cares. In this respect he resembles Achilles, who had cherished anger, though it meant death to the Achaeans, and now belatedly defends them for the sake of Patroclus. ... Hector has become an alien because of his shame, Achilles was isolated from the Achaeans out of shamelessness. Both are driven to a combat each had sought to avoid. Achilles' vain effort to re-establish his honor corresponds to Hector's attempt to correct his mistake: as if Achilles could balance the death of Hector against the loss of Patroclus, and Hector, in clinging to his civil shame, could maintain his renown. ... Each has made his own excellence contradict itself. In his desire to be the perfect hero, each has ceased to be a hero at all. (121-22)

Benardete points out persuasively, then, how the hero is in a no-win situation. A strict integrity with regard to one ideal compromises another ideal. Hector would be shamed by a lack of courage in failing to meet Achilles, but meeting Achilles means that he violates his responsibility to his city. Achilles could have properly aided his comrades-in-arms, but doing so would have shown weakness in his dispute with Agamemnon. In such contradictions can be found the tragedy of the Homeric hero. Within a hero is the negation of the hero.

Benardete does not discuss the significance of his work beyond simply understanding Homer. The hero, however, has been an important theme in the work of some of Benardete's friends and colleagues at the University of Chicago, most famously in Alan Bloom's book, *The Closing of the American Mind* (1988). In his controversial best-seller, Bloom bemoans the demystification of heroism in contemporary society. Bloom may be right or wrong in his analysis, but I believe he certainly could have benefited from an engagement with detailed discussions of heroism like that found in Benardete. He could have discussed, for example, this tragic element of heroism. For Homer and for us, heroism not only seems to demand tragic and perilous circumstances for its existence, but it also usually involves strict allegiance to principles that will necessarily conflict. Worries about a culture of heroism go beyond the modern demystifiers that Bloom despises in contemporary universities; Homer himself worried about such things.

The themes Benardete addresses are significant in other ways. Benardete not only has much to say about heroes but also the context in which heroes are found. He traces with intricate detail how the rationale for the Trojan War changes during the *Iliad*. At first it is a dispute about Helen. As that rationale for war diminishes, however, the war becomes an arena for the winning of honor. And finally, it becomes a revenge match again, but not between Menelaus and Paris. The war, in the end of the *Iliad*, is all about Achilles and his search for vengeance. In tracing this development, Benardete not only helps us to understand the *Iliad*, but also to understand the nature of warfare. World history and Benardete's Homer unite to show us that war has a momentum of its own; rationales given for war at first will not be those given at the end. Even when original justifications for war become publicly recognized as flawed or irrelevant, one should not expect the conflict to draw to its logical closure. The practice of warfare will itself have created a multitude of reasons to keep on fighting, be it for vengeance, greed, or shame. "From personal revenge to impersonal ambition and back again to revenge is the *Iliad*'s plot,"

Benardete writes. "The love for Helen turns into the love for fame, which in turn becomes Achilles' love for Patroclus" (90). One reason for war spawns others; war breeds its own rationalizations. Perhaps we are not so distant from the Greeks and Trojans as we might expect. Benardete does well to warn us about ourselves.

Chapter Sixteen

On the Being of
The Being of the Beautiful

Michael Davis

khalepa ta kala

I.

Seth Benardete's *The Being of the Beautiful* combines a precise translation and a comprehensive analysis of the three Platonic dialogues: *Theaetetus, Sophist*, and *Statesman*. The book brings to mind two questions, one
specific and one general. As the subject matter of none of the three dialogues seems on the surface to be the beautiful (Benardete implies as much
by prefacing his book with an interpretation of Plato's *Hippias Major*, of
which the explicit theme is the beautiful), why is *The Being of the Beautiful*
an appropriate title? And why is a book which contains so little technical
vocabulary as to be almost idiomatic in its parts, so difficult to grasp as a
whole?

These two questions, while not the same, are connected to one another
by the question of appearance. Benardete calls our attention to the connection
between the beautiful and appearance in a section of his analysis of the *Hippias* called "The Seemly."

> The beautiful has so far come to light as something that is both
> complete in itself and a pointer beyond itself.... The beautiful,
> then, looks as if it is the impossible togetherness of the necessarily
> apart. Deceptiveness belongs to the beautiful in truth; it is the

Reprinted from *Ancient Philosophy* 7 (1987), 191–200. Page numbers in parentheses
refer to *The Being of the Beautiful: Plato's "Theaetetus," "Sophist," and "Statesman"*
(Chicago: University of Chicago Press, 1984).

necessary consequence of its privileged position as the unique being which discloses itself in perception. (xxxiv)

And somewhat later in the same section,

Beautiful things declare in their appearance that they are beautiful. Appearance conveys the message of being. (xxxvi)

The beautiful then calls attention to the importance of appearance. Philosophy's ultimate question would seem to be, What is Being?, but for us who ask about being the question of knowledge comes first (I.85). The question is never simply being, but also asking. Wonder about being leads to wonder about wondering, that is, about the way in which being appears or does not fully appear. This in turn leads to wonder about what it is about being that makes it appear as it does. If the beautiful accounts for why beings appear as they do, it would seem to be the "being of the beings" (xv). *The Being of the Beautiful* then would be about the being of the being of the beings, that is, about the way it is possible to say that being is. While this comes close to a conventional understanding of the concern if not of the whole trilogy, at least of the *Sophist*, it does not account for why, if this is his central concern, Benardete does not simply identify it in the traditional way. This brings us back to the question of the difficulty of his book. Why is it written as it is? What necessity makes it appear as it appears? What is the being of *The Being of the Beautiful*?

This problem could be stated in a different way. In the *Theaetetus* Socrates raises the question, What is knowledge? The question suggests that we cannot know the beings until we know something about knowing, and so about the being in which knowing comes to be. Self-knowledge seems to be the necessary precondition for knowledge of being. On the one hand, Socrates seems to have discovered the priority of epistemology to metaphysics. The *Theaetetus* precedes the *Sophist*. On the other hand, Socrates has discovered that self-knowledge, knowing who we are, is connected with knowing where we are and at what time we are (unlike Theodorus Socrates is interested in all the local gossip); he has discovered the power of *doxa* and so of "orthodoxy." Plato has learned from Socrates the importance of political philosophy. And so the *Sophist* must be read in light of the *Statesman*. The separation of the issues of the two dialogues is only apparent. The *Theaetetus*, where metaphysics and political philosophy are already together, is therefore not simply an inquiry preliminary to raising the question of the *Sophist*. Socrates' penultimate question is his ultimate question. Understood correctly the problem of appearing is the problem of being. What holds the three dialogues together is the centrality of appearance.

II.

The connection between the problem of writing and the problem of appearance is one with which Benardete, following Plato, begins.

> All Platonic dialogues are written, but only the *Theaetetus* presents most of itself as written. Its author is not Plato. The voice is the voice of Plato, but the hand is the hand of Euclides. (I.85)

The dramatic structure of the *Theaetetus* is difficult. There was an original conversation between Socrates, Theodorus, and Theaetetus shortly before Socrates' trial. Socrates then related this conversation before his death in a series of conversations he had with Euclides. Euclides took notes on these conversations and then transformed these notes into a dialogue in which the fact that he was not present and the fact that he has gotten his information from a narration are suppressed. We therefore witness the transformation of a real event into an account of the event and finally into an account of the event that presents itself as though it were the real event. We are given all the intermediate steps so as to see that what we finally get cannot help but be quite deceiving, albeit quite like a Platonic dialogue. But Euclides presents Socrates' interpretation of what happened as what happened. He makes the mistake that characterizes the mathematicians, Theodorus and Theaetetus; he takes for granted the possibility of a true account because he suppresses his own role as an account giver.

> In calling our attention to the dialogue as written, and the almost Thucydidean effort Euclides spent on translating his notes into a complete record, Plato rehearses on the level of historiography the problem with which the dialogue deals. Does the recording of what happened stand to what happened as the knowledge of what is stands to what is? (I.87–88)

Any account must stand apart from what it is an account of in order to serve as its description. If it loses this apartness it cannot be an adequate re-presentation. It would be indistinguishable from that of which it was supposed to be the representation. Where this apartness is lacking there can be no reasoning and without reasoning there is no knowledge. On the other hand this very distance ensures that all reasoning will be subject to distortion; it will be imperfect reasoning. Socrates' narration is in a mediate relation to the conversation it describes. Euclides' dialogue presents that conversation as though it were actually happening, suppressing the difference of space and time. He thus unwittingly represents for us the problem of the dialogue he has written: how to represent the immediate.

Benardete shows this problem reemerging in a variety of ways within the dialogue. To persuade Theaetetus to converse, Socrates must convince him to feel secure enough to assert what he admittedly does not know. Toward that end Socrates introduces the image of himself as a midwife of the offspring of the soul. His purpose is two-fold. On the one hand he lays claim to an art so as to convince Theaetetus that he is competent or experienced. On the other hand Socrates asserts his own barrenness of offspring so as to assure Theaetetus that he has no experience of his own to prefer. Socrates' image, therefore, is an impossible combination of things necessarily apart. He must claim both innocence and experience, the former to assure the purity and the latter to provide the content for his knowledge.

The difference between knowledge understood as opinion and knowledge understood as perception runs parallel to the distinction between narration and dialogue and the distinction between experience and innocence. That knowledge is perception, Theaetetus's claim in the first part of the dialogue, has an immediate appeal because we sense that knowledge has to be an account of what is and that perception is a passive rendering of what is as it is. Instead of examining this view directly Socrates connects it with Protagoras's doctrine that man is the measure of all things. Protagoras's view, in turn, undergoes a series of revisions that lead finally to Homer and Heraclitus. The buck continues to get passed because the view that perception is knowledge is something one could never know directly from experience. Theaetetus had to learn it from a book.

Benardete points out that there are two ways in which human beings might be the measure of all things. On the one hand things might be only as they are for me. So I am the measure in the sense that I make the world what it is. But then everything in the world would be perfectly as I made it. While I would be the measure, I could never know that I was the measure. On the other hand, suppose that it means something to me that I am the measure,

suppose it gives me a certain self-confidence, then I can be that kind of measure, a term of distinction, only if I am not the measure of all things, that is,
only if I feel some resistance from the world. It looks, therefore, as though
either I am the measure of my world and cannot say so or I am not the measure of my world and so can claim to be. In response to Socrates' suggestion
that Theaetetus was in labor, the boy had said, "I do not know, Socrates, what,
however, I've experienced I say."

How is this connected to the question of knowledge and perception? It
is tempting to identify knowledge with perception because of the purity and
immediacy of the relation between the perceiver and what is. But if the relation of the perceiver to what is were that pure and immediate the question of
knowledge would never even come up. If we formed our world we would not
be in it. Protagoras is, therefore, made an issue in the *Theaetetus* because, by
attempting to combine the two notions of measure, he points to the fact that
we assert the first, the measure as universally determining what is, in order
to affirm the second, the measure as allowing me to do what I wish. Socrates
introduces Protagoras in order to show that Theaetetus's innocent epistemology conceals Protagoras's sophisticated power politics.

At the center of the *Theaetetus* there is a long digression on the nature of
philosophy. Benardete points out that this depiction of the philosopher looks
much more like Theaetetus or Theodorus than Socrates. This philosopher is
so detached from the world, he so little "knows his way to the marketplace,"
that he could never understand politics well enough to present the argument
about the difference between the political man and the philosopher in which
he is disclosed. His purity marks him as defective in knowledge because knowledge is of that which is defective. The naïveté of Theaetetus and Theodorus,
like Euclides' dialogue, is innocent in the sense of self-forgetting, but only
speciously pure. Ignorance of political life does not mean one is less governed
by it. The innocence of Theaetetus and Theodorus is not the purity of knowledge as perception, but their failure to be aware of the extent to which their
perceptions are governed by opinion. For them knowledge means knowledge
of opinion, of *doxa*.

If perception were knowledge, there would be no possibility of error.
What Theaetetus does not see is that the possibility of error is as necessary
for the possibility of truth as is evil the necessary condition for the good.
Otherwise their very inquiry is unintelligible. Having discovered that knowledge cannot be perception, Theaetetus ventures the opinion that it is true
opinion. But if what he says is true then he knows what knowledge is and need

go no further. If his opinion needs confirmation it is not knowledge and is false. What is impossible according to Theaetetus's new view is what Socrates claims about himself at his trial—that he knows that he know nothing. For if knowledge is true opinion then knowledge of ignorance would be either the true opinion that one had false opinion or the true opinion that one had no opinion. The former case, knowing that one's opinions are false, would mean that one ceases to hold them, and so it reduces to the latter case. But the true opinion that one holds no opinion is self-contradictory. Theaetetus's new view makes knowledge of ignorance, and so knowledge of knowledge, impossible. One can have true opinion, but one can never know it to be true. The problem of the immediacy of perception has simply been reproduced on the level of opinion.

The problem of false opinion seems at first merely an obstacle to be overcome, a necessary detour in our attempt to answer the question, What is knowledge? But as in the case of the *Theaetetus* itself such appearance is deceiving. The necessary condition for false opinion, taking the other for the same, is identical to the necessary condition for thinking as such. Thinking is always a putting together of things which to be understood as together must first be understood as apart. For Theaetetus that is simply impossible; the soul is for him *a* being. For false opinion to be possible the soul must be understood as two, as something which asks and then answers itself, as not knowing and knowing. It must be understood as a "we." In his discussion of the beautiful in the *Hippias Major* Benardete had made the following two remarks:

> The beautiful, then, looks as if it is the impossible togetherness of the necessarily apart. (xxxiv)

> "We" is thus the plainest example of the impossible togetherness of the necessarily apart. (xlvi)

We began with the question of the peculiar form of the *Theaetetus* in hope that it might shed some light on the form of *The Being of the Beautiful*. That question led us to the distinction between perception and opinion, which in turn led us to the question of the false opinion. But the necessary condition for false opinion, which turns out to be the same as the necessary condition for thinking, and so for knowing, points to the necessary twoness of the human soul. This in turn has led us to the beautiful. The question is why.

The twoness of the soul involved the simultaneity of knowing and not knowing. Socrates in his knowledge of ignorance stands as an image of the human soul. What might it mean then that the "double meaning of Socratic dialectic is the double of the beautiful" (xlvi)? On the one hand the beautiful is what makes it possible to see things as wholes, as perfect instances of their kinds. It is, therefore, what makes beings countable, what renders them distinct from one another. It is, even though he does not know it, what underlies Theaetetus's first "definition" of knowledge as the countable. But the completeness of the beings as presented to us by the beautiful is an illusion. The beautiful is the necessary illusion of the wholeness of the part. It frames beings for us and so makes them seem perfectly self-justifying. If everything were seen as connected nothing would ever be seen. The beautiful thus obscures our vision in order to make our vision possible. But the "knowledge" made possible in this way is always based on an oversimplification. Knowledge of the parts is always partial and, therefore, in part false. It is always accompanied by false opinion. The beautiful makes it possible to know in part because of an illusion of wholeness, which, because it is an illusion, makes pure knowledge impossible.

Left at this, the beautiful makes partial vision intelligible but leaves unexplained our awareness of the partiality of our vision. However, there is another half to the doubleness of the beautiful.

> The beautiful has the structure of an indeterminate dyad: anything beautiful jumps its class and at the same time remains a member of the class it jumps. This unresolvable duality indicates why the beautiful and image-making are inseparable. (xxvii)

The beautiful simultaneously enchants and disenchants. We are at once made aware of beings as complete and as pointing beyond themselves. The beautiful, the impossible togetherness of the necessarily apart, is the necessary condition for both false opinion and the awareness of the falseness of opinion.

The irony of the *Theaetetus* is that in the first half of the dialogue Socrates appears to attack Protagoras while in fact giving the thesis that man is the measure of all things its due. In emphasizing the power of opinion to shape our perceptions Socrates approximates the view of the sophists. In the second part of the dialogue, while Socrates appears to come closer to the skeptical views of the sophists, in fact he provides the foundation for the distinction between opinion and knowledge. That distinction is not so much visible in what the dialogue says as in how it is said. The problem of the dialogue, then, is the elusiveness of Socrates. Socrates and Theaetetus are look-alikes. The question is how to tell them apart. That Theaetetus the mathematician looks just like Socrates the philosopher has something to do what the way philosophy must necessarily appear. This in turn has something to do with the inability of Athens to distinguish philosophy and sophistry; it has something to do with the trial and death of Socrates.

The *Theaetetus* means to give an account of knowledge that will show that knowledge must be publicly indistinguishable from opinion. It is, therefore, an attack before the fact on the Enlightenment understanding of the solution to the tension between philosophy and the polity, that is, universal education. The *Theaetetus* suggests that the best universal education can do is to create a society of mathematicians. But this is not to diminish the tension between knowledge and opinion; it is only to exchange one kind of opinion for another. In fact, this is how the dialogue begins. Theaetetus has just exchanged his unreflective mathematics for an unreflective politics.

But why can knowledge not be distinguished from opinion? The relation between knowledge and opinion is something like the relation between consonant and vowel. The vowel can manifest itself alone, but the consonant, while being something apart from vowels can never show itself alone. The first part of the *Theaetetus* deals with perception and shows that it cannot be knowledge. It is not independent of opinion, which can exist independently of something like perception, but, which when it does so, lacks something. Knowledge requires that the two parts be put together, but every time they are put together the result is something that looks like opinion. It is to say the least ironic that perception, which serves as a model for what is "added" to opinion to transform it into knowledge, should in doing so become necessarily immanifest. Only the invisible can certify what is visible.

This is the problem of *logos*. I can say something and understand what I am saying, but for that very reason it is also possible for another to say exactly what I have said and not understand. The sign of this difficulty is the manner in which the conversation is being transmitted to Terpsion. No one expects the slave boy who is reading Euclides' dialogue to understand what he is reading. To know may mean to be able to say, but to be able to say does not mean to know. Knowledge depends on something that is immanifest and must remain immanifest. It is as though knowledge were opinion plus a little something added, but a something that cannot really be understood as added. One can list the parts of a whole, but all the parts by themselves do not make the whole. What makes the whole cannot be listed alongside as another part. This would merely create another all. The wholeness of a whole is accordingly immanifest in the whole. How then do we know wholes?

> Wholes become most manifest as wholes when there is something missing from them (cf. 186a4), but numbers are never caught short. Counting has the double character of always being complete and never being complete. To begin to count is never to stop and already to stop counting. Theaetetus, therefore, cannot avoid agreeing that whole and all are the same, for at any moment the number is a total, and just as in a whole nothing is missing. (I.174–75)

This relation between all and whole parallels the relation between opinion and knowledge. It points to the problem of Socrates' defense. As there is no sure way of distinguishing between knowledge and opinion, there is no sure way of distinguishing between philosophy and sophistry. To defend himself Socrates would have had to make the difference clear. He would have had to *say* the difference between knowledge and opinion. Since he cannot do this, he knows that he will be condemned.

Knowledge, like a misprint, cannot be illustrated. There is something essentially accidental about it. Only when it is brought to life is it knowledge. What brings it to life is soul, a sort of *skutalē*. (A *skutalē* was a staff used for secret dispatches. A message was written on a strip of leather wrapped slantwise around it so that when the leather was unwrapped the letters of the message were unintelligible. It was read by rewrapping it around a *skutalē* of identical thickness.) Without the soul *logoi* are like letters arranged meaninglessly on a page. The soul is the *skutalē* that puts them together in such a way as to render them meaningful. This is the truth underlying Protagoras's *Truth.* That means, however, that there can be no account of knowledge without an account of soul. The problem of knowledge is, therefore, on a different level just the problem of confusing Socrates and Theaetetus. The *Theaetetus* is a memorial to Socrates that is mistaken for a memorial to Theaetetus. Even Socrates' former disciples misunderstand and are full of praise for Theaetetus. They call beautiful and good an ugly man dying of an ugly disease. If they cannot tell the difference, how much less can one expect it of Athens?

At the beginning of the dialogue Euclides had claimed to have given us "all" the speech (143a). Not the whole but the all is gotten by stringing together the parts. By removing the explanations proper to narrative, Euclides removes Socrates' reflections on the conversation as a whole and gives us an all. At first this seems a shame until we realize that since a true whole requires to be put together, Euclides has given us something that feels incomplete so that we have an incentive to complete it. Were it obviously complete it would be too easily appropriated. We would, like Theaetetus, get our opinions from a book. The form of the *Theaetetus* is, therefore, a reflection on the necessity of presenting the motion (question) to which a stop or rest (answer) is a response, in order to know what the stop in question is. While not a complete solution to the problem of the transmission of knowledge, a Platonic dialogue is an acknowledgement of the problem. Like beauty, knowledge is a verb and not a noun. However, "verb" is a noun. When this sort of incompleteness is presented to us in way that is perfectly premeditated and whole, we may have the deepest possible expression of the beautiful as the illusory wholeness of our partiality.

III.

We began with two questions—the title and the mode of presentation of *The Being of the Beautiful*. A brief glance at the *Theaetetus* has confirmed that the doubleness of the beautiful is its primary theme. A more complete reading would have to show how that theme is both the same and different in the *Sophist* and *Statesman*. Benardete indicates the way.

> The *Sophist* and the *Statesman* are needed to show that the *Theaetetus*'s negative determination of Socrates obtains of necessity for the philosopher simply. The universalization of Socrates as a problem brings in its train the problem of being. The discovery through the perplexity of nonbeing of the equal perplexity of being is the *Sophist*'s equivalent to Socratic ignorance. Being, too, is not wholly countable. (I.183)

One example must suffice of an issue that reemerges in the other dialogues. The problem we have been particularly concerned with, the form of the *Theaetetus*, reemerges in the *Sophist* as the distinction between eikastics and phantastics. Benardete discusses it in his section "Appearing":

> Eikastics has nothing to do with the beautiful, for the paradigm can be either ugly or beautiful; it simply re-presents the paradigm. But phantastics necessarily involves the beautiful, for if

perspectival distortion were left uncorrected, the parts of the copy would look ill-proportioned, and if the paradigm were itself ill-proportioned, the copy might then either re-present it in its ugliness or by chance present the ugly as the beautiful, contrary to the intention of the artisan. Neither eikastics nor phantastics has the slightest trace in them of the spurious. Eikastics assumes knowledge of what is perceived, phantastics knowledge of the perceiver as well. (II.109)

And two pages later,

> All Platonic dialogues are *phantasmata*. They are images of what is and what is biggest, which are made ill-proportioned in themselves in order to appear perfectly proportioned. (II.111)

And finally,

> Platonic phantastics is the art of making thinking manifest and therefore immanifest, but thinking is the soul's silent conversation with itself as question and answer. To know how phantastics is possible is to know how thinking is possible, in which the soul is the same as itself when it is other and other when it is the same. (II.112)

If the problem of Socrates is universalized as the problem of the relation of nonbeing to being in the *Sophist*, the problem of the form of the dialogue *Theaetetus* is universalized as the problem of re-presenting as such in the *Sophist*.

Plato wrote three books concerned in part with the connection between the beautiful and images. Only if he had lacked self-knowledge could he have failed to see that these books had to be examples of what they were about. The beginning of the *Theaetetus* points to this without calling any attention to it. Benardete's analysis of course calls attention to it and along the way points to itself as an example of what it is about. The problem of the title of Benardete's book is in the end the same as the problem of its mode of presentation. There are two ways of seeing this—one apparently unthematic and playful, and one thematic.

The playfulness begins at the beginning. In the first sentence Benardete informs us of how many articles were written on the *Theaetetus*, *Sophist*, and

229

Statesman over a period of seventeen years and then proceeds to reflect on the unevenness of the distribution. Given the discussions of the inadequacy of mathematical knowledge in the *Theaetetus* and of the difference between the arithmetic measure and the measure of the mean in the *Statesman*, it is striking that Benardete nevertheless begins with what one can learn in a comprehensive way by reflection on the precise. Later Benardete appears to make a grammatical error, substituting "who" where he ought to have used "whom" (xxiv). Can it be accidental that the very next paragraph is a complicated analysis of that part of the *Hippias* where Socrates doubles himself and where we are seduced into mistaking the relative reality of Socrates as subject and Socrates as predicate? As a general rule, in the introduction Benardete does what Plato does just prior to calling our attention to the fact that Plato has done it, thereby pointing to his own way of writing without calling attention to it.

But Benardete also knows about the intimate relation of the serious and the playful. He tacitly makes his own mode of writing thematic when in his introduction he deals at some length with the problem of translation. By discussing the difficulty of the translating *sophistēs* and *politikos*, he points to the ambiguity in their natures owing to which this difficulty exists. He thus prepares us to see that while the *Theaetetus* can be understood as a combination of the other two dialogues, each of them nevertheless reflects the doubleness of the *Theaetetus* within itself. That *sophistēs*, which can mean wise man, can also come to mean one who manipulates others points ahead to the dual meaning of man as measure of all things.

But it is in his discussion of the two principles of translation that one learns the most about Benardete's mode of writing.

> The two principles of translation, which have just been illustrated, do not consist with one another. One is the principle of all imitative art: that the translation appears to let the original shine through and leave no tell-tale sign of its own unoriginality. The second principle is that everything in the original be rendered as it is in the original, for the sake of keeping the original at its proper distance. The inevitable conflict, therefore, between the idiomatic and the literal cannot except speciously be resolved. The verb *sumpheromai* means either "move together" or "agree" but the perfect translation "concur" obliterates the double meaning while containing both. In the case of Plato, however, this conflict does

not have to be resolved perfectly in order to show how Plato himself practiced in his writing these two same principles of translation. It was the necessary consequence of showing philosophy in the city. (xii)

The problem of translating is the problem of re-presenting, of phantastics and eikastics, of opinion and perception. Benardete suggests here that the problem cannot be resolved "except speciously" directly before calling our attention to a "perfect translation," an English word derived from the Latin equivalent for the Greek word to be translated. The English "specious" also derives from Latin, from *speciosus* (meaning showy or beautiful), and ultimately from *species* (meaning look, show, appearance, or *eidos*). The resolution of the tension between the idiomatic and the literal, the comprehensive and the precise, cannot be resolved except by showing the two as already together. Benardete's example of that is the word "specious," which embodies the way in which the beautiful, the element of which is false opinion, is the vehicle for knowledge. In a later passage and in connection with the word *ontōs*, Benardete rejects the "perfect translation," "really," because it "fails just as 'concur' did, by camouflaging its own rightness" (xiv).

We are now in a somewhat better position to see why the book is written as it is. A strictly literal translation, even were it possible, would make explicit things only implicit in the original; it would consequently conceal the character of the immanifest by making it altogether manifest. Part of what one learns about what one must work to get at is learned from the work one does to get at it. Benardete once called the beautiful a verb. A translation that was perfectly idiomatic would entirely conceal the literal. The immanifest would be rendered invisible. Benardete's translations attempt to be idiomatic while keeping the literal in mind. His commentaries attempt to make the implicit explicit, but to do so in such a way that their implicit character is not altogether sacrificed. Benardete's commentaries try to camouflage their own rightness at crucial places because some things can only be understood on the basis of how they appear. The beautiful cannot be understood except speciously.

It is unusual in our age for a book to be written with this much care for the concurrence of its form and content. *The Being of the Beautiful* is not an easy book, but then that should not surprise us for "the beautiful things are difficult."

Chapter Seventeen

Review of *The Being of the Beautiful*: *Plato's* Theaetetus, Sophist, *and* Statesman

Stanley Rosen

Seth Benardete is one of the very few contemporary classicists who combine the highest philological competence with a subtlety and taste that approximate that of the ancients. At the same time, he has set himself the entirely modern hermeneutical task of uncovering what the ancients preferred to keep veiled, of making explicit what they indicated, and hence (to apply a thesis from the volume under review) of showing the naked ugliness of artificial beauty. The exemplification of this conflict between the ancients and the moderns is Benardete's style, which somehow reminds me of someone rowing into the sunlight with muffled oars. "Somehow" and "someone"—these terms are not chosen by chance (remember the Aristotelian *pōs*). The problem faced by Benardete is to give a comprehensively precise account of what he identifies in Plato as the incompatibility between the comprehensive and the precise.

Stated with maximum concision, Benardete holds that, for Plato, the beautiful is "the being of the beings" (xv), and is problematically related to the good. He takes the *Symposium* and *Phaedrus* to prove without arguing that, whereas the goal of philosophy, knowledge of the whole, is not feasible, the task of philosophy is "a wresting away from the poets of the beautiful and an establishing of it as the philosophical question" (xix). The *Theaetetus, Sophist,* and *Statesman* "supply the full support" of the twin visions that the beautiful is both "the culmination of philosophy's quest" and "the sole means available to philosophy in its quest" (ibid.). In the course of his preliminary discussion of these claims (via a reading of the *Hippias Major*), Benardete conjectures

Reprinted from *Graduate Faculty Philosophy Journal* 10, no. 2 (1985): 163–66. Page numbers in parentheses refer to *The Being of the Beautiful*: *Plato's "Theaetetus,"* *"Sophist,"* and *"Statesman"* (Chicago: University of Chicago Press, 1984).

that the beings themselves may not be beautiful, "but the beautiful, like light, is still that which discloses them to us." And again: "The beauty of things would thus be due to the manner of their disclosure," namely, to Socratic dialectics (xxxiv). According to Benardete, "the beautiful is the impossible union of the eidetic and dimensionality" (xxxv).

From this, it is immediately evident that contrary to the apparent contention of the Eleatic Stranger in the *Sophist*, phantastics is deeper than eikastics, since it contains the beautiful, i.e., knowledge of the soul, or of the proper way in which to render things beautiful to the multiplicity of perspectives (II.109). Philosophy is thus the true or noble sophistry: "All Platonic dialogues are *phantasmata...*" (II.111). The most important theoretical consequence of this view of Plato concerns the nature of being. In a crucial section of his *Theaetetus* commentary, Benardete says, a propos the Homeric thesis that everything flows (including Theaetetus): "Being...is the mutual bonding together of whatever two are indispensable for each other" (I.115). This entails the negation of the thesis, to be developed in the *Sophist* by the Stranger, that being is itself an eidetic atom and (in my opinion) it opens the door to the historical process culminating in Hegel's dialectico-speculative logic, or the *Aufhebung* of the beautiful *qua* perspectival into the conceptual structure of perspectivity. (I note in passing that the rejection of Hegel's logic led in turn to a rehabilitation of the thesis of the noble sophistry, now called noble nihilism by Nietzsche, that the beautiful is the perspectival.) That the Homeric thesis, maintained initially by Theaetetus, is not fundamentally different from the Stranger's doctrine of being, is suggested for me by passages like that on II.140 of Benardete's *Sophist* commentary. Benardete here refers to the problem that "the hypothetical singularity of the being seems to be at odds with the factual plurality of its predicates...." Benardete relates this problem to the case of nonbeing, which can enter speech only if it is one, "which is contrary to its being nonbeing." This problem does indeed relate to speech, but not, I would hold, to the eidetic atoms or elements, and not to non-being. The problem is that *nothing* can be said of any of the "greatest forms" except by combining them, and then by replacing their combinations with predications. In other words, speech that is ostensibly about the eidetic elements, including being, seems in fact to be about speech, i.e., about predications. The fundamental error of the "analytical" Plato scholars lies in their overlooking what Plato is actually talking about. They don the protective covering of discourse without understanding what it is that they are protecting. On the other hand, if "eidetic" discourse is in fact about the greatest forms, then it is necessarily about these as interconnected in a dialectical structure of the Hegelian type.

I do not find the problem posed in this way in Benardete's commentary, nor do I find the explicit admission that, strictly speaking, nothing can be said of Plato's eidetic elements, and so, that they are indistinguishable from nonbeing. Nevertheless, I agree with his conclusion that Platonic philosophy is phantastics, and would add that it is production or poetry rather than theory, whether for his reasons or for mine. As Benardete observes, the eidetic elements are intelligible only from the phenomena, not in themselves prior to these (II.143). This being so, discursive analysis, and especially the now fashionable use of mathematical formalisms, to "explain" the "theory" of forms, is poetry once removed from itself. Benardete's epigrammatical style, which will no doubt be scorned by the analytical "hard-heads," is in fact much closer to the spirit of Platonic royal sophistry. I only wish that Benardete had clearly recognized the poetic nature of what, for example, he calls "partial sharing" (II.145). One atom can share neither partially nor entirely with another atom. I therefore agree with Benardete that the Stranger does not replace myth "with a *logos* about being that is simultaneously comprehensive and precise," but deny that the Stranger nevertheless "solves the riddle of nonbeing" (II.128). Phantastics is indeed the art "of bringing to light the other as other" (II.160), but not as the Other. Plato is not Emmanuel Levinas.

Benardete holds that "the *Sophist* and *Statesman* are needed to show that the *Theaetetus'* negative determination of Socrates obtains of necessity for the philosopher simply" (I.183). In the *Statesman* commentary, the impossibility of philosophy is expressed as the impossibility of combining teleology with an eidetic analysis of the whole (III.117). Benardete rightly regards the *Statesman* as more profound than the *Sophist* (III.142). On his interpretation, this is confirmed by the Stranger's refusal to employ phantastics, and the consequent "ugliness" of the dialogue (III.118). Benardete says that the ugliness of the *Statesman* is necessary in order to bring to light the necessity of the ugliness of *nomos*, an ugliness equivalent to the lack of self-knowledge (III.137). This in turn is evidently connected to the failure of the law to reconcile precision with comprehensiveness (ibid.). Yet Benardete closes his study by defining the doubleness of the beautiful as the opposition between courage and moderation in the soul, and precision and comprehensiveness in metrics (III.146). He apparently believes that the soul can resolve this opposition, whereas the duality of metrics is irresolvable ("The soul can thus be whole, while knowledge for us cannot...." ibid.). Self-knowledge thus seems to be equivalent to the beautiful recognition of the ugliness of being or (as I would put it) to the replacement of ugly ontology by beautiful rhetoric (of which dialectic is a species).

I have no space to do more than to mention the utility of Benardete's translations, or to list the countless observations in his commentary that are penetrating and, if not true, certainly beautiful. Unlike the great majority of books about Plato, this book is actually *about Plato*. Ortega says somewhere that Plato has not been fortunate in his modern disciples. But then, Ortega did not live to read this extraordinary book, which is urgently recommended to those who love to think, despite its muffled oars.

Chapter Eighteen

Thirty-nine Reasons for Reading Benardete on the *Republic*: Review Essay on *Socrates' Second Sailing*

Will Morrisey

Professor Benardete has been around long enough to have established a reputation. His writings are reputed to be hard to understand. This reputation has led to certain worries. "He is so difficult. He commits philology. He gives me a headache; Socrates never gets a headache; Benardete makes me feel unSocratic. *Must* I read Benardete?" By no means. But you may want to, anyway. His commentary on Plato's *Republic* consists of thirty-nine chapters, each of which contains at least one reason for reading the book.

Socrates' second sailing means the Socratic turn in philosophy from the attempt to understand nature directly, in the Anaxagorean manner, to the recognition that one must also understand oneself, the would-be understander of nature. The need for this turn proceeds from the need to know the good. The attempt to see the good in nature by considering nature directly founders on the problem of teleology. If the good is somehow independent of the series of events or developments that led up to the good, then why is the series necessary? And if the good is somehow the amalgamation of lesser goods within the series, do we not need to know the entire series in order to know the good, or even to know that the lesser goods really are good? Yet we do not know the supreme good of nature in this way because nature continues to percolate: Where will it end? Socrates resets the ship's compass and sails again by considering his own life as a philosopher, as a would-be understander. He is forcefully brought to see that there are two opposing opinions about himself: the opinion of the majority of his fellow Athenians—an opin-

Reprinted from *Interpretation* 23, no. 1 (Fall 1995): 89–100. Page numbers in parentheses refer to *Socrates' Second Sailing*: *On Plato's* Republic (Chicago: University of Chicago Press, 1989).

ion whose *telos* (end) is the cup of hemlock conceived as punishment—and his own opinion, whose *telos* is also the cup of hemlock, but not conceived necessarily as a punishment for him in certain circumstances. Socratic philosophy looks not at things, initially, but at opinions about things, to determine whether those opinions are fragmentary or whole, self-contradictory or coherent. This procedure involves pairing opinions (in the case of the *Republic*, opinions about the just) with other opinions, for comparison. The procedure also involves parting, setting opinions about the just apart from other things, for contrast.

Benardete has many things to say about the long course of the arguments Socrates and his interlocutors make in the *Republic*. With Spartan-like austerity, I shall restrict myself to identifying one insight or set of insights per chapter.

1. The form of the *Republic*—a dialogue narrated by Socrates—fits the substance of the *Republic*—the teaching that the thought of the one best regime "guides one's understanding of political life even if it never shapes one's actions" (9). "Socrates is himself and plays all the parts," just as the best regime, whether or not "concretely" realizable, "comprehends the manifold of all inferior regimes" (9).

2. Socrates tells Cephalus that those who make things tend toward overfondness for their productions: poets for their poems, fathers for their children, moneymakers for their money. "Socrates after all is the maker of his own city, and perhaps he is too fond of it" (14). But perhaps not: "When the poets are finally banished in Book X, perhaps Socrates the poet goes into exile with them" (14). What gives each citizen a claim to rule—the good thing he produces for the city—also inclines him to excessive "pride of authorship" with respect to the production, and with respect to the city in which that production is deemed essential. Socrates must liberate himself from such self-regard while working through it.

3. To show that justice is patriotism—benefitting the city's friends and harming its enemies—then one must first prove that the city is good (assuming that the city's reputed purpose, justice, is a good, or a part of the good). "[I]n philosophy, the ideality of things must precede the reality of their good" (17). Yet, if justice is an art, a kind of knowledge, it is not clear that justice is good. Is knowledge ever anything more than, as one says today, "value-neutral"? The best doctor is the best poisoner, thanks to the same knowledge. Is the most just man therefore potentially the most unjust?

4. Thrasymachus gives every appearance of being a most unjust man. Yet "Socrates soon forces him to face the difficulty that he cannot win for himself

any pupils if they believe his sole consideration is his own advantage" (21). Socrates' irony, although denounced by the apparently indignant Thrasymachus, does not stop his interlocutors from discovering the truth about the good. "Thrasymachus sees no difficulty in combining law and knowledge; but we are made to wonder whether his savagery is not due to his belief in their perfect compatibility" (22). If no good lies outside the lawgiving city, the real and the shamming *enragés* who leap to the defense of the law will finally know no lawful limits. Thrasymachus represents religiosity without the gods; the departure of pious old Cephalus marks great danger as well as philosophic opportunity.

5. Thrasymachus and Socrates agree to the principle of specialization, that for every doable task there is or can be some natural or artificial instrument whose function is to perform that task. "Does the city have a function?" (30). If so, is the city the best instrument to perform that function? Even if philosophy is not the city's function, it might be that philosophy is a byproduct of the city, that the city is both necessary to the discovery of philosophy and an impediment to the full exercise of philosophy.

6. Glaucon "prepares the way for a confrontation between the philosopher and the city" (41) by restating Thrasymachus's argument in terms of the story of Gyges. Gyges' ring, which makes its wearer invisible when he twists it in a certain way, "stands for the veil the law wraps around the foundation of the city" (37). The foundation of the city is adultery and murder. Why not *Realpolitik*, if one is wise? Adeimantus "prepares the way for renewing the ancient quarrel between poetry and philosophy" (42) by noting that the gods can be propitiated with material things, bribed. So, why not keep one eye on clever injustices, another on camouflage for them?

7. The need to found a city in speech arises from the inability to find justice directly: by introspection or by contemplation of the cosmos. A founded or made city does not pose the dilemma of an origin given by someone else whose intentions may be obscure. "Making in speech cuts out time and place, both of which are indispensable for becoming" (47). In founding the city in speech, the dialogue, the *Republic*, "is the philosophic city in which Socrates is already king" (47). Glaucon's disdain for the simple, healthy city, which he calls the city of pigs, and his preference for what Socrates calls the feverish city, the city whose citizens eat meat and recline on couches, make possible both war and philosophy—both of which require delaying the satisfaction of such desires as may be gratified instantly or easily.

8. *Thumos* (the spiritedness of the human soul) is a Homeric word, fallen into disuse by Socrates' time; Socrates "first confronts" Homer by "taking over from him this old-fashioned word" (55). Although "the philosopher's best friends are his opponents" (57), Glaucon doesn't know that. The philosopher-dogs or guardians-called-philosophers appeal to Glaucon, attaching him to the city in speech. "The heart, says the heart, is the mind" (57). It is enough for now for Glaucon to be less mindless. "Political philosophy has become political" (58) for the sake of inducing the very political, hearty Glaucon to begin to see that the mind has secrets unknown to the heart.

9. *"The Republic* is a story that slips into Glaucon in the form of a story about stories" (58), that is, an account of the stories appropriate to guardians. Their education *apparently* transforms *thumos* into eros, for the edification of Glaucon, although one notices that the story itself is told with the help of Adeimantus. The problem with existing, Homeric, stories is a moral one. Homer and the epic poets generally begin in the middle of things, in contrast to the moral book, the Bible, which begins at the beginning. Beginnings are humbling to man, glorious to God. Morality requires a beginning, a middle, and an end, but Homer, it is regrettable to say, "has the beautiful determine the very sequence of events" (62). Homer and the other poets are insufficiently moral and insufficiently immoral, for they allow Zeus to live on after inventing Athena, their representative. *Their* city in speech is accordingly ill-founded, a self-contradictory mixture of old and new.

10. Socratic theology comports with Socratic education of the guardians. This is not an education through suffering. The gods are not to be represented as dispensing evils to men, as poets would have gods do. The Socratic gods "are as indifferent to friendship as they are to enmity," "models of self-sufficiency" rather than cosmic cops or "models of care" (62). "Perhaps they are beautiful but invisible statues" (64), a thought that makes one wonder at Socrates' previous criticism of Homer as an amoral esthete. Be this as it may, the guardians must not be taught fear, and potential philosophers must not suppose fear of the Lord to be the beginning of wisdom.

11. Socrates and sober Adeimantus exile tragic and comic poetry from the city. "The language of death is to cease to be affective and become neutral," like an art (67). "Life is mere life": extreme moderation, as it were, yields equality and freedom. Freedom is a problem for the city because "the city ... in duplicating its own freedom and self-sufficiency in its warriors cannot help but detach them from the city," making each warrior " a city unto himself" (68). And therefore *un*equal to other citizens?

12. *Mimēsis* means both emulation and imitation. If the city in speech is to inculcate the opinion that every man has his own natural job, the poet, who imitates everyone while emulating no one, presents a problem. But the city is also a problem. In the city, "Education sets out to produce the integral self—no one can be anyone else—and ends up by producing the collective self: each one is everyone else. The city thus aspires to reproduce the anonymity of knowledge on the level of corporeality," of mere opinion (72). Therefore "the city impersonates wisdom. It is the sophist of all sophists" (72).

13. Musical education moderates the soul by separating "love of one's own (*philein*) from the love of the beautiful (*eran*)" (73). One loves the beautiful but cannot have it, cannot make it one's own, cannot direct filial love at it. Most souls cannot sensibly want to defend the beautiful to the death, to act thumotically with respect to it. This therapeutic teaching complements the teaching about gymnastic, medicine, and the body—the latter of course being the thing that is most one's own. It is all very well to perform a severe and effective therapy upon a body that is diseased but fundamentally healthy. But to sustain a body diseased through and through for year after year, a body whose maintenance requires too much of the soul's attention: this is not what Socrates' "statesmanlike" Asclepius had in mind.

14. The noble lie yokes together being and opinion. One's being or nature is said to coincide perfectly with the good of the city. The lie has two parts, autochthony and natural division of classes. The first incorporates Polemarchus's view of the distinction between us and them, citizens and foreigners. The second incorporates Thraysmachus's view that there are rulers and ruled. "The first part of the lie naturalizes the law, the second legalizes nature" (77); "the soil makes the city one, the metals structure it" (78).

15. Problem: "justice and happiness do not go together," as happiness consists of "goods the core of which was not justice" (79). A solution of sorts: the members of the *dialogic* city are happy while *contemplating* justice.

16. An "idealizing excursion into foreign affairs" (81) induces Adeimantus to succumb to a sort of idealizing or "Platonizing" in domestic affairs, overemphasizing music education's effectiveness as the crucial determinant in the perpetuation of the regime.

17. "Moderation is the virtue of knowers who acknowledge the right of those who have only opinion to rule them" (87). As for justice, it is "that principle which adjusts the rulers' soul-structure to that of the other two classes" (91). The city's justice is not identical to the ruler's justice; the ruler has "no

justice that is not identical with his wisdom" (91). The city's justice is a compromise with the auxiliaries and artisans.

18. The principle of noncontradiction has as its illustration the spinning top that moves on its axis but whose axis does not, in the imaginary/geometrical sense, move. In nature a real top's axis does move. "The principle of noncontradiction helps meet the objections of the captious and evade the difficulties of understanding the nature of things," and Socrates knows this (95). "Socrates has replaced nature with syntax," philologist Benardete observes (96).

> An analysis of soul, if done imprecisely, leads to a proliferation of ideas, for it takes its bearings by language. Speech, because it admits of greater precision than fact, produces greater imprecision about facts. Political philosophy would seem to be caught in this paradox, and its imaginary republics rightly subject to Machiavelli's strictures. (96)

Benardete at his most shocking sublimates the philology his accusers complain of.

Machiavelli is an unusually thumotic or leonine philosopher, as well as a vulpine one. Socrates approaches the theme of *thumos* through the story of Leontius, whose name Benardete uses as the title of this chapter. "Anger generates syntax; it needs to understand things eidetically, for it knows nothing of nature or the body" (99). Anger refuses to give in, "denies the existence of the body" (100). Oedipus, a greater Leontius, knows what man is through eidetic analysis but does not know himself. Machiavelli evidently claims to know himself as the prince of war, not the prince of peace, implying that the prince of war is the prince of princes, the lord of lords. Yet Machiavelli rejects eidetic analysis and prefers the sense of touch to the sense of sight and also to the sense of hearing, which brings words into the soul. Perhaps some of Machiavelli's strictures are wiser than others?

19. In the city in speech the warriors ally themselves with the rational, governing the moneymakers. Without reason or desires of their own, "they are the core of the city because they belong to it as a particular city" (104). Therefore, "The core of the city is alienation" (104), a radical denaturing.

20. To gaze at dead bodies is shameful; to gaze at live bodies, particularly those of wrinkled old men, seems ridiculous. But the conventional sense of the ridiculous must be overcome in a regime requiring communism or women among the guardians. The nakedness of legally required coeducational gym-

nastics counterpoints the concealment from the guardians of knowledge of nature. "The essential communicability of knowledge misrepresents the reality of its secretiveness.... The tension between the city and philosophy is ultimately due to the philosopher's selfishness. He does not measure up to the idealism of opinion. He minds his own business" (111). The philosopher devotes himself to what is truly his own, the truth (hence "*philo*-sophy"). For the philosopher, unlike the lover of the beautiful, what is truly one's own is not the body. This is why philosophy is learning how to "die." The philosopher is reluctant to denature himself for the city's sake. This is the central chapter of Benardete's book.

21. This city requires, then, a kind of radical equality among the members of its guardian class. To achieve equality, human nature must be atomized and then reunited along communistic lines. This operation in the city of speech is *philosophically* crucial because it "puts in question any simple teleology and radicalizes the issue of nature" (117). The *political* logic culminating in communism forces Socrates' second sailing, "the search for truly intelligible species"—rather than merely conventional ones—"and the whole to which they belong." The radical questioning of conventional divisions entailed in overcoming one's feeling that coeducational gymnastics is unthinkably silly makes the philosopher see that he cannot have confidence in the belief that he has "immediate access to the nature of things" (117). "Without the twin sophistries of art and the city, the descent of philosophy would be as unnecessary as the ascent of philosophy would be impossible. The divergence from the truth converges with the truth only through the city" (117).

22. "The city may ultimately make its citizens, but it will never make the philosopher. Nature in the form of chance frustrates the true city" (119).

23. The discussion of community shifts to a discussion of war (hatred of barbarians) and faction (hatred of Greeks). The discussion of faction is especially pertinent because it shows how a unity (Greekness) can nonetheless split apart, have tensions within it. The same danger obviously threatens any city, no matter how communal. "Socrates' intent... seems to have been to show how the massive contradictions in the city come to light in practice" (122).

24. "The dialogic city"—that is, the city constituted by dialogue itself—"is already real and Socrates is its king" (123). The city in speech constructed by the interlocutors *within* the dialogue is another matter, and a city in existence physically is another matter still. A philosophic writer, Plato, can attempt to "maintain the survival of the dialogic city," but as for the other two cities,

Thrasymachus "cannot be banished from that whose essence he is" (124). "Philosophy is not a means for realizing the impossible; it is a means for ridding Glaucon"—"the disaffected offspring of a regime," democracy, "that renders everything feasible unattractive"—"of the desire to realize the impossible" (126). In so doing Socrates must lyingly or, shall we say, mythologically transform philosophy into an image of "perfect wisdom" so that it can exert enough influence on Glaucon for him to remain content with Athens as it is" (126).

> Socrates pulls philosophy out of the dialogic city into the city in speech in order to make it manifest; but it is unlikely to be, as manifest, the same as what it was when it was invisibly at work. Socrates is the king of the dialogic city, he is not the philosopher-king of the city in speech. (127)

Even in the city in speech, "the coincidence of political power and philosophy requires a miracle; but the gods, who are beautiful and good, do not listen to prayers" (129).

25. "The philosopher cannot put into the city the order of his soul..." (129). This is true even of the city in speech. In the *dialogic* city, the analysis of the difference between knowledge and opinion is a matter for *eidetic* analysis. In the city in speech, by contrast, the analysis is carried out in terms of being and nonbeing. The city in speech talks in the language of being and knowledge. In order to realize the city in speech one would have to replace eidetic analysis with metaphysics. This cannot be done, inasmuch as the city as city must engage in hypocoristics, those endearing names or euphemisms "uttered everywhere and always to disguise the love of one's own" (138). "The discovery of the difference between knowledge and opinion is a discovery of philosophy..." (138). Can the philosopher, having "detached unreal subjects from real predicates," then "reattach real subjects to them" (139)?

26. The philosopher-king is un-Socratic. He descends from the beings, "bear[ing] an uncanny resemblance to the Homeric gods" (139). Socrates, in contrast, ascends from the particulars to the beings, and brings back little that is useful, when he must descend. He minds his own business. "'I can't be bothered' is the philosopher's version of morality" (142). Moderation and courage are "trivial consequences" of his nature (143). Books VI and VII contain a "rival account of philosophy and at the same time contain Socrates' refutation of it" (148).

27. When the philosopher-king enters, can Adeimantus be far behind? Glaucon intervenes with challenges, Adeimantus with "wait-a-minute." Philosophers are such oddballs—how could they ever rule a city? "Adeimantus is vaguely aware that justice is the dyad of philosophy and city, and that conjunction can never become an equation" (144). For Adeimantus's sake (or perhaps for Socrates' sake) "Socrates convinces Adeimantus that the pre-Socratic Socrates"—the Socrates who aspired to direct knowledge of nature—"should rule" (146). Socrates

> convinces Adeimantus that pre-Socratic philosophy is competent to do what it never dreamed of doing. The Anaxagorean rule of mind over body was as far as it had gone. Socrates has never been wittier. (146)

The philosopher conceived as one who knows nature and benefits his city by coming down from the realm of being with this knowledge that he somehow makes useful to his countrymen: what adamantine respectability is this! The people should positively *beg* him to rule them, but far be it from *him* to impose. He is such a gentleman. And rather a technocrat, too: Thrasymachus himself will submit to his beneficent sagacity. Of course, "the pleasure [the city] knows it attributes to the body, and the virtues it promises it believes are of the soul" (146). Indeed, "A city whose motto was 'A life not passed in examination is not worth living' could not be happy" (147). Therefore, "Justice and injustice are necessarily co-present in the city" (146):

> Any attempt to root out injustice will take justice with it. For Glaucon and Adeimantus, who have not followed this argument, the doctrine of the 'ideas' is an easy way to inculcate the same lesson. It is an instrument of political moderation and not only of political moderation. (146–47)

Even the best regime, the city in speech, the highest politics, cannot make even one philosopher. Nature does that. Socrates' *daimonion* or guardian spirit kept him *out* of politics.

But not out of the city. The city does serve the young philosopher's purposes precisely by impeding his progress, dragging him down, making his quest difficult, thwarting his ascent to the clouds. Evil is "the toughening element of the good, and the innocence of the good nature is the same as its ignorance of good and evil—and *a fortiori* of its own nature and limits" (150). Because "the sophist is the spokesman of the city," the philosopher must converse with him, he who calls necessity "morality" and "freedom" (150). Socrates knows that the city is "necessary for all men and cannot make any man happy" (153). Because he knows this about the city, Socrates knows that he does not know the whole, for he knows that the city necessarily thwarts his attempted ascent from the city. In so knowing, Socrates differs from those who deny that philosophy can exist, claiming that the city's conventions are all-encompassing. The city is "the place where the true difference between the necessary and the good can be discerned, and where the question of man's good and the question of the whole coincide" (153). Hence the necessity of constructing the city in speech.

28. While "morality is idealistic, happiness is not" (153). Happiness is realistic. Every man really wants the good, which alone can make his soul happy. In addition to really knowing the city, Socrates also really knows that it is good to know the good, although he also knows that no one has adequate knowledge of the good. Socrates' knowledge plus Socrates' ignorance add up to Socrates' self-knowledge.

The good is the measure of the beings and the conventions with regard to their usefulness for someone or some thing. Theoretical and prudential wisdom share in the good. The good makes it possible for the beings to be parts of the whole; it also and equally makes them detachable, knowable as parts without some impossible knowledge of the whole or omniscience. One does not need an omni-science to know something. Both fox and hedgehog really know part of the whole. "What Nietzsche calls the optimism of Plato may not be unreasonably connected with this double claim for the good" (156). It is, Benardete immediately adds, a limited optimism.

29. Socrates' images of the sun, the divided line, and the cave do not suggest that the conventions of the city are anything but snares and delusions. Where does this leave *political* philosophy? "At the center of the *Republic* stands an account that is alien from its own setting. It pretends to be prior and is posterior to the discovery of political philosophy. It is the second sailing in the guise of the first sailing" (161). Political philosophy acknowledges that the many, contradictory opinions are the foundation from which "one begins the ascent to the unity of the *idea*" (162). In the cave, however, "Our waking life is a dream, and everything is inside our heads" (171), puppetry by firelight. "The cave thus represents the city as if the noble lie had succeeded completely" (171)—the noble lie with the nobility subtracted. In this me-

and-my-shadow world, "Man is the self-ignorant measure of all things" (172). Law and art unite to keep nature out.

The imagery represents *pre*-Socratic philosophy. Socrates agrees with his predecessors in distinguishing nature and convention. The pre-Socratic, however, believes he can replace conventions with "their true originals" (174): four elements, or "strife," or "love," replace the gods. To the pre-Socratic, "The city has mislabeled the beings, it has misidentified them" (174). The pre-Socratic "horror of unreality begs the question of the goodness of the real that the denizens of the cave, Glaucon and Adeimantus, are at least aware of" (175). That is why descent is as important as ascent, why a second sailing is philosophically needed after the philosophically needed first sailing. Socratic philosophy does not conquer its predecessors. It looks at the first sailing's sailors in the spirit of gratitude as well as in the spirit of correction.

30. "There is no science of wonder" (179). Philosophers can be produced neither by habituation nor by art. Philosophy is a conversion, an abrupt and radical break. "It is the practice of dying and being dead" (179). Philosophy is not concerned with the life of the city, with ruling. "Socrates startles us into this realization: no one has a nature designed to rule in the city" (181). The philosopher can, but does not want to. "'Philosopher-king' rejects in its very formulation the principle of one man/one job" (180), and is therefore unjust—to the philosopher. While the descent or return to the cave may be philosophically necessary, ruling the cave is not.

31. Where is the human to be located? Poetry, especially tragic poetry, locates the human in the pre-political and the pre-Promethean. Poetry is an art about something prior to the arts. Political philosophy is at least initially mathematical, not poetical. Mathematics itself is of course pre-philosophic; "all the arts of the city make use of number" (182). Mathematics and the city may lead to philosophy because contradiction inheres in both. The city has its contradictory opinions. Mathematics features the contradiction of the one and the many; it rests on the problem-laden perception that the many different fingers are all one thing, "finger." Arithmetic makes this problem apparent by treating each item counted as a "one," undifferentiated from every other "one." Thinking about mathematics (as distinguished from thinking mathematically) is periagogic, rather as thinking about the city (as distinguished from thinking politically) is periagogic. Anticipating the coming discussion of democracy, one might observe that democracy poses this problem of the one and the many by treating each one as undifferentiated from, equal to,

every other one. Both philosopher and sophist, to say nothing of the tyrant, see that one can be worth more than ten thousand if he is the best.

32. If "philosopher-king" is a sort of contradiction, and the best city is impossible, how will justice ever come to light in its real context? Or must an erotic young man like Glaucon choose the unjust life in order to be happy? A new defense of the city is needed, and, because the rational city has been shown to be infeasible, it will have to be a new kind of city, a city fallen away from political perfection. This city will not be rational but religious; hence the renewed discussion of poetry.

33. On Socrates' tour of regimes and their geneses, Benardete remarks, "Virtue in itself is not the principle of any actual regime; it is always a retrospective interpretation of those who come later and who, having fallen further, ascribe it to motives that have ceased to be intelligible to them" (195). Political life depends upon nostalgia.

34. In order for the just man, Socrates, to become manifest, timocracy must decline into oligarchy and oligarchy into democracy. Democracy in its multicolored variety brings out *all* the souls, the better to be seen and studied. In treating each citizen as equal, democracy brings out individuals. This is why democracy doesn't last long. Unfortunately for democracy, "Evil and power are to it unreal" (200); its "failure to enforce its decisions and protect itself parodies philosophy, for which everything is open to revision" (200).

35. The tyrant comes into being as the punisher of the rich, who stand in the way of full equality even in a democracy. The tyrannical soul will always condemn "economic royalists" while clearing the way for its own supremacy. "[T]he truth of the thumoeidetic comes to light slowly by the gradual casting off of the Leontius story, which denied that *thumos* and desire are ever in alliance against reason" (204). On the contrary: "The tyrant is the embodiment of all democratic wishes—he does whatever he wants—and the object of all democratic desires. He is Eros" (205). The tyrant "is the true believer in the lie of the city stripped of everything that made it noble and good"; his is "the bestiality of unalloyed patriotism" (207).

36. The tyrant "represents the complete politicization of desire" (208). "Anger and love are one" in his soul (208). Glaucon had started out like that. Socrates has cured him. It is in that cure, and not so much in any doctrine or in any city in speech, that justice may be found in the *Republic*.

The tragic poet teaches the democratic/tyrannical man "to grieve for his unsatisfiable longings"(208). By contrast, the philosopher has no self-pity. He has a longing that is partially unsatisfiable, but sheds no tears over it.

37. Poetry "is interested less in courage as the repository of all lawful opinions than in envy and willfulness, and less in the socially useful love of money than in the polymorphism of desire" (214–15). Its piety contradictorily supports and subverts the laws. It is in between, "outside the city but not outside the cave" (218). It prefers justice and beauty to the good.

The rational response to grief is to recognize pain as "an impediment to deliberation" and misfortune as an evil accident. This being the case, "one can pick oneself up and go on, for one can determine on one's own what is best" (221).

38. Glaucon is not a philosopher. He "needs the immortality of the soul because he needs injustice to be altogether terrifying" (224). As for Socrates, he prefers to concentrate on the good.

39. "To figure out the best life is the best life" (229).

Benardete reports that *Socrates' Second Sailing* began as a review of Leo Strauss's book *The City and Man*. The review was the lead article in the 1978 number of *The Political Science Reviewer*. Setting Benardete's commentary next to Strauss's chapter on the *Republic*, it appears that Strauss is somewhat more open to the possibility that the philosopher might also be a lover of his country.

Chapter Nineteen

Review of *Socrates' Second Sailing*: *On Plato's* Republic

Arlene Saxonhouse

As with much of Benardete's other work, this is not an easy book to read. To say that it is dense, boldly paradoxical, replete with hellenized English, and abjures the standard expectations of expository writing only hints at the difficulties one must face in reading this text. Sentences such as "The true city is the true lie" (66) or "By the omission of the line [of Homer] the poets are forthwith expelled, though by the same token they are allowed to stay" (68) or "Socrates has used the eideticizing power of the thumoeidetic to get rid of the gods. The falsity of the thumoeidetic is its truth" (102), can leave the reader—or, at least, they left me—baffled. And yet this is also classic Benardete, where cryptic allusions, startling paradoxes, new questions (that seem obvious once they are asked) about long-accepted passages all work to give brilliant new insights into the Platonic text and therewith as well the possibility or impossibility of combining politics and philosophy, practice and theory. Benardete notes that this book began with a review of Leo Strauss's *The City and Man*, and while it owes its thematic concerns to Strauss, the execution is all Benardete's own. At its better moments, Benardete's style becomes the modern writer's version of the Platonic dialogue. The perplexities induced by the paradoxes presented make us aware of the inadequacy of the model of rationality favored by many—if not most—readers of the *Republic*, for whom the forms exist as an external standard of value, accessible to the mind ascending, and brought down by the philosopher to the world of the city. Although Benardete's spare prose allows no references to the scholarship he rejects, it is just such readings of the *Republic* that must yield to Benardete's analysis.

Reprinted from *Political Theory* 18, no. 4 (Nov. 1990): 690–705. Page numbers in parentheses refer to *Socrates' Second Sailing*: *On Plato's* Republic (Chicago: University of Chicago Press, 1989).

Benardete begins by taking us back to the *Phaedo* and Socrates awaiting death in the prison of the Athenians. Why is Socrates here? Mind cannot be the cause, since the mind of the Athenians—execution—is one, that of Socrates—suicide—another, and yet they both lead to the same action. Similarly, mind as the explorer in search of mechanical causation cannot and does not order for the sake of that which is good. And so, we must look elsewhere to explain what mind itself cannot: we embark on a "second sailing," a methodology that Benardete calls "eidetic analysis," one that eschews teleology "without giving up on either mind or the good" (4). Eidetic analysis, always opposing, always joining, and associating, entails two opposed analytic approaches which Benardete says control his reading of the *Republic*: "burst-like" and "filamentlike." Yet the insights and interpretations he offers, irrespective of the name he may assign to it, emerge from his own subtle questions, his own subtle reflections, his own deep knowledge of the Greek language. A missing *eta* raises questions about the identity of justice found and the justice sought (88), or a misplaced alpha-privative removes doubt from a verb of desiring (96). Who, for instance, has asked before: to whom do those who hold the figures reflected on the wall of the cave speak—to the cavemen or to themselves? Benardete uses this question to suggest that "the speeches of the carriers do not necessarily have anything to do with the artifacts they carry" (173), which in turn suggests to Benardete "the arbitrariness of speeches in the cave" and thus the possibility of examining "predicates without subjects" (177), or the many without the one. This becomes the starting point for the second sailing, for it leads forward to one of Benardete's central themes about the nature of the constructed city in speech: It need not exist as an idea for it to reveal "the envelope of unreality in which every city exists and without which none could exist" (185).

Elsewhere, Benardete notes the inordinate amount of time that Socrates seems to spend on isolating the desiring part of the soul from the reasoning part—inordinate since this opposition seems so obvious. But, as Benardete remarks, the problem sets Socrates against Socrates, for Socrates has argued elsewhere that we always desire the good and that, therefore, desires could not oppose our reason. "Socrates against Socrates is a conflict that only the highest principles could resolve" (94). Those highest principles are, in part, the desiring of what we do not know that we want and the implications of discovering what it is that we want (e.g., not just drink to quench thirst but drink that is good for the human being, who is not only soul but must have body as well). The process is one that brings us more to the joining than to the separation of body and soul, to the replacement of "nature with syntax" (96); this, in turn, underscores Benardete's point that the city of speech, or the city as *idea*, cannot exist apart from the "dialogic city" where Socrates rules over the young men in Cephalus's house. The *ideas* are created by ourselves.

This interaction between the dialogic city and the city created by speech is at the core of Benardete's analysis. The latter is "made," the former comes into being and while the contradictions emerge in the "made" city, the dialogic city becomes the *Republic* itself. But the two cities exist not in simple opposition to one another. Rather, the process of creation entails the politicization of the dialogic city as the interlocutors metamorphose from a "we" of production (in the city of pigs) to the "us" against "them" of politics (in the fevered city). And as the ruler in the dialogic city, Socrates can turn Glaucon and Adeimantus into defenders of justice in the created city before in the dialogic city they know what justice is. Such is the power of speech. Further, by placing his interlocutors outside the constructed city, Socrates can make them see its beauty from without and be happy with that beauty, although were they to exist within the city, they might, as Adeimantus indeed does, question the unity of beauty and happiness. As the dialogic city always "shadows" (169) the city in speech, the latter city is undermined throughout and, with the questioning of that constructed city, we question the *ideas* created as well, the education that such *ideas* would require, the separation from the physical world entailed in such *ideas*—and we become aware of the joining of the mind and the physical worlds, of practice and philosophy as we would not were the focus only on the city of speech. This emphasis on the dialogic city as necessary for uncovering the true lesson of the *Republic* makes us aware of the limits of the city of speech; it is in this conclusion that we see most vividly the debt to Strauss's reading. But Benardete goes beyond Strauss in questioning not only the city in speech; we are left at the end of his analysis deep in the cave where "[t]he images of things are the truth of things" (228) and where philosophy as a "rare strand in the bond of the cosmos" may only arise "if babies who die at birth [and] choose a life at random sometimes get lucky" (229).

Benardete's interpretations are always novel, sometimes outrageous. Often, he will posit a reading that then becomes the untested basis for further claims. Having posed the question about the audience for the figure-holders of the cave, he accepts his own proposal that they *may* be speaking to themselves as the grounds for the subsequent analysis. One must be willing to follow him, as Adeimantus and Glaucon do with Socrates, though we may then find ourselves exclaiming with Adeimantus, "[W]hen the littles are collected at the end of the argument, the slip turns out to be great and contrary to the first assertions" (487b, Bloom translation).

As one reads Benardete's book, one is reminded of the Platonic dialogue as a model: The content cannot be abstracted from the form in which it is presented. But I fear that while the form of Plato's dialogues may draw us into the discourse of the characters, Benardete's style may establish a barrier for many. "Clarity makes us surreptitiously the standard," Benardete comments during his discussion of the divided line. "It is the subjective side of Truth" (166). Though in Benardete's reading, Socrates is turning us toward this subjective side as the beginning point for our philosophic search, Benardete does not see this as an injunction to clarity on his own part. This is a shame, for the novelty of his readings could do much to draw many back into the *Republic* as a work far richer even than the one that has enchanted readers for millennia and far more engaged in controversies of current theory and practice than is usually acknowledged.

Chapter Twenty

Review of *The Rhetoric of Morality and Philosophy*: *Plato's* Gorgias *and* Phaedrus

Abraham Anderson

Students of moral and political philosophy sometimes seem divided between those who seek truth through arguments without regarding their influence on human beings and those who think that argument, whether in political life or speculation, is a mere mask for power. Since the first abstract from human emotion and temperament, and the second deny the possibility of rationality as such, neither group attends to a central concern of Platonic and Aristotelian philosophy, rhetoric as the dimension which mediates between reasoning and emotion. In the book under review, Seth Benardete has chosen to investigate this dimension by studying the two dialogues of Plato most explicitly concerned with rhetoric and its powers: the *Gorgias* and the *Phaedrus*—the first being, he argues, Plato's meditation on moral rhetoric, the second Plato's meditation on philosophical rhetoric. Benardete himself, who has among the pupils of Leo Strauss the highest of reputations for his classical scholarship and subtlety of interpretation, is distinguished from many of Strauss's disciples by his readiness to go beyond commentary and address general questions directly and in his own person. He does so repeatedly in this work.

Benardete's discussion of the rhetoric of morality is organized around the fundamental Socratic paradox: Moral indignation must claim to be founded on knowledge, or it is unjust; but if moral judgment is founded on knowledge, then indignation has no place in it—those who act immorally are just ignorant, and therefore not blameworthy. Thus moral indignation, insofar as it involves a claim to knowledge which is both indispensable to it and

Reprinted from *Ancient Philosophy* 17, Issue 2 (Fall 1997): 443–47.

incompatible with it, is not only not founded on knowledge but is always founded on a particular sort of ignorance, the ignorance of one's own ignorance. Moral indignation invokes philosophy, since it seeks justification for moral judgments. But moral indignation also resists philosophy, since it must avoid the recognition of its own basis in ignorance. If there is a science of the just which leads us away from mere indignation to a theoretical knowledge of the nature of justice, such a science would not only not be just, it would be unjust—if, that is, "just" means disposed to moral indignation.

If rhetoric is the capacity to persuade the many of opinions about justice, then rhetoric, Benardete points out, might seem like the solution to the problem of the *Republic*: the solution to the problem of achieving a political order founded on knowledge. For rhetoric holds out the promise of uniting the authority of knowledge with the power of political persuasion and prudence; indeed, it claims to be a knowledge which consists in or is manifested through the ability to persuade. This promise is not realized. According to Benardete, however, the purpose of the *Gorgias* is not to show Socrates refuting the claims of rhetoric. It is rather to give a playful anatomy of rhetoric through his encounter with his three interlocutors, Gorgias, Polus, and Callicles.

Gorgias, according to Benardete, floats between science and opinion. He wishes to lay claim to an art—naturally, since he wishes to possess something teachable. He also wishes rhetoric to be powerful, indeed all-powerful, since the value and importance of that art, and hence his own value and importance, depend on its power. Gorgias claims that rhetoric is a knowledge, and at the same time the highest good. But Gorgias must defend rhetoric against the imputation that it is unjust. If his ability is to be effective, however, it cannot simply be a science of the just; such a science would not be suitable for public persuasion, which takes place under circumstances that leave no room for teaching.

Gorgias's rhetoric is in fact effective not because it is based on knowledge of truth, but by means of a capacity for giving pleasure. But Gorgias does not want to acknowledge that the power of rhetoric is based simply on the capacity to give pleasure; he wants it to be based on knowledge, and on a capacity for invoking justice, which appears to transcend the concern with pleasure through its appeal to moral indignation. Gorgias's inattention to pleasure blinds him, Benardete suggests, to the peculiar motivation of Socratic conversation, which is a conscious pursuit of pleasure through refuting and being refuted; though Gorgias too—but without being able to explain how or why—delights in his own activity. Whereas Socrates' activity is directed towards

254

self-knowledge and begins from a consciousness of ignorance of oneself, Gorgias's art is without self-knowledge, and by fostering pleasure in indignation it acts to prevent self-knowledge and knowledge of one's own ignorance. Socrates' destructive investigation of rhetoric's (or Gorgias's) claim to knowledge leads Polus to break in. Polus, unlike Gorgias, does not care about rhetoric's claim to be based on knowledge, in particular on any knowledge of the just and unjust; what interests him is simply its power, and power which culminates in the rhetorician's ability to exile and punish as he sees fit.

Polus, Benardete suggests, represents not the scientific aspiration of rhetoric, its claim to knowledge, but rather its moral element, its relation to indignation or the sense of justice; as well as the self-deceptive nature of the sense of justice, its relation to the concealment of one's own desire or pursuit of advantage—and in particular of any pleasure we might take in punishing. Polus's passion for punishing expresses the curious willfulness or abstraction of the moral, the belief that justice is always clear and that the activity of punishment, which expresses the anger of the punisher, can always discover and strike at the guilt of the punished, which is thus present and known via the indignation of the punisher. Polus insists, against Gorgias, that happiness and wisdom need not involve justice. His praise of Archelaus, Benardete argues, is intimately connected with his belief in Archelaus's injustice. Benardete suggests that the case of Polus is meant to show the relation between moral indignation and the attraction to tyranny; moral indignation both depends on the belief that injustice makes one happy and itself involves an impulse to punish others, an impulse allied to the belief in the happiness of the tyrant. Socrates' task in dealing with Polus, Benardete suggests, is to tame Polus's indignation by teaching him to turn it against himself; in teaching him to attend primarily to punishing his own vices and arrogance, rather than those of others, Socrates induces a version, at the level of moral self-government, of the philosopher's knowledge of his own ignorance.

Polus, Benardete says, represents what everybody thinks about the relation between happiness and injustice, but nobody dares to say. Callicles, on the other hand, represents not the thoughts or speeches of anybody and everybody but what is "said" by imperial Athens itself: the conjunction he makes between the praise of prudence and courage and the praise of gratification makes sense only as a representation of the spirit of Athens whose bold and clever activity of conquest and exploitation serves to provide it with wealth and gratification. He argues that Callicles' expansiveness of spirit is related to that of Pericles' funeral oration. The three speakers correspond, Benardete suggests, to the three parts of the soul in the psychology of the *Republic*, though they overlap, since Gorgias's interest in science contains an implicit moralism that leads to Polus' indignation, and this latter contains an implicit pleasure in willfulness which shades into the erotic. Both Polus's willfulness and Gorgias's belief in the power of words thus issue in Callicles' desire to escape all conditions or limitations through an unrestricted exercise of desire. The impossibility of distinguishing sharply between the three interlocutors of the *Gorgias* thus shows that the description of the soul as tripartite was illusory.

Benardete's problem in the *Phaedrus* commentary is: What is the relation between the discussion of writing and the discussion of eros? How does the problem of eros illuminate the problem of writing and vice versa? He begins with a characterization of Phaedrus. Phaedrus's attraction to Lysias, he argues, derives from Phaedrus's desire for a speech that transcends the erotic, a complete subjection of the erotic to the power of the Muses. Socrates' problem, if he is to lead Phaedrus in the direction of philosophy, is to disrupt his confidence in the sufficiency of the Muses, his tendency, as Benardete puts it, towards the state of a cicada, caught in an eternal and mindless enjoyment of music. Those who love speeches taken apart from everything else (lovers of "literature," as we would say nowadays) are not philosophical, according to Benardete.

Socrates' first long speech, Benardete proposes, suggests an intrinsic connection between political justice and moderation and the eros and hubris of the tyrant: the lover induces submissiveness in his beloved as the tyrant does in the many, by his own passionate pursuit of his own good: this, Benardete says, is what Thrasymachus wished but was ashamed to say about justice. But it is with the second long speech and its discussion of eros, the gods, and the beings beyond the visible that Benardete's discussion of the dialogue comes to a climax. Benardete's treatment of Socrates' discussion of the soul and its ascent is centered on the relation between the human mind and human form. The Olympian gods (and their inventors, the poets) humanized the Greeks by teaching them to represent the divine and the first principles it represents in a human form, and thus to couple the thought of divine law and first principles with attention to the visible world and to human desire, and the love of speeches with the love of sights. This claim leads Benardete to his discussion of writing and of the effect of Socrates on Greek religion: Socrates will have the effect of destroying the Olympian gods and bringing back their predecessors, of which they are humanized or beautified versions: the gods of Egypt. Benardete associates the Egyptian gods with writing and with divine law as written. In so doing, he seems to allude to the victory of Hebraic over Olympian religion, though he illustrates the victorious return of the Egyptian gods not by reference to Judaism or Christianity but by reference to Apuleius. *The Golden Ass,* Benardete suggests, is concerned with the return of the Egyptian gods in the wake of Socrates' destruction of the Olympians.

The other great theme of Benardete's discussion of the soul and the divine is the superiority of eros and imperfection to divine perfection, which lacks purpose or intrinsic meaning. The Olympian religion makes possible Socratic philosophy because it supports human eros against the strangeness or inhumanity of pre-Olympian divine law, and thereby makes possible Socrates' pursuit of the "divine," a pursuit which (in contrast to the speculation of the natural philosophers or the teaching of pre-philosophical priests) begins from the human. But the humanized gods of Olympus are subverted by the Socratic realization of the priority of human eros and pursuit of the intelligible to the Olympian gods, whom Socrates reduces to the figurative expressions of eros and the intelligible. The problem of divine law, Benardete suggests, is that it is antinomian: the strangeness of the divine which gives it authority also subverts it by transcending the law and inspiring curiosity about its extra-legal origins. Olympian religion tempers this effect by humanizing the gods, but, Benardete says, Olympian religion is impossible without the lingering authority of the pre-Olympians, though they are unintelligible in the light of Olympian religion. Eros too is antinomian with respect to human law: in leading us towards the "divine" as embodied in the beloved or in any other object of eros, it leads us beyond the law and beyond obedience generally. The extra-legal character of eros helps explain its importance for philosophy: one who, like Phaedrus, simply relies on speeches or on what everyone knows, never moves beyond opinion; only a use of words conjoined with eros for the visible and the "reminders" it affords us can lead the mind beyond conventional thoughts. Thus it is not surprising that Benardete holds the black horse of the soul-story (eros) to be decisively superior to the white horse (opinion or spiritedness); he goes so far, in fact, as to say that the white horse is a disguised imitation of the black horse, a projection of it outside itself. He also identifies the black horse with Socrates and suggests that the hooked nose of the white horse is Meletus's, as the snub nose of the black is Socrates'.

Benardete's discussion of eros leads to his discussion of writing: writing is shown by the *Phaedrus*, he says, to be superior to speech because of its capacity for repeating at once the living whole of a conversation and the logical order of its parts, the analytic or spatial order embodied by that temporal process. Speech alone cannot do this. It is the written imitation of the Socratic dialogue, invented by Plato, which best solves the problem of how to unite the claims of scientific invariance made by writing and the acquisition of self-knowledge apparently possible only through speech or conversation.

Benardete's discussion of the treatment of writing emphasizes the antinomian character of the *Phaedrus* itself, and of Socratic philosophy generally. Law is merely a plaything. The reason for this is its rigidity, which means that it, unlike Socratic dialogue or Platonic writing, cannot adjust itself to the different sorts of souls. In any case law does not reason freely as philosophy does, since it must seek to establish and enforce a stable opinion. But this antinomian character of Socratic philosophy does not exclude the ability to create a stable teaching. Because it can "show" us speeches and their parts as speech itself cannot, Platonic writing, Benardete says, is superior to oral philosophical tradition; Benardete contrasts the survival of Socrates and Plato through the written text with the degeneration of the Academy in and after Plotinus, though he also indicates that sects may be necessary for preserving consciousness of the unity of a writer's oeuvre over time. Sects have the disadvantage, he says, of discouraging those who are not followers by nature from seeking access to the thought of the philosopher who founded the sect. This is regrettable, because it is precisely those who are not followers by nature who might learn from the founders of sects in a higher degree than do their followers, and thereby become the rivals of those founders. In speaking of founders of sects Benardete is speaking of Plato, but perhaps also of his teacher Strauss.

Chapter Twenty-One

Review of *The Bow and the Lyre*: *A Platonic Reading of the* Odyssey

Martin Sitte

Benardete's book investigates the possibility that the Socratic turn in philosophy, that which enabled philosophy to inquire into the human and political, had been anticipated by and perhaps learned from the poets. Benardete asks in particular whether Homer had not fully understood the peculiar character of that indirection which, according to the "second sailing" of the *Phaedo*, is needed for access to the truth. He reminds us that according to Socrates' second speech in the *Phaedrus*, the ascent to the beings always requires the detour through "the fiction of the Olympian gods." The book is intended to initiate us into Homeric dialectic.

Benardete acts on the assumption that Homer is as aware of the implications of all he says as, say, a philosopher would be. For example, the stories of Nestor, Menelaus, and Odysseus about the return of the heroes from the Trojan War do not quite cohere. Where many scholars take Homer to be combining disparate traditions, Benardete takes Homer to be indicating on the level of narrative the re-isolation of the cities after their joint effort; common authority for both action and speech has disappeared. Benardete's procedure frees him to take seriously the problems of the surface on their own terms.

The central event of the *Odyssey* is Odysseus' choice, when faced with Calypso's offer to make him a god, to remain human. The *Odyssey* is deliberately structured to avoid presenting the deliberation leading to that choice. It is an extended reflection both on the choiceworthiness and meaning of human life and on the obstacles to discerning that meaning, presenting the former primarily through the latter. Odysseus is shown to have to undergo

Reprinted from *The Review of Metaphysics* 51, no. 4 (June 1998): 911–13. Page numbers in parentheses refer to *The Bow and the Lyre: A Platonic Reading of Homer's* Odyssey (Chicago: University of Chicago Press, 1997).

self-misunderstanding before achieving such self-understanding as he does; Benardete tries to show that Homer similarly leads the reader through error, intended to precipitate misinterpretation, as necessary preparation for true understanding. Even this is misleading if the reader assumes that forewarning of such a procedure suffices in order to bypass the need for such indirection. Precisely the necessarily unanticipatable consequences of necessary error are what is necessary; else the reader is likely to seek answers only to the questions, and only in the way, that he already knows. (We may compare Socrates' investigating the truth rather through refutation of opinions than directly.) In this, Benardete gives Homer's wisdom the benefit of the doubt: his book consists primarily in articulating the perplexities with which Homer attempts to ensnare and prepare the reader, and he is extremely chary of suggesting how these are to be resolved; he seeks to induce confrontation with the problems—one may be tempted to compare an aporetic dialogue. The epigraph, from Eustathius, reads: "The *Odyssey*: Depth of thought with a surface simplicity"; Benardete dispenses with the latter. Homer's readers have the choice to lose themselves in the charm of the story and not raise such questions, Benardete's do not. Why, then, are his readers likely to think the challenge of this difficult book worth undertaking?

We illustrate the complexity of the puzzle with Odysseus' choice. The reader is given the immediate consequences of that choice, a retrospective account of the experiences leading up to it, and an account of the principal event of the life defined by that choice. It is further necessary, in the story of Odysseus' adventures preceding his choice, to disentangle his self-understanding at the time of those experiences from that resulting from seven years' reflection on them, and from any distortion due to his purposes in telling his story to the Phaeacians, while always remembering his agility in the telling of lies. In the land of the forgetfulness-inducing lotus, Odysseus chooses memory and the particularity it entails, whereas in the very next adventure he seems to understand himself as embodying the rootless anonymity of mind (in calling himself "No One" to the Cyclops, he puns on "mind"). He held back from his first urge to inflict (just) punishment on the Cyclops, realizing that, were he to kill him, he would have no means of escaping the cave, and he understands his holding back as reason triumphing over anger—although thereby reason also causes necessity to triumph over justice. However, he cannot refrain from gloating when beyond the Cyclops' reach, at the cost of bringing down on himself Polyphemus' curse: reason has not triumphed over anger as much as he had thought; perhaps it was animated by a subtler form of anger. One of the main themes of the book is this subtle interplay of will and reason. When Odysseus' men have been turned into swine, in his first act not aimed at his own advantage, Odysseus risks trying to rescue them, and this act is immediately followed by Hermes' revealing to him that things have natures; Benardete interprets the passage concerning the nature of the moly, the "peak" of the *Odyssey*, as pointing to knowledge of the necessary invisible unity of the nature of man, the indivisibility of human form and human mind. Benardete at first speaks of the knowledge of nature as a reward for Odysseus' "completely just and daring action, with its implicit recognition of what he shares with other human beings" (84). Yet on pages 85 and 87 he restates this thought with a qualifying "seems." Is the first observation something that the reader would want to be true, and are the subsequent remarks a way to let that reader down gently, if indeed the quiet qualification is noticed? Or is the first statement a truth very difficult to hold onto in the face of experience? Or is Homer suggesting that the actor himself cannot be certain of the demarcation between the contributions of reason and of will; is Homer's understanding of that truth different from Odysseus'? To answer the latter requires both the account of Hades and of Odysseus' return. Like the *Republic*, the *Odyssey* concerns the contribution to wisdom of reflection on the relation of justice and wisdom. What is the relation within Odysseus of the wanderer after knowledge and the avenging punisher of the suitors? The encounter with the Sirens suggests that Odysseus' deepest desire is for knowledge, but he seems to be reborn a different man when brought home.

The *Odyssey* prepares the withdrawal of the gods from direct intervention in human life; it ushers in the post-heroic age, with a corresponding increase in the harshness of life. The gods will govern by threat and terror instead; humans will live under law and not easily moderated human desire to punish. The killing of the suitors and disloyal servants stands in stark disproportion to the apparent pettiness of their offenses; it sends a dire warning to all who hear of it, but the justice behind it is very difficult to discern. The latter part of the book hovers between two interpretations of Odysseus' motives which are nearly impossible to combine. On the one hand, Odysseus is faced with the political problem of resentment for having lost the best of a whole generation of Ithacans during his absence, a resentment whose most prominent representatives are the suitors. Securing the throne for Telemachus and lawful succession would seem to require the removal of the incurably hostile. Is Odysseus capable of cold-blooded killing solely on the basis of political calculation—in spite, for example, of the suitors' offer to pay back the property they had consumed? Or is Odysseus stirred by a just anger, and if so, how does he understand the suitors' offenses to be such as to merit this degree of punishment? The earlier question is thus restated in the second half of the *Odyssey*. Benardete leaves the reader in as much suspense as he can. He demonstrates the extent to which the presentation on the narrative level imitates the difficulties of self-knowledge for Odysseus. In choosing to be human, Odysseus chooses some degree of self-opacity. Self-justification interferes with self-knowledge. Odysseus in his desire to be a Somebody sacrifices not only the "No One" of mind; to establish the new harsh justice, to reestablish rule which can no longer be on the grounds of the natural right by which he somehow took over the rule from his father, he is also forced to be the messenger of the new piety, the furtherer of faith in things unseen, all the more terrifying for being unseen.

Homer understands by way of negation, not to say double negation. The human cannot be articulated on its own, but only as neither the divine nor the bestial; the divine and bestial can in turn only be put together in their own negation. The human propensity to interpret events in the light of justice, and the mysteries of the workings of the will, which Homer in bringing Greekness to the Greeks expresses together through the gods, point to different modes of understanding: the patterns of right and experience do not simply cohere. Odysseus' name derives from the verb for anger, ambiguously as to whether object of anger or subject to it. As the indispensable element of his sense of justice and his experience of justice, anger would stand as the limit to his self-understanding, if not to Homer's.

None of this is to deny that Benardete gives occasional hints toward resolutions. For the working out of the connection to Plato, the reader is referred to his several books and articles on Plato, in particular his interpretation of the *Republic—Socrates' Second Sailing* (Chicago: University of Chicago Press, 1989).

Chapter Twenty-Two

Review of *The Argument of the Action*: *Essays on Greek Poetry and Philosophy*

Steven Berg

The Argument of the Action is a collection of essays by Seth Benardete on Greek poetry and philosophy selected and introduced by Ronna Burger and Michael Davis. We must be grateful to the editors for making these remarkable essays available to readers once again. The collection encompasses the greater part of the most significant authors of Greek antiquity: Homer and Hesiod, the tragedians, and Plato and Aristotle. Each essay opens up the work under consideration and illuminates its essential concerns in such a new and yet convincing way that the reader is forced to experience simultaneously a shock of surprise and a sense of recognition. In interpreting these works, Benardete never repeats himself, never foists an alien schema upon the text, and never merely rests upon the laurels of an insight previously won. Yet, and this is one of the most admirable aspects of the book, despite the range of their topics and the individuality of each interpretation, the essays exhibit a rare unity of intellectual purpose. They constitute an exploration of a single terrain of reflection which includes, on the one hand, the character and meaning of Socrates' "turn to the speeches" or his "second sailing" and, on the other, the setting and preconditions of that turn displayed in the works of the Greek poets.

Benardete understands Socrates' turn to be the genuine discovery of philosophy (408) that is, nevertheless, essentially consequent to the "historical" beginning of philosophy. Thought, he argues, necessarily begins with a false articulation of the question which is nonetheless that without which its true articulation would prove impossible. According to Benardete's analysis, this is a consequence of the "mutual interference" of the double starting point

Reprinted from *The Review of Metaphysics* 55, no. 1 (Sept. 2001): 119–21. Page numbers in parentheses refer to *The Argument of the Action*, eds. Ronna Burger and Michael Davis (Chicago: University of Chicago Press, 2000).

of philosophy: reflection on the nature of the beings, on the one hand, and on the nature of the good, on the other (411). For the attempt to reveal the being as a part works at cross-purposes with the attempt to comprehend the whole of which it is a part. As a consequence we conceive as separate what can only be understood as together—a one is taken for a two—or as one and the same what is in fact irreducibly different—a two is taken for a one. Socratic dialectics (collection and division in speech), as Benardete understands it, constitutes the way to overcoming both the false unities and the false divisions of opinion in an ascent to the truth of the whole.

According to Benardete's interpretation of Socrates' own account of his discovery of this way (287–93), Socrates came to understand that all "presocratic" causal analyses of becoming are in fact versions of the erroneous starting point of opinion. Such analyses understand the togetherness of parts in a whole to be the result of a process of aggregation that is modeled on the operations of counting as commonly understood (287). In the light of this realization, Socrates saw that the problems inherent in the attempt to understand the coming-to-be of two from the addition or division of ones pose insuperable difficulties for all causal accounts, since opposite causes must be supposed to produce one and the same effect and the same cause opposite effects (286–87). When he found this same problem, however, embedded in the relation between the teleological and efficient causation that lies at the heart of the Anaxagorean account of mind as cause (290), he realized that causal accounts as such are unintelligible or merely "mythological," that is, they treat as separate—or as an aggregate—what can only be understood as essentially together or, as Benardete has it, they understand a "disjunctive two" in terms of a "conjunctive two" (289; compare 316).

Socrates, therefore, came to see that not only the togetherness of things, but their separation as well can be understood only as operations of mind, not as final or efficient cause but as at work in the speeches. Thus he was compelled, in Benardete's words, to "jump to logos away from fact" or "the things" (288). He turned from a causal analysis to what Benardete calls an "eidetic analysis" (371). Ceasing to attempt to account for how two are together, he sought instead to demonstrate that they cannot be what they are apart from their being together (296). Yet Socrates' new way incorporates the error of the old within it: the conjunctive two is retained not as a mode of directly understanding the beings, but as an event within the speeches, namely, the starting point of dialectics in the ideality of opinion which the argument of the action of dialectics cancels or overcomes (286, 320, 329, 346–47, 372).

Benardete shows how, in the works of Plato, this "mythological" starting point is dictated by the dialogic situation. Socrates is paired with a particular interlocutor whose limited perspective conditions and partially determines the character of the speeches. The erotic aspect of Socrates' philosophy—his coupling in speech with another—therefore ensures that the arguments of Plato's dialogues are always together with a particular set of conditions apart from which they cannot be understood. At the same time, the understanding of the truth of those arguments equally requires that one tease apart the argument from the distorting influence exercised by these same conditions. This separating of the speeches from their conditions, however, is the "dialogic equivalent" or the truth of the separation of soul and body: the "practice of dying and being dead." When these two partial aspects of Socrates' philosophizing are put together they amount to the "double practice . . . of collection and division . . . whose single name is dialectic" (167). The togetherness of Socratic *dialektikē* and *dialegesthai* (350) means that Socrates' starting point is the political opinions of his interlocutors or the "idealism" of the city and that the initial assumption of the apartness of the beings is a function of the false political understanding of the good: its reduction to the just or the beautiful. Socrates' turn to the speeches, therefore, is also the discovery of political philosophy (413).

That Benardete's work is devoted not simply to Socratic philosophy, but also to an analysis of the works of the Greek poets that preceded Socrates is explained in part by his conviction that the poets, long before Socrates' revolution in thought, had undertaken similar inquiries—the tragic poets in formulating the nature of the city (215) and Homer and Hesiod in their recognition of the relation of argument and action (416). Hesiod, Benardete remarks, knew as well as Socrates that no direct access to the beings is possible, but that "the recovery of the beings is through the meaning of the beings" (11). Socrates' discovery of political philosophy is, therefore, in fact a rediscovery (415). Benardete's remarkable insight in this regard is that philosophy as such cannot have a perfectly original starting point, but is always and necessarily the recovery of a prior possibility.

In the two final essays of the volume, Benardete acknowledges his debt to Leo Strauss, whom he understands to be the first to have succeeded in recovering political philosophy since the similar and comparably momentous efforts of al-Farabi in the tenth century. In doing so he identifies his own work as an extension of the renewal of political philosophy that the thought of Strauss represents. Benardete's accomplishment in this regard is extraordinary. His interpretations of the Greek tragedies, the poems of Homer and Hesiod and, above all, the dialogues of Plato, while proceeding on the basis of Strauss's own principles, illuminate in unprecedented ways the central concern of Platonic political philosophy as both Strauss and Benardete understand it: "to articulate the problem of cosmology" in answering "the question what philosophy is or what a philosopher is" (416).

Chapter Twenty-Three

A Classicist's Starting Point:
Putting Aside Interpretations

Edward Rothstein

Confessions of ignorance are not usually in a critic's best interest. But in this case, perhaps, an exception can be made. Ignorance, after all, is now common when confronting Greek literature. Beginning with ignorance is also an approach recommended by many of these demanding essays by Seth Benardete, a classicist at New York University, who died to relatively little notice in November. Because of his difficult and idiosyncratic interpretations, that notice is not likely to expand beyond a small group of philosophers, political scientists and classicists.

Yet testimonials are unqualified. Pierre Vidal-Naquet, the respected French historian, has proclaimed of Benardete, "I have long believed that he deserves glory—that of the heroes of Homer, to be precise." Harvey Mansfield, a political scientist at Harvard, said Benardete was "the most learned man alive and, I venture to assert, the deepest thinker as well." According to several anecdotes, T. S. Eliot heaped praise on his brilliance. At a memorial program at New York University earlier this month, encomiums for the man—who spent his career writing translations and commentary on Plato, a book on *The Odyssey* (*The Bow and the Lyre*) and essays on Sophocles, Euripides, and Aristotle—were offered by philosophers and classicists, including Ronna Burger of Tulane University and Michael Davis of Sarah Lawrence College, both of whom edited the current collection.

But why the broad devotion to so specialized a scholar? Why the praise for a writer whose gnomic vocabulary about gnomic material uses phrases like "eidetic analysis" and "indeterminate dyad"?

Review of *The Argument of the Action*, eds. Ronna Burger and Michael Davis (Chicago: University of Chicago Press, 2000). Reprinted from *The New York Times*, "Shelf Life," February 16, 2002.

The Argument of the Action provides some answers by collecting essays written throughout Benardete's career. They are so intimidating in their minute attention to Greek tragedies and Platonic dialogues that they can barely be read without following the works themselves (only some of which I have studied). The essays ornately weave allusions, analyses and images, engaging in close textual analysis while venturing unsettling hypotheses.

The first step, Benardete stressed, is indeed to approach the works as a beginner, to read, say, *The Republic* or *Oedipus Tyrannus* free from millennia of interpretations. At first, the arguments and plots might seem fairly transparent. Sophocles' most famous Oedipus play, for example, has long been regarded as a story about a man who unknowingly kills his father, the king of Thebes, and marries his mother. When he discovers the truth, he blinds himself. Such are the tragic consequences of desire and fate.

Such plays have, of course, been analyzed for their literary structure. But Benardete goes further. He looks not for unity but for peculiarity. Why does the queen apparently marry Oedipus before she knows about her husband's death? Why does the witness to Oedipus's crime contradict the known facts? We think we understand the action, but the closer we look the less seems clear. For Benardete the play forces the reader to blunder into its familiar world as unknowingly as Oedipus does in his, to engage in a detailed inquiry and to discover the unexpected. Consider, he suggests, the great riddle of the Sphinx that Oedipus must solve to stop the plague that has come to Thebes: what walks on four legs in the morning, on two at midday and on three in the evening? Oedipus's answer is man, who first crawls as a baby, then walks upright and in old age uses a cane. That answer would seem to show him a master of the human. But Oedipus is more like its victim. The problem in Benardete's view is that he sees only the general not the particular. His notion of the human is outlined by the Sphinx's riddle. All variation and difference is lost; even Oedipus himself, partially lame, does not fit the Sphinx's pattern. Yet he persists in focusing purely on the abstract. He becomes a tyrant, seeking to establish public order as if it could be created by formula. The play, Benardete argues, is about tragic consequences of political blindness.

In such a reading the surface is closely examined to reveal unexpected depths. This was also the approach of Benardete's mentor at the University of Chicago, Leo Strauss, a charismatic scholar. Students of Strauss, including Benardete, have had an almost cultic relationship to him. Many have also become influential conservative intellectuals—most famously, the late Allan Bloom, author of *The Closing of the American Mind*. Strauss has, in fact, been attacked for conservativism: his unmitigated elitism and supposed antidemo-cratic temperament, which some say included the suggestion that Nazism was a product of the Enlightenment. But this view of the Nazis—and of Soviet Communism—was not as bizarre as it might seem. It was held by Isa-iah Berlin as well, because the ideals of the Enlightenment included the belief that reason had utopian powers and that humanity could be reconstructed under its guidance. That belief in the malleability of the human, Berlin argued, ended up leading to totalitarianism.

Strauss's dismissal of the reasoned perfectibility of society did not, as many have claimed, lead to a belief that the quest for justice should not be attempted. It did mean that any attempt to attain justice could only approach its goal by taking into account the ambiguities, unpredictability and variability of humanity. Strauss stressed the inherent difficulty of the project, not the need for its abandonment; that was one reason for his elitism. This view does not seem far from Benardete's. Oedipus, again, is a political leader who mis-takenly believes that justice can be attained and suffering relieved by the nar-row application of reason and will alone. The word sphinx means binder or constrictor, Benardete argues, which is just what such a narrow view of the human will do: bind rather than liberate. That was Benardete's response to the Sphinx's riddle.

Chapter Twenty-Four

At Homer's Diner:
Conversations with Seth Benardete

Mark Blitz

There's a joke that goes: "'Do you know where we're supposed to go?' I said, 'No.' So he said, 'Well let's go together.' That's how we met."

This joke—an all-purpose metaphor for youth, love, education, friendship, and thought—appears in *Encounters and Reflections*. The book is a remarkable collection of accounts of Seth Benardete's encounters with various people, now mostly obscure, and his reflections on topics, more obscure still. Benardete, the classical scholar and philosopher who died last year, sat down in the early 1990s with three of his students to recapture their conversations of twenty years before. The resulting discussions are both spontaneous and well ordered: a lovely achievement brought about by the editor's skill, Benardete's wizardry, and the familiarity of friends. Of course, they don't quite have the unity of one of Plato's dialogues. But it's nonetheless presumably no accident that many of them occurred in a place called Homer's Diner.

The first part of *Encounters and Reflections* treats the reader to Benardete's stories about his friends and teachers, occupants of lost worlds of scholarship and intellectual passion, with some of their attendant eccentricities: "Didn't you once tell us that Strauss didn't know how to boil water? No, that was Wachs, in the sociology of religion." Benardete's anecdotes and descriptions often are punctuated with compressed analyses of his colleagues' leading traits and their cause. The remarkable Allan Bloom saw the meaning of the 1960s more clearly than Benardete and had extraordinary sensitivity "to people's defects." Yet, "he got impatient if you could not say what you wanted to say in more than half a sentence," and the vanity of which he accused others (such

Review of *Encounters and Reflections: Conversations with Seth Benardete* (Chicago: University of Chicago Press, 2003). Reprinted from *The Weekly Standard* 8, no. 29 (April 7, 2003).

as the late philosopher Richard Kennington) might better be attributed to Bloom himself.

In fact, Kennington's questions always seemed to Benardete "to be so much deeper than anything I was doing that I couldn't catch up" (which must make Kennington so deep as to be literally unfathomable). Benedict Einarson, a professor of classics at Chicago, "knew more than anybody else. Absolutely amazing knowledge." But "he looked like the Michelin tire ad," and "everything he said was punctuated by a laugh." Peter von Blanckenhagen, the art historian, understood himself as Goethe understood Winckelmann, "the notion of the eternal moment being preserved by the work of art," two things "completely at odds." Yet "he was eager to be accepted by people who did not have the same capacity as he did, like those who were at the top of the American archaeological profession, who were unimaginative, or imaginative in a very professional way, not like him at all." The classical historian Arnaldo Momigliano also knew everything but was never satisfied with the number of his honorary degrees. Renato Poggioli, who studied comparative literature, would always conclude his conversations by saying, "Now you see the point," more charming if less honest than Jacob Klein's characteristic "By Zeus I don't know." And that's not to mention Benardete's discussions of rats, dogs, deer, and T. S. Eliot.

There is an untold amount to learn from any of Benardete's books: works like *The Argument of the Action: Essays on Greek Poetry and Philosophy*, or *Socrates' Second Sailing: On Plato's* Republic, or *Herodotean Inquiries*. But to read them is to be forced to overcome a real denseness and compression that sometimes blocks access to them. *Encounters and Reflections* is attractive because the clear, straightforward, and charming Benardete of its first part makes us confident of the accessibility of the master magician of textual interpretation. In the second part, moreover, Benardete is still answering questions. When he says something dense about Plato's *Phaedrus* or *Republic*, his friends ask what he means, and they keep on asking until it comes clear. Robert Berman, Ronna Burger, and Michael Davis's own considerable learning and intelligence allow them the luxury here of seeming occasionally to be ignorant—and thus to ask out loud the question one sometimes mutters when reading Benardete: What could you possibly mean?

Still, the discussions in *Encounters and Reflections* are difficult. They cover many poets and thinkers, chiefly Plato. We see remarkable reflections on the connection between the gods and the ideas, the political-theological problem, love and spiritedness, existence, and the good. The major theme is Benardete's view that, in ancient poetry and Plato's dialogues, the plot embodies its own logic. It cannot be explained simply as exemplifying or modifying in detailed action a formal structure or list of topics. "Well, if the Platonic dialogue and ancient poetry always have to do with the oddity of the individual, what is being reflected in these imitations is the fact that something is being disclosed in a particular that is incapable of being disclosed in any other way. It looks as if the Platonic enterprise is based on a thesis about the nature of the world—that there is something I would call the encounter with the question, which can't be determined by formula or concept."

The bulk of the book discusses this point, in various guises. The inevitable duality in things, their being what they are but not only that, is the major issue. Benardete's students press him, trying to work this problem out in specific cases. He makes clear how his initial formal analyses of books (for example, that Herodotus follows the pattern laid out in the Divided Line of Plato's *Republic*) is modified by his new understanding. Needless to say, we can clarify this understanding more completely only by reading Benardete's other works, and the books he is discussing.

A second theme of *Encounters and Reflections* is the idea of "beginning"— beginning to think and to learn. Benardete sketches throughout his remarks a notion of how original questions, perplexities, or crises launch inquiries that when pursued uncover the deeper cause of what has launched them. The Greek discovery of the singularity of nature over the multiplicity of laws, conventions, and cultures is the necessary condition for the philosophical quest. Yet, the individuality of one's beginning retains a certain independence. The particular is not wholly subsumed in the general, practice not wholly subsumed in theory, the lover not wholly subsumed in what is loved. Socrates' political philosophy puts philosophy in crisis by involving it with political risk and desire for what is best for oneself. This seeking of what is good here and now, and not just what is good generally, keeps philosophy alive.

Encounters and Reflections not only discusses the importance of the individual, it exemplifies it. In fact, the occasional and accidental element in things may make us despair over our own condition. We apparently have nothing with which to replace the marvelous combination of accidents—academic parents, undergraduate friends such as Stanley Rosen and Bloom, attention to the great books, and the presence of Leo Strauss—that helped make Benardete what he was. Indeed, given the state of the academy today, we may well wonder whether the passion of the scholar that he exemplified will ever revive. Intense and brilliant thought may still exist, but will it again be as significant individually or as dominant generally as once it was? One by one our intellectual giants disappear, and their memories seem to shrivel in the gloomy and endless cave of our mediocrity.

It is more hopeful to say instead that in books like this they continue to glow. The humor and intelligence in Seth Benardete's *Encounters and Reflections* make us long for the world it remembers. This world can be recovered because none of the elements that constitutes it is simply an accident. Each reflects or exemplifies things more lasting: love, friendship, natural wonder, intellect, and courage.

Chapter Twenty-Five

Review of *Encounters and Reflections*: *Conversations with Seth Benardete*

Vincent Renzi

As Ronna Burger notes in her preface [to *Encounters and Reflections*], the present volume is "a project that falls outside the usual categories" of scholarship (x). While listing him as author, it is in fact an edited transcript of interviews with Seth Benardete, late of the New York University Department of Classics, conducted during 1992 and 1993 by Burger, Michael Davis, and Robert Berman, three of his former students from the Department of Philosophy at the New School for Social Research, where Benardete had also frequently taught during his long career in New York. It falls into two major sections, each of five chapters. The first, "Encounters," is primarily reminiscences of persons Benardete had known. It will be of interest to many classicists at least for the anecdotes concerning eminent philologists of the past. In the second half, "Reflections," the conversations turn to discussion of Benardete's major interpretative contributions, especially in regard to ancient philosophy, and Plato in particular.

Benardete was certainly one of the leading classicists of his generation. He possessed an encyclopedic learning and an unsurpassed mastery of Greek, and, as a translator, demonstrated a rare combination of fidelity to the original and fluid English idiom of great literary merit. For his provocative and insightful analyses especially of Plato, which comprised the central concern of his career, he was well known; yet his own originality as a philosophical thinker has not been easy to appreciate.[1] As a kind of compendium of his

Reprinted, with updated notes by the author, from *The Bryn Mawr Classical Review* 2003.11.31.

1. Even when the profundity and influence of Benardete's work is appreciated in the abstract, frequently missed or misunderstood is the playfulness of his writing and the deep philosophical reasons for his style of close commentary. See, e.g.,

thought, *Encounters and Reflections* provides a welcome occasion for such an assessment. While Benardete had read the penultimate draft of the book prior to his death in November 2001, there is much of his work subsequent to the interviews—then eight or nine years before—that is not reflected here. I shall try therefore to round out an account of his career with a view to his later work and from my own conversations with him, which began with my arrival at N.Y.U. in 1997.[2]

Part I of *Encounters and Reflections* is arranged to follow the chronology of Benardete's life and starts with his answers to some queries from the interlocutors about his upbringing and early years. These preliminaries quickly yield a store of vignettes about fellow students, former teachers, and others with whom Benardete was acquainted from his time as an undergraduate at the University of Chicago (where he began in 1948), through his graduate education there, fellowships in Rome and at Harvard and his first faculty positions, to his arrival at N.Y.U. in 1964 and subsequent career.

For those who were fortunate to have heard them from Benardete himself, these stories will bring back fond memories. Quite apart from this personal appeal, the interviews also form a remarkable historical record; but to collect and arrange them in this way necessarily misses the natural context in which Benardete would have told these tales. To anyone who had extended conversations with him, they will be familiar, for Benardete often adduced one or the other of them to punctuate discussions. Those of his experiences which

---

Edward Rothstein's article on Benardete's collected essays, *The Argument of the Action*, in *The New York Times* (February 16, 2002), reprinted in this volume. For an appreciation of his typical style, see the review by Michael Davis of Benardete's *The Being of the Beautiful*, reprinted in this volume. See also Richard Velkley, "In Memoriam: Seth Benardete, 1930-2001," *The Claremont Review of Books*, Winter 2002.

2. During this period, I sometimes had occasion to audit Benardete's philosophy courses at the New School, each of which formed the basis of a later paper of his. —Heraclitus, Spring 1998; "On Heraclitus"; —*Timaeus*, Spring 1999; "On the *Timaeus*"; —Parmenides, Spring 2000; "'Night and Day,...': Parmenides"; —Plato's *Parmenides*, Spring 2001; "Plato's *Parmenides*: A Sketch." These papers are now published in either *The Argument of the Action*, 2000, or *The Archaeology of the Soul*, 2012. (See "Works by Seth Benardete" in this volume.) (At the time of his death, Benardete was planning a course on the *Euthydemus* for Spring 2002.) In addition to having been a colleague of Benardete—albeit one trained in philosophy, not Classics—I should also acknowledge my acquaintance with Michael Davis, who kindly provided copies of some of Benardete's papers before they were published.

Benardete would recall on these occasions were of interest to him because of what they revealed—more comically than tragically—of human nature and the human condition. In retrospect, however, it seems clear this was rather of a piece with his interest in Herodotus—the subject of his first book, and an author with whom he remained concerned throughout his career.[3] Indeed, the whole first part of *Encounters and Reflections* is, I think, best understood, as a kind of Herodotean inquiry. In Benardete's view, Herodotus is of interest not for his "history" (in the modern sense), but for the way his narratives unfold within his work as a whole: What they communicate must be understood as something beyond their content. It concerns the interplay of contents and occasion—what Benardete called the tension between "pattern" and "dynamic."[4] Through this tension, Herodotus' stories reveal enduring sources of continuing inquiry into human affairs, rather than solutions to the puzzles of "history." In the same way, the interest of the stories collected by Burger et al. is not so much for what they tell us of Benardete *qua* individual—and in any case, Benardete was or makes himself out always to be a bystander of their action. Their interest lies rather in what they reveal to be the source of his understanding of philosophy—concrete encounters with the unexpected in human life.[5]

Since the point of the stories anthologized in *Encounters and Reflections* is not autobiography, they provide little direct sense of Benardete's intellectual development. Chief among the influences on him was his relationship—as a student and subsequently—with Leo Strauss, whose importance is clear from the frequent references to his work in the "Reflections" section, as opposed to his nearly complete absence from the "Encounters." Benardete readily acknowledged his teacher's impact on him; but Strauss's own work is so commonly and completely misunderstood that little is to be gained merely by attaching the term "Straussian" to Benardete.[6] Benardete did clearly take

---

3. *Herodotean Inquiries* (Nijhoff, 1969), reprinted with an appendix "Second Thoughts" (St. Augustine's Press, 1999). Benardete returned to Herodotus again in "Freedom: Grace and Necessity" (2001), reprinted in *The Archaeology of the Soul*. (See "Works by Seth Benardete" in this volume.) Discussion of Herodotus also informs his commentary on Plato's *Laws* (Chicago, 2000). See especially the Preface to that work, xii–xvii.

4. Cf. "From Pattern to Dynamic," chapter six of *Encounters and Reflections*. For the discussion of Herodotus therein, see 118–20.

5. Cf. Burger's preface to *Encounters and Reflections*, vii.

6. Cf. the recent spate of commentary that seeks to hold Strauss responsible for the

from Strauss an appreciation of philosophy's place in human affairs and an approach to engaging texts philosophically; and these are evident already in his readings of the *Iliad* (the subject of his dissertation at Chicago in 1955), Aeschylus's *Persians* and *Suppliant Maidens* (translations of which were his first publications, in 1957), and Herodotus.[7] Some forty years later, in his *The Bow and the Lyre: A Platonic Reading of the* Odyssey (1997), Benardete remarked that he had come to understand why this interpretative method had proven fruitful: The power of these interpretations was due to the fact that Plato had inherited from his predecessors his understanding both of the domain of philosophical problems and the range of solutions he addresses. This insight, Benardete writes, he owed ultimately to Strauss.[8]

In other words, it might be said (to use the useful terminology of literary theorist Harold Bloom) that Plato's "strength" as a poet obscures for the tradition his dependence on his predecessors, and none among them more so than the "historical" Socrates.[9] By the end of his career, Benardete's thinking-through of this thought had given him in turn a highly nuanced sense of the literary character of Plato's work in particular and of his predecessors' more generally. This allowed him remarkable insights on the methods by

---

politics of the current administration in the United States. See, e.g.: James Atlas, "A Classicist's Legacy: New Empire Builders," *The New York Times* (May 4, 2003), Week in Review section, page 1; and Jeet Heer, "The Mind of the Administration," *The Boston Globe* (May 11, 2003), page H1. For a helpful corrective see "The Real Leo Strauss," by Jenny Strauss Clay, *The New York Times* (June 7, 2003), page A15.

7. See also his Master's thesis on the *Theages* (Chicago, 1953). Benardete accepted this dialogue as Platonic, as he was typically inclined to accept as authentic—in the case of the *Theages* and the *Minos* explicitly—Platonic works of the Thrasyllan corpus whose authorship is now disputed. For discussion of the latter, see his commentary on Plato's *Laws*, especially 3–7. Cf. also his "Plato, True and False" (review of Plato, *Complete Works*, edited by John Cooper), reprinted in *The Archaeology of the Soul*. (See "Works by Seth Benardete" in this volume.)

8. *The Bow and the Lyre* (Rowman and Littlefield, 1997), xiv. For an extended appraisal of Strauss's influence on him, see Benardete's "Strauss on Plato" (1993), reprinted in *The Argument of the Action*, 407–17.

9. Cf. Charles Kahn's *Plato and the Socratic Dialogue* (Cambridge, 1996). Kahn's Plato could likewise be said to be a "strong poet," dominating our view of others working in the same literary genre of "dialogues with Socrates." Already before this, Strauss was remarkable among modern commentators on Plato for the weight he gave to the accounts of Socrates to be found in the works of Xenophon.

which these authors can be approached, their epistemological and metaphysical commitments, and the importance of Plato's distinction between "poetry" and "philosophy," as well as the importance of Plato's undercutting of that distinction, even as he makes it.[10]

While Benardete's whole career might thus be seen as an exploration of an interpretative approach suggested by Strauss, in his last major work, his commentary on Plato's *Laws*, subtitled "The Discovery of Being" (2000), Benardete pushed this insight yet farther, to seek the "concealed ontological dimension" in Plato's political philosophy, and "why it is concealed and how it comes to light" (xii). In doing so, he was pursuing something of a "second sailing" of his own. Just as Plato says Socrates turned away from beings to speeches (*Phaedo* 99d–e), Benardete moved from his earlier concern for Plato's conception of the Being of the beings (in his translations and commentaries on *Theaetetus*, *Sophist*, and *Statesman*, published as *The Being of the Beautiful*, 1984) to a more subtle sense of Plato's metaphysical skepticism.[11] Beginning with *Socrates' Second Sailing: On Plato's* Republic (1989), which itself began as a review of Strauss's *The City and Man*, and up through the *Laws* commentary, Benardete was increasingly concerned to show that the whole metaphysical problematic of Being is an unavoidable epiphenomenon of human life, most particularly arising in our use of language as we

---

10. Benardete suggests that Plato learned this dialectical understanding of the opposition of poetry and philosophy from Heraclitus: "Plato's *Parmenides*: A Sketch," *The Archaeology of the Soul*, 231.

11. In his preface (ix) to *The Tragedy and Comedy of Life*, his translation and commentary on the *Philebus* (Chicago, 1993), Benardete said he had meant with that work to complete "his account of Plato's understanding of the beautiful, the just, and the good" (treated, respectively, in *The Being of the Beautiful*, *Socrates' Second Sailing*, and this work on the *Philebus*). This is certainly an accurate description of the project of those three studies, but Benardete leaves out of consideration here a number of his other publications during the same period, particularly his 1986 translation of the *Symposium* (a dialogue on which he went on also to comment in 1994), and his commentaries on the *Gorgias* and *Phaedrus* (*The Rhetoric of Morality and Philosophy*; Chicago, 1991). Moreover, in his introduction to the latter (3), he writes: "The *Gorgias* and the *Phaedrus*, then, pick up as their theological counterparts the *Protagoras* and *Symposium*, respectively. I propose to treat the latter pair in another book, 'The Gods of the Poets,' which will explicate the theological dimension of the *Gorgias* and *Phaedrus*." That proposal was never brought to fruition, but I believe the impetus behind it found expression in Benardete's subsequent work, as I am characterizing it herein.

seek to know and represent the world.[12] To continue this line of inquiry, Benardete then turned to readings of Heraclitus and Parmenides, and to the vision of the latter in Plato's *Parmenides*.

The Plato who emerges from Benardete's work is not simply the Straussian philosopher of minimal metaphysical commitments; rather, he is an author profoundly concerned to investigate the necessary forgetting of philosophy that linguistic usage effects, while at the same time constantly creating anew the possibility of philosophy's manifestation in the unexpected circumstances he portrays in his poetic and dialogical art. To put it more analytically, Benardete reveals that Plato is not a "Platonist," in the sense that the dialogues neither expound nor refine a doctrine of ideas. It may well be that idealism, as it is articulated by Plato, is a marriage of putatively Parmenidean ontology with Pythagorean number-theory, as Aristotle is wont to see it; but to say this much is yet to say nothing of Plato's interest in such a synthesis. Benardete's view, as I understand it, is that Plato sees such idealism as the condition for the possibility for technical knowledge. I use the Kantian terminology deliberately, though Plato seems already to be beyond transcendental idealism.[13] For Plato, it is not that idealism is the (presumably) preferred metaphysical solution to philosophical problems. It is rather that ideas are hypothesized by humans in our search for knowledge; but however necessary they may be to that pursuit, their reality remains only a fiction.

We might then say, as Benardete once remarked in person, "there are as many ideas as questions"—as if one could enumerate either; but the point of this obiter dictum is really to remind us that philosophy, for Plato, is not a doctrine but therapeutic to the search for technical knowledge. Such knowledge at once entails eidetic analysis—collection and division of phenomena into species or forms (*eidē*), the class characteristics of which are the ideas—

---

12. Benardete thus sees Plato as already aware of and transcending the criticism of commentators like Jacques Derrida. Benardete spoke to the Derridean misprision of Plato in a lecture "Derrida and Plato" delivered in October, 2000, at N.Y.U (reprinted in *The Archaeology of the Soul*). The Derridean reading had also already been differently criticized, e.g., by G. R. F. Ferrari in *Listening to the Cicadas: A Study of Plato's* Phaedrus (Cambridge, 1987). Benardete's review of Strauss's *The City and Man* is reprinted in *The Archaeology of the Soul*. (See "Works by Seth Benardete" in this volume.)

13. In the summer before his death, I was fortunate to have had the opportunity to discuss with Benardete Plato's achievement in this regard, as well as the views of Paul Natorp and Leon Robin.

and genetic analysis, which aims at identifying causal principles.[14] The practice of philosophy is to comprehend the confusions that arise in such pursuits,
which may be slight in mechanical arts—though these help provide perspective—but are of the greatest seriousness when the claim is to knowledge of
human things, e.g., an art of ruling the city.

Plato's "positivism" in this regard would be close to that of Wittgenstein
from the time of the *Philosophical Investigations*, for, if some problems may
be dissolved, what remains is the constant possibility of manifestly philosophical inquiry. In his turn back to Heraclitus and Parmenides, Benardete found
these concerns in them already. Heraclitus, already before Plato, had come to
the understanding that speech makes both inquiry and error possible; and
Parmenides had already shown that the metaphysical assumptions of the natural historians were untenable.

Parmenides' poem is not to be understood, then, as promulgating a doctrine of Being, but rather as articulating "Being" as the idealist hypothesis
that makes possible the inquiries of the natural historian, a hypothesis which
is then shown to be incoherent, because it at once admits the necessity of non-
Being while denying its possibility: without non-Being, the technical project
of collecting and dividing is impossible. The paradox of eidetic analysis—
that things must be both like and unlike, both be and not be what they are—
is both the ground and limit of knowledge. Returning to Plato's treatment of
this Eleatic legacy, as we see it in Plato's *Parmenides*, Benardete is able to make
excellent sense of this difficult dialogue. He dissolves the apparent problem
here of developmentalist readings of Plato—why Socrates at the end of his
life, as shown in the *Phaedo*, returns to an idealist doctrine already discredited
in his youth, as portrayed in the *Parmenides*. What Benardete sees, instead, is
a confirmation of the power of Plato's authorship: Socrates, as characterized
by Plato, signifies the paradoxical, accidental nature of philosophy; and philosophical practice is only made to seem logical and necessary on a particular
occasion through the art of the Platonic dialogue.

---

14. Benardete used these concepts frequently, if not always with as clear a statement
    of them as we find in chapter 1 of this *Laws* commentary (entitled "The Eidetic
    and the Genetic"), 18 n. 18. These terms of analysis are grounded particularly in
    his reading of the *Timaeus*. Benardete's late paper on this dialogue (published in
    The Argument of the Action) followed an earlier piece, "On Plato's *Timaeus* and
    Timaeus' Science Fiction," reprinted in *The Archaeology of the Soul*. (See "Works
    by Seth Benardete" in this volume.)

This illusion Benardete sometimes calls the "logographic necessity" of Platonic dialogues (borrowing Plato's own term from *Phaedrus* 264b). Its interpretative counterpart is finding what he calls the "argument in the action" of a work.[15] It is an approach which, rather than faulting Plato for the unsound arguments he frequently gives his leading speakers, asks instead why Plato does so, what pattern the arguments form, and what he means to communicate by having the interlocutors accept or reject them. The result is to replace our conception of a dogmatic Plato—or Socrates—with one in which we recognize Plato not so much de-mythologizing the poets as demonstrating how the demands of a progressive project aiming at technical knowledge trade the necessity of the poets' Olympian gods for the necessity of ideas among natural historians and sophists alike. The poets had shown why we needed the fiction of the gods to understand human experience. Positing ideas of the just, the good, and the beautiful as terms for understanding the characteristically human—and in particular this means the political—is not an advance of philosophy, but rather a renewal of the need for philosophical practice to remind us of the essentially mythical status of these metaphysical entities.

It is impossible here to do more than sketch the movement of Benardete's thought; and I have passed over much in silence, most notably his studies of Greek tragedy, his remarks in *Encounters and Reflections* concerning Christian and Roman writers, and his conception of law, which Benardete's sudden passing prevented the interviewers from including.[16] While he certainly changed his mind about various details over the course of his career, that movement, as may also be the case in the work of Plato, is not to be understood developmentally, but rather was the result of the profound thinking-through of a fundamental insight about the nature of philosophical thought. That insight is precisely not reducible to a proposition, but it is hinted at in formulas like the "second sailing," and Benardete's remark once that "There is only surface. Depth is an illusion of surface."[17] Or, again, it is an openness

---

15. Cf. "The *Logos* of the Action in the Platonic Dialogue," *Encounters and Reflections*, 124–28. The phrase "the argument in the action" echoes the title of Strauss's commentary *The Argument and the Action of Plato's Laws* (Chicago, 1975). At least once, Benardete also writes "the action of the argument" (*The Tragedy and Comedy of Life*, 90).

16. See Burger's preface to *Encounters and Reflections*, ix–x.

17. He thus revises a remark of Strauss, from *Thoughts on Machiavelli* (lectures at the University of Chicago, 1953; published at Glencoe, Ill.: Free Press, 1958, p. 13): "The problem inherent in the surface of things, and only in the surface of things,

to the unexpected as the accidental occasion for remembering that the ideas which appear to be necessary for us to make sense of our experiences are themselves fictions the "philosophers" have substituted for those of the poets. In this view, the "ancient quarrel between poetry and philosophy" is both the mark of this and the continuing possibility of its recognition; and, Benardete may best be understood to be a "poet" of the same sort as Herodotus, one recognizing the need for a history of such mythologizing, even when it is one's own. Beautifully produced, *Encounters and Reflections* is recommended to those wishing to embark on such an inquiry into Benardete's work themselves.

---

is the heart of things." Benardete cites this remark in his review of Strauss's *The City and Man*. See also *Encounters and Reflections*, 125.

Chapter Twenty-Six

Review of *The Archaeology of the Soul*: *Platonic Readings of Ancient Poetry and Philosophy*

Steven Berg

The Archaeology of the Soul is a collection of essays by the late Seth Benardete compiled and arranged by the editors of the volume, Ronna Burger and Michael Davis. A helpful introduction composed by the editors and a concluding coda—Benardete's memorial speech for Leo Strauss—frame the collection. The value of this publication is inestimable, since it brings together in a single place those essays of Benardete that had either remained unpublished or fallen out of print. The editors, therefore, have performed a great service to those devoted to classical learning, the study of philosophy, or both.

The title of the collection has been chosen by the editors and, as they explain in their introduction, is a variation on a phrase that Benardete himself employs in the first essay of the volume, "The Poet-Merchant and the Stranger from the Sea": "The archaeology of the human spirit is one of the characteristics of ancient poetry." This "spiritual" archaeology, Benardete explains, is "the attempt to consider the origins of things in the light of the current experience of those things" and thereby "expose the criminality of the presumably lawful." The case in point in this essay is sailing, which, though now as routine as the plowing of the soil, signified at its origin the "uncanniness of man" in his "transgression of all limits" (1). Homer, in Benardete's view, is the first to reveal this original meaning of sailing in his portrayal of "Odysseus' search for wisdom," a search that, in an attempt to uncover "things as they are," must of necessity violate "the prohibition [of the law] not to look beyond one's own." This "transgressiveness of know-

Reprinted from *Polis: The Journal for Ancient Greek Political Thought* 30, no. 2 (2013): 340–43. Page numbers in parentheses refer to *The Archaeology of the Soul*, eds. Ronna Burger and Michael Davis (South Bend: St. Augustine's Press, 2012).

ledge" (2) culminates in "philosophy's desacralization of everything" (249), when, for example, Heraclitus denies the validity of the sacred law of burial by declaring that corpses should be thrown out faster than dung.

Homer and his influence are themes that run like a golden thread throughout Benardete's thought and the essays of this book. As Benardete makes clear, Homer is not only the first to show the necessity of philosophy's transgression of sacred limits, but, in a seeming paradox, also appears as the source for the meaning of the sacred as it was experienced by the Greeks. This experience of the meaning of the sacred is encapsulated in the "tragic formula...*pathei mathos*, by experience, understanding" (268). It is represented paradigmatically by Homer's account in the *Iliad* of the deeds and suffering of Achilles through which he arrives at the insight that "even in the house of Hades there is left something, a soul and an image." The rite of burial and the sacred status of the corpse are the sacred law's acknowledgment of this "fact." Through his insight Achilles arrives at an understanding of both the necessary limits on human action (beyond such limits man is not a god, but a beast) and man's need, therefore, for the gods. The return of Hector's corpse to Priam for burial is the belated return of Achilles to the humanity he sought to discard (72). By this account, Hades distinguishes man from both god and beast. It is the negative and lawful determination of man.

It is Benardete's contention that *pathei mathos* exhibits itself not only on the sub-philosophical level of Greekness in the insight into the meaning of the sacred, but on the philosophic plane as well. Here again, in Benardete's view, Homer first paved the way. His portrayal of the manner in which Odysseus' experiences at sea prepared him for the discovery of the nature of the human represents just such a philosophical version of understanding through suffering. Odysseus' discovery, however, is the antithesis of Achilles' insight, insofar as his uncovering of the truth of human nature meant the recognition that "he was mind and shape together" (228), a two that though apparently opposed, are in fact inseparably united by an invisible and intelligible bond. The knowledge of nature that made Odysseus resistant to both the enchantments of Circe and the blandishments of Calypso, is, therefore, also a denial of the central premise of the sacred: Hades or the separate existence of the soul.

In the essays collected here on Greek philosophy, Benardete shows how Heraclitus, Parmenides, Plato, and Aristotle are the inheritors and elaborators of this original Homeric discovery of nature. As for displaying, however, the necessity, if insufficiency, of experience for philosophical understanding—the philosophic version of *pathei mathos*—this is given its most complete articulation in this volume in the essay "'Night and Day...': Parmenides." At the opening of the poem, as Benardete shows, Parmenides portrays himself as on the way to truth unencumbered by opinion. He is pure mind able to read off directly from the experience of things, the first principles of things. A "presocratic" materialist cosmological "theory" (225) would have been the inevitable result of such an effort were it not for the fact that Justice blocked his path (204). According to Benardete, this Justice must be understood in terms of the punitive justice of the law and the "punitive understanding man has of himself" that is derived from the violent application of the law. This punitive understanding is identified by Benardete with "tragic knowledge," namely, that man is the paradigm of non-being (207): at the core of man's lawful humanity is the understanding of man as corpse rather than carrion or a mindless shadow in Hades.

Parmenides shows, on Benardete's reading, how any materialist cosmology must reproduce this nullity of the human insofar as both the human experience of the human and nature in its Homeric or philosophic sense evaporate in the glare and heat of such "theory." It is Justice then that blocks the path to such "theory" precisely through "theory" being displayed as justice, that is, as lawful opinion: the "direct way to truth" is shown to be no way to the truth at all, but merely a reiteration of the punitive understanding of man.

Once he has "passed through" the gateway of Justice that blocks his path, Parmenides encounters the goddess who discriminates between truth and opinion and thereby makes clear that Parmenides' original understanding of himself as pure mind was pure opinion: "he was of the opinion when he set out that he was without opinion" (209). In her precise discriminations between truth and opinion, being and non-being, and mortal and immortal, however, the goddess offers an account of the truth and oneness of being that renders impossible Parmenides' own reception of that account: he, along with all other mortals, is consigned exclusively to the realm of untruth, opinion, and non-being. Parmenides is informed upon hearing the truth of being that he cannot be hearing the truth of being—he is non-being through and through. The punitive understanding of man thus returns once again in the goddess's most manifest statements regarding being: the account of the goddess that points out the saturation of the original "way to truth" with opinion is also suffused with lawful opinion.

There are not then, as the goddess apparently insists, two ways—the way of truth and being and the impassable way of opinion and non-being—but one and only one way along which truth and opinion are thoroughly mixed. How then to make one's way upon this jumbled way becomes the issue. Within the goddess's manifest argument, Benardete shows, is lodged a second argument that leads not to "the truth" of being, but to the problem of being and at the same time displays the only way for thought to articulate that problem, namely, the necessity, through speech, of cutting away a part of being from being in order to examine it apart from the whole of being. "He must let a part apart from being be non-being" (215). The articulation of the problem of being, therefore, requires equally the articulation of the problem of non-being. "The non-beings of experience are all [he] has" (216). Speech or *logos*, even as informed by lawful opinion, proves to be the only way to uncovering the truth. The false partings and pairings of speech and lawful opinion provide the sole means to thinking the true partings and pairings and the invisible unities of nature, the one day of night and day.

The experience of such a "break" and "reorientation" vis-à-vis experience (204) is what Socrates called his "second sailing." Benardete shows, therefore, that Parmenides had already charted those waters before Socrates set sail. Perhaps for the first time, Benardete makes intelligible Plato's representation of Parmenides as *the* catalyst for the young Socrates' turn to the speeches. The greatest of the "pre-Socratics" was already "Socratic" through and through. As noted, however, Benardete traces what we generally understand to be the Socratic turn to the very origin of Greekness: Homer was there before them all.

The power of Homer's sun to enlighten and generate inevitably gives rise to the question as to how the world must appear once that sun has set. Benardete illuminates this dark landscape in a series of articles devoted to the Latin poets, Horace, Virgil, and Apuleius. In these essays he shows that Rome (both old and new), with the absence of poetry at its founding and philosophy as a "native growth," must display the forlorn spectacle of suffering without meaning and experience opaque to understanding, that is, "human" life at its most brutal. In Benardete's view, the Latin poets, with full consciousness of what is lacking, provide a complete analysis of this benighted world.

Towards the end of the collection we find an essay devoted to Jacques Derrida, through whom Benardete shows that it has been left to the contemporary degradation of modernity to give us a taste of a new, and strangely articulate, though thoroughly unself-conscious, version of experience opaque to all insight and significance. This last expression of modernity's decay is found, according Benardete's presentation, in Derrida's celebration of the "apocalyptic" decline of the West and his effort to hasten that decline by effecting "the entire destruction of the possibility of philosophy." Derrida pretends to accomplish this destruction through the denial of the primacy of the Homeric distinction upon which philosophy is founded: nature versus law. Benardete detects here a quasi-religious motivation for Derrida's denial of philosophy: he seeks to prepare the ground for the advent of a "new revelation" (351). Benardete amply demonstrates the ignorance that lies behind Derrida's efforts to eliminate the possibility of philosophy. The Frenchman, he shows, systematically misunderstands the character of philosophy, conceiving it as a dogmatic science of being, rather than an aporetic inquiry into the problem of being. Benardete here employs literally and to great effect those passages from his study of Parmenides that show him to be at one with Socrates in his understanding of philosophy as necessarily exhibiting a first and second sailing structure. By these means he demolishes Derrida's presupposition, borrowed from his master Heidegger, that the Socratic understanding of *eidos* is identical to an understanding of being as presence. In the pieces on Strauss included at the end of the volume, and in the eloquent testimony to his own philosophizing that Benardete has left behind him in his writings, we are given the alternative to Derrida's and Heidegger's "destruction" of the philosophical tradition: "the restoration of political philosophy" in its original meaning (360).

Chapter Twenty-Seven

Review of *The Archaeology of the Soul*: *Platonic Readings of Ancient Poetry and Philosophy*

Svetozar Minkov

This is a posthumous collection of essays and reviews by the philoso-pher-classicist Seth Benardete. Unlike the previous collection edited by Burger and Davis (*The Argument of the Action*), *The Archaeology of the Soul* could not have Benardete's stamp of approval, but the range and depth of (occasionally oracularly expressed) interpretation are unmistakably his. The volume, properly studied, in some sense completes Benardete's lifetime body of work and confirms him as one of the most philosophically penetrating thinkers of recent generations. Its highlights include Benardete's astonishing recovery of the self-reflective wisdom of Heraclitus and Parmenides (arguably exceeding the insights of the avid proponent of the Pre-Socratics, Heidegger); his intensive interpretations of ancient tragedy on the city and the gods (per-haps surpassing the interpretations by Hegel and Heidegger; cf. 238 n. 6); his unfolding of the meaning of Roman poetry (in its unique placement between classical philosophy, the Roman empire and law, and the coming of Christianity, 309); his uncovering of the philosophical nature of the ancient historians; and the discussion of the psychological core of Plato's and Aristo-tle's "metaphysics" (e.g., 354, 242, and 244); not to mention his reflections on Cicero, Nietzsche, and Derrida.

In the brief but very helpful preface, the editors offer the following as the key to the unity of the book and thus the plausibility of its subtitle and of Ben-ardete's "platonizing" approach to non-Platonic works, which take up about half of the book: "Only because Plato seemed to [Benardete] to come so close

Reprinted from *The Review of Politics* 75, no. 4 (Fall 2013): 682–85. Page numbers in parentheses refer to *The Archaeology of the Soul*, eds. Ronna Burger and Michael Davis (South Bend: St. Augustine's Press, 2012).

to the truth of things could he hope to learn so much by unearthing Platonic resonances in other thinkers—whether earlier or later, poetic or philosophic" (x; cf. Leo Strauss's *Studies in Platonic Political Philosophy*, most of which is not on Plato). To be sure, there is something arbitrary or anachronistic in calling these resonances "Platonic" since "Benardete came to see that the discovery of philosophy through the 'Socratic turn' was really the rediscovery of an understanding already present in some form in the Greek poets" (xii; and ibid.: "Heraclitus or Parmenides is a genuine philosophic thinker precisely to the extent that a Socratic turn can be found in some form within his own thought."). Now, one could justify calling Parmenides Socratic or Platonic insofar as Plato has made the philosophic experience more conspicuous or even rendered it more intelligible. But while in his essay on Parmenides' poem Benardete refers to Plato's *Parmenides* for clarification, those references are not central to his interpretation. And in his reading of Heraclitus—in addition to relying, as he does in all his readings, on a meticulous reflection on the text itself—he begins with Lucretius and introduces Plato in the footnotes in apparently the same manner in which he brings up Herodotus or Sophocles. In fact, Benardete's heightened appreciation of certain pre-Socratics is perhaps the greatest change from his earlier understanding (see 328 and 375). In the case of ancient poetry, another non-Socratic alternative, Benardete does not claim that "philosophic reflection" is poetry's core element. Rather, "the relation between the local and the universal, between law and the transcendence of the law, which is at the heart of ancient poetry, recurs in the element of philosophic reflection in Plato" (6). In his essay on Parmenides' poem, Benardete compares Parmenides to Hesiod and suggests that Parmenides succeeds in integrating love and justice with rationality whereas Hesiod's *Theogony* culminates in the triumph of mind over eros and teaches that the Sun and Justice come from different families (224). Nevertheless, Hesiod and Parmenides agree that "the beautiful and the just are at the heart of the human" (ibid.). While perhaps not going beyond what is suggested in the essay on Parmenides' poem, the essay "Socrates and Plato: the Dialectics of Eros" articulates most directly the relation of eros to mind (but also law, justice, and the gods): "Plato has two themes, justice and love, both in their relation to one another and in their relation to mind.... The soul of man is the problem" (259; see also 239). Benardete uncovers a Socrates who is "immune from illusions, hopes, and ideals, and is eros itself united with mind" (259).

The title for the collection the editors have chosen appears to be a version of Benardete's statement in the extraordinary essay on Greek and Roman poetry, "The Poet-Merchant and the Stranger from the Sea," the first chapter of the volume: "The archaeology of the human spirit is one of the characteristics of ancient poetry" (1). The collected essays, however, point beyond such an archaeology to what the editors call "a lifetime of philosophic reflection on the human soul" (xiii). "Archaeology" is also used in the last chapter of the volume, "Memorial Speech for Leo Strauss": "'Archaeology' was the only path still open to any possible 'physiology'" (375; cf. 355: "The impossible is our sole access to that which is"). In this way, "archaeology" frames this volume. The greatest density of "archaeology" occurs, however, in Benardete's comments on the Thucydides chapter of Strauss's *The City and Man* (370–72). The main theme of that archaeology is the origin of Greekness in barbarism. One wonders, then, about the place of the historian Thucydides (and Herodotus) in this volume of "Platonic readings of ancient poetry and philosophy." In a sense, Thucydides' history is a "chastened" version of Homer's fabulous patterns. But this formulation is "much too fragile, too poetic to capture the whole of Thucydides' thought," in which "elusive patterns" are mere means to thought. Thucydides' "archaeology" is ultimately not history, but a heuristic device (370); Thucydides completes the transition from poetry and history to philosophy. As for Herodotus, Benardete remarks that in reaching Herodotus' understanding of law, one is led to "an appreciation of Aeschylus' *Persians*, in which no word for justice . . . ever appears" (335). The poets and the historians expose the amoral roots of the city and display an "indifference to the issue of right in itself" (263). Plato, however, radicalizes or completes the poetic-historical thought—as perhaps Parmenides and Heraclitus do too—and shows that, though "the good city lives in the element of justice while it violates justice from the start," "this veil of false opinion is on the whole good as well" (but cf. 41).

The reference to Strauss as an "archaeologist" raises the question of the relation between Strauss and Benardete (whose remarkable correspondence is yet to be published). "Political philosophy"—Strauss's crucial catchphrase—is not used much by Benardete except in reference to Strauss (375, 359, but see 245). And one might receive the impression that Benardete addresses the uncanny, the sacred, the tragic (e.g., he wrote on Homer and Sophocles while Strauss wrote in a sustained way only on Aristophanes among the ancient poets, 375), the soul, nature, *eidos*, *phantasia*, and many intricate literary puzzles, while Strauss operated in the "rich middle" of political philosophy. But this would be misleading: in going to the pre- and trans-political, Benardete always clarifies the political. (And conspicuously, the essay "Freedom: Grace and Necessity" offers a sharp analysis of the essence of modernity—in its scientific and political dispositions and hopes.) Strauss and Benardete also share a focus on "the problem of the gods" (e.g., 330; see 356–57 on Plato's *Republic* in relation to the Bible and Christianity; cf. 61, 260, 283, 308, 346, 359, 375, as well as 380: "writing poses the issue of divine revelation of the law"). Another way to see Benardete's affinity to Strauss is to say that the ontological psychology that Benardete outlines (242, 199) is in agreement with Strauss's "anti-historicist historical psychology" (376). For both, at any rate, political philosophy is linked to "first philosophy." If anything, one might be tempted to say that Benardete turns all his authors into Strauss's Plato. But this facile claim is immediately belied by the originality and sheer power, as well as filigree subtlety, of Benardete's readings. Benardete's demanding work is less likely to reach as broad an audience as that of Strauss. Still, while this collection is unlikely to change that situation radically, in "pointing the way to understanding," it extends a "lifeline to the rest of us" (358).

Chapter Twenty-Eight

The Bed and the Table

Seth Benardete

The *Republic*, insofar as it is concerned with the city, consists of three parts, II–IV, V–VII, VIII–X; II–IV and V–VII are each generated out of a Thrasymachean suggestion in I—a) his theatrical anger, b) his distinction between precise speech and speaking loosely (*akribes logos* and *hōs epos eipein*). Socrates has taken theatrical anger and made it both central to the city and that in light of which the soul's structure is to be understood. He has likewise taken the standard of precise speech and brought it to the conclusion that wisdom in the strict sense is to rule the city. Socrates has thus split the connection between reason and spiritedness by considering each separately while still giving the impression that the alliance claimed between reason and spiritedness is maintained. Now, the adjustment of the soul's structure to political necessity entails the adjustment likewise of wisdom; philosophy is replaced by wisdom, and wisdom is allied with mathematical studies, the locus of precision itself: the education preparatory to dialectic turns out to be fully possible within the confines of the cave, and of which solid geometry is the big example because it duplicates body and leads to a kinematics wholly independent of cosmology.

What Socrates has done so far is to articulate the necessity for his own "second" sailing as second, while he presents the second sailing as first: political philosophy hides itself in its own discovery. This is due to the narrative form Socrates adopts: the city in speech comes forward at the expense of the dialogic city (consisting of the participants in and the conditions of the discussion) that Socrates has truly founded in a different way—it is not politically realizable. Socrates' deliberate self-effacement indicates the actual

---

Transcribed from a handwritten document (probably composed for a lecture during the time Benardete was working on his *Republic* book). Material in brackets is from the reverse of the manuscript pages. "The Bed and the Table," SB 03–15, Seth Benardete Papers, New School for Social Research Archives and Special Collections.

self-forgetfulness of pre-Socratic philosophy. The utopianism of the *Republic* squares with the utopianism of the city as well as with philosophy as a first sailing.

From another point of view, II–IV can be understood as education in the beautiful: but for that very reason, the primacy of eros in the education— education without punishment—does not fit with the centrality of *thumos* and *to thumoeides*: the difficulty shows up in Socrates' acknowledging the natural relation between justice and anger and yet proposing a way of treating *to thumoeides* as if its nature were the unity of courage and moderation. Justice thus emerges as a principle but not as a virtue identifiable as such. This difficulty is ultimately connected with the implicit relation between knowledge as *technē* and need, with which Socrates started—the true city—and what would have emerged once need became understood as desire in the city of fevered heat; for the need to split desire as a class principle of the city from the formation of the class can only be overcome through the practice of Socrates' erotic art, which would eliminate the core of the city and the bond of the soul.

Books V–VII, in turn, can be understood as being on *t'agathon*, the emergence of which is coupled with the principle that "good" can only be predicated of the real: the city cannot be happy unless it is realizable. Curiously, the understanding of the city that does not require its reality yields to a lower demand that is then combined with the highest of all principles. This principle is not cosmological either, for it is not tied in with a psychology; it's a non-teleological teleology and hence divorced from becoming. It is linked only with mind and not soul. The precise itself as a principle is the obstacle to a precise account of soul. [Socrates at the end of Book X explicitly distinguishes between the true nature of soul, which is linked with philosophy, and *soul itself* and *justice itself*, with which the *Republic* deals.]

It would seem that Books VIII–X must deal with *to dikaion* in the context of degeneration, some version of becoming. Justice, then, must be connected with that which is not, and that is why it vanished in the previous analysis, since we were concerned with eidetic structures (city and soul) or beings. Although the original question had been the *genesis* of justice, justice had been lacking at the beginning as a principle and hadn't come to be at all. If this is so, Socrates is going to prove to Glaucon that justice cannot be and be an "idea." The issue then is whether Socrates can show any longer the goodness of justice, that it uniquely makes one happy, if it necessarily comes to light in the context of defectiveness: the first citizen of any city that is said to be just

293

is the oligarch, and he only seems so. In the myth of Er punishment and reward are connected with *to dikaion*, but choice with *t'agathon*. Does justice become "that without which" and no longer of primary importance? Does philosophy as human, Socratically understood, emerge as itself only in the context of degeneration and defectiveness? There is, in Socrates' scheme, philosophy only in democracy.

The city spans two different things: non-bestiality and knowledge. The city is justified through both, but not together. The city is closer to non-bestiality than it is to wisdom: there is no connection between the rationality of technology and non-bestiality—the true city is the city of pigs—anymore than there is a connection between the human as Glaucon understands it and rationality. There is no *art* of freedom. The abandonment of the rational city brings back the issue of poetry: VIII begins with the invocation of the Muses—Socrates never says they stop singing—then goes on to the truth of Oedipus the tyrant in IX, the second discussion of poetry in X, and the myth of Er.

What happens in the last three books is this: the displacement of spiritedness in II–IV on behalf of eros and knowledge is shown to be a fundamental misreading of the city. Books VIII–X reveal that poetry is as much allied with spiritedness as with eros, and that Socrates' interpretation of justice in light of knowledge and class analysis, which was necessary to establish philosophy as justice, is a distorted revision of the duality of justice as it is in the element of *to thumoeides*. The introduction of Truth in the central books has the effect of making it possible to understand the truth of the eidetic structure of soul and breaks once and for all the alliance between spiritedness and reason. Insofar as the *Republic* is directed to Glaucon, Glaucon's *Republic* ends with VII: after that it becomes a critique of Glaucon and the possibility of any unity between his being both erotic and spirited. After Book VII, Glaucon never laughs.

Socrates' account of the degeneration of regimes is presented superficially almost entirely as the understanding of desire until the tyrant emerges as the incarnation of the god Eros. The account, however, is really that of *to thumoeides* as it assumes various guises and by adapting the language and posture of desire keeps itself pure. This is built into the very structure of the city inasmuch as Socrates uses the appetitive and the money-making as equivalent characterizations of a part of the soul and of the city. All of this was foreshadowed by Thrasymachus, whose express desire to get money out of Socrates concealed his will to triumph over him. A far more telling example is Glaucon, whose express desire for meat led him to call the true city "the city of pigs"; but the truth of that desire emerges in his demand that Socrates supply beds upon which to lie and tables from which to take food. In the true city there are neither beds nor tables: its citizens slept and ate on the ground. The "ideas" are the ultimate in luxuries (cf. 596b). Glaucon wants to be off the ground and to eat not without mediation. He wants the possibility of being proud of being human, for there are no men whom the poets can celebrate in the true city.

Socrates tries to show them that the city's banishment of eros—of the possibility of there being any other whole than itself—leads to its interpretation of desire in light of its own essence, and this distortion necessarily culminates in the presentation of the tyrant, who is the truth of all political men, as the very opposite of the political, or Eros.

We pick up Socrates' account at the end of Book VIII, where the tyrant enslaves the *dēmos* through his running out of the rich to plunder. The involvement of the *dēmos* is depicted as a beating. Socrates thus presents the tyrant as an unholy father-beater (*patroloias*). The *dēmos* is the father, the tyrant its son. This presentation depends on Socrates' grafting the genealogy-model of the individual's transformation onto the regime-transformation. The city becomes one family. The political becomes charged with the pre-political—religion and the family. This is the context in which tragedy is introduced as a digression. The destruction of the family (patricide and incest) in tragedy is the equivalent to the non-existence of the family in the best city. Adeimantus here alludes to Euripides' *Trojan Women* 1169, where Hecuba regrets that Hector's son was killed before he enjoyed *isotheos tyrannis*. Tragedy thus operates at the same time democratically and non-democratically, by assigning to figures of the heroic age contemporary language, so that *tyrannis* is both legitimate as an oriental term and illegitimate as a Greek term; but even legitimately it implies that no one but the king is free. So the assignment of democracy to the heroic age is not just an accident of the Hesiodic scheme Socrates has adopted: it is now used to point to the peculiarity of the presentation of the heroic age before a democratic society in Athens. The audience is persuaded to sorrow for a barbarian's loss of a godlike tyranny. They are made to imagine the immoral amorally, as the beautiful separated from justice. The outstanding survive the onslaught of democratic equalization through its translation into the imaginary: tragedy prepares the way for tyranny by denying the outstanding any reality. Rebarbarization becomes possible through the assertion of its conquest.

To set up tyranny as the *seeming* split away from the *reality* of the effect of injustice in the soul, Socrates has had to transform the audience into a theatrical figure whose son is the tyrant. The tyrant becomes poeticized in order to get at the tyrannical soul by itself. This poeticization requires the sanctification of the *dēmos*: the *dēmos* becomes a non-generated eternal being, and the tyrant becomes the embodiment of everything the *dēmos* loves. The object of democratic desires is the offspring of those desires: the tyrant is the beloved son of the *dēmos*.

In order to account for the genesis of the democratic man, Socrates had to distinguish between necessary and non-necessary desires; in order to account for the genesis of the tyrannical man, he has to divide the non-necessary desires into the non-necessary simply and the non-necessary that transgress the law. These desires are revealed in dreams, where such a man "as he believes," tries to have intercourse with his mother, any other human being, god, and beast. But the tyrant cannot in reality have intercourse with a god—it can only happen in poetry. The unlawful desires have nothing to do with possibility; they are unlawful but not punishable by law. They are desires determined by the law itself, inasmuch as the law must first establish the beings which are then imaged as being violated. In this case, the non-being is safe from violation both as a non-being and as a lawful being. Desire, then, is wholly disengaged from real capacity; its objects are not necessary because they are neither necessary for survival nor for well-being; but they have become objects of desire through the law: the law, in establishing them, attaches prohibitions to them; these prohibitions imply a prior desire: their existence thus gets rooted through the prohibition. Unlawful desires are desires that violate the fundamental requirements of the city, but fully acknowledge the fictions of the city. [Their taking over the tyrant is prepared for by democracy, where the absence of a class structure fosters the total absorption of the principle of the regime into the makeup of each individual. It's the pleasure in its own variety that democracy grants its spectator—and hence everyone plays everyone else and lacks all substance. The tyrant finishes this process.] The tyrant is the true believer in the city as such: "fatherland" (*patris*) occurs first in connection with the tyrant: "He will punish, if he can," says Socrates, "the fatherland," but he can't, for the fatherland too is a non-being. The tyrant, Socrates says, is the only one who cannot see the sights outside his city; he is the only one for whom there is only the cave, without any opening into the light. He alone does not hate the lie in the soul. [He is in love, as Socrates puts it, with the image of Helen. And at the same time, the tyrant, in his desire to be loved for himself alone, is the pure expression of the fatherland.]

The tyrant is thus the embodiment, not of eros, but of the god Eros, a non-being that combines the perfect beauty of the beloved with the total neediness of the lover. Eros as an invention expresses the double modality of Master and Slave. It occurs through the lover infusing desire with right. He makes the beloved into an active agent of his own interpretation of his shame—the lover can then slip out of his shame and attribute his abjection to another. He becomes forced to punish, and so becomes as slave his own master. This double movement is nothing else but Socrates' understanding of *to thumoeides*. When somebody pushes us aside, we say, "Who do you think you are?" We imply by this, at the same time, that he is no better than we are and if he were, he *would* have the right to push us aside. Everyone wants his own space and believes he has a right to it, and this is the individual equivalent to the fatherland, a country without any regime, without any claim to superiority. What the tyrant reveals, however, is that the claim to the fatherland is a claim to nothing, and the awareness of the nullity of the claim requires complete domination: only when the possibility of the exposure of *doxa* as *doxa* is wholly eliminated can the tyrant be satisfied. [Achilles' wish that he be the slave of a poor peasant rather than king of all the dead is an impossible wish for Achilles to make.]

What has slowly emerged is this: Socrates established justice as being a dyadic structure. It was, on the one hand, identified with perfect knowledge, insofar as any artisan had his art as his sole ticket of admission into the city, and on the other hand, it was identified with the principle of the class structure of the city, minding one's own business. This dyad is now seen to be the cognitive equivalent to the duality of *thumos* itself, for which man is both everything and nothing. The tragic formula, "Not to be born is best," is not the expression of an impossible wish but of the experience of nothingness. When Socrates says that the entire lifetime of a man from childhood to old age is small in comparison with all time, Glaucon corrects him: "No," he says, "it's nothing."

The consequence of putting the city back on its own axis through the analysis of the tyrant is that Socrates presents the soul at the end of IX as a monstrous natural fusion of many bestial forms into one; one form is of a complex and many-headed beast, with heads of both wild and tame beasts, another is of a lion, and a third is of a human being, and this is covered over by an envelope with the appearance of a human being. Man then is in the image of man, and since that man is said to be divine, man is an infinitely receding being. This rendering of the soul and man is a consequence of the gradual dismantling of the eidetic structure of soul with which Socrates began; it then turns out that what Socrates put at the beginning is the consequence of education: the eidetic structure of soul is, as Socrates already hinted at in Book III, truly possibly only by way of philosophy, of which the class structures of cities are poor copies, and without either philosophy or the city in its resistance to being nothing but a fatherland, the inhumanity of the human soul in itself is the subject of poetry, for which the Furies are of no less interest than Athena. Poetry, then, is now in its most powerful position; in the myth of Er, the man brought up in the best city chooses tyrant, which condemns him to eat his own children, and Ajax, Agamemnon, and Thersites choose the life of beasts. And there is no life of philosophy to be chosen. The ancient quarrel between poetry and philosophy can at last be drawn.

The confrontation with poetry takes two forms: in the first, poetry's fictions are contrasted with the gods as makers of the unique beings; in the second, poetry's knowledge is contrasted with the knowledge of the user. Poetry, then, is found wanting with respect to both being and the good. Socrates' next argument is about the immortality of the soul, in which he implies that the soul is the unique being in which being and being good belong together of necessity. Soul, then, is the focus of the two separate arguments against poetry. We can now turn to those.

Socrates chooses to illustrate the ideas with bed and table. In calling our attention to their absence in the true city, he calls our attention to Glaucon's demand for them. "Bed" and "Table" were the carriers of meaning. As ideas, their being is solely their meaning, since the idea table cannot support our food and the idea bed cannot support us. Each is so much its meaning that neither can serve any other purpose, and whereas tables can support us and beds things, neither idea can ever be abused. They thus give an ontology to Thrasymachus's demand that words be used in their precise sense. This Thrasymachean demand had been taken up by Glaucon at the beginning of the second book. There he proposed a kind of justice which, though it embodied the common opinions about justice, did not show itself as such to anyone. It was *doxa* without meaning. Now Socrates connects Glaucon's positing of justice itself with his objection to the true city: Glaucon wants to be somebody regardless of justice and he wants justice without appearances. He wants the false city and true justice: the "idea" is what we know perfectly and are not perfectly. The idea table is the truth of the idea justice, as justice without human beings. Glaucon, then, in rejecting the true city, discloses in his hunger that he wouldn't be satisfied with the satisfactions that city affords. He wants possibility; he wants unrealized possibility, and unrealized possibility is unqualified being: to be is to be an eternally unrealized possibility. It is to be free.

The god, says Socrates, either did not want to produce, or a kind of necessity was upon him not to produce, more than one bed in its nature, because if he should make only two, again one would come to light in which both of those would have the *eidos*, and that would be *the* bed and not the two he made. And the god, knowing this, wanting to be in his being (*ontos*) the maker of a bed that is in its being (*ontos*), and not a maker of some bed or some kind of bedmaker, he made grow one bed by itself by nature. One is struck at once by the stress on the will and the absence of any claim that the god had an art. Neither god nor any of the bedmakers or tablemakers are said to have knowledge or know-how. Glaucon and Socrates posit the idea for the purpose of inquiry, but the bedmaker looks to the idea "bed" without any understanding. What, then, prevents you or I or even the poet from looking at the same bed? So the god freely made the idea and the bedmaker freely copied it. Each individual then has his own perfect idea which is the same for all eternity. This is the consequence of the total collapse of the class structure of the city, so that each member of the city ceases to have a craft and to belong to the class of craftsmen but becomes wholly himself while losing his art.

We should not be surprised, then, that when Socrates confronts the imitator with the maker, he no longer speaks of the image of the artifact but of the image of the maker. The bedmaker is an imitation of the god bedmaker, and the painter in painting the human bedmaker cannot deceive him, for what he truly is, is wholly concealed within. This then is Glaucon's just man who, we recall, was just but had no knowledge by which to show himself as just. Knowledge belonged only to the unjust man, the imitator at three removes from the god. [The bedmaker knows that the painted picture of himself is not real because it is neither himself nor his god. The painter, as Socrates said in V, is indifferent to the real because his pictures are of the perfect. You, he says to the human bedmaker, are not as beautiful as the illusion I make, but the individual wants to be himself without being either good or beautiful.]

In the conclusion of this argument Socrates compares the poetic devices of poetry to the charm of youth that supervenes on those who are not beautiful. He implies that poetry presupposes the non-beauty of the original. As

Napoleon said, to speak continually of virtue in novels is to induce the conviction that it is by a mirage. It is precisely in its enhancement of individuality, so that it appears as a type, that poetry declares the individuality it celebrates to be mean and low. No mother has ever mourned her son as Thetis did Achilles once she is made to say "Woe! I am wretched. Woe! Unhappy mother of the best son" (*Iliad* 18.54).

The shift from god the maker to the user—the shift from the democratic to the architectonic perspective—occurs when Socrates changes the question from whether Homer was a competent physician to the issue of virtue. The poets are not makers of true individuality, since they make gods of too general a type, and they do not know virtue, since they defer to the law. It's not clear, however, why in the case of flutes there is the same flute for both flutist and flutemaker, and another which the painter makes. What happened to the flute in truth? Once more, it seems, the good is only in reality and not as a hypothesis. But still: if the painter paints the flute that the flutemaker makes in conformity with the flutist's prescriptions, why shouldn't the flutist find it good? The painter, then, no longer solely looks to the flutes; he adjusts them to the opinion of the many with regard to the beautiful. The painter, in short, does not accept the strictly Socratic proposition that virtue, beauty, and correctness are solely determined by use, and of which the most striking assertion in the *Republic* was that the most useful marriages were *ipso facto* sacred (458e4).

Imitation fosters that in us which is far from prudence, from the calculation of our own good. We can easily imagine in the case of the horse's bit that the painter played down its harshness or exaggerated it, as in the story of the painter who could not get the foam flooded with blood just right before he threw a sponge at his picture, but in any case, ignored its purpose in taming the horse. In the case of flutes, perhaps a painter would minimize the ugliness they cause the player and thus go against their rejection by Athena. In the case of the tragic poet, his power goes further: he makes public the private grief of the decent man and thus fundamentally alters it. The law orders the decent man to do something that he cannot do; it does not mind, or at least it can do nothing about it, if he does not keep up appearances in private. Or rather, does he not experience the fact that the law needs a sanction—his obedience to it needs to be backed up by others? He is forced to realize his criminality, his submission to something that he would not obey by himself. Furthermore, the poet's representation of the inside exposes the decent man to the view of everyone. The poet reveals that he knows him, and he knows that he is not as poetic as the poet is: he knows that so noble a being in suffering does not exist. The poet presents a version of an event that, on the one hand, is wholly unknown except as silence strictly enjoined by the law, and on the other, takes on a wholly private character that cannot be known by another: poetry therefore has the privilege of depicting it as it vanishes; it becomes known to us through poetry. [Consider the catachresis, as old as the poets, of the word "tragic."] The necessary falsification of guilt is our only access to guilt (see 605d–606c).

The primary function of image-making is the suspension of our own—there are fears, Socrates says, that can calculate that it is a necessity for us in seeing images to absorb into our own that which is another's. We sympathize without identifying and we do so because of the recognized alien character of the image—it is not ourselves. We stand outside ourselves in *ekstasis*—so that there is no ordered self, but a spurious identity with another combined with a delight in breaking the law without breaking the law. Poetry's suspension of the real is the suspension of self-knowledge (it is the absence of self-knowledge as a theme that labels the *Republic* as pre-Socratic); it thus looks like the denial of the self, for the spectator-self, who engages the alien, fails to recognize the self in the other. Though the pleasure belongs to that which has been forcibly restrained, the best part of us believes the pleasure belongs to it as onlooker, and this is the reflexive self: it fails to recognize the pleasure of crying as belonging to spiritedness, because it pretends that in judging a man to be pitiable, it judges that he deserves it; it never lets up its guard on the dirge-like, which it would if it acknowledged any pleasure in it. It is poetry that establishes the spurious alliance between reason and spiritedness. Poetry thus takes hold of a duality in *to thumoeides* and splits it apart. Grief is like a painting of flutes, for their lack of any capacity to function matches the experience of purposelessness in grief. [In the Fifth Ode of Bacchylides, immediately after Heracles says "not to be born is best," he adds, "There is no doing (*prēxis*) for those who lament" (160–63).]

The ancient quarrel between poetry and philosophy, in which all the abuse is on the side of poetry, leads to a presentation of it in terms of two partisans. Philosophy : poetry :: lovers of wisdom : lovers of poetry. The lovers of poetry are to speak on her behalf, without meter, just as poetry or the poets are to defend it in verse and song; but philosophy does not herself speak, and she has as her mouthpiece only the philosophers themselves, who defend what seems true (*to dokoun alēthes*). Poetry can be seen through Homer, philosophy cannot be seen through anything but itself. The poetry-lover is enchanted by the poetry and praises the poet: he splits apart the pleasant and the good. This split constitutes the insidious power of poetry, for it makes one believe one is superior to oneself: one believes one is with the poet while being in fact with the poem. Philosophy does not discriminate in this way, for it is not a making. There is for it no artifact separate from the artifice: Socrates tells his own story. Philosophy is not an "idea" to which one looks and in light of which one makes oneself. If the gods are, they are philosophers and not makers of the idea of philosophy. [X: the psychology of imitation implies a pseudo-ontology, which alone justifies the rejection of imitation.] The poet, however, enchants because we are beside ourselves and yet are not the poet; the story does not lead to the poet but away from him to a future version of ourselves. The poet induces in us an admiration for him without emulation, while he turns us into his inventions. We become those products while disguising them and praising their producers: we thus end up by making ourselves according to the prescriptions of the poets. They are, as Shelley said, the *unacknowledged* legislators of mankind.

Chapter Twenty-Nine

Two Paradigms

Seth Benardete

What I want to explore is how a stated pattern or paradigm in Plato is related to the argument in which it is embedded. It is characteristic of any paradigm—in Plato at least—never to match perfectly that which it exemplifies. The transposition of elements from the argument to the example leads initially to the intrusion of elements of the example that either are not to be found in the original or are related to what Socrates wants to illustrate in a different manner from what its paradigmatic function requires.

In the *Theaetetus*, Socrates makes an elaborate comparison between his own art and that of his mother the midwife. He asserts that the two arts differ in only two respects; his deals with the soul and not the body, and he detects phantom offspring of thought while there are no phantom children. However, Socrates claims that he has *one* art, and this art consists in three things: 1) he knows whom he is to bring together with whom for fertilization—this corresponds to the correlated art of matchmaking; 2) he knows how to ease or intensify the pains of those who are pregnant—this corresponds to the obstetric part of the midwife's art, which also includes abortion; 3) he knows how to detect the true from false thought or *eidolon*. If his third practice has no counterpart in midwifery strictly understood, Socrates cannot claim that it is part of the same art as the first and second. If he wants to keep the unity of his art, he must allow there to be the equivalent of phantom offspring in human birth; clearly they would be children whom the midwife aborts, and these are not only defective children but also children produced by the mismatchings of mother and father. Good children, then, are equivalent to true thoughts, bad children to false thoughts; but now that we have vindicated the

Transcribed from a handwritten document (probably composed for a lecture during the time Benardete was working on his *Gorgias* and *Phaedrus* book). "Two Paradigms," SB 01–74, Seth Benardete Papers, New School for Social Research Archives and Special Collections.

unity of Socrates' art, we have to deny to Socrates the description of false-hoods as phantom images, for by analogy false children are as real as good children. Socrates, then, can be vindicated only if we allow the false to be real: the issue of the *Sophist* is thus completely inside the *Theaetetus*.

In the *Gorgias*, Socrates introduces an even more elaborate schema in order to explain to Gorgias and Polus his understanding of rhetoric (465c): Two things are immediately obvious: 1) the phantom images are compre-

	psychē	*sōma*		*psychē*	*sōma*	
politics *politikē*	legislation *nomothetikē*	gymnastics *gymnastikē*		sophistics *sophistikē*	cosmetics *kommsōmatikē*	experience *empeiria*
	justice *dikaiosunē /* *dikastikē* (520b)	medicine *iatrikē*		rhetoric *rhetorikē*	cookery *opsopoiikē*	
	no *technē!*			flattery *kolakeia*		

hended by a single name, flattery, and the genuine arts are not: there is no single art that determines how the four *technai* are to be deployed: body and soul are completely split by art; body and soul are together and partly con-fused in the element of the spurious. 2) This is equally startling: not a single word is said about *nomothetikē*, and how it is related to *gymnastikē* (beautiful and strong); no one asks Socrates about the meaning of *politikē*, or about what he means by saying that justice is an art.

We have, then, the peculiar fact that cries out for an explanation, of how pleasure in its four-fold form attempts to duplicate the four genuine arts. What in fact happens in the dialogue is an experiment on the part of Socrates that tests the formal picture of the two paradigms and proves that he was right. The first piece of evidence that this is going to occur is that Gorgias accepts the notion that to know justice is to be just, i.e., Gorgias takes on a Socratic position in an unthinking way: the *morality* of rhetoric *looks like* the knowledge of Socratic justice. This happens through Gorgias's identifying knowledge and the will; he is forced to make that identification because he accepts the notion that if one has learned something, one has been equally persuaded of that something; and since to be persuaded of something means nothing unless one behaves in accordance with one's conviction, it necessarily follows for Gorgias that if one knows, i.e., has reached an even higher level of conviction, one must be a man of principle. The *Gorgias* thus starts out with an illustration of the peculiar status of morality in opinion: if one knows what is right, one does not necessarily do what is right, but the proof that one has a firm opinion about what is right is that one acts in accordance with one's opinion. No one denies that opinion is inferior to knowledge, but almost everyone identifies morality with opinion.

This leads us to what is the most remarkable feature of the *Gorgias*. Socrates begins by distinguishing between what X is and whether X is good or bad, and he claims one cannot argue about the second unless the first issue is settled; but though he applies this principle to rhetoric, no one asks Socrates to say what justice is, and more than two thirds of the dialogue is taken up with arguing about whether it is better or worse to suffer or do injustice. Accordingly, if Socrates is right, the *Gorgias* is entirely rhetorical, and Socrates attacks rhetoric while defending justice rhetorically.

We should, then, look into how the deformation of Socrates' original structure occurs. Socrates' schema confirms this equation: *t'agathon* equals *to kalon* plus *to dikaion* (the good equals the beautiful plus the just). What then happens is that Polus identifies *to dikaion* with *to kalon*, i.e., *nomothetikē* as the counterpart to *gymnastikē* drops out and justice becomes the sole virtue. Rhetoric exaggerates justice.

Once Polus identifies the just and the beautiful, he splits the beautiful into the pleasant and the beneficial (or Socrates' original good):

		the beautiful	..... divided into	the pleasant
t'agathon	=	identified with		and
		the just		the beneficial

Polus is then queried about punishment: Punishment is always just. (Polus's tyrant never punishes.) Socrates introduces the notion of agent and patient, and gets Polus to accept the view that whatever adverb qualifies the action of the agent equally qualifies the patiency of the patient. So if the agent cuts deeply, the patient is cut deeply. Accordingly, if to punish is to punish beautifully, and that is to punish justly, then it follows that one who is the patient of punishment must be benefited, since it is obvious that he receives no pleasure, and the beautiful must consist in either pleasure, benefit, or both. Polus, then, has failed to observe that the punisher in punishing must either be receiving pleasure or being benefited, and if he is not being benefited, he must be receiving pleasure, and by his receiving pleasure punishment is beautiful by definition regardless of whether the patient of punishment is benefited or not. Polus, then, is blind to his own pleasure in punishment and believes that punishment is effective; but Polus cannot believe that unless he believes that the intention of the punisher goes directly into the one punished: the punished accepts, i.e., is persuaded by, the will of the punisher to make him just and therefore he becomes just. Rhetoric thus duplicates in the spurious mode of the will the knowledge of justice. Polus is shown to believe that the pain the punished suffers through the body is translated into benefit for his soul by his belief in the will of the punisher. Socrates thus shows that rhetoric is spurious because it takes the connection between the pain of surgery and the resulting health of the patient as a causal relation, whereas in fact it is merely experiential, and experience is incapable by itself of rendering an account.

In the third part of the *Gorgias*, Callicles wants to accept only the pleasure part of the beautiful and drop the beneficial; but at the same time he wants to claim the superiority of prudence and manliness (*phronēsis* and *andreia*) to justice and moderation. Consequently, Callicles, on the one hand, says that the good is the pleasant, and on the other, that the beautiful is courage and wisdom. That means that Callicles takes the upper part of *nomothetikē*, the counterpart to *gymnastikē*, as *phronēsis* and *andreia*, and sneaks in for the lower part, *t'agathon* as *hēdonē*. This becomes absurd because he makes the higher sense the lower, and he does not show that *phronēsis* and *andreia* are at all needed for pleasure; but surprisingly, when Callicles finally admits that all pleasures are not the same, he drops courage and wisdom together, so he has good and bad pleasures but no virtues either to discriminate them or to obtain them.

The reason for this is that Callicles, contrary to his initial presentation, is not at all concerned with the beauty of criminality—that is Polus—but with the fear of suffering injustice. It is not the doing of injustice but the suffering of injustice that concerns him, and the injustice that concerns him is not obvious harm, like the breaking of a limb, but the strictly psychic form of injustice, the insult that takes the form of a slap in the face. He is not concerned with getting through to the unjust man in the form of punishment, but with his interpretation of the slap in the face: the slap says to him, "You are nothing!" He fears that if he does not retaliate, the slapper has correctly evaluated his worthlessness. Callicles thus reveals why throughout the *Gorgias* no one ever asks Socrates for a definition of justice: they all know what justice is through this interpretation of injustice: the man who experiences something as unjust does so through tracing back his experience of injury to the one who injured him in the form of his will to do him an injustice. Justice is known only through the experience of injustice, and thus the will parades as knowledge.

What then of Socrates? Does he simply leave it as the uncovering of the will? No. He reveals what he meant all along by justice by remarking at the end: to act justly is to make another perplexed (521d–522c; cf. 458a–b). Therefore, it is better to be punished, i.e., to be made perplexed, than not to be punished, i.e. to be left in a state of dogmatism. In short, Socrates vindicates philosophy in the guise of morality.

There is more one could say about how Socrates' schema is fully unfolded and displayed in the *Gorgias*, but I want to turn to the *Phaedrus*, where Socrates accounts for the structure of the dialogue in another way. The most notorious difficulty of the *Phaedrus* is the split between its two parts, despite Socrates' remark about the perfect writing being like an animal; it looks as if the dialogue is split between a rhetorical part and a dialectical part, and the rhetorical part is mainly an occasion for the dialectical, but any rhetorical *topos* will do and there is no necessity that it be eros.

Lysias wrote a speech in which he recommended the nonlover. This speech attracts Phaedrus, because by definition the nonlover is the beloved and Phaedrus is a beloved. Phaedrus recites a speech which proves why the beloved should not grant his favors to any lover simply because he is a lover, i.e., the beloved is not a patient simply because the lover looks like an agent. Nothing happens to the beloved simply because the lover utters the magic words, "I love you." The lover believes otherwise; the lover is so humiliated by his surprise recognition of his radical defectiveness that he charges the beloved with a crime, the only compensation for which is sexual gratification, since the lover now declares that the beloved has incurred a debt—he owes his superior status to the lover who alone acknowledged his superiority. Lysias's speech, then—and this is not surprising coming from a man who wrote speeches for the law courts—is a condemnation of eros in light of justice.

Socrates' first speech, which is designed to prove that Lysias did not exhaust the topic as Phaedrus believes, resumes the attack on the lover in terms of the good. The lover is simply bad for the body and soul of the beloved. Surprisingly, however, the blame of the lover involves the admission that the tyrannical disposition of the lover is effective in inducing justice and moderation in the beloved. The condemnation of the lover thus goes along with the condemnation of moderation. Consequently, Socrates' second speech praises madness and not moderation, and appeals to the goodness of eros in light of the beautiful. The three speeches thus display the three kinds of rhetoric: forensic, deliberative, and epideictic, with the good set between the just and the beautiful.

Now comes the surprise. When Socrates begins to analyze Lysias's speech and his own, he presents his first speech as part of his second speech and together they make one speech. Furthermore, Socrates argues that one cannot deceive unless one starts with the truth; so he implies that the truth of his single speech was in the first part, in which he condemns eros, and the false is in the second part, in which he praises it. Now clearly, Socrates' first speech cannot be part of his second speech unless he can detach it from Lysias's speech; but how can that be done, since it shares with Lysias's speech the same intention and the same premise, that eros is a human disease? In order to solve this, one begins by observing that Lysias's speech cannot be spoken but only written, for in order to be spoken it would have to have an addressee, but if the nonlover had an addressee, he would have thereby admitted that he was a lover who was only pretending to be a nonlover. Accordingly, the premise of Socrates' first speech is precisely that the speaker is a lover who has previously convinced the beloved that he is not a lover. A lover, then, makes a speech that presents to the beloved the beloved who is the nonlover. The beloved falls for a speech which matches perfectly himself. Socrates' first speech, then, is the speech of the lover; it therefore has the same speaker as his second speech, which is openly the speech of the lover. The lover, then, has split himself into lover and nonlover or beloved.

Now in his second speech, Socrates describes the soul as divided into three parts, a charioteer (*nous*, mind), a white horse (moderate lover), and a black horse (immoderate lover). The black horse looks like Socrates. The black horse alone tries to speak with the beloved, the charioteer and white horse join to prevent not only sexual intercourse but any kind of intercourse. The lover then as such is the black horse, the white horse is the beloved when he is finally persuaded to join with the black horse. The white horse is Socrates' first speech, the black horse is Socrates' first and second speech.

The proof for this is several: 1) When beloved and lover are united, they are said to share the same wings, and that would only be possible if the beloved was incorporated into the lover. 2) The beloved is said to fall in love not with the lover but with himself, more accurately, the higher version of himself,

308

which has been invented by the lover; but this higher fiction is simply a preferred version of the beloved. Thus the beloved falls in love with himself in the form of the lover's higher version of himself. Socrates says that the beloved's experience is like looking into a mirror without knowing one is doing so. But if the beloved is looking at himself, mirror-wise, and does not know it, he will mistake his own left and right and believe the image's right is on his left and its left on his right. But that means that the black horse will show up as white, and the beloved will never know that there was only one black horse, and what he takes in is its phantom image.

Now the central myth of the *Phaedrus* is that, on the one hand, there are hyperuranian beings, and on the other, there are Olympian gods, and one cannot get to the former except through the latter: the discoveries of mind arise through the diversions of soul. This means that the structure of any Platonic dialogue consists in a hyperuranian *aporia* and a white horse image, which presents that perplexity in a complete and finished form. That means that Plato made a higher religion out of the Homeric gods: the dialogues are the new deities behind which are the truth about the beings—what we do not know.

Chapter Thirty

Herodotus' Understanding of *Barbaros*

Seth Benardete

The perplexity at the heart of Herodotus' understanding of *barbaros* comes to light at once in the first sentence of his *Histories* or *Inquiries*: "Here is the showing forth of the inquiry of Herodotus of Halicarnassus, in order that the things done by human beings may not vanish in time, and the deeds, both great and wonderful shown forth, some by Greeks and some by barbarians, may not prove to be without fame, and it is the showing forth of everything else as well as of the cause of the wars they waged against one another." Herodotus' own "showing forth" (*apodexis*) has three functions: first, it is designed to prevent the disappearance of "the things done by human beings" (*ta genomena ex anthrō-pōn*)—Greeks and barbarians are indifferently human beings, and what they did could presumably comprehend indifferently whatever they said no less than what they did; second, his *apodexis* is aligned with and separated from the *apodexis* of deeds that Greeks and barbarians equally produced, for Herodotus is responsible for their being not without fame (*kleos*)—nothing they did gains *kleos* on its own; and third, his *apodexis* supplies the cause why they waged war against one another: we automatically assume that the Persians are the barbarians Herodotus has in mind.

Herodotus separates out three purposes of his *Inquiries*: two consist in narrative, one in causal explanation. The two narrative purposes seem to coincide, but the first is as neutral to the difference between Greeks and barbarians as it is indifferent as to whether their deeds deserve fame or not, for *ta genomena* implicitly comprehend the trivial and not particularly wonderful things that constitute most of human life. No one would deny that Herodotus

Taken from a typewritten manuscript (perhaps written in the summer of 2001, judging from correspondence with Ronna Burger, in which Benardete quotes the passage from Bacon cited in the note to this essay). "The perplexity at the heart of Herodotus' understanding of *barbaros*," SB 03–07, Seth Benardete Papers, New School for Social Research Archives and Special Collections.

includes many things unworthy of a serious historian. Indeed, he begins with a series of funny stories about the ultimate cause of the Persian Wars. They are funny because they turn the heroes and heroines of Greek mythology, on the one hand, into ordinary men and women and insert them, on the other, into a grand scheme of crime and punishment. The Persians who tell these stories, while they deny that any nonhuman causality is at work in human history, magnify the importance of the principles at stake in it. They are more rational than any other people in Herodotus and as crazy as anyone else. The Persians propound a strict morality without any theodicy to back it up.

Herodotus tells us soon afterward that he is not as ambitious as the Persians, and he has no intention of tracing things back into a mythical past. His understanding of the human is free from any grandiose scheme of justice; rather, human happiness is necessarily at odds with justice, for human happiness depends on greatness, and greatness cannot be achieved without imperial expansion, and imperial expansion in turn necessarily involves the unjust enslavement of foreign peoples. So the great and wonderful deeds of Greeks and barbarians are primarily the unjust deeds they severally performed that laid the foundation of their temporary happiness. The fame Herodotus wants to bestow on their deeds as either Greek or barbarian is not going to wipe out the criminality that has its common root in the all too human. There is nothing glorious in the human, there is nothing just in the exploits of Greeks or barbarians. Themistocles, who preserved Greek freedom, paved the way for the Peloponnesian War, which was, according to Herodotus, nothing but a struggle for empire; and Themistocles himself was as ready to sell out the Greeks for money as to offer to enslave them all to the Persian king. The Spartan Pausanias was no better; he was simply less prudent and resourceful.

This very abbreviated account of Herodotus' understanding of the political links up with the theme of *Hellēn-Barbaros* in the following manner: it once again involves the Persians. After the seven conspirators around Darius managed to kill the false Smerdis, who looked like Cambyses but was a Persian priest, they went on to kill every magus that happened to be around, and the Persians, on hearing the story, approved of their action and killed every magus they could find, and, Herodotus adds, "if night had not come over them, they would have left no magus alive." The Persians, he goes on to say, hold this day of magus-killing in the highest esteem, and when it is celebrated no magus is allowed to come into the light. Five days after the liberation the conspirators deliberated about all matters, "and speeches were spoken, though unbelievable to some of the Greeks, all the same they were spoken." These speeches concern the possible excellence of three regimes: democracy, aristocracy, or monarchy. None of the speakers mentions the sacred as a consideration nor alludes to Cambyses' various acts of impiety: he is hubris incarnate, not irreligion. Just as the greatness of the city is at the expense of justice, so the discovery of the political order as such is at the expense of the sacred. Only the suppression of the priests allows the political to come to light. This is human freedom. Nowhere is it to be found except in speech, or more precisely, in a speech about free speech. The abstraction from the sacred on this single occasion points to its ineradicable presence everywhere and always. It is for Herodotus one of the two roots of the city. Herodotus calls the other root "iron." In the first half of the first book, immediately after the Persians have implicitly denied the existence of a heroic age, are one-third of all occurrences of the word "iron." Indeed, in a story about the Spartan search for the bones of Orestes, bones more than life-size are found underneath the forge of a blacksmith who, to the astonishment of a Spartan, is working in iron. The word for blacksmith in Greek is *chalkeus*, a worker in bronze. Just before Herodotus turns to Croesus, whose expansion was the first to enslave Greeks (before Croesus, Herodotus says, all Greeks were free), he puts the sacred and iron together in a single sentence: "Alyattes was the second of his house to make dedications at Delphi: a large silver crater and a welded iron crater-stand, which is more worthy of seeing than all the dedications at Delphi; it is the fabrication of Glaucus a Chian, who was the only one of all human beings to discover the welding of iron." A barbarian recognizes a Greek god; a Greek is unique among all human beings.

Herodotus constitutes the city in three ways: its purpose is freedom and empire; its double root is art or invention and the holy, and its regime is how these elements are given their form and the citizens their way of life. These three ways cut across the distinction between Greek and barbarian. That distinction is essentially ambiguous, for the Egyptians call everyone who does not speak the same language as they do barbarians. "Barbarian" is merely a way of singling out oneself and collecting everyone else together. It is *the* example according to Plato of a cut not made at the natural joint. It thus expresses the essence of convention: though the earth is one, Herodotus says, he will use the three conventional names for its arbitrarily distinguished parts. "Barbarian," then, is in one sense merely convenient and conveys nothing. It is in itself completely neutral and yet in usage completely loaded: *barbaros* occurs most frequently in the relatively short eighth book, for there the struggle for Greek freedom is tied in directly with the Greek gods. There the Athenians use two words for home, *oikos* and *oikēma*, for temple; and the only other time they have this meaning in Herodotus is in the book about the Egyptians, who are, he says, *theosebees perissōs*, "excessively reverent of gods," and *thrēskeuousi perissōs*, "excessive in their worship." Herodotus speaks of *thrēskeiē* and *thrēskeuein* only of the Egyptian religion. It is Egypt that compels Herodotus to break his wish not to discuss the divine; it was his silent way of being in accord with the free speeches of the Persians after the killing of the magi.

Three countries shape Herodotus' understanding of the barbarians: Egypt, Persia, and Scythia. Egypt stands for the thesis that there is nothing but body, Persia nothing but soul, and Scythia poses the issue of the image and poetry. Each of them represents a distinct alternative to Greekness, which thus emerges as something more than a label for a language. Greekness becomes something that can only be recognized through others. Homer set this way of looking at Greekness. In the seventh book of the *Iliad* the Achaeans and Trojans hold a truce and bury their dead; both armies weep as they collect the hardly recognizable corpses; Priam forbids the Trojans to weep. Homer says nothing about Agamemnon. The Trojans cannot weep without losing their fighting edge; the Achaeans can weep and still fight the next day: Vergil speaks of the Trojans' broken strength on a similar occasion. In Herodotus the barbarians alone, with one exception, shed tears. At the beginning of the third book of the *Iliad* the war resumes. The Trojans advance with a noisy shout, just like birds, "as is the clamor of cranes that goes up to the sky when they flee winter and unspeakable rain, and they fly with a clamor toward the flowing of Ocean, bringing death and slaughter to the Pygmies, and they in the early morning challenge them to evil strife; but the Achaeans went in silence breathing might, eager in their heart to defend one another." The Trojans get the simile; there is nothing to which the Achaeans can be likened. In Herodotus the phrase *mega ambōsas*, "with a great shout," occurs three times of barbarians, never of a Greek. On the second of those occasions, Darius puts this question to some Greeks at his court: "For how much money would you be willing to eat your dead parents?" The Greeks reply that they would not for any amount. Darius then called some Indians who eat their parents, and with the Greeks present asked them through an interpreter for what money they would burn their dead parents. They shouted aloud and urged him not to speak in an ill-omened way. The Greeks did not shout when the question was put to them, and the Indians were not present when the Greeks were asked whether they would choose to practice the ways of the Indians. The Greeks' silence is of a piece with their presence at the questioning of the

Indians. They can face the other without becoming the other. The Greeks represent the turn to pure theory.

The Greek discovery of difference begins with the *Odyssey*. Its subject is a man who wandered very far and saw the cities of many men and knew their mind. The man has no name, and he himself gives himself a nameless name, *Outis*, "No one." *Outis* is no one; he is not *outidanos*, a nobody. His being *outis* has a deep connection with his being *mētis* or mind. It is mind that comes to know minds. These minds are the laws and conventions of diverse people: an ancient variant, known to Horace, for the *noos*, mind, of the third line of the *Odyssey*, is *nomos* or law. Herodotus has set out to be Odysseus. Odysseus represents two things, the quest for human wisdom, unsupported by the gods, and the quest for justice, which cannot dispense with divine support. Herodotus' version of the connection and divergence between these two quests is to impose a pattern of right onto events and at the same time take the pattern apart in order to discover the nature of human things. In doing so Herodotus has refused to separate moderation from wisdom. Herodotean wisdom has its roots in the soil of Greek moderation.

In the most obvious sense, Herodotus rehearses the structure of the *Odyssey*. Odysseus away from home is to Odysseus at home as Herodotus among the foreign peoples of his first four books is to Herodotus the historian of the Persian Wars. The wars are his way of coming home. The self-discovery of Odysseus through others prepares but does not complete the Odysseus who returns home to punish the suitors and set Telemachus on his throne: Odysseus must undertake another journey immediately after his homecoming. He is most himself in exile. The highest achievement of Greekness is to be at home in homelessness. It is to live without nostalgia. It consists of the Nietzschean paradox of the cheerfulness of Greek tragedy. Herodotus has the Greeks in tears only once: the Athenians were looking at a tragedy. Greek tragedy represents the nonassimilating incorporation of the other into the same. Aeschylus' *Persians* is of the essence of Greek tragedy: the barbarians who would enslave Greece are shown in their noble suffering without a word about their injustice. Neither *dikē* nor any of its cognates occurs in the play. Herodotus' version of this Aeschylean reticence is never to apply *dikē* or its cognates to Athens and the Athenians. His story about Athens begins with Pisistratus dressing up a tall woman to look like Athena; his story about Sparta begins with their consultation of Delphi.

At the heart of Greek moderation lies Greek poetry. The image-making of the poets replaces the religious authority that the poets have everywhere else.[1] The gods are now known only through the Muses who tell lies like the truth. Self-aware stories stand between divine law and human truth. The *kalon*, the beautiful and noble, occupies this between for the *kalon* is essentially indifferent to the real. It always shows up in an image: according to Homer's old men, Helen has the terrible likeness of the deathless goddesses, and according to Stesichorus, not Helen herself but her image came to Troy. The beautiful is forever elusive; it is, as we say, the ideal. Herodotus believes that the origin of the Greek gods is to be found in Egypt, where the ritually clean is the precursor to the beauty of the Greek gods; and the makers of the Greek gods are Homer and Hesiod. They beautified the holy obscenities of Egypt and took away the bestial disguises of the gods. Hera is now merely ox-eyed. In Egypt everything is holy except man; in Greece nothing is divine except man. Egyptian piety is identical with man's contempt for man; Greek piety is the same as man looking up to man. Egypt, Hegel says, posed the riddle of the Sphinx, Greece solved it.

Egyptian life is lived in the shadow of death. Among the wealthy, after dinner, a wooden corpse in a casket, made as like as possible to the life, is carried around among the guests, and on showing it to each the bearer says, "Look! Drink and enjoy; you will be just like it once you are dead." Since there is no human soul as such in Egypt, for the soul in its immortality passes in a regular cycle through all living things, the human body is all there is to man, and of the body everything corruptible has to be dissolved in the process of mummification in order to achieve an immortality that in the most elaborate process goes by the name of a god. Man is nothing but corpse and as corpse he is god. Egypt, even while it sets them apart as far as possible, cannot separate life and death, man and god. One of the last things Cambyses did in Egypt before he went mad was to kill a god and declare the Egyptians deserved a god of flesh and blood that was sensitive to iron. The first thing that Herodotus calls divine in Egypt is the suicide of cats.

---

1. Cf. Francis Bacon, *The Advancement of Learning*, II.25.19: "The matter informed by divinity is of two kinds; matter of belief and truth of opinion, and matter of service and adoration; which is also judged and directed by the former: the one being as the internal soul of religion, and the other as the external body thereof. And therefore the heathen religion was not only a worship of idols, but the whole religion was an idol in itself; for it had not soul, that is, no certainty of belief or confession: as a man may well think, considering that the chief doctors of their church were the poets: and the reason was, because the heathen gods were no jealous gods, but were glad to be admitted into part, as they had reason. Neither did they respect the pureness of heart, so they mought have external honour and rites.

Just as Diogenes was called Socrates gone mad, so Cambyses is Herodotus gone mad. He is the truth-seeker without self-knowledge. His lack of self-knowledge is at one with his unawareness of the sacred in ordinary human life. Herodotus' proof of Cambyses' madness is his laughter at sacred things. "If," he says, "one should propose to all human beings to select the most beautiful of all laws, each and every one would on inspection choose his own." This remark echoes and explains the meaning of the story of Gyges with which Herodotus almost begins his *Inquiries*. In that story Candaules, because he was in love with his own wife, told his chief bodyguard to see the queen naked for himself in order to confirm presumably that his eros had not affected his judgment. Gyges shouted aloud and refused, for, he said, "the beautiful things have been discovered long ago, and one of them is this: each is to look to his own." Law is the concealment of the naked truth. The Persians paradoxically have a law to tell the truth. Consequently they must lie, for they assert that no one ever killed his mother or father, and if anyone ever did, it would be found on further investigation that the child was of necessity either the offspring of an adulterous relation or suppositious. Oedipus and Orestes are impossible in Persia; they are necessary for Greek poetry. The Persians are compelled to lie in deed as well. No conspiracy can succeed unless lying is permissible, and Darius, in urging the indifference of lying and truth-telling if the false Smerdis is to be overthrown, corrupts Persia irremediably. Immediately after the successful restoration, Intaphernes, one of the seven conspirators, wanted to consult Darius, and though the chamberlain denied him admission strictly according to the law, he believed he was lying, mutilated the chamberlain, and Darius, suspecting it was a common enterprise among the six, had him killed.

The truth-telling of the Persians, in its aim and falling short, is decisive for Herodotus. It allowed him to cancel the heroic age at the beginning of his *Inquiries* and tell the story of Cyrus straight without the enhancement of divine causation. In the absence of such causation the story of Cyrus' birth is the story of Oedipus'. The Persians thus pay a high price for truth-telling. The blindness truth-telling settles on them enhances their demand for justice. When Xerxes stations his fleet at Salamis he has only to wait for the Greeks to disperse to have all of Greece fall into his hands; but Themistocles tempts him with the possibility of punishing the Greeks. He sacrifices his imperial ambitions for the exaction of right.

Works by Seth Benardete

"The *Daimonion* of Socrates: A Study of Plato's *Theages*." Master's thesis. University of Chicago, 1953.

"Achilles and Hector: The Homeric Hero." Ph.D. dissertation. University of Chicago, 1955. Published in *St. John's Review* in two parts: Spring 1985: 31–58; Summer 1985: 85–114. Reprint, *Achilles and Hector: The Homeric Hero*, edited by Ronna Burger with an Introduction by Michael Davis. South Bend: St. Augustine's Press, 2005.

Aeschylus, *Suppliant Maidens* and *Persians*. Translation. Chicago: University of Chicago Press, 1957.

"Plato *Sophist* 231b1–7." *Phronesis* 5, no. 3 (1960): 129–39. Reprinted in *The Archaeology of the Soul*, 2012.

"Vat. Gr. 2181: An Unknown Aristophanes MS." *Harvard Studies in Classical Philology* (1962): 241–48.

"Achilles and the *Iliad*." *Hermes* 91, no. 1 (1963): 1–16. Reprinted in *The Argument of the Action*, 2000.

"The Right, the True, and the Beautiful." *Glotta* 41, nos. 1–2 (1963): 54–62. Reprinted in *The Archaeology of the Soul*, 2012.

"*Eidos* and *Diaeresis* in Plato's *Statesman*." *Philologus* 107, nos. 3–4 (1963): 193–226. Reprinted in *The Archaeology of the Soul*, 2012.

"Some Misquotations of Homer in Plato." *Phronesis* 8, no. 2 (1963): 173–78. Reprinted in *The Archaeology of the Soul*, 2012.

"The Crimes and Arts of Prometheus." *Rheinisches Museum für Philologie* 107, no. 2 (1964): 126–39. Reprinted in *The Archaeology of the Soul*, 2012.

"Sophocles' *Oedipus Tyrannus*." In *Ancients and Moderns*, edited by Joseph Cropsey, 1–15. New York: Basic Books, 1964. Reprinted in *Sophocles: Twentieth Century Views*, edited by Thomas Woodard. Englewood Cliffs, N.J.: Prentice Hall, 1966; and in *The Argument of the Action*, 2000.

"XRH and DEI in Plato and Others." *Glotta* 43, nos. 3–4 (1965): 285–98. Reprinted in *The Archaeology of the Soul*, 2012.

"Two Notes on Aeschylus' *Septem.*" *Wiener Studien*, in two parts: NF 1 (1967): 22–30 and NF 2 (1968): 5–17. Reprinted in *Sacred Transgressions: A Reading of Sophocles'* Antigone. South Bend: St. Augustine's Press, 1999.

"Hesiod's *Works and Days*: A First Reading." *Agon* 1 (1967): 150–74. Reprinted in *The Archaeology of the Soul*, 2012.

"The *Aristeia* of Diomedes and the Plot of the *Iliad.*" *Agon* 2 (1968): 10–38. Reprinted in *The Argument of the Action*, 2000.

Herodotean Inquiries. The Hague: Martinus Nijhoff, 1969. New edition with "Second Thoughts." South Bend: St. Augustine's Press, 1999. Paperback, 2009.

"On Plato's *Timaeus* and Timaeus' Science Fiction." *Interpretation* 2, no. 1 (Summer 1971): 21–63. Reprinted in *The Archaeology of the Soul*, 2012.

Review of H. Lloyd-Jones' translation of Aeschylus' *Oresteia*. *American Journal of Philology* 93, no. 4 (1972): 633–35.

Memorial Speech for Leo Strauss, 1974. Published in *The Archaeology of the Soul*, 2012.

"Aristotle *de anima* III.3–5." *The Review of Metaphysics* 28, no. 4 (June 1975): 611–22. Reprinted in *The Archaeology of the Soul*, 2012.

"A Reading of Sophocles' *Antigone.*" *Interpretation*, in three parts: vol. 4, no. 3 (Spring 1975): 148–96; vol. 5, no. 1 (Summer 1975): 1–55; vol. 5, no. 2 (Winter 1975): 148–84. Reprinted in *Sacred Transgressions: A Reading of Sophocles'* Antigone. South Bend: St. Augustine's Press, 1999.

"Euripides' *Hippolytus.*" In *Essays in Honor of Jacob Klein*, 21–27. Annapolis: St. John's College Press, 1976. Reprinted in *The Argument of the Action*, 2000.

"The Grammar of Being." Review of Charles Kahn, *The Verb "Be" in Ancient Greek. The Review of Metaphysics* 30, no. 3 (March 1977): 486–96. Reprinted in *The Archaeology of the Soul*, 2012.

"Glorifying the Archaic." Review of Hermann Fraenkel, *Early Greek Poetry and Philosophy*. *New York Review of Books*, March 17, 1977.

"On Wisdom and Philosophy: The First Two Chapters of Aristotle's *Metaphysics* A." *The Review of Metaphysics* 32, no. 2 (Dec. 1978): 205–15. Reprinted in *The Argument of the Action*, 2000.

"Leo Strauss' *The City and Man*." *The Political Science Reviewer* 8 (1978): 1–20. Reprinted in *The Archaeology of the Soul*, 2012.

"On Greek Tragedy." In *The Great Ideas Today*, 102–43. Chicago: Encyclopedia Britannica, Inc., 1980. Reprinted in *The Argument of the Action*, 2000.

"Plato's *Phaedo*." Manuscript, 1980. Published in *The Argument of the Action*, 2000.

"Physics and Tragedy: On Plato's *Cratylus*." *Ancient Philosophy* 1, no. 2 (1981): 127–40. Reprinted in *The Argument of the Action*, 2000.

"*The Furies* of Aeschylus." Manuscript, 1982. Published in *The Argument of the Action*, 2000.

Review of J. Dudley, *Gott und "Theoria" bei Aristoteles: Die metaphysische Grundlage der Nikomachischen Ethik*. *The Review of Metaphysics* 37, no. 1 (Sept. 1983): 112–13. Reprinted in *The Archaeology of the Soul*, 2012.

The Being of the Beautiful: Plato's "Theaetetus," "Sophist," and "Statesman." Translation and commentary. Chicago: University of Chicago Press, 1984. Paperback in 3 volumes with a new introduction, 1986.

Review of Stanley Rosen, *Plato's Sophist: The Drama of Original and Image*. *Graduate Faculty Philosophy Journal* 10, no. 2 (1985): 167–69.

"On Interpreting Plato's *Charmides*." *Graduate Faculty Philosophy Journal* 11, no. 2 (1986): 9–36. Reprinted in *The Argument of the Action*, 2000.

Symposium. A translation by Seth Benardete. In *The Dialogues of Plato*, edited by Erich Segal, 231-86. New York: Bantam Books, 1986. Reprinted in *Plato's "Symposium."* A translation by Seth Benardete with Commentary by Seth Benardete and Allan Bloom. Chicago: University of Chicago Press, 2001.

Review of M. Giraudeau, *Les notions juridiques et socials chez Herodote.*
Gnomon 58, no. 5 (1986): 546–57. Reprinted in *The Archaeology of
the Soul*, 2012.

"Cicero's *de legibus* I: Its Plan and Intention." *American Journal of Philology* 108, no. 2 (1987): 295–309. Reprinted in *The Archaeology of the
Soul*, 2012.

"Protagoras' Myth and *Logos*." Manuscript 1988. Published in *The Argument of the Action*, 2000.

Socrates' Second Sailing: On Plato's Republic. Chicago: University of Chicago Press, 1989. Paperback, 1992.

The Rhetoric of Morality and Philosophy: Plato's "Gorgias" and "Phaedrus."
Chicago: University of Chicago Press, 1991.

"The Plan of the *Statesman*." *Metis: Revue d'anthropologie du monde grec
ancien* 7, nos. 1–2 (1992): 25–47. Reprinted in *The Argument of the
Action*, 2000.

"Plato's *Laches*: A Question of Definition." Manuscript, 1992. Published in
The Argument of the Action, 2000.

The Tragedy and Comedy of Life: Plato's "Philebus." Translation and commentary. Chicago: University of Chicago Press, 1993.

"On Plato's *Sophist*." *The Review of Metaphysics* 46, no. 4 (June 1993):
747–80. Reprinted in *The Argument of the Action*, 2000.

"The Poet-Merchant and the Stranger from the Sea." *The Greeks and the
Sea*, edited by Vryonis Speros, 59–65. New York: Aristide Caratzas
Publishers, 1993. Reprinted in *The Archaeology of the Soul*, 2012.

"Strauss on Plato." Opening lecture in series, "The Legacy of Leo
Strauss," The John M. Olin Center, University of Chicago, 1993.
Published in *The Argument of the Action*, 2000.

On Plato's Symposium. Munich: Carl Friedrich von Siemens Stiftung, 1994.
Reprinted in *Plato's "Symposium."* A translation by Seth Benardete
with Commentary by Seth Benardete and Allan Bloom. Chicago:
University of Chicago Press, 2001; and in *The Argument of the
Action*, 2000.

"On Plato's *Lysis*." Manuscript, 1994. Published in *The Argument of the
Action*, 2000.

"The First Crisis in First Philosophy." *Graduate Faculty Philosophy Journal* 18, no. 1 (1995): 237–48. Reprinted in *The Argument of the Action*, 2000.

"The Play of Truth." Review of R. B. Rutherford, *The Art of Plato: Ten Essays in Platonic Interpretation. Boston Book Review*, Nov. 10, 1995: 11–12. Reprinted in *The Archaeology of the Soul*, 2012.

The Bow and the Lyre: A Platonic Reading of the Odyssey. Lanham, Md.: Rowman & Littlefield, 1997.

"Plato's *Theaetetus*: On the Way of the Logos." *The Review of Metaphysics* 51, no. 1 (Sept. 1997): 25–53. Reprinted in *The Argument of the Action*, 2000.

Review of Michael Tanner, *Nietzsche: A Very Short Introduction*. In *The Great Ideas Today*, 454–58. Chicago: Encyclopedia Britannica, Inc., 1997. Reprinted in *The Archaeology of the Soul*, 2012.

"Plato, True and False." Review of *Plato: Complete Works*, edited by John M. Cooper. *The New Criterion*, Feb. 1998: 70–74. Reprinted in *The Archaeology of the Soul*, 2012.

"'Night and Day...': Parmenides." *Metis: Revue d'anthropologie du monde grec ancien* 13 (1998): 193–225. Reprinted in *The Archaeology of the Soul*, 2012.

"On the *Timaeus*." Lecture at the Hannah Arendt/Reiner Schürmann Memorial Symposium in Political Philosophy: "The Philosophy of Leo Strauss," New School for Social Research, 1999. Published in *The Argument of the Action*, 2000.

"Metamorphosis and Conversion: Apuleius's *Metamorphoses*." In *Literary Imagination, Ancient and Modern: Essays in Honor of David Grene*, edited by Todd Breyfogle, 155–76. Chicago: University of Chicago Press, 1999. Reprinted in *The Archaeology of the Soul*, 2012.

"On Heraclitus." *The Review of Metaphysics* 53, no. 3 (March 2000): 613–33. Reprinted in *The Archaeology of the Soul*, 2012.

The Argument of the Action: Essays on Greek Poetry and Philosophy, edited by Ronna Burger and Michael Davis. Chicago: University of Chicago Press, 2000.

Plato's "Laws": The Discovery of Being. Chicago: University of Chicago Press, 2000.

"Socrates and Plato: The Dialectics of Eros." German translation in *Über die Liebe*, edited by Heinrich Meier and Gerhardt Neumann. Munich: Piper Verlag, 2000. Published in *Socrates and Plato. The Dialectics of Eros* (German and English). Munich: Carl Friedrich von Siemens Stiftung, 2002. Reprinted in *The Archaeology of the Soul*, 2012.

"Derrida and Plato." Lecture delivered at New York University, in series, "Derrida and his Non-Contemporaries," Oct. 19, 2000. Reprinted in *The Archaeology of the Soul*, 2012.

"Plato's *Parmenides*: A Sketch." Manuscript, 2001. Published in *The Archaeology of the Soul*, 2012.

"A. E. Housman." December 15, 2001. www.greekworks.com.

Foreword to Leo Strauss, *On Plato's "Symposium,"* edited by Seth Benardete (Chicago: University of Chicago Press, 2001).

Encounters and Reflections: Conversations with Seth Benardete, edited by Ronna Burger. Chicago: University of Chicago Press, 2002.

Aristotle. *On Poetics*. Translation by Seth Benardete and Michael Davis, Introduction by Michael Davis. South Bend: St. Augustine's Press, 2002.

"The Plan of Odysseus and the Plot of the *Philoctetes*." *Epoché* 7, no. 2 (Spring 2003): 133–50. Reprinted in *The Archaeology of the Soul*, 2012.

"Freedom: Grace and Necessity." In *Freedom and the Human Person*, edited by Richard Velkley. *Studies in Philosophy and the History of Philosophy*. Washington, D.C.: The Catholic University of America Press, 2007. Reprinted in *The Archaeology of the Soul*, 2012.

The Archaeology of the Soul: Platonic Readings of Ancient Poetry and Philosophy, edited by Ronna Burger and Michael Davis. South Bend: St. Augustine's Press, 2012.

"On Reading Pindar Platonically." Manuscript, undated. Published in *The Archaeology of the Soul*, 2012.

"Horace C.I.xv." Manuscript, undated. Published in *The Archaeology of the Soul*, 2012.

"The Bed and the Table." Manuscript, undated. Published in this volume.

"Two Paradigms." Manuscript, undated. Published in this volume.

"Herodotus' Understanding of *Barbaros*." Manuscript, undated. Published in this volume.

Seth Benardete Papers. Collection NA.0005.01. New School Archives and Special Collections, The New School, New York, New York.